A Place in History

PRINCETON UNIVERSITY PRESS IS PROUD TO INCLUDE
Michael Herzfeld's
*A Place in History: Social and Monumental Time
in a Cretan Town*

in two of its established series
(a list of titles in these series appears
on the last printed page of the book):

PRINCETON MODERN GREEK STUDIES

PRINCETON STUDIES IN CULTURE/POWER/HISTORY

PRINCETON STUDIES IN
CULTURE/POWER/HISTORY

A Place in History

SOCIAL AND MONUMENTAL TIME
IN A CRETAN TOWN

Michael Herzfeld

PRINCETON UNIVERSITY PRESS

PRINCETON, NEW JERSEY

Library of Congress Cataloging-in-Publication Data

Herzfeld, Michael, 1947–
A place in history : social and monumental time in a
Cretan town / Michael Herzfeld.
p.   cm. — (Princeton studies in culture/power/history)
(Princeton modern Greek studies)
Includes bibliographical references and index.
1. Rethymnon (Greece)—History. I. Title. II. Series.
III. Series: Princeton modern Greek studies.
DF951.R4H47 1991
949.9′8—dc20   90-28755

ISBN 0-691-09456-X. — ISBN 0-691-02855-9 (pbk.)

Για όσους πονάνε
το παλιό το Ρέθεμνος

To all those who feel
for old Rethemnos

CONTENTS

LIST OF ILLUSTRATIONS

PLATES

Photographs (except plates 2–6, 8, 12, and 24) are by Cornelia Mayer Herzfeld; the remainder are by the author.

Figures

PREFACE

THIS BOOK is about the disputed ownership of history. In recent years, various scholars have begun to treat history as a negotiable good rather than as an objective entity. The study of European constructions of history in situ offers an exceptional opportunity to examine what has been meant by both "Europe" and "history." From this perspective, the claim that Greece is the ancestral land takes on a new kind of interest, far removed from the jaded philhellenism of the past century and a half, and calls out for ethnographic investigation.

This study of a Cretan town is not about Minoans or even Classical Greeks. It is about the efforts of the present-day inhabitants of an old but well-preserved town, Rethemnos, to come to terms with the significance that others have foisted on the physical fabric of their homes. Possibly the best preserved example of Renaissance Venetian domestic architecture to be found outside Italy, the Old Town of Rethemnos survived the economic boom of the early 1970s and the frantic development mania that came with it. Not that its inhabitants did not want to join the boom. They were prevented from doing so, in part by circumstances—the lack of a good harbor, fierce competition from the two larger towns on the island—that condemned Rethemnos to poverty for a little longer. When, from about 1970 on, the Rethemniots found the prospect of money coming their way, so that they did not have to chase after it in distant places, they also encountered a severe setback. The government had not only forbidden virtually all new building within the Renaissance limits of the town but had strictly enforced a ban on even minor alterations to the fabric of their homes.

That prohibition saved the Venetian core of the town and may have worked to many residents' long-term economic advantage. It also provoked bitter fury. As the conservation effort got under way, moreover, much of the fury turned to frustration, disillusionment, irritation—pettier emotions, perhaps, but capable of moving political mountains. Some residents were happy that their town was taking its rightful place in an official, monumentalized history. Others cared far more about the personal and family histories that they had hoped to carve out of the land according to their own commitments: dowry houses, extended homes to incorporate elderly parents and a large brood of children, business premises that signaled aggressive entrepreneurship.

In this struggle, a cultural debate has insistently set the tone. It is very much a debate about the relationship between Greek culture and the idealized entity called "Europe." In looking at the fortunes of the historic conservation effort in Rethemnos, we are thus also looking at the embodiment of this debate in social practice. We shall be following the same debate through other arenas: contrasts between social and official norms of economic interaction, for example, and between the historical ideals of the bureaucracy and the personal histories embedded in the battered, familiar walls of the Old Town.

Throughout the ramifications of this debate, there runs a thread of symbolic opposition. This is not an abstract binarism in the purely theoretical sense. It is, however, historically related to the latter. The formalism (Mouzelis 1978) of the Greek state is born of the same kind of logic as the binarism that we associate with certain modes of anthropological analysis. If ever a place cried out for inspection of the dialectical relationship between structure and process, Greece must be an outstanding candidate. For, as we look at the social practices associated with so intense a struggle between "Europe" and "the Orient," the sense of opposition—negotiable, labile, debatable, but always a dominant theme in the agonistic rhetoric of the modern Greeks—acquires an immediacy that is more than academic. It is a rhetoric that permits access to the complex relationship between state ideology and the exigencies of everyday life.

In 1970, I visited Rethemnos and attempted a very modest study of the incised patterns with which poor residents were decorating their homes in lieu of tiling or other costly surface materials. Even at that early point, I was made aware of the locals' resentment at being forbidden to dismantle the few remaining Turkish wooden window boxes (Herzfeld 1971:189). In the course of several return visits, my interest in the town continued to grow. Finally, in 1984, I encountered the more obviously political contours of its changing architectural face. My wife was taking photographs of some of the old houses when an elderly man came out to inquire why anyone could possibly be interested in such things. When we explained that we found them attractive, he began to declaim a litany of complaints against the "communists"—actually the PASOK (Panhellenic Socialist Movement) government then in power—who were preventing people from doing what they wanted with their private property. Further conversation convinced me that here was a place in which I could pursue an interest in the local ramifications of bureaucracy and nationalism. Indeed it was.

It was also much more. It was, above all, an often surprising initiation into the rhetorical strategies with which townspeople and civil servants battle over the inhabited history they call home. Much later on, another resident—a self-declared communist himself this time—gave vent to his fury at the government's unconstitutional interference in his right to manage his own property. This same individual also complained that the gov-

ernment was suppressing the architectural expression of national sentiment through various motifs. By this point, it was clear that the lability
of the national symbolism might both explain its penetration of local discourse and shed some light on the locals' ability—partial and temporary
though it is—to resist the conformist pressures of the bureaucracy.

The book is dedicated to all who love Old Rethemnos. Some may read
into my account interpretations of motive that I would not presume to
make. There are many ways in which people can express their affection
for the town, and of these some must inevitably clash. This does not necessarily make them ill intentioned or damaging in their effects. There is
also a good deal of indirection in the way residents and bureaucrats alike
handle their mutual relationships, but this does not signal hypocrisy so
much as awareness, on the part of a variety of theorizing actors, of the
possible consequences of their actions for others as well as for themselves.
Perhaps some of the people I met *were* dishonest—anything else, in a
community of about seven thousand people, would be astonishing, and it
would be arrogant to dismiss the criticisms that Rethemniots made of
each other as "mere" strategies in a combative social game. Since, however, I have the warmest memories both of the local residents and a wide
range of bureaucrats and of scholars who are involved in the town's problems, I can only express the hope that I have made clear my deep enthusiasm for their tolerance, their kindness, their generosity, and their extraordinary patience.

The problems that face Rethemnos are not unique to that town, although its special circumstances throw them into high relief and open
them up for comparison. Archaeologists and historians everywhere face
a set of interconnected moral dilemmas whose magnitude is only now
becoming clear. To what extent may the desire to preserve an ancient
heritage impinge on the lives of those who inhabit it? Whose heritage is
it, and who makes those decisions? Can the state act as a guardian for the
future, or is that paternalistic image simply a disguise for the uncontrolled
use of bureaucratic authority? What, finally, *is* history—and who makes
it?

Rethemnos is a lens that brings these issues into peculiarly sharp focus.
Moreover, it does so in ways that make nonsense of the old distinctions
between observers and observed. It has been a university town for a decade now. Many of its people hail from the mountain villages, yet their
town was famous in centuries gone by for its devotion to both letters and
international commerce. The interplay of Venetian cornice and Ottoman
crescent, of loggia and minaret, of severe stone doorways and smoke-
blackened wooden interior beams—these contrasts put us in mind of others, less tangible, that also carry the same ambiguities about the past. The
formal models of official culture and the informal practices of social life

all evoke this sense of complementarity. They are both essential to being Greek or Cretan, or to being a member of this local community. They represent the particular embodiments of the theoretical pair that recent anthropology has made so much its own: structure and process.

The Rethemniots, as social actors, theorize about these symbolic resources and translate their thoughts into political action. Their engagement, in other words, is far from passive. They realize their identities, not simply *within* the framework of nationalist discourse and official procedures, but—at least as much—*against* it. Since for most of them criticism of the national ideal is unthinkable, the alternative must suffice. They fight against the bureaucrats—people like themselves, and, as such, fair game for any attempt to divert them from strictly legal procedure. Fighting to redefine one's history, especially when it also happens to be one's physical home, is an appropriate response to bureaucratic procrastination and obstinacy. In so doing, however, the Rethemniots have ended up playing a game that they did not start and whose terms of reference they do not control.

These are delicate matters. The Rethemniots' willingness to engage with me in exploring them was at times overwhelming, and I am more grateful than words can say. A Rethemniot might find the words more easily, perhaps, sitting off the narrow street opposite the municipal library, sipping grappa and eating olives, dried beans, and hot, salted and lemon-drenched baked new potatoes, or catching from some coffee shop the appetizing smells of fried fish and charcoal-roasted meat and the high warbling throb of the three-stringed *lira* that accompanies raucously improvised verses. Those would probably be mischievous words, perhaps sometimes ironic words, but always words of an amiable camaraderie in which the cares of a backbreaking day's work, or of the corrosive hostility of a bad neighbor, suddenly become simply the joke that life plays on all good people. They would be words of welcome to a sociability that few can match and none surpass.

Writing this book has given me all the pleasures of fond reminiscence. It has also allowed me to engage with a number of critical readers, some of them Rethemniots themselves, and all generous with their advice at various stages of the writing process: Joëlle Bahloul, Jane K. Cowan, Loring M. Danforth, Dafni Gondica, Michael Jackson, Pandelis Kalaitzidakis, Eleftherios Pavlides, Maria Emm. Tsirimonaki, and Michalis Tzekakis. Cornelia Mayer Herzfeld also provided a careful reading, one that was based in part on our shared sojourns in Rethemnos. My debt to her is incalculable on many fronts, and her photographs (all the photographs, except plates 2–6, 8, 12, and 24, are hers, while the others are my own) clearly show that engaged warmth which she brought to all our interactions with the Rethemniots. Among the series editors, Geoffrey Eley and Sherry Ortner provided both encouragement and close critical readings, and I am indebted to the editors of both series for permitting the arrangement whereby they share publication of the study. Gail Ullman and Lauren Lepow made the editorial process pleasant and interesting. I am indebted to John M. Hollingsworth for the artwork on figs. 1.1, 1.2, 7.4, and 7.5, to Janis Kearney for redrawing the architectural drawings by Kostas Iliakis (figs. 7.1, 7.2, and 7.3) for publication, and to Janis Kearney and Thomas Hubbard for carefully preparing prints of the photographs for the production process. Della Collins Cook gave generously of her time and expertise in helping to assess the statistical significance of the population data used in this study. George Nikolakakis provided collegial stimulation at many times during the fieldwork. Officials of the National Archaeological Service of Greece and the Greek Ministry of Justice were helpful in facilitating my search for relevant data in both Athens and Rethemnos; I am particularly indebted to Despina Kakoyannaki. Several public servants, mentioned in the text, granted interviews that proved to be an invaluable complement to the more conventional field data. The main period of research was undertaken while I was on sabbatical leave from Indiana University in 1986–1987 and generously supported by a Fellowship for Study and Research from the National Endowment for the Humanities. Grants-in-aid from Indiana University also supported a "prospecting" visit in 1984 (see Herzfeld 1985:xviii). Such a rich variety of personal as well as professional support creates powerful obligations to give the best account I can, a debt that I feel especially strongly toward the Rethemniots whose lives this book partially describes. For the deficiencies that undoubtedly exist, I willingly assume the responsibility.

The issue of whether to use real names remains a contested one in anthropology. Here, because I am writing about research that brought me into contact with a number of public figures, I have drawn an approximate line between these individuals, who are named, and those whose interests seemed better served at this stage by the use of pseudonyms. The decision to publish ideas in print or to run for public office of any sort carries certain risks; I hope I have not inadvertently realized anyone's fears. I have been greatly moved by the forthrightness with which active public figures across the political spectrum spoke to me of their concern for Rethemnos, and their views mingle here with those of more self-effacing commentators to, I believe, the mutual enrichment of all.

Rethemnos gave me wonderful friendships, memories, insights. In dedicating this book to those who, as I have come to do, feel for the Old Town in its extraordinary vicissitudes, I recognize that there are many ways of expressing that emotion, many ways of turning it into practice. This is mine. I offer it in infinite gratitude and affection.

Note on Kinship Abbreviations

I have adopted the following conventions:

B =	brother	M =	mother
D =	daughter	S =	son
F =	father	W =	wife
H =	husband	Z =	sister

and combinations thereof (e.g., MBS = mother's brother's son).

A Place in History

———————————

Chapter One

THE TOWN OF THE *TALE*

Exploring the Old Town

"Rethemnos is, if you will, built on the boundary between domestication and wilderness." With these words, the Greek novelist Pandelis Prevelakis places the small Cretan coastal town of Rethemnos,[1] where he was born in 1909, in cultural as well as natural and geographical space. His extended reminiscence, the title of which has been rendered into English as *The Tale of a Town*, might no less appropriately have been called *The Chronicle of a Way of Life*. For the word *politia*, used by Cretan authors to mean both place and activity,[2] suggests the physical architecture that clothes and embodies a living people and its memories.

It is an uncomfortable garb—damp, smelling of mold and urine, some parts crumbling under the inexorable press of indifference, others patched up with obvious signs of careful restoration or obscured by the transient fabrics of a tawdry, makeshift modernity. People work hard here; leisure to observe, to sunbathe and wander aimlessly, is the recent and intrusive privilege of outsiders.

These outsiders are the latest, both in daily time and historically, to add their distinctive presence to the succession of odors. Early in the morning, above the fading dankness of the night, the warm spiciness of baking bread announces a long-established local craft. Another craft answers as, with the shrilling of their equipment, the carpenters' sawdust adds a distinctive sharpness, later drowned in the still more nostril-dilating acridity of varnish. As the shadows shorten toward late morning, the vacuous sweetness of warming olive oil, wafted from dark windows, draws rich savor from meat, tomato, garlic, onion—and the neighbors' alert noses judge the wealth and care that goes into each household's dining that day. Meanwhile, an exigent modernity encroaches. The narrow streets have begun to reverberate to the screech and roar of motorbikes and the impatient horns of trucks trying to squeeze a passage through. Finally, with the leisurely, strolling tourists comes the chemical scent of suntan oil from, especially, the foreign women now heading for the beach, intensifying the scented soap and aftershave that the more modish local men have already spread generously round—a faint echo, perhaps, of the perfumes that Turkish men lavished on their bodies a century ago?—as others exude the sweat of backbreaking labor and a whiff of mutton fat emanates from some passing villager's heavy, dark clothes. The hours of this "smellscape" reproduce the larger changes in the town's history in a sensual, embodied, social time that risks losing itsef, finally, in the packaged pollutants of the newest comers.

This battle over time is a battle over the possession of identity. The people within the walled space of old Rethemnos resent the town's compression of their lives and at the same time defend it against all critics. Encircling their conflict of values and emotions is a still larger politia— the state. The state is a humorless machine that—sometimes literally— stamps its rigid bureaucratic formulae on every moment of carefree sociability. It is also the guardian of that national identity most Rethemniots would, and in the past countless thousands of Rethemniots did, defend to the death. In Rethemnos, the contest of nature and culture becomes an ideological clash between an oppressive Turkish past and a timeless European history, between armed parochialism and urbane cosmopolitanism. The Old Town of Rethemnos, with its contrasts of stately architecture and anarchic rebuilding, clothes and embodies these conflicts. They are the dilemmas of civility beset by violence, of a stately past beset by the social facts of self-interest and betrayal in the present, within as well as beyond the town's time-stained walls.

Prevelakis (1938:7) describes the Rethemniots as "good people, respectful and proud at the same time, well read and well mannered, in a word a desirable type in this violence-ridden island." But the stereotypical violence of the Cretan hinterland still enters the town as well. A year before I began fieldwork there, a car bomb nearly killed the mayor. Physically and in the origins of many residents, Rethemnos is close to rural society. It shelters within its walls such rude embarrassments as the highest urban illiteracy rate in Crete, despite its proverbial status as a town of letters.[3] Nature itself is never far away. Inside the sturdy Venetian fortifications that dominate the town, luxuriant grass partly disguises the litter left by tourists and locals. On the elegant Renaissance houses and walls, sculpted reliefs of helmeted heads and noble insignia (plates 1, 2) defy the battering of time and the salt-laden sea spray borne by gusty winter winds far into the heart of the town.

These walls and houses are the familiar context of a social life that is full of affection, distrust, loyalty, hatred, amused tolerance, fierce exclusion. The patches of plaster incised with wildly asymmetrical squiggles and heart shapes or elaborate geometries struggle to renounce the poverty of the materials (plates 3–6). Scraps of posters still adhering to the walls recall the ephemeral fury of past elections. In places, this amiable disorder yields to unblemished and carefully regimented pastel shades; old blue-painted wooden doors that have decayed comfortably in the sun give way to brightly varnished new versions of the old (plate 7), and hitherto taken-

1. A helmeted head flanks a Venetian stone doorway.
(1986)

for-granted domes and arches are suddenly thrust out of jumbled anonymity by sparkling plasterwork and gaping spaces. Then there are the
other voids, left by ancient buildings that disappeared overnight when
their owners could no longer bear the disfiguring caries of neglect and
erased their memory with brand-new concrete. These are the signs of ebb
and flow in the battle with which this book is mainly concerned.
   That battle is over the future of the past. Rethemnos does not only
belong to its citizens. It is also part of a modern nation-state with a monumental conception of history. These two aspects and identities come into
frequent conflict. On the one side, bureaucratic modernity strives to represent familiar domestic spaces as monumental. This is a well-established
tradition of nationalist thought. In nationalist folklore, for example, the
effervescence of performance was reduced to the category of "monuments of the word" (as in Politis 1909). Like song texts, however, the

2. Two dolphins decorate the base of a stone window frame of Venetian date. (1970)

spaces that people inhabit are actually shifting and unstable. Like songs, too, they succumb to the bureaucratic nation-state's insatiable taxonomic appetite. By recasting past and future in terms of a monolithic present, the state creates "traditional neighborhoods" and "archaeological monuments" out of what, for residents, are the streets where their friends and enemies live and die. As the state encroaches ever further, residents increasingly adopt its rhetorical tactics in self-defense.

Soon, people are talking about history in monumental terms, and the awareness of social time—a time defined by both formal relationships (Evans-Pritchard 1940:107) and daily interaction (Bourdieu 1977:5–8)—appears to slip away. To complicate matters still further, the social management of time has also changed through time. No more does a barrel maker take an hour and a half off to sip his coffee as in a fondly recalled "liturgy" (*litouryima*); no more do customers accept the imprecise promises of craftsmen as an excuse to sit patiently by. But *were* they ever so patient? Or is that claim simply a modern way of romanticizing the past to ensure that it will never return? In this book, which is about the social context of a massive historic conservation effort, we shall find that the social uses of time and its monumentalization by officialdom are entangled in a struggle of sinewy complexity.

Monumental time is calibrated in well-defined periods. The bureau-

3

3–6. Poor householders used designs incised in the plasterwork of their houses in place of expensive materials such as tiling. (1970)

4

5

6

7. A carved stone lintel tops a new door modeled in
the local tradition of woodwork. (1986)

cratic measure of history, it is no less *managed* than social time, and its
proprieties are no less contingent on access to sources of power; but it has
the power to conceal the props of its management and to insist on the
rightness of its results. That, at least, is the theory. The monumentalization of history exemplifies what de Certeau (1984:36) has called "the
mastery of time through the foundation of an autonomous place."
Houses of technically questionable age are now definitively Venetian and
thus part of a larger European cultural space. The contexts of social experience have become an anonymous archaeological site. In resisting this
official appropriation of their lived space, Rethemniots have in effect disputed a much wider range of bureaucratic arbitrariness—the control of
history writ large. They have tried to reclaim their lives from a detempor-
alized past and a desocialized present, and to develop other kinds of his-

torical consciousness: a counter-archaeology, to adapt Foucault's (1972) terminology, of social knowledge. This study is an attempt to render that counter-archaeology explicit, to explore its evocation of familial and non-European pasts in defiance of the etiquette of official history, and to document its complex engagement with the symbolism and meanings of official discourse.

CONTESTED TIME

Between social and monumental time lies a discursive chasm, separating popular from official understandings of history. Social time is the grist of everyday experience. It is above all the kind of time in which events cannot be predicted but in which every effort can be made to influence them. It is the time that gives events their reality, because it encounters each as one of a kind. Monumental time, by contrast, is reductive and generic. It encounters events as realizations of some supreme destiny, and it reduces social experience to collective predictability. Its main focus is on the past—a past constituted by categories and stereotypes. In its extreme forms, it is the time frame of the nation-state. To it belongs the vicarious fatalism—the call to submit to one's ordained destiny—that marks all authoritarian control. As Anderson (1983:19) wisely remarks, "[i]t is the magic of nationalism to turn chance into destiny." That magic turns tea leaves into temples, tarot cards into tables of law, and social experience into eternal truth.

In Rethemnos, this imposed predestination shores up the very fabric of the physical environment. The state has declared the Old Town to be a national, historic "monument," although monuments are exactly what residents adamantly insist they do not want to inhabit. They resist the erosion of the uncertainty in their lives and of the transience of their physical surroundings. In their everyday lives, they resent others' attempts to focus too precisely, or to impose order, on their activities. Why, indeed, should they welcome the state's much more radical permeation? In later chapters, I shall point to specific kinds of regulation in which, from the residents' point of view, official intervention resembles nothing so much as the evil eye cast by an envious neighbor—the "undue attention" (Spooner 1976:79), the hubristic desire for perfection, that runs counter to human sociability. Turning people's homes into a collective monument forces this socially anomalous objectivism into the most intimate recesses of their lives. It is an extreme case of the "enhancement of value through the diversion of commodities from their customary circuits" (Appadurai 1986:28), in which the state has initiated the diversion and where the advantages of enhanced value only accrue to those who are willing to comply with the new rules.

The conversion of chance into destiny displaces intimacy in favor of form. If the play of chance is what enables everyday experience to grow out of imperfection and spontaneity, destiny must ultimately render human action socially meaningless and reduce it to the status of a cipher in some immovable grand design. Materially, this reduction is enshrined in that triumph of place over time—here, monuments over social experience—that characterizes ideas about propriety (de Certeau 1984:36). In other words, the "undue attention" with which the state intrudes into ordinary people's everyday affairs is part of a reductive process: the evil eye of a few nasty and antisocial neighbors has given way to the all-seeing eye of bureaucratic authority. Once everything is knowable and reduced to measurements and categories, the countless idiosyncratic traces of social practice recast as "normative frameworks" (de Certeau 1984:21), and memory-saturated homes are formally catalogued as historic houses, all socially experienced sense of time disappears in favor of a set of banal, bureaucratic verities. The idea of historic conservation, especially in an inhabited town, always risks this suspension of real time: wear and tear give way to pretensions of indestructible physical presence. But in reality cultural value is never so static (see also Appadurai 1986:29). Neither social life nor physical reality comes to an end, because neither bureaucrats nor buildings are incorruptible.

As a result, the new authenticity is experienced as fakery of both fabric and motives. The monumentalization of private homes attacks widely held values of ownership. This symbolic deprivation may be reinforced by economic pressures. Sometimes the poor find themselves forced out, as has happened with many "gentrification" programs. Their erstwhile homes shift, in Thompson's (1979:35–36) terms, from the status of "transient" to that of "durable" possessions. These are not objective states of being, but cultural evaluations. The rise to durable status "is accompanied by an increasing aesthetic value" (Thompson 1979:32). The terms of this transformation correspond to the respective cosmologies of social life and the state: chance is transient, destiny durable.

The revaluation of the Greek past displays the full force of this transformation. Antiquities, which counted for naught among the peasantry, became a key to the legitimation that the state sought in the family of nations. The state and its scholarly supporters battled mightily against the idea that "old things" were to be discarded and replaced—not, in Rethemnos at least, with full success. In particular, rebuilding the Classical heritage was the path to European identity. This was not only true in Greece; neo-Classicism was, for example, "pre-eminently suitable as the vehicle whereby Britain's historic entry into the European Community could be effected" (Thompson 1979:98–99). In Greece, it appears, ironically, more intrusive than it usually does elsewhere. Successive waves of economic and political domination hide, to use a peculiarly germane metaphor, behind its facade of cultural restitution. In modern Rethemnos, with its—at best—skimpy Classical vestiges, prefabricated Parthenon frontages appear on the crumbling walls of venerable, historic buildings: transient images of the durable, rendering the durable transient. Official and elite disapproval of such accretions only shows how successful the dominant cultural ideology has been, not only at reproducing itself, but at forcing its consumers to play by its arbitration of the rules. Such cultural ironies map out larger power structures: Greek Cypriots living in elegant Georgian houses in London ignite their upmarket British neighbors' cultural moralism by redecorating their homes with metal-frame windows and pink and blue paint (Thompson 1979:50). Far more ironic yet is the contestation of the European heritage when, as in Rethemnos, it is played out in the Greek landscape itself.

Local rejections of elitist antiquarianism are statements, by Greeks, of cultural values that differ quite radically from those wished upon them from above. To their indifference to baroque or neo-Classical architecture we should add their resistance to the *social* analogues of these styles: the highly conventionalized "individualisms" of European nationalist ideologies (see Handler 1988; Herzfeld 1987a; Kapferer 1988; cf. also Dorst 1989:167). The owners' ideas about style conflict with the official regulation of color, form, and ornament. This cultural argument is simultaneously a contest over social identities: *my* house or *our* national monument?

Much of the recent literature on the management of the past, especially of its physical remnants, has concentrated on the various attempts that political elites have made to "fix" history in a partial, highly selective presentation. These formulations, while useful as a critique of statist ideology, entail two closely interwoven dangers. First, such terms as "the invention of tradition" (Hobsbawm and Ranger 1983; but see Dorst's [1989:110] much more nuanced use of "veneer") suggest the possibility of an ultimately knowable historical past. Although traditions are invented, the implicit argument suggests, there ought to be something else that represents the "real" past. But if any history is invented, all history is invented. We should not view one kind of tradition as more invented than others, although its bearers may be more powerful and therefore more capable of enforcing its reproduction among disenfranchised classes—a different issue (on which, see Cowan 1988). Indeed, if we deny the consumers of tradition any role in recasting them or investing them with distinctive meanings, we simply reproduce the state's own denial of ordinary people's participation in real history.

Dorst's admirable attempt to "read" an American suburb illustrates the problem. He sets out to document the hegemony of a particular kind of postmodernism, the ahistoric reification of the past that he calls "traditionizing," and he explores the ways in which that hegemony is constructed. In his account, however, social actors largely disappear. As he rightly notes (1989:189), such impersonality is itself all of a piece with the postmodern dissolution of the individual as an ideological construct.

The difficulty with this approach is that it ends up risking complicity with the forces of hegemony to which it is critically addressed. Ethnography can empower voices not usually heard in discussions of tradition, historic conservation, and the like, the voices of those who live in the spaces decreed as monumental by the state. It can recover the unofficial meanings that people often read into official discursive forms (see de Certeau 1984:xiii; Herzfeld 1987a:144–151). In this way, it places in question official interpretations of past and present.

It is because I agree with Dorst's (1989:166) view that the anthropologist should not end up co-opted by the logic of rival claims to authenticity that I would insist on investigating as many of the competing (and often submerged) authenticities as possible. Histories range from highly personal and subversive to some that are broadly and obviously hegemonic. The contest among them is written in the inhabited spaces. As a poor rural migrant to Rethemnos told me in 1970, the neatly scratched wavy designs on the plaster surfaces of his house represented his blood—the blood of crushing labor—"flowing in the building" (Herzfeld 1971:192). When at last the authorities persuade such a householder to strip these accretions away from the ancient stone beneath, the new format must also represent an interpretation, perhaps even a compromise between a "strict" reading of the law and the neighborly relations that the conservation bureaucrat wants to preserve with the householder. If postmodernism is truly a "regime of surfaces" (Dorst 1989:104), any challenge to its legitimacy demands that we probe beneath the surfaces. Who lives behind those reconstituted "historic" doors? What do movements in and out of the structures signify? What history of mediation and accommodation does the present surface reflect? The official management of an inhabited environment is liable to irreverent and unruly interpretations by those who reside within. The effects of this failure of official intentions may be entirely tangible, but we need local knowledge to make sense of them. Otherwise, as Rabinow (1989:299) also implies, we may seem to endorse hegemony by crediting it with too much success.

By the same token, we should also recognize that most bureaucrats are neither the heartless lackeys nor the choiceless victims of some generic teleology—the state, postmodern hegemony, colonialism. They, too, are situated actors struggling to bend partly recalcitrant boundaries. While their assigned task is to reinforce the monumentalization of official time, through acts of commemoration on the one hand and through their insistence on the eternal validity of law on the other, in practice they must confront an enormous array of decisions to be made and risks to be taken. They must work with conflicting official guidelines on the one side, and under constant social pressure on the other. In widely acknowledged practices that popular and official detractors alike treat as relics of Ottoman corruption, they reinsert " 'popular' techniques of other times and other places" (de Certeau 1984:26) into the normative present. Their actions, no less than those of ordinary citizens, are subject to various degrees of uncertainty, often interpreted by disgruntled clients as caprice but welcomed with sympathy by those who have benefited from it. We can read the functionaries' necessary compromises between grand ideology and exigent sociability in the spaces cleaned, excavated, scratched, plastered, and painted on the architectonic landscape, and especially in the parade of inconsistencies that these various interventions present to the critical eye.

Conservation—in Greek, *anapaleosi*, literally, "reantiquating"—encapsulates and defines the forms of tradition and history. From the perspective of residents who have gradually modified their physical environment without making radical changes, it is a shocking destruction of the familiar: not continuity, but radical change. Maurice Halbwachs (1980:135), a French social thinker who was himself directly implicated in town planning for the state (see Rabinow 1989), observed that destruction of a town's physical fabric may generate considerable anxiety, and that after a while the elements of familiar society will reappear, imprinted afresh on the new setting. It is this resilience of social practices that ever eludes the grasp of total monumentalization. Even now, when it may seem that the economic advantages of the conservation program have proved persuasive to many Rethemniots, the signs of differing opinions and bureaucratic complaisance are everywhere.

Monumental time is, in practice, never immune to contestation. The fact that bureaucrats are rarely consistent in their use of it repeatedly wrecks its claims to absolute validity by exposing them to ridicule. In scale, it is cultural rather than social, although its local imposition obviously has social consequences. It is the time in which an entire cultural identity is framed. By definition, it is always retrospective—a grand afterthought, significantly like destiny in this regard. Experience frequently undermines its claims. Actors exercise choice and struggle to change the way things are—the very aspects of collective existence that monumental time, with its intimations of unalterable destiny, categorically denies. Because actors pursue individual or interest-group goals, the untidiness of social time repeatedly intrudes into the streamlined orientation of monumental time to the collective achievement of an entire nation.

To understand social time in these terms, and to understand how it affects the development of a historic conservation program such as that of Rethemnos, it is not enough simply to record acts of resistance against conservation alone. On the contrary, we must see how time is apprehended in a wide variety of contexts. In these terms, we shall see that the monumental version of time is in fact extremely vulnerable to creative reuse by the same social forces that it seeks to control. Bureaucrats do not "impose" it equally; local landowners do not necessarily go along with the view of "tradition" that it implies, although they may use its rhetoric; and certainly those who claim to suffer most from its imposition also adopt its rhetoric and turn it in a variety of unexpectedly inventive directions of their own choosing. Power is always diffuse to some degree. Its rhetoric is usually fairly uniform, but the uses to which that rhetoric is put may not be uniform at all. It is important, then, to recognize that a shared rhetoric of the past, however official it may seem on the surface, can conceal multiple interpretations and experiences of time. This is what the ethnographic evidence most strongly suggests.

Historic conservation is an increasingly common phenomenon globally. It appears to serve a fairly consistent set of social, economic, and ideological goals. The houses of Rethemnos, with their echoes of Classical Greece and of the European Renaissance, present a theme that colonialism has carried around the world. Ancient Athens surfaces, sometimes sketchy and spindly and sometimes bluntly vast, in domestic as well as monumental architectures from the creole traditions of the New World to fascist railway stations and stately homes in the Old. Rethemnos is exemplary of a tendency to conflate all earlier styles as a celebration of European identity through the spread of an increasingly stylized image of European power. Even the neatly framed preservation of Turkish elements resuscitates "Western" ideals of tolerance (see also Rabinow 1989:300) and a desire, expressed in endless public statements, to join in the global drive to preserve great architecture of all periods and civilizations. In this way, Turkish elements can be contained within "traditional architecture" and "local heritage." I do not mean that the act of preserving Turkish remains is necessarily misguided. I do want to suggest, however, that it has largely become possible as the expression of a cultural liberalism that is itself one of the diagnostic forms of European identity. It certainly does not represent a particularly common attitude among those who must today carry the burden of being "traditional," the residents of old Rethemnos.

David Lowenthal (1985:xvii; see also 404–405) has drawn our attention to the way in which the twentieth century, by treating the past as a "foreign country" radically different from our own time, has made its relics practically irrelevant to modern concerns. His argument can be extended, I believe, to the people who are forced in one way or another to live in these monumentalized relics. They, too, to borrow his evocative phrase, feel themselves to be "prized as vestiges." Lacking an easy means of escape, their alienation from the sources of power marked by the otherness of anachronism (cf. Fabian's [1983] "allochronism"), the poor inhabit an increasingly marginal space, a condition they resent for the economic limitations it imposes on them in a world where social values are increasingly defined by a consumer economy. It is not necessary to charge that their dispirited condition springs from deliberate social management from above. That they perceive themselves in these terms, however, shows that they fully appreciate the degree of their entanglement in processes over which they exercise virtually no control.

This assessment of their present condition takes the form of evoking a categorically despised past. Residents attribute their most familiar economic habits to "Turkish" cultural models, especially in such economic practices as bargaining and usury. Such perceptions are at once the cause and the effect of their remaining, economically as well as residentially, more or less where they are. Theirs is the ultimate "otherness within," the bitter cultural gift from the crypto-colonial Great Powers. Thus, the creation of an increasingly marginalized underclass and the monumentalization of its residential space spring from a common Eurocentric impetus. Small wonder, then, that Rethemniot shopkeepers resent those tourists who persist in such petty but ubiquitous acts of "practical orientalism" (to extend Said's [1978] usage) as bargaining with them. Such perceived condescension adds cultural insult to economic injury.

So, too, does the government's insistence on obstructing the residents' attempts to modernize their homes with endless bureaucratic restrictions, and on interfering with the ebb and flow of social intimacies through its imposition of rigid tax laws and legal restraints on public ebullience. Once again, we should not expect to decipher the complex meanings that conservation acquires without attending to the larger but more private social contexts into which it pries with a persistent and heavy hand.

FRAGMENTS OF THE PAST

Rethemnos might seem a poor choice for the neo-Classical ideology of official Greek cultural policy. Although there is some evidence of habitation in nearby villages in Minoan times, the earliest extant remains in Rethemnos itself date to the Hellenistic period. Of these earliest phases, little survives today: odds and ends of masonry, dispirited shards in dusty glass cases indifferently laid out in the gloomy interior of the delicate Venetian Loggia, side by side with fake Egyptian ushabti statuettes and, in the garden, shattered marble fragments from the graves of long-departed Turks. (For many years the museum has awaited removal to more dramatic display quarters up by the old Venetian citadel: an apt allegory, this inertia, of the tale we are going to explore.) Among the fragments on display in the garden are two that attest to another vanished presence, that of the Jews—one from the local community and dated 1768, the other the tombstone of a Jewish member of the Russian peacekeeping force who died in Rethemnos in 1907 (Ankori 1968:321–323). Especially noticeable, however, are the many Turkish fragments, with their scrolling Arabic monumental calligraphy, representing a long occupation (1646–1898) whose traces reappear throughout the town, in fountain inscriptions, minarets, domes, and house decorations of clearly Islamic inspiration.

The Turkish armies attacked Crete in 1645. Rethemnos fell early, and the Turks eventually overwhelmed even the tough defense of Candia (Iraklio). Thus ended over four centuries of Venetian rule (1210–1669). At the end of the Venetian era, Rethemnos boasted a population of about 8,500 (Nenedakis 1983:79; Manousakas 1949:58 gives 8,038, from the Trivan census). By late 1646, the town, its citizenry depleted by more than four-fifths, was in Turkish hands. So, too, was most of the rest of Crete, although Candia (Iraklio) held out until 1669. The Turks immediately consolidated military and administrative presence in the town. Despite its now much smaller population, it seems to have been a significant commercial post, and by the time Pashley visited it in 1833 it contained "upwards of three thousand souls, of whom only about eighty families are Christians" (Pashley 1837, I:104).[4] It had several substantial mosques and, it seems, a thriving community of Dervishes whose ecstatic possession rituals combined—an apt metaphor for Rethemnos—with alternations of passive neighborliness and wild religious fanaticism against the infidels in their midst. Occasions for strife were certainly frequent, for the Cretans rose in bloody revolt several times as they had against Venetian rule.

The most notable insurrections were that of Daskaloyannis, a local Sfakiot chieftain, in 1770, which ended in abject failure when a promised Russian fleet failed to come to the aid of the beleaguered Christians; and the 1886 revolt that culminated in the self-immolation of the besieged monks and villagers at the monastery of Arkadi. During the half century following Pashley's visit, the continuing violence drove increasing numbers of villagers into the towns and sent the Muslims to Ottoman centers whose future seemed less at risk. While the overall population grew rapidly to 7,000, the Christian component reached one-third of the total (Khatzidakis 1881:66; cf. also Stavrakis 1890, II:30, giving a figure of 7,929 in 1881). On Crete as a whole, the Christian population, hitherto roughly equal to the Muslim, now became three times as large as the latter (Detorakis 1986:401). The total population continued to grow, reaching by century's end almost the same level as on the eve of the Turkish invasion. Much of the town's commerce came into Christian hands during this phase, reversing the decline in Christian fortunes that began early in the Turkish period in response to the discriminatory taxation of all non-Muslims (see, e.g., Stavrinidis 1986, I:98). For some fifty years, too, Christian artisans and merchants had begun taking charge of their economic situation by creating urban professional guilds of their own (Detorakis 1986:297). By 1899, when Crete began its fourteen-year experiment with autonomy, many of the Muslims left in Rethemnos seem to have been unemployed, although others were still among the richest citizens of the town and clearly hoped that their personal wealth would preserve them from harm.

Documents from the turn of the century illustrate the rapid decline in the Muslim population.[5] Of sixty-four property sale contracts from 1900 that I was able to examine, thirty-one are from Muslim to Christian owners, while not a single one bears witness to a sale from a Christian to a Muslim. Only one out of the twelve, mostly poor properties on the Fortezza (Venetian citadel) that changed ownership in this period was initially owned by a Christian, while a mere four remained in Muslim hands. In the slightly more elegant quarter of Skridloff Square—formerly the Muslim quarter of Ak-Serai and now renamed by the Russian authorities who in 1898 oversaw the local transition to independence under an international four-power agreement[6]—five out of seven hitherto Muslim properties ended up under Christian control. The documents, which also indicate who owned the abutting properties, show a steady Christian erosion of a virtual Muslim monopoly in this neighborhood.

One after another, once exclusively Muslim districts became mixed. People of all classes were involved, whether as direct parties to sales or as witnesses. The sale documents mention Muslim coffee and tobacco merchants, laborers, religious officials, grocers, shoemakers, a builder, a "rope-knitter" (a profession already known on Crete in Venetian times [Dimakopoulos 1977:39]), a blacksmith, a knife maker, a barber, a porter, a boatman, and a fisherman. Christians included a lawyer, a teacher, a priest, a wine merchant, a pastry cook, an ironworker, carpenters, and bakers. In many cases, the wealthier Muslim owners have already left for Smyrna and the Dardanelles; still-resident coreligionists wind up their affairs for them with the sale of their erstwhile homes. The Greek documents sometimes introduce a solemn rhetoric into this dreary tale of decline. Sometimes the background seems to be one of desperate speculation over minute properties. An "Ethiopian [i.e., black] slave," freed upon the death of her master, gets a pittance for the property she sells to an out-of-work coreligionist in the slum where most such former slaves, originally brought to Crete by the armies of the Albanian Mehmet Ali of

Egypt, eked out a living. This was the poorest quarter, Çikur Bostan (Aetoudakis 1986:133), huddled inside the walls of what the document grandly calls the "Acropolis"—that is, the Fortezza. Official Hellenism has already quietly begun, a mere two years after liberation and thirteen years before union with Greece, to tune the often shabby recent past to the neo-Classical sonorities of an irredentist present.

The property sale documents give an interesting picture of Muslim-Christian relations. The common language seems usually to have been Greek. The notaries were of both faiths; one Muslim, a certain Pertiv Dhervisakis ("son of the Dervish"), was especially active in sales involving his coreligionists. When Muslim women appeared as parties to a contract, they "had their faces covered in accordance with Ottoman [*sic*] custom."

Veiling supposedly impeded identification. In a late nineteenth-century photograph of a young urban Muslim woman, however, we see only a gauzy partial drape, which suggests that she did not literally have to hide her identity even before a Christian male (who happened to be the French consul general). Another of his photographs, this time portraying female Muslim migrants from North Africa (*khalikoutisses*), shows several of these women full face and completely unveiled (Louloudakis 1984:15, 44, 61). The law, it seems, recognized the formal implications of veiling rather than its sketchy implementation in practice. Thus, for each Muslim female party to a contract, two additional male witnesses—beyond the two required for the actual transaction of the contract—had to affirm that she was indeed who she said she was. Such witnesses to women's identity were almost always Muslims themselves and often included a husband or brother; but one Christian doctor, doubtless a person of privileged intimacy, was also permitted to serve in this capacity. When female parties were Christian, the notary could register them as "unknown to him" without requiring any further attestation of their identities. As the Muslim exodus accelerated, notaries may have become increasingly nervous about incurring responsibility for unknown defaulters. When we turn to modern legal practice in a later chapter, we shall again see this bureaucratic concern to evade personal involvement, and to hide personal motives behind the formal rhetoric of the law—a rhetoric not vastly changed from that of the turn of the century.

When Crete finally became part of the Greek state in 1912, the irredentists in Athens seemed on the verge of realizing as a political reality the so-called Great Idea. This was the dream of recapturing all the territories once and presently inhabited by Greeks, and, emblematically, of resuming the Mass in the Church of Agia Sophia at the point at which it had broken off when the Turks sacked Constantinople in 1453. At first, when the Greeks invaded Asia Minor in 1920, all seemed well. With the Turkish defeat of the Greek armies in 1922, however, the irredentist vision evaporated in ignominy and recrimination (see Llewellyn Smith 1973), and the Treaty of Lausanne (1923) sent a flood of refugees from Asia Minor into Greece. Rethemnos, a poor and confined space now in commercial decline, was not attractive to the more ambitious and entrepreneurial of the newcomers, and many of them stayed only briefly. From the beginning of the century to the 1928 census, the population dropped by nearly 3,000. A mere 1,350 refugees from Asia Minor (Malagari and Stratigakis 1985–1986:64) finally settled in the Rethemnos houses vacated by the Muslims, who had been similarly required by the terms of the treaty to depart for Turkey.

The departing Muslims regarded Crete as their home. Their language, for the most part, was Greek. Their departure was as bitter an exile as the reverse flow of Christians, some of them Turkish-speaking, into the Greek territories. The forcible exchange of populations made a harsh human sacrifice to the Realpolitik of national homogenization. Its insensitive logic of equating religious with ethnic identity was one of the bitterest of historical ironies, given that the Turkish state was about to adopt a deliberate domestic policy of banishing Islam to the margins of secular life.

Refugees do not easily sever all ties with the lived places of their memory. Today, in a more peaceful era, Cretan Muslims and their children, many still Greek-speaking, occasionally visit Rethemnos. The Asia Minor Greeks go on similar pilgrimages to their former homes on the Turkish mainland. Each meets a refugee presence in what once was home, each understands the other's longing. Categorical enmity yields to common social experience. And the points of reference are indeed common places: homes, walls, the towering citadel. It matters little whether one is returning on a visit from exile, or from a day's toil in factory or field. For nostalgic refugee and exhausted worker alike, the eroded grandeur of the Fortezza still rears out of heat haze or winter mist to offer the returning Rethemniot the first sight of home (see plate 8).

ARRIVING IN PLACE

To this sight, dominating an ancient walled town whose population was some three-quarters of its present size at the turn of the century, I found myself repeatedly returning along the coastal road from the Khania airport or from villages to east or west. By 1986, I already knew Rethemnos as the commercial capital of the prefecture in whose mountainous hinterland I had worked earlier ("Glendi" [Herzfeld 1985]; see map, fig. 1.1). Here were the police headquarters, the prefecture offices, and the pervasive evidence of municipal pride: statues of a bewhiskered preindependence resistance hero and of the urbanely smooth-cheeked Pandelis

8. View across the rooftops toward the Fortezza, with a mosque dome looming above the walls and the former Venetian prison in front, right of center. (1970)

Prevelakis, a carefully watered and weeded park and modern squares, bus terminals and business offices, traffic lights and fire hydrants. Much earlier still, I had noted the attempts made by Rethemniots, many of them newly arrived from villages in the intermediate hinterland, to beautify their plastered walls with the incised designs already mentioned, ranging from simple alternating bands of straight and wavy lines to complex combinations of geometrical fantasy (Herzfeld 1971). Here was the struggle over the physical body of Rethemnos: a modern medium, dressing the distinctive contours of rubble soon to emerge as a precious heritage of Venetian architecture (map, fig. 1.2). The narrative thread of this ethnography is written in such revisions of perspective.

My several return visits in the course of my work in the mountainous zone provided a different view of Rethemnos, as the seat of officialdom. Although I was slowly becoming aware of the local tensions occasioned by official efforts to conserve the historic Old Town and had indeed been attracted by them to conduct research there, I still saw the rebellious village and the seemingly decorous town as to some extent culturally discrete. I had accepted at face value the "well-mannered" image behind which, says the local novelist Yiannis Kaloyerakis (1982:38), Rethemniots "try to hide the wildness of the Cretan, which you can make out in their eyes if you are a Cretan." True, I had become interested in the apparent cultural borrowing between these polarized topoi of the anthro-

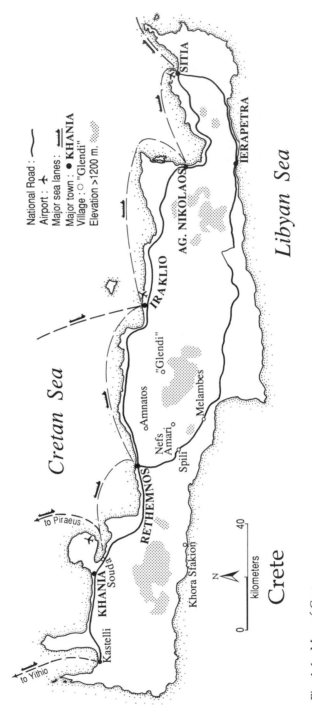

Fig. 1.1. Map of Crete

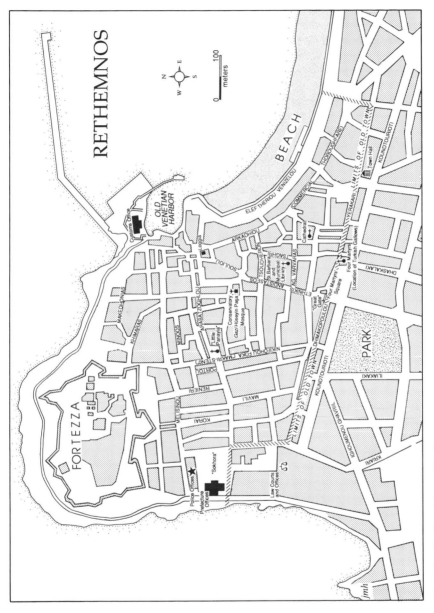

Fig. 1.2. Outline Map of Rethemnos

pological imagination: the wild and the tame, the rural and the urban. But the municipal order that I found inscribed everywhere affected my own perceptions even as I became fascinated with the marks of a competing disorder: the roughly incised plaster patched up and covered with unrelated serendipities of electrical wiring, the informality with which one made the acquaintance of local musicians and shopkeepers.

With time, the wildness and the domestication began to merge, to interact. A little over two years after I began the present project, I learned that some of my friends from the mountain village had helped to ransack the local offices of the Ministry of Agriculture at the end of a day of raucous protest and were being sought by the police. Meanwhile, a local newspaper reviewed my study of the rural community (Tsirimonaki 1988)[7] and interviewed me about the new work I was now doing in town (Pitsidianaki 1987). Gradually, I stopped thinking about village and town as separate entities. Each is situated within the other's experience; each claims an identity that at once incorporates and rejects the self-image of the other. An elderly resident, growing tired of his own tirades against official attempts to preserve the town's historic fabric, admitted to hopes of reconciliation: "I'm an old man, but I believe that the animals will be found (*tha vrethoun ta oza*), as we say in Crete"—an evocation of reciprocal animal theft in the mountain villages, and of the social solidarity that transcends its daily outbreaks. While the binarism of town and country is a part of local perceptions, moreover, it becomes entwined with the many other ambiguities of local identity.

This is indeed a study of how people negotiate their sense of place. It is about situating moral identity, about battling the form and future of the physical environment, about shoring up familiar cultural spaces against the encroaching, encompassing strangeness of larger worlds. Rethemnos is not merely a physical place. It is also a literary topos—the word means "place" too—that animates the writings of major Greek poets and novelists. Prevelakis himself recognized this textual entailment when he chose as his epigraph an ode to Rethemnos by the poet Angelos Sikelianos.

In Prevelakis's *Tale*, nostalgia for a lost past echoes regrets still voiced, while both his and the other major novel set in Rethemnos—Lilika Nakou's *Madame Do-Re-Mi*—sensuously explore the complex intertwining of town and village, European and Oriental, foreign elegance and local roughness. Rethemnos exemplifies the often stormy tension between a powerful model of a monumentalized "European" culture and the lovable imperfections of experienced social life with its more fragmented, polyphonous pasts. The poems of Yoryis Kalomenopoulos (1964) are descriptive tableaux that revive the intimacy of Christian-Muslim interaction in the marketplace, the harbor, and the coffee shops of Rethemnos before the enforced departure of the Muslims in the mid-1920s. They, too, portray the precarious balance between East and West, rusticity and cosmopolitanism, the rough Cretan camaraderie and the "pâtisserie-confiserie" that was still a fond memory for one of my older and more conservative friends and that was the last trace left by the "international [peacekeeping] forces" that briefly occupied *to Rethemnaki* ("little Rethemnos") in 1898 on the eve of Cretan independence (Kalomenopoulos 1964:126).

Lilika Nakou, perhaps more than anyone else, provoked these passions of identity during her own sojourn. Her largely autobiographical novel (1955) relates her cosmopolitan, Paris-polished inability to come to terms with the easily outraged ideas of respectability of the townspeople whose children she had come to teach. Her book still excites lively controversy. A retired civil servant objected to her representation of the schoolboys of her time (1932) as wearing the *vraka* (baggy trousers) and carrying guns,[8] although he did confirm the central incident in which the hapless young teacher accidentally led the adolescent girls in her charge to the Fortezza for an educational stroll, not realizing that it was the brothel zone!

Another elderly gentleman, the same who yearned for that old pâtisserie, more sentimentally recalled her French ways. She made little bows, while the locals were still "barbaric" in their ways—"it was [like] East and West!" Yet this was a town where the community leaders still spoke French among themselves, affected European dress styles, and imported only the best English suitings. True, Rethemnos suffers from neglect. It is not what it might have been. But this was the very wound that Nakou irritated. She too forcibly brought the Rethemniots up against what they were not (see also Tannen 1983:103). Today, ironically, the garish seafront, with its brash pursuit of the tourist trade, prompts the remark: "Here it's not Rethimno now, the Old Town. It's—[*dramatic pause for effect*] Paris!" But this Paris is no gain. European culture is both a goal and an imposition, a dream of incorporation into the civilized West and a nightmare of cultural colonization. Ultimately, Madame Do-Re-Mi and the tourists represent the same invasive breach in the walls of parochial respectability and sexual morals. She took the local schoolgirls to the brothel zone up beside the Fortezza, the Venetian citadel; the tourists, say nervous citizens, bring promiscuity and drugs that all too easily prey on the boredom of the town's youth.[9] It is not mere chance that those who were most offended by the television serial of *Madame Do-Re-Mi* were the elderly and the politically conservative—people whose lives and vision have straddled the most violent awakening to the multiple meanings of "Europe."

When the national television service broadcast a serialized version of the book, its offense was to display disreputable aspects of Rethemnos to the rest of the world. As a conservative parliamentary deputy for the region objected in an official question in Parliament, the serial "crudely insults the history of Rethimno [and] the tradition, the courageous strength, the pride and the hospitality of its inhabitants, representing their town as an inhospitable, filthy village used as a place for [political exile] and its people [as] unrefined bumpkins, cowardly, thuggish, antisocial, ready to commit crime." This, at least, was the reaction on the political Right, and it found support particularly among the older citizens concerned with maintaining a respectable image. Irritated also by the serial's brief focus on the practice of exiling communists to out-of-the-way places, the supporters of the Right elicited sympathy by translating their political ire into cultural dudgeon. The socialist government responded that the book was "just a novel." Not so, responded the Right: it is a false portrait of a community. The past treatment of *local* communists by the politically dominant Right, especially from the Civil War until the collapse of the military junta in 1974, invisibly but surely animates what superficially appears to be a discussion of culture and above all of mores. The protests in fact began before the television serial had reached the point when the protagonist took her charges to the brothel zone and fell to her ultimate disgrace. Yet the moral dimension remains implicit in reactions to Nakou's account of Rethemnos. Those in power seek to monumentalize and eternalize the "European" values of Greekness, respectability, and order.

The Fortezza is an ambivalent presence for Rethemniots. On the one hand, it is an impressive remnant of their links with the West European awakening, which the Renaissance Festival (begun in 1987) attempts to resuscitate. But it is also a reminder of past tyrannies, Nazi as well as Venetian and Turkish, its last real inhabitants the destitute and the formerly enslaved, and its physical proximity to the brothels an unsavory memory. A local town-planning official has suggested that only full restoration and recontextualization—with a "green zone" replacing the brothel district—can dispel its darker shadows.

Respectability is not a concern for the official world alone. Rather, it provides a generic metaphor for the exercise of power. A few years ago, a desperately poor family refused to occupy its ancestral property in the street where the few remaining houses of ill repute linger; they had young daughters and would not expose them to this bad example. They only agreed to move there when it became clear that the state authorities, in response to local agitation, were making a decisive effort to suppress the brothels once and for all:

> And there are three women [i.e., prostitutes] up there, and [each one] tells you, "I'm not leaving!" What's to happen now—is the tourist to go up, and with this lady coming out [of her house] with her improper behavior, and is he—the tourist—to ask, "What's this here?"

Exposure is the offense, a disrobing of sexuality and privacy:

> The woman will come out onto her veranda to sit and drink her coffee, the customer will come up; one will kiss her, one will caress her, another I don't know what! At a certain moment [one] will open her dressing-gown (*roba*) and she's completely naked within.

This, then, is the voice of outraged respectability: bodily exposure is also the exposure of the community, a breach of collective decency. The strategy of the Right is to displace its own embarrassment at being caught "with its trousers down" (as we might say) by outrage at the fallen women—prostitutes or tourists—who "go about without their trousers on" (as they say). At least the Fortezza was isolated. On the sole occasion when a brothel opened in the main part of the town, in a temporary shelter on one of the open spaces left by the demolition or collapse of an old building, it was swiftly cleared away.

The novelist Kaloyerakis, however, makes it clear that the prostitutes' presence was also very central to the lives of young men, at least until the arrival of the tourists. In his first novel, *The Killing God*, he draws largely from his own experiences, as he told me, to present the insider's view. Men, he said, would form real friendships with these women, and such attachments were recognized and respected. *The Killing God* was not a novel to endear Kaloyerakis to his fellow townspeople; and it did not. Here again, commonly heard insinuations about the author's political motives are inseparable from the local reactions to his writing.

In Kaloyerakis's novel, too, women's sexuality—a familiar theme in descriptions of Greek society—works as a metaphor for the twin passions of intimacy and embarrassment. Women are the locus of male pride and the means of their collective fall. A woman once sued her husband for divorce on the grounds of the latter's adultery. Everyone in Rethemnos, men and women alike, was furious with her: it was a disgraceful embarrassment (*dropi*)[10] to expose *the town* in this way when so many other men did the very same thing without being shamed in public! In the male-dominated discourse of public discussion, women cannot win. They are always the source of humiliation, whether by virtue of their own sexual downfall or on the rare occasions when they dare challenge men's actions.

It is consistent with this androcentric localism, in which the collective identity is imbued with specifically male pride, that the prostitutes are never Rethemniot women and may even be from outside Crete. The public purity of the male image thus informs that of the town. No local father would tolerate the humiliation that a daughter's prostitution would bring. To avoid being killed, a local "fallen woman" (for this is the category from which most prostitutes are recruited) goes elsewhere. In the early years of the Turkish occupation, as perhaps also at a comparable

stage of the Venetian period, prostitutes were sometimes women raped by
the invaders or their officials and therefore unable to marry (Stavrinidis
1986, I:94–96). While the Turkish authorities sometimes attempted to
limit both the prostitution and concubinage of Christian women, as well
as the infanticide that often ensued from unwanted pregnancies (Detorakis 1986:288–289), their efforts were often cursory and ultimately un-
successful. Turkish official documents show that some Turks made free
with Christian virgins, to whom they effectively left no other option than
prostitution. Not all unions between Christian women and Muslim men
were illegitimate; as in the Venetian period, when the Catholic invaders
often took Greek Orthodox wives, marriage was a cause of large-scale
religious conversion, as was the desire to escape the heavy capitation tax
levied on all infidels.[11] Once a woman had been raped by a Turk, however, she had little choice but to become a prostitute if he refused to marry
her.

Not all prostitutes were Christians. The Rethemniot poet Kalomenopoulos (1964:116) describes the triumphal passage of one Nuriye
through the streets of the town: "Hodjas [Muslim clerics] and [Christian]
priests, old men, middle-aged and young, pupils and teachers, merchants and secretaries, craftsmen and apprentices stand admiring Nuriye's charms." Nor did prostitution cease with the departure of the
Turks. In spite of the silence that surrounds the subject, there are hints
that the military commanders representing the Great Powers in 1898 recognized it as a problem as well as a necessity (Malagari and Stratigakis
1985–1986:62), and the local authorities are still in the final throes of
trying to eradicate it altogether.

Illicit sexuality, so intimate in practice, must always be presented in
public as foreign to local values.[12] There has indeed been some recent
concern that prostitutes would come in from foreign countries, especially
the Far East, and tourist women are often generically dismissed as
"whores." From this perspective, then, Nakou transgressed the boundaries of "Europe," the emblem of both respectability and licentiousness.

In Rethemnos, at the turn of the century, most of the prostitutes' customers were unmarried men of military age. The police checked to make
sure that adolescents were kept away. The brothels were situated among
Turkish-owned houses, and this additional touch of the exotic was often
sufficient reason for the younger boys to fear going there. The prostitutes'
neighbors included three or four "troglodytes"—garbage collectors who
made their homes in caves and ruins on the Fortezza until the Municipality finally swept their ramshackle habitations away, causing a veritable
treasure hunt as coins and other artifacts came to the surface.

The prostitute population has almost disappeared since Nakou's day.
Under the Metaxas dictatorship, in the immediately pre–World War II

period, there were seventeen women operating on the Fortezza. After the war, the Plastiras government introduced compulsory registration. Successive attempts to clear away the houses as they became derelict has allowed the Municipality to close down the entire zone, and all that is left today are a few squalid houses and some quiet outpourings of male nostalgia.

Today, moreover, other sexual adventures beckon. Some local women regard all tourist and student women as prostitutes. This is not a facile display of prudery. It springs less from a *shared* moral indignation on the part of Rethemniot women and men than from the local women's perhaps realistic fear that their husbands and brothers may be seduced away from their marital beds and—what is perhaps more important—from their economic role as central breadwinners by the charms of these sirens (see Herzfeld 1991). Students and tourists, moreover, provide access to nonlocal wealth and work, opportunities from which the prostitutes of an earlier day were completely isolated.[13] They compete with the local women's sole sources of support. Similar concerns animate local wives' reactions to the men's gambling. Men's huge self-glorification does not win much female applause, not because it is immoral, but because it is highly destructive.

But, from the men's point of view, social life has its wild underside, and good fellowship means recognizing this in oneself and others. A village saying claims that "too much cleanliness is halfway to pollution" (*i poli pastrikosini ine misi ghoursouzia*). The town's peculiar combination of dilapidation and neatly maintained houses (compare, for example, plates 9 and 10) is the locus of its familiar life. This intimate, postlapsarian sociability opposes the petty precision of bureaucracy and of a too careful focus on appearances. Formal respectability is only the public face of the town.

ROOTS AND CUTTINGS: RETHEMNOS AS AGRO-TOWN

There is another sense in which Rethemnos occupies frontier territory between nature and culture. It is a true agro-town. Most of its inhabitants hail from hinterland villages and represent immigration to the town within the past quarter of a century. While the same process has been going on for years, the yearning for urban comforts certainly fueled a considerable acceleration from about 1960 on. Virtually all the Rethemniots who immigrated within two generations of the present own land in their ancestral villages; moreover, since a common pattern is for marriage between people from different villages to lead to residence in town, most such families have agricultural properties in at least two different places and continue to assume responsibility for their cultivation. A further link

9. A view toward the Venetian harbor, with the restored lighthouse on the right. (1987)

with the home village comes at election time: voting is compulsory, and many Rethemniots, like other recently urban Greeks, have not bothered to transfer their electoral registration to the town.

Olives require year-round care. Most of it, however, is not very time-consuming in comparison with the demands made by vines. The busy time is in late summer and autumn. Early spring pruning is only needed every ten or fifteen years. Annually, at the end of March, light pruning provides useful firewood; other light work in April can be undertaken by a paid laborer. The first nets are usually spread on the ground in the autumn. A family owning a restaurant on the touristy seafront closes it down each November to harvest their olives; others start in October. Those who have vines must collect the grape skins to make grappa (*tsikoudhia*) in September. Few claim to make much profit on this kind of agriculture, but it does protect poorer townspeople from some of the effects of inflation. In a good year, a household might even expect to make a little profit, with which it can purchase oil of a better quality than it produces itself; in an off year, it might still only have to acquire a hundred kilos or so to cover the year's domestic needs (about 250 kilos for a family of five).

Viticulture is immensely more labor-consuming than olive cultivation, to which it has increasingly given way in the Cretan countryside with the demise of true subsistence farming. Viticulture not only calls for more specialized knowledge, it is also far more inconvenient for town dwellers. In January, the vines must be carefully pruned. After fertilizer has been laid down, the cultivator must watch the weather; if there is too much rain, spraying and sulphur dusting become urgently necessary. For many, the main crop is raisin grapes, for which the August harvest calls for immediate drying on open-air frames; if, as happens quite often, the first autumn rain comes down before the harvest is dried and bagged, all the work has been for naught. To compound the difficulties, vines require a much greater financial investment than do olives; one Rethemnos resident, for example, found himself paying 17,000 drachmas as many as ten years ago for the digging over and weeding of his slightly less than half an acre of vines, whereas it only cost him 1,500 drachmas to have the whole area dug over for olives. Even olives create problems: if the couple's home villages are far apart, the crop may require two days' work instead of the one it would have taken to harvest the same yield in a single place; but this is a minor nuisance when set beside the recurrent inconveniences of vine cultivation.

Vines are thus a high-risk activity with potentially good profits but also frequent setbacks and heavy expenses for the rural farmer; for the town dweller, unless local laborers can be employed at a reasonable wage, they mean probable and repetitive disaster. Thus olives, the less profitable crop, are more viable for those self-employed small merchants who have to work hard, long hours in the town; only civil servants (who work regular hours) and the very rich (who control their own time) can really afford the speculation that viticulture entails. The ultimate effect is that the combination of village agriculture with residence in the town accentuates differences between rich and poor—a tendency that we shall see markedly present in other domains of experience as well. Indeed, as one small-time manufacturer grumbled, many people here go "and make sure of a loafer's job (*mia dhoulia loufa*) in the Civil Service" just so that they can run inherited property in this way; those who cannot afford to do so rip up their vines and plant olives instead. A few lowly civil servants—a postman, for example—may instead hire themselves out as wage laborers on agricultural properties near the town, as a means of eking out their insufficient wages. One leftist, sourly observing that the collapse of agriculture in the 1960s had led certain lesser individuals to enter the gendarmerie, noted that for greater security of employment such a person "will profit at the expense of incurring most people's contempt!"

A constant in these calculations is the reluctance to sell off ancestral land, a sentiment doubtless compounded these days by the growing realization that the city does not necessarily offer a secure future or reliable real estate investments. A middle-aged couple quarrels: the husband has converted all his father's vines to olives, reversing his father's actions simply in order to be able to make use of the land at all. His wife would rather do without any of these rural burdens, but her husband reminds her that she had been keen enough in the old days, before the pressures of their small business in Rethemnos made visiting their respective home villages a nuisance.

Sentimental attachments to property aside, decisions about redistribution are largely a matter of location. A man who hails from a more distant village, say in Sfakia, may give his ancestral land away to kinsfolk, thereby keeping the property in the family, and acquire a few olive trees closer to town—an increasingly common practice as some entrepreneurs acquire new houses in the outer suburbia of New Rethemnos. Those who live there can often keep a few goats and sheep near their homes. Among those who do live in the Old Town, it seems usually to be the women who want to make a complete move to the amenities of the New Town, their husbands who cling sentimentally to their Old Town residences or to ancestral village properties.

A recurrent problem is created by the inheritance patterns that obtain in the rural areas: since, in theory at least, all children inherit equally, the harvest of properties that are nominally held in common may be problematical. For example, one village father gave property in Old Rethemnos to all four daughters and five out of his six sons (the exception being a man who resided abroad and preferred to take money, which he then converted into Old Town real estate in his own good time). The children all inherited equal shares of some hundred walnut trees in the village as well. These trees are on a continuous slope, so the harvesters must work in close coordination from top to bottom. One brother has had bad relations with the others and will not work with them; he is obliged to take laborers with him, an expense that his brothers and sisters are able to avoid by working together, sharing the labor as they harvest each sibling's trees in turn. Any of them who must be absent in a given year allow the sibling who happens to be in the most straitened circumstances (*ksepes-menos*) at the time to collect their shares.

In the villages around Rethemnos, the practice of dowering daughters with town houses in Rethemnos is of long standing. Some villages exhibit a strong agnatic preference for dividing the property exclusively among the sons ("so that the father's property will not pass to another line"), but in practice daughters do also inherit land. Nonetheless, since the object is to "catch" grooms of some education and prospects, a town house is more important, and village land may even create problems. A groom would have to sell the land to his brothers-in-law whether he wanted to or not, as they control the water supply on which the salability of the land depends. Thus, while land here could be transferred from mother to son (and so go outside the patrigroup), the transfer contracts make it impossible to move land to complete non-kin. Women therefore tend to marry into more urban families, while their brothers remain at home. Brothers who do migrate usually return to the natal village at harvest time. Those who hail from more distant villages may find it worthwhile to build a village house as a base for agricultural labor. When one of the siblings is unable to participate in the work, another does the work on a *simisako* basis: the yield is divided equally between the owner and the sibling who undertook to harvest it—an arrangement that can also be done with unrelated workers when the basic yield is likely to mean actual profit.

The continuing cultivation of village lands is only viable as long as the owners remain in Rethemnos or the village itself. Village produce is extremely labor-absorbing. One man, who came to Rethemnos as a boy and worked as a waiter there, was one of six children who divided their paternal property of 200 olive-trees and a few carob trees into equal parts; he also inherited "two laborers' vines" (*dhio n-erghaton ambeli*, i.e., as many vines as two laborers could harvest in one day). When he left Crete for Athens in 1957, he gave equal parts of the latter to the siblings whose properties bordered his own. Until then, he had been able to make enough oil for domestic consumption, as well as 500 *okadhes* of carobs at 2 drachmas per oka (= 1.27 kilos or 2.8 pounds); the annual income of 1,000 drachmas that the latter gave him would be worth, he thought, about 10,000 drachmas at today's prices. After his departure for Athens, his siblings felt obliged to continue sending him a can or two of oil from time to time. Once he had made himself economically self-sufficient, however, he wrote to tell them not to do this any more.

Agricultural activities are dirty and tiring, and contravene notions of urbanity. While this certainly does not prevent even relatively wealthy townsfolk from tending their rural properties, it gives a sense of ambivalence to even the most enthusiastic endorsement of rural life. It is not the way of the politia.

THE INTRUSIVE STATE: CONSERVATION AS DECAY

Politia, as I have said, is both a place and the way of life that it embodies. The physical politia of Rethemnos consists in dignified dilapidations of wall and garden, buttressed cornice and heraldic doorway, that together make up the best-preserved domestic architecture of the Venetian era outside Venice itself. The ornamental and architectural reminders of that grandiose imperium are chipped, overgrown with grassy weeds and electrical wiring (see plate 10). Venetian cornices and buttresses preserve their stately contours through coats of plaster and glossy marble shop facings. At least two shops have sprouted glossy fake Classical columns (plate 11), an unconsciously ironic reminder of another part of the nation's collective—but in this case not particularly Cretan—past. These and other invasions of historical propriety may raise a few knowing eyebrows among the visitors; worse, they draw the intervention of a protective but often heavy-handed national bureaucracy.

To many residents, the profusion of antiquarian sights is a tiresome irritant. True, for those increasing numbers who rent rooms to tourists, the picturesque pays. But others resent the idea that the state, by disrupting their lives in the name of conservation, places them at the mercy of gaping tourists who would do nothing to protect them—as one man grumbled—if war broke out! The national bureaucracy, never popular on Crete, confronts local ideas about ownership and history that depart significantly from official perceptions.

The national Archaeological Service has waged a principled battle against the heedless pursuit of comfortable modernity and the consequent destruction of the architectural heritage. It is important to see the value and integrity of its goals from the outset, especially as we shall be examining in some detail the distortion these undergo in the course of implementation. The Old Town of Rethemnos is arguably the best-preserved and largest domestic complex of late medieval and early Renaissance architecture anywhere in the Mediterranean. The effort to preserve this heritage is not the capricious choice of some bureaucratic entity in Athens, then, but a reasoned decision that, as one of its local functionaries admitted, might most fairly be criticized as too little, too late.

It has encountered many setbacks. These reflect the inability of a centralized bureaucracy to come to terms with local circumstances. Of the bitterness that has arisen, there can be no doubt. Inhabitants often call the historic conservation agency a "cancer" and a "gangrene." For these angry Rethemniots, *Arkheoloyia* is an obscenity in their mouths and an economic sickness in their lives: "Here people have terrible problems with the word 'archaeology' (*edho o kosmos eši fovera provlimata me ti leksi aršeoloyia*)" (see also Margaritis 1986). Against this, we must set the experience of those other Rethemniots for whom it is the source of new opportunities and of a new pride in the past. One ten-year-old girl informed me that she wanted to become "an archaeologist or a pathologist" when she grew up—a revealing comment, given the high prestige of the medical profession. Technically, those who staff the historic conservation office are not archaeologists at all; but the news that a (genuine) archaeologist had run afoul of the bureaucratic conservators occasioned much glee. Divergent interpretations vie for supremacy, each the pragmatic realization of specific interests in a conflict that twists and turns but

11. "Rooms for rent," souvenir shops, and an imitation-Classical frontage grace the old shoemakers' quarter, Souliou Street. (1989)

10. Crumbling Venetian doorway fragments frame a Pramateftakis poster for the 1986 municipal elections. (1986)

never goes away, a conflict that is often further fueled by political and administrative events which lie far beyond the immediate horizons of the town.

Until the late 1960s, when the promise of tourism heralded economic growth, buildings that had stood for three or four hundred years were repaired as best people could manage, then allowed to decay because they served as storerooms for rough tools and materials that would not suffer greatly in the seeping damp, and finally mined for masonry when they could no longer serve even this humble function. The so-called *kalderimi*, a street leading down from the south side of the Venetian fortress (Fortezza), formerly paved with a mosaic of carefully graded cobblestones, is now a ragged, weed-infested, and uneven path:

> I was already alive and saw that kalderimi when the Germans came here, and it was completely undamaged. You saw a [wonderful] thing, and you said, "But what craftsman was this who placed each boulder, each stone?" It was like a mosaic!

The steel of German tanks ripped through this ordered old paving as the harsh invaders took charge of the fortress, then oversaw the systematic demolition of the small neighborhood that had remained intact within the fortress walls throughout Turkish rule, and turned the entire ravished space into a military command post.

The German occupation left Rethemnos in a miserable economic condition. While Rethemnos still had some resources, mostly through the merchants' control of olive oil supplies from the hinterland, its lack of a viable harbor was a major disadvantage. The cessation of hostilities in 1944–1945 put an end to the use of oil as an alternative currency, and the demand for Rethemnos soap—the major local oil product—suddenly collapsed in the early 1960s as mass-produced soap products invaded Greece and the Balkans, sending many of the local producers into bankruptcy and their dependents to Athens in desperate search of work—any work. Other major towns, including Iraklio and Khania on Crete, began to participate in the larger economy more actively, and construction efforts soon signaled this development. Not so Rethemnos. It was the very stagnation and progressive depopulation of Rethemnos that saved it physically. The houses themselves came to mean dank, poverty-stricken, degrading misery. When conservation began after 1968, and still more with the restoration efforts from 1974 on, it would take a long, painful adjustment before the Rethemniots could so much as conceive of these collapsing ruins as a place to live "like a human being," still less as a source of future wealth.

Few Rethemniots then had enough basic funds to equip the interior of a house comfortably, let alone undertake major repairs. There were faint intimations, however, of a desire for ornament on the part of people for whom the old was certainly not also the beautiful. It was in the decades after the war that patterns incised on the plasterwork on house exteriors started to appear. They were a sign of several things: that villagers were again moving into the town, bringing with them decorative techniques born of poverty and the sudden availability of cheap modern materials, and replacing those Rethemniots who had fled to the economically more rewarding allures of Iraklio and Athens; that these newcomers, like those who had stayed on in the Old Town, were too poor to afford tiling or even glossy paint; that still, whatever the aesthetic that drove them (in their own view) to "beautify" their homes, it was not a scholastic regard for the architecture of Venetians and Turks based on its historical interest, its elegance, or its purity of line, but an assertion of spirited life on its own terms.

Conversely, these designs are not part of the officially recognized "past." An official of the historic conservation office to whom I mentioned them dismissed them as "the easy way out," and as "not very pleasing aesthetically" (*dhen in' ke poli kalesthita*), and showed no interest in the idea of preserving a few outstandingly elaborate specimens. They are too redolent of economic stagnation and neglect, too far from the ideals of mainstream art history, and, quite simply, too new:

> But, from the moment that we intervene in a building, and its historic testimonies are revealed, its historic phases, we always try to conserve, to keep, to display the most prominent (*tin epikratesteri*) as far as possible.

Clearly, these designs have no place in the official definition of history. They are in a very technical sense *interior*, a hidden undergarment, the architectural equivalent of social embarrassment, for they are the scratchings that hold an outer layer of painted plaster on to the inner wall. They bear witness to the pain, the "blood," embedded within. Few Rethemniots could afford the plaster or tile facings to which these scratchings were meant to give a better grip. In Greek, what I have translated here as "most prominent" (*epikratesteri*) also means "more powerful" and "more durable"—an admission, far from tacit, of the political implications of heritage conservation and its censorship of distress.

When I made that 1971 visit, the historic conservation that forms the major theme of this account had begun only three years earlier. The inhabitants were mystified, apprehensive, occasionally hopeful, always wary. They spoke unaffectedly of both the "beauty" (*omorfia*) and the "blood" in the plaster designs. Now, however, the conservation effort brought a new civility, one in which the monumentalizing of the past left no room for contemporary individualities. Even though the craftsmen who incised the designs were all recent or current rural dwellers, moreover, work in such a modern medium could not count as "folk craft." The designs show increasing neglect, with rusty rain stains and partial over-painting, or have been replaced. A new past is eclipsing the aging present.

SPACES AND COVERS: THE ARCHITECTONICS OF RESPECTABILITY

Rethemnos is small, and conscious of it. People know each other—not as well as in a small village, to be sure, but well enough to necessitate some of the same stratagems of secrecy. As in the mountain village, I was told that groceries should be wrapped so that people would not see what we were going to eat at home. In a small community, the most disconnected fragment of information may be the thin end of a prying wedge.

Possessing intense knowledge of their neighbors, informants have re-peatedly betrayed their fellow townsfolk to foreign invaders and dictato-rial rulers alike. In the aftermath of the Civil War, a vindictively victori-ous right wing hounded all suspected "communists," barring their children from good jobs and interfering with their access to social ser-vices. One union activist who won priority in a lottery for state-subsi-dized workers' housing was told that his draw did not count; today, he faces the hardships of old age in a ramshackle ruin. Alleged leftists were subject to continual petty harassments, which intensified under the mili-tary junta of 1967–1974 until the restoration of democracy brought with it the legalization of communist parties.

Such bitter experiences fuel the more diffuse apprehension with which citizens view the state's functionaries in general. The role of the conser-vation office filters through this dark prism. In the face of the historical conservation office's rather desperate attempts to punish those who alter and demolish the old buildings, people speak somberly of the fear that "the Archaeology" inspires. The tax office inspires similar nervousness. Few Rethemniots can afford not to take illegal risks. Indeed, rather like farmers who distribute their crops among many tiny fields so as to avoid total dependence on one zone (see Forbes 1976), so in the political ecol-ogy of small-town life most Rethemniots expect to get caught from time to time for moonlighting, tax evasion, or mispricing—but they calculate the resulting fines into their balance sheets. Such calculations must remain highly evasive, however, since neighborhood rivals might easily stoop to informing.

Prosperity reinforces this growing fragmentation of social life. Privacy becomes more than just a day-to-day tally of secrets breached and guarded. Economic necessity dictates a more bureaucratic mode of pro-fessionalism. It makes sense to have one's business in the heart of the Old Town, with its direct access to the tourist trade. With economic advance-ment, private life parts company from business. Social capital weighs ever less in the calculations of those who do business with outsiders, for there is no continuing interdependence to warrant investments of intimacy. As more and more merchants actually live in the New Town or the suburbs, moreover, the solidarity of neighborhoods gives way to a more brusquely economic calculation.

These changes are visible as one walks along Arkadiou Street, one of the two main commercial thoroughfares. Small traders in everything from clothes to glass and china, electrical supplies, and books, present a restrained face to the street, their goods organized in rarely changing, chaste displays in dusty windows. These businesses operate in a quiet, unobtrusive way; their custom is local and regular. Jostling them, the food shops display meat, fish, and vegetables to the open street. Most aggressively open of all are the tourist shops, some of which take up enormous stretches of the sidewalk, forcing passersby to step down in the way of the impatient single-line traffic. The life of the market has shifted to the tourist trade, where some of the visitors expect to be able to bargain. The demure commercialism of the more locally useful shops better suits the Rethemniots' respectable self-image as well as their desire to do their business in privacy. Bureaucratic regulation fuels the mutual mistrust that earlier generations tempered with obligations of hospitality and neighborliness. It is only in bargaining with transient outsiders that one has nothing to lose except money.

The desire for privacy both derives from the closing down of residences in the tightly clustered neighborhoods of the Old Town and contributes to it. Ties with the Old Town do not disappear; they just become more completely commercial. People understand the social consequences of the residential exodus. Moving calls for considerable delicacy. A specialty baker, for example, hoped to return to the Old Town, where he felt more comfortable than in the sterile modern apartment he bought to dower his daughter, and where he, his wife, and the daughter were living, causing themselves a half-hour trudge to and from work every day in place of just coming downstairs each morning to open up the shop and work space; but his wife, who had originally insisted on the move, felt initially that she could not return to full residence in their old quarters because the neighbors would have some unkind things to say about people who thought they were better than their old friends but could not manage their new luxury after all. Notwithstanding these fears, practicality has supervened. Now, with the daughter's marriage accomplished, they have, after all, returned to their old abode.

One of this man's regular customers, a pastry cook, is now contemplating a similar move. Like the baker, the pastry cook claims a preference for staying in his old house, similarly located above his shop in the heart of the Old Town, although on a noisier street. His justification for moving is that his two daughters and infant son should grow up in a good environment, not one in which visitors to the house have to pass through the work spaces of the shop.

Such pragmatic concern with display and concealment is a key to the front and back doors of Greek culture: recall again the embarrassment expressed at the brazen behavior of the remaining prostitutes. This, rather than the more specialized notions of "honor and shame," provides the social architectonics of Greek life. It conjoins the strategies of pride and gossip with the large ideologies of nationalism. Architecture and town planning not only embody it (see especially Hirschon 1981, 1989; Pavlides and Hesser 1986; Herzfeld 1987a:117–119); they provide some of its most compelling prototypes. In looking at the struggles of the Rethemniots with the architects and archaeologists of the national bureaucracy, we shall be following a richly tropological struggle over the penetration and protection of various kinds of space: individual, household, monumental. Rethemnos is not merely the site of an especially accessible interaction between local social values and bureaucratic regulation. It is, because of its architectural specificity, the locus of dramatic tensions between concealment and display, between daily strategies of advantage and the recasting of history as a monumental topos, between socially experienced time and administratively reified place.

At the level of national identity, these tensions are played out in the residents' reactions to the tourists. But it is the immediate realities that primarily concern people like the pastry cook. Since his house and shop are on a relatively busy commercial street, he becomes very visible during the slack weeks of September when he takes an extended rest and relaxes on his all-too-public balcony. People ask sarcastically whether he is some kind of fool because they see that he does not work for such a long period. This is a man who fills orders for *kolliva*—the ritual food used for funerals and memorial services—every Friday and Saturday night until about 3:00 A.M.! But the issue is not one of accuracy so much as of effective backbiting; by appearing to work hard, he could just as easily attract charges of being too devoted to mere money, and the avoidance of this slur must be at least a partial incentive for his generous hospitality in the public area of his shop. (Both he and his supplier-baker originally moved into their current Old Town premises precisely because they wanted to be near their work, and so not lose any time.) In this concatenation of seemingly incompatible strategies against the gossip of neighbors and rivals, the pastry cook exemplifies the consummate balancing that inhabitants of the Old Town are constantly compelled to perform, and from which the relative privacy of the New Town allows them to escape into the comforts brought by economic self-improvement.

His worries and tactics also point up the social constraints that no amount of bureaucratic finesse can adequately compensate. Whether the concern is with privacy, or with the adequacy of a dowry (now even more difficult for officialdom to recognize, as a result of the abolition of dowry as a legal category), or again with creating a distinctive facade for the house and thus also for family, the interest of Rethemniots runs counter to that of an intrusive national bureaucracy.

SMALL SPACES AND LARGE WORRIES

It also runs counter to the physical constraints of place. Until about 1965, Rethemnos was a self-contained, small town that barely overran the enclosure of its Venetian walls. Pirate raids in Venetian and Turkish times, town limits that closed down from dusk to dawn (Aetoudakis 1986:110) and would not admit even the visiting foreign dignitary after hours (Pashley 1837, I:100), the lack of economic incentives to expand beyond the walls—all these circumstances created a sense of enclosure. For two decades after World War II and the ensuing Civil War, there were few opportunities for economic expansion. Then, however, the lure of quick wealth began to draw Rethemniots to Athens and abroad, especially to Germany. Returning *Gastarbeiter* invested their sudden wealth in real estate. Within half a decade more, the military's heavy-handed promotion of large-scale tourism (see Greger 1988:108; Hopkins 1977:235–236) had also created new models for emulation. The pressures of family expansion and the desire for more modern and comfortable quarters wrought a dramatic change in the economic topography.

Until these changes set in, most couples with growing daughters would try to create an upper storey for them to inhabit with their own husbands and children when the time came. With the new expansion, once-desirable Old Town properties suddenly lost their allure, and formerly useless beachside fields became immensely valuable properties. In exchange for a plot of land on which an entrepreneur could build a high-rise apartment block, the owners would now receive, in the new building, four or five fashionable apartments and a couple of shops to rent out. Those who owned such properties now had a home in the New Town, although most continued to do business in the Old Town, which has remained the hub of local commerce. Those whose houses in the Old Town had been extensively refurbished by the historic conservation office could now turn a profit by converting them into tourist boardinghouses. They had, in effect, turned their homes into business premises and were therefore in a position to buy modern homes in the New Town for themselves.

This artificially heated local economy, however, faces the threat of sudden collapse. The number of small, barely profitable shops has increased suddenly and dramatically. The number of tourists has not kept pace.

Above all, the Old Town is too cramped for significant development: "If the divisible [economic base] doesn't increase, things are going to be very, very cramped _(stenokhoremena),_" observed one shrewd entrepreneur who had already lost most of his property in the 1960s collapse of the soap industry.

The cramping of which he spoke is a spatial metaphor for economic compression. There has long been a sense of closed space in Rethemnos. An early nineteenth-century traveler noted, "[T]he by-streets consist of walls, with doors; the fronts being turned the other way" (Sieber 1823:48). In part, this was a direct consequence of the architectural veiling with lattice windows, also noted by the same visitor. Then, as now, many of the buildings enclosed pleasant gardens, protected from prying eyes by these thick "walls, with doors." While there is a public life on the street, the alleyways _(sokakia)_[14] have come to mean constraint in another sense, one of a more psychological order. These local perceptions guide much of the hostility to the government's historic conservation program, since the vagaries of the latter only add to the daily anxiety. Not coincidentally, the usual Greek term for anxiety or frustration is _stenokhoria,_ literally, "having narrow space" (see Danforth 1989:78; Hirschon 1989:236):

> Look here, it isn't only the houses that create a problem. People have begun to think that they're being stifled in the Old Town. The Old Town's choking them. There's no way out _(dhieksodho[s])._ You go out to your window [and] you see the house opposite. You go to the window upstairs, again you see a house opposite. At a certain moment you feel you haven't air to breathe. You are _near_!

Children, too, echo their parents' complaints about the lack of space. Over a century ago, when the local climate was viewed with less concern than modern worries about the effects of pervasive damp generate today, a traveler could nevertheless be struck by the airlessness of the walled old town (Khatzidakis 1881:66). Today, the mean spaces of Rethemnos, ever more crowded in on themselves both by expanding families and by changing perceptions of acceptable living room, are the source _and_ the substance of a pervasive distress. Life becomes a consuming attempt to break out. Some fled to Athens, where they found a life that was no less "enclosed," confined, by anxiety:

> You began to be shut up in Athens too, in the constant motion, the bothersomeness _(taleporia),_ all those things, and at some moment you think that perhaps "it's better to get up and leave."

Between the impersonality of Athens and the social pressures of Rethemnos, there was ultimately little to choose. The boredom of Rethemnos life, especially during the longer winter months, makes the town's youth an easy prey for drugs and drink, although the very active Cultural Association provides an outlet for the more studious or artistic. Rethemniots returning from Athens resent the burdensome social reciprocities of earlier days. "Young people now shut themselves up at home," goes the complaint, and they evade much of the neighborliness that was once a focus of concern and interest:

> One used to be interested if the neighbor woman was sick today: "Why hasn't she come out today, to sweep around her door? Perhaps something's wrong with her?" *Tak-tak!*: one would go and knock on her [door].

To many young Rethemniots today, such involvement is a nuisance, the very walls an oppressive screen behind which avid noses identify cooking smells and eager ears register every angry altercation and every audible detail of domestic life. The open spaces of social life, repositories of a treasured sociability (see Hirschon 1978), have narrowed oppressively on younger residents who have come to value living apart, limiting them to ever more introverted resources. The centrifugal possibilities of modern life have stranded them on centripetal whirlpools of anxiety and frustration.

The domestic unit turns in on itself in palpable ways. Until a few years ago, for example, men were embarrassed to appear too uxorious. People thought it "completely unnatural" for a man to sit in the street with the women. It was the women who, with their gossip, would probe the defenses of each other's domesticity; men had no place in this exchange except as objects of rivalrous discussion. Today, a husband may spend long hours at home and may sit with his wife and her friends in the street on the long summer evenings when such social gatherings still occur. This urban, "European" model of family life is a new idiom and, to many, still a source of unease.

Balance between the privacy of domestic information and the intensity of social interaction in the street was once valued in terms of a virtually theological reverence (Hirschon 1989:237). Now, however, the security that one formerly sought in social life and built into homes and land must be eked out from the fickle caprices of a paper economy: the houses are worth too little; the fields were sold to more adventurous speculators long before they would yield their present price. For those who must remain within the Old Town, the *makri-steno* (the "long-narrow" Nikiforou Foka Street) epitomizes the oxymoron—intimacy that is also oppression—that its residents feel the Old Town to be. It has all the discomforts of the old, to which it has now added the dangerous, noisy, polluting traffic that is the hallmark of the new conditions and disrupts what little inclination to reciprocity remains.

It is not entirely clear, however, that this sense of loss, of an open neighborhood now irrevocably fragmented and closed in upon itself, represents more than nostalgia for the past. A woman who grew up in Kallithea, one of the present suburbs that was then quite separate from the town proper, attributes the sense of closure and isolation in the Old Town (where her parents also owned property) to characteristics that are certainly not new. She recalls that in Kallithea, with its open spaces and little gardens, a sense of neighborhood was much more prevalent than in the Old Town:

> I don't know, just the way these houses here are built isolates the family. When we lived in Kallithea, our house had a very low wall around it, and the gates were always open—the gates of the courtyard. The neighbor women came at whatever moment they wanted. Almost without knocking on the door. From the time we settled in the house in Ksanthoudidou Street, I remember that we were a family but completely isolated. There's this perimeter wall (*mandrotikhos*), the courtyard is [in the] interior.

And her sister similarly recalled that they had enjoyed few neighborly relations there, in contrast to Kallithea.

It is possible, then, that those who remember an older, more open society are just grafting an idealized past on childhood memories. For these sisters, who did not live in the Old Town, there is no need to posit a better, more sociable past there: the displacements of place, as they moved their home, substitute convincingly for those of time. At five or six years of age, whenever they visited their father's property there, the Old Town nonetheless had a magical appearance that obscured their parents' less pleasant experiences of the place:

> And we used to see through the walls, where the date palms showed, and oaks, oaks, oak leaves, and I remember—I at least believed it then, I believed it, that it must be Paradise. In one courtyard . . . a great deal of greenery appeared within.

Their great joy was to run around in the narrow alleyways until they managed to get quite lost, the children's pleasure in the closeness and secrecy of it all the source of their parents' anxiety and pain. For the children, the place was big enough to lose themselves in, its walls a vision of adventure and eternity, boundaries and restrictions abolished for all time. For their parents, these same, close-leaning walls brought the prying eyes and ears of neighbors too close to the intimacy of their lives, suggesting that the oppressiveness of the close neighborhood is not as new an experience as some younger Rethemniots may think.

All the more likely, then, were those who had lived only in the security of the suburb—then a village—to reconstruct its past in terms of reconstituted reciprocities: neighbors were more neighborly than in town, kinsfolk recognized their mutual obligations. The sisters were aware that the town, in which they found such pleasure, was a source of distress to their elders. In the town, they recalled, the gossip of passersby could be vicious, as indeed it often still is. There has certainly long been tension between the ideals of sociability and the desire to pry; but memory always seems to locate one's own childhood in a time and place where that tension remained more evenly in balance and where the walls admitted people while still secluding the intimacies of family life. The physical and notional topos of the Old Town embodies the paradoxes and contradictions of a moral topography.

This nostalgia for a balanced past perhaps explains the success of more official kinds of folklore at gaining a foothold. Several Cretan dance troupes provide performances, mostly by schoolchildren, in which stylized dance steps match highly idealized renditions of the Cretan costume of a century ago. Such ventures routinize and unify the past, turning local feuds into objects of nationalistic pride. The irony can be palpable. In a coffeehouse that used to be a stable, local laborers in shirts and trousers noisily treat each other to endless bottles of wine while one of their number quietly takes down a lira (three-stringed fiddle; see plate 12) from the old manger shelf and begins to challenge the company to a round of song dueling in the rhyming couplets that have for centuries enjoyed a respected place in vernacular Cretan culture. Opposite, to recorded music,

12. Musicians play the three-stringed lira and the base lute (*laghouto*). (1970)

boys and girls in almost invariant Cretan vrakes (baggy pants) and long dresses learn the steps of the old dances with pedantic determination. The scene is a parable of improvisation repressed. The lira player will desist if one offends his modesty by treating his entertainment as a set performance—by applauding, for example, or actually *asking* him to play. The dancers are trying self-consciously to symbolize the old devil-may-care Crete of the wars against the Turks, while the skills of invention and personal memory cower in the shadows of the old stable across the narrow street. When the passing tourists look at all, it is almost always at the diminutive dancers; or, when they do turn to the coffeehouse, it is because the appetizing whiffs of the workers' food excite the hardier among them to try something local.

This dance troupe was the first one to come into existence. Its founder, a local woman, had come to appreciate the possibilities while she lived for several years in Athens, and today she takes great pride in the accuracy of her costume reconstructions. Her daughter, a prominent official of the historic conservation office, remarked without irony that perhaps her mother was "to blame" for the fact that she "fell in love" with the old houses of Rethemnos. It was a love of "tradition" (*paradhosi*)—not "invented" tradition (Hobsbawm and Ranger 1983), so much as images of the multiple and often mutually contradictory pasts that a modern and bureaucratic national society has tried—not always successfully—to monumentalize as an affective unity (see Anderson 1983; Löfgren 1989; Lowenthal 1986). Like the small tourist guest-house operators of the Old Town, she saw the refurbishing of old houses as a strengthening both of the traditional culture and of the economic viability that it seems to offer. This is the kind of tourism in which "the [kind of] foreigner (*ksenos*)[15] who will be coming, will come to enter the Greek family (*elliniki iko-yenia*). He'll eat with them, go hunting with them, go fishing with them. He won't be alienated (*dhe th' apoksenothi*)[16] entirely" as in big hotels. One owner even argued that his new hotel was a Byzantine building, and he used the claim to suggest that the intimacy of small hotels was of a piece with the older traditions of the town. He identified his small-scale entrepreneurship with a vision of history that, for him, surpassed the narrow perceptions of the bureaucrats who insisted that he restore the building according to their specifications. In the Old Town of Rethemnos, one cannot separate history from its uses, for the age of a building stakes an ideological claim.

The Venetian glories and the folklore traditions merge in the collective representation of a single Cretan past, grandly European in its architectural culture but folksily small-town in the intimacy of domestic space. The official attempts to reframe Rethemnos at various times as both an "architectural monument" and a "traditional neighborhood" reflect the same suppression of unruly histories in favor of an encompassing monu-mentalism. Some of the arguments are motivated by political party loy-alties. The criticism of Nakou, and of the televised version of *Madame Do-Re-Mi*, seems to have sprung mostly from the political Right. But the Right does not have a monopoly of monumentalism: it was the moder-ately left-leaning leadership of that first dance troupe that provided the costumes and some of the actors for the film. The construction of a uni-fied past does not necessarily consist in unified efforts. It is a competition to define history writ large. As an ethnographer, I encountered many pasts. Present interests vied for that unifying, monumental control, their tactics and discourse increasingly homogenized by the inexorable cate-gorical logic of the bureaucratic nation-state.

ETHNOGRAPHER, TOURIST, SPY: PROBING OTHERS' SPACES

The context of a tourist town provides special challenges for anthropo-logical research. Unlike a remote village, such a town has developed re-sources for confining foreigners to places of display and restricting access to the intimate sociability that challenges the public assumption of re-spectability. The tourist's determination not to *be* a tourist plays right into the hands of local entrepreneurs, who supply variegated packaged formulae—package tours—for instant, domesticated adventures in oth-erness.

As an ethnographer, I did not fit this pattern. I was hard to place. Flu-ency in Greek—a language of supposedly near-insurmountable diffi-culty—and a working knowledge of local dialect especially confused the boundaries. A shopkeeper who did not know me at the time, when I thanked her for giving me directions, told me that people always did this for tourists and should therefore do it "all the more for the Greeks." When people realized that I was in fact a foreigner, they found this both flattering and suspicious. In some of the coffee shops, I became a regular, which meant being charged local prices and being expected to sit with the locals rather than the tourists. But in one of them I was also rather se-verely informed that, aside from the fact that time would erode whatever demonstrations of respect I might have enjoyed as an educated outsider, I would have received better treatment there if I had *not* spoken Greek; and that, on the other hand, being recognized as a foreigner did not pro-tect me from being thought a government agent, employed by the author-ities to spy on Greeks.

The suspicion of espionage is a common hazard in fieldwork. I encoun-tered it in my earlier work in the mountains; indeed, my landlord from those days provided a good character report on me when one of my Re-themniot acquaintances decided to check up on my account of myself. It would be easy enough to dismiss the suspicion of spying as merely the irrational and ill-informed paranoia of people who do not understand one's work. I prefer, however, to recognize in it the political sensitivity and realism of the Rethemniots. Their more or less veiled allusions to spying make sense in the larger context of the social strategies they use to deal with the ever-present, ever-oppressive bureaucracy. And indeed, I was much less often thought to be a foreign agent than suspected of prying on the government's behalf—a fair indication, were one needed, of the mutual suspicion that now subsists between the citizenry and the bureaucracy which supposedly serves it. I was, in fact, warned of certain "two-faced" individuals who thought me to be a spy, but this most commonly turned out to mean "government agent." If I *had* been a spy, there were plenty of willing friends to warn me (or was the most forthcoming of these merely being "two-faced" [*dhiprosopos*] himself?).

Reactions to my fluency in Greek were thus emblematic of my ambiguous standing. As an ethnographer, I could hardly manage without it. Until word got around that the newspapers had given some publicity to my work, however, it was also a potential liability. It violated the usual sense of "foreigner"; but I was certainly not "local." One well-disposed friend, a proud communist, reported that I had sworn on the Cross (*sic*; this with a dramatic version of the appropriate gesture) that I was not Greek, and that I had sworn I was a "genuine" (*ghnisios*)[17] Englishman— a double recasting of what I had actually said that occasioned me only marginally less discomfort than another communist's angry claim that I was a representative of the destructive presence (as he saw it) of Jews on Crete.

The warnings about those who suspected me of spying were interesting in their own right. One of the communists made a big point of the fact that those who did so were mercenary and hoping to gain thereby. This was my first, and very personal, introduction to the constant, if no longer very convincing, fear of police informers in the town. As we shall see, the communists have particularly good reason to remember the surveillance (*fakellosi*, literally, "filing") of left-wing unionists and others by earlier, nondemocratic regimes. This kindly man claimed he told those who were still suspicious that I was obviously not watching airplanes or anything of that sort, and insisted to me that he was not a *keratas* ("cuckold"), a *roufianos* ("pimp"; a common metaphor for an informer), or a *poutanas* (a masculinized form of the word for "prostitute")—in other words, not someone perverted enough to sell a friend for lucre. (Anyone who *was* caught spying would, of course, be quite appropriately described in these same uncomplimentary terms.) The metaphorical range of sexuality is never irrelevant to social relations here and provides a means of moving metonymically from the personal to the political with ease. Motives are always suspect, but never wholly decipherable. Less than a week later, the very man whom this communist had particularly earmarked as a venal spy spotter himself told me that his accuser had pointed out that I couldn't really be a spy because I was not watching airplanes. Who was trying to bluff whom? Who was trying to trick an admission out of whom? Was I perhaps beginning to join in an empty game of suspicion and countersuspicion, the goals of which had nothing to do with espionage but had everything to do with local social tensions?

But the suspicion that was perhaps hardest to dispel held that I might be an agent of the Archaeological Service. This was understandable enough: my interest in historic conservation problems sometimes collided uncomfortably with deep mistrust, based on unhappy personal experiences in the past, of both government and foreign agencies. In one such confluence, a communist veteran of the Civil War, having learned that I was interested in hearing about his illegal restoration of the house in which his father had been killed by nationalist police troops, refused to talk to me; a well-disposed go-between—and next-door neighbor of the old warrior—decided to try indirectly by getting me to his own house, assuring the other man meanwhile that he had not seen me again. The idea was to organize a "chance" meeting, which would protect the mediator ("I don't want to be exposed [to accusations of meddling]," he remarked) while giving me the opportunity of establishing a personal link that would overcome suspicion. In the event, the ruse failed because the suspicious and somewhat nervous ex-guerrilla, frightened that he might be caught out either by the local authorities or by the "English" descendant of his erstwhile persecutors (for such is the logic of association), worked on his house late at night and otherwise managed to remain virtually invisible; there was thus no time at which I could have approached him *without* seeming to persecute him—something that I emphatically wanted to avoid.

This unsatisfactory nonencounter illustrates some key themes. First of all, the palpable fear of the conservation office affects people's daily actions. Another recurrent aspect is the conflation of my own categorical roles, in the eyes of a citizen who had never met me, as English (and therefore ipso facto an "agent") and as government-employed pest. On the other hand, countering this, the mediator unequivocally maintained that direct acquaintance would overcome such suspicion, to the point at which, even if his neighbor finally suspected him of setting things up for my benefit, the new relationship would supervene and the tactical machinations that led to it be forgotten. The mediator cast himself in the role more often attributed to me: he was going to lure his neighbor over by leaving his own light on one evening when I "happened" to be visiting, and, as he said, this is "like espionage" (*kataskopeftiko*)!

Spying was a constant theme, and as a charge it as often linked me to the current (socialist) government as to foreign espionage. My research served to focus fears of the government bureaucracy. These fears were thus a significant part of what I was studying. They seemed especially strong among those of right-wing persuasion. Although there is no reason to suppose that there was any high-level involvement in local intimidation, it was all too clear that PASOK (the ruling Panhellenic Socialist Movement) enthusiasts delighted in hinting at what they could do to those who dared complain; it is also true that some right-wingers expropriated the postjunta rhetoric about civil liberties for their own ends. One disaffected PASOK supporter and unionist indicated to me that I might write down anything he said; I might not record him on tape, however, as that would make him too identifiable—given that, as he saw matters, there was no democracy in Greece.[18] Such fears did not seem to be particularly directed at me in any personal sense, and one elderly man, who was extremely secretive about his political affiliations in general coffeehouse conversation, confided that he had told me his views as, being an outsider (ksenos), I did not pose a real risk to his standing.

There were frequent discussions of my presence in town. Friends told my landlord about my visits to them, significantly including the detail that I had refused the offer of a drink on the grounds that the information provided had been sufficiently generous. On another occasion, a local friend remarked to another townsman how impressed I had been with the fact that gamblers could get credit in the coffeehouses: instances of everyday routine to locals, now "made strange" for them by the puzzlement and interest of a curious visitor. These tales fully agreed with my own recollections. The emphasis on gossip in the ethnographic literature on Greece might give the impression that there is little substance to the stories that people tell about one another. In practice, however, people tell stories as a sort of tracking device—as an identifiable narrative whose progress they can follow through the gossip network. For this reason, there must always be a good measure of verifiable fact. People told me stories about other Rethemniots' views of me, sometimes out of a kindly concern that I should know what my current standing was, more often— or so it seemed—as a test of my attitudes. It is not always easy to separate the effects of lingering fear from well-meant advice, and townspeople often used strategies that might plausibly involve both. We were outsiders of an extremely ambiguous kind. Incorporation could on occasion amount to a polite form of exclusion, as when our first landlady offered us hospitality and announced that we should not feel kseni (foreigners, outsiders) but, on the contrary, *dhiči mas anthropi* (*our* people).[19] This is gentle, and effective, irony (cf. Chock 1987).

Because people are constantly trying to get information out of each other at minimal cost to themselves, a high premium is placed on indirection. My landlady once told a good friend that he was especially deft at going at any topic in a "sideways" manner. That judgment clearly did not offend. This may seem odd, however, in a society where the ethos of manliness entails a mien of utter forthrightness. Yet the two dimensions are not mutually exclusive. Rather, they are contextually appropriate. They also show how people could contemplate the possibility that I was a spy without necessarily thinking less of me for it, and without allowing their fear of such an identity to cloud the equanimity of their actual dealings with me most of the time. Their hospitality ensured them the moral high ground whatever my real role might be.

It is in the male fellowship of the coffeehouse (see plate 13)—and especially in the act of *kerasma*, or aggressive mutual treating of drinks and food (see Herzfeld 1985; Papataxiarchis 1991; cf. also Kapferer 1988:159, on the male Australian equivalent, "shouting")—that we find a dramatic illustration of the ambivalence which subsists in relations among social actors. At one level, it is a celebration of the ideological egalitarianism of the *parea* (company of friends), of all Cretans, and of all Greeks. At another, it marks the possibility of symbolically subordinating a powerful guest (Herzfeld 1987b). Among women, too, as Cowan (1990:63–67) has demonstrated, the seemingly casual intimacy of treat-

13. Coffeehouse conversation ranges from the intensely serious to this style of aggressive banter. (1987)

ing is rife with subtly coercive implications. As a foreign visitor who spoke Greek and engaged in aggressively rustic forms of kerasma,[20] I unintentionally played on this ambivalence—not necessarily to my disadvantage.

Thus, at least one townsman thought I was generous in kerasma because I wanted to gain social acceptance, whereas he—a rather irascible older man—justified his *avoidance* of giving kerasma on the grounds that he would be insulted by the greater familiarity toward him that others would think it entitled them to. He thus delicately condescended to me, implying both that I was adapting well to local custom, and that I had much more need to observe the conventions than he did! Kerasma is normally a means of creating forthright relations. But to use it diplomatically for ulterior purposes is not necessarily bad or contradictory. As another man told me, while insinuating that perhaps I had motives that no one in Rethemnos could fathom, I was a "professional," and that entitled me to a degree of deviousness if I judged it necessary. In particular, he claimed to disbelieve my assertion that I had not tape-recorded him secretly, "because you're a professional." The defining characteristic of the professional, he confided, is an ability not to give away the secrets of one's work. Being professional, then, is a denial of reciprocity—the antithesis of kerasma. But it may use kerasma and other forms of reciprocal sociability in order to achieve personal goals.

If kerasma is a means of creating affectionate male relationships, withholding it can be a means of avoiding unwanted ones. This is what my irascible older friend had meant. But such withholding is also liable to multiple interpretations. A coffee shop owner was visited one day by a certain colleague. I knew the visitor slightly and offered him a drink. After he left, the proprietor told me that he had tried to make a signal (*noima*)[21] to me *not* to treat this man, which I had failed to notice or understand. He said that if one got into a conversation with the visitor, one would too easily end up in a noisy and profitless squabble, and if that were to happen, the only thing one could do, as a *kirios*,[22] would be to get up and leave. It is dropi (a cause for embarrassment) to do otherwise. He went on to say that the visitor had come into the coffee shop some five years earlier and smashed everything in sight. "I saved him," said the proprietor—that is, by pretending to the authorities that the visitor had paid for the damage.

After the proprietor left, the elderly man who had explained his reluctance to treat volunteered the comment, "Write down a motto: many words are poverty." He went on to explain that while the proprietor might claim not to want the rowdy visitor in his establishment, and to have thrown him out on past occasions, he always greeted him most heartily; he always claimed (continued my rather malicious companion) that he'd thrown people out when in fact it was his own bad behavior and management that had driven them to take their custom elsewhere.

Forthrightness and diplomatic evasion are not absolute qualities of men's behavior. They are *stances*. As such, they come into existence, emerge, only in moments of performance and interpretation. One man's forthrightness might well be recast by another as a form of indirection. The coffeehouse proprietor wanted his hearers to *think* that he had thrown the offender out; but he also wanted the offender to think him a good fellow on whom he could rely for friendship and cooperation; and the last thing he wanted to do—especially as some thought he had special influence with the police—was to make an open complaint to the authorities. There are few more unambiguous acts than that.

Social success lies in *balancing* the stances of indirection and forthrightness, in such a way that actions do not too obviously belie words. Any inconsistency between the two can be *either* a failure of forthrightness *or* an excellent demonstration of "diplomacy." (*Dhiplomatia* is a very double-edged virtue in local eyes.) Serious men should also use few words— "many words are poverty," as my sour friend remarked. The coffeehouse proprietor tried to communicate with me by means of a noima—a "gesture," but the word also means "meaning." After the event, however, he overstated his claim to the silence of diplomatic indirection, turning it into the noise of unmanly boastfulness.

Forthrightness and indirection, self-display and evasive self-concealment, heroic wildness and devious urbanity, gossip and secrecy: these contrasts, so explicit a part of the image in which Rethemniots cast themselves, realize in everyday social interaction those other contrasts between a gloriously austere European past and an engagingly familiar Oriental one. They do not precisely gloss those larger antinomies, nor do any of these conceptual pairings have any meaning outside those given them by social actors—the Rethemniots themselves. For the people of this politia, however, those meanings are as immediate as they are shifting and elusive. This persistent binarism, arguably a direct consequence of the degree to which the Greeks have been made to internalize European self-other tensions, sometimes also appears as a simplistic urban-rural polarity that arguably stamps nation-state ideologies around the Mediterranean (Davis 1977:8). It is, finally, the boundary between the wild and the tame on which Prevelakis has situated his Rethemnos.

Many of the most wrenching cultural dichotomies have been exacerbated, given immediacy, by the Rethemniots' often painful engagement with the bureaucratic establishment. A struggle that from one angle appears to be over the ownership and control of property consists, from another perspective, in an intense argument over the definition—and above all the control—of history. Whose history is at stake? *Which* history is at stake? To these political questions, the daily twisting and turning of Rethemniot etiquette between the opposing models of civility and toughness, between smooth urbanity and the fatal rhetoric of the vendetta, is far more relevant than the monolithic discourse of official history would have us believe. Nor is that discourse as static as its claims to eternal verity would suggest. It, too, partakes of the negotiated qualities of social experience, albeit at a slower pace imposed by its pretensions of monumentality. Official discourse centers on the ownership of monuments, physical proxies for a collective past. Social discourse resists this bureaucratic impertinence (which is also a *lack of pertinence*—that is, to everyday concerns). It centers on the ownership of homes, physical embodiments of a multiplicity of individual and family pasts. These homes are, for those who live in them, landmarks of life rather than an abstract celebration of eternity. Yet the Rethemniots would justly claim to be loyal Greeks, and officialdom equally claims to be the preserver of the local heritage. The remaining chapters move the focus by stages to this dispute over present-day rights to define and portray time past.

Chapter Two

HISTORIES IN CONFLICT

MULTIPLE PASTS, MULTIPLE PRESENTS

Rethemnos has many pasts. Its citizens hail from varied backgrounds, although its former ethnic heterogeneity has all but vanished. The population is overwhelmingly Greek-speaking and Greek Orthodox. The majority either come from the villages of the hinterland or represent the substantial influx of refugees from Asia Minor that culminated after the Turkish victory over the Greek armies in 1922. Some representatives of the old merchant class persevere. Especially few are the remnants of the local nobility created by the Serene Republic of Venice in the course of its long and rebellion-ridden occupation (1210–1645).

Surnames are only a partial guide to origins. Families with names like Ghavalas, Kalleryis, and Vlastos claim descent from the twelve Byzantine families with which the emperor Alexios Komninos repopulated Crete after Nikiforos Fokas's savage defeat of the Saracen occupiers in 961. The several Venetian family names like Renieri and Dandolo attest a no less ennobled past. Few of these names, however, have been passed along in an unbroken succession. In many cases, it seems more likely that the honorific bestowal of surnames on retainers and even serfs may have made such names commoner than they would otherwise have been, and it is also virtually certain that at least some of the Venetian names belonged to soldiers of the Serene Republic who intermarried with local Orthodox women and settled on Crete to farm in the fertile lands of the Amari Valley and elsewhere. Their immediate descendants fell into penury under Turkish rule (see Moatsos 1974:221), and over the centuries that followed their more distant descendants came to Rethemnos in search of a bare but decent living.

The remnants of the "Cretan nobles," a category of squires created by the Venetians, are today scattered throughout the length and breadth of Crete, although a few family names remained unique to Rethemnos into the present century (Moatsos 1974). Such knowledge as present inhabitants have of their supposedly ancient roots comes from books and from instruction by an elite anxious to restore the general claim of Crete to a noble history. A workman who boasted the surname of one of Komninos's twelve families told me that his ancestors came from "one of the fourteen [*sic*] families," and that he thought they had owned a "title to nobility"—an indicative compound of mangled Byzantine history and Venetian images. Faithful to the agnatic ideology that prevails in western Crete, he maintained that all bearers of his surname recognized each other as theoretical kin, but that the family had been "broken up" so that they no longer knew each other. This reduction of grand lineage history to experiential terms continued: his brother had moved to Iraklio, while their sister, in Athens, has more contact with their patrilateral first cousins in Thessaloniki because they are physically closer. Even if such individuals are actually the descendants of noble colonists, their perception of this relation to the past is the refraction of a modern, schoolroom historicism through the experience of two generations of their immediate family. We shall later see this agnatic localism at work on the architectural history of the town as well.

The Catholics who lived in Rethemnos before World War II had Italian family names that recalled their Venetian roots, and they are remembered today as "aristocrats." This label recognizes a style and an identity. Any suggestion that such mores are "Venetian" belongs to the rhetoric that claims a "European" identity for the economically stronger elements in Rethemniot society. Prevelakis recalls a merchant of the old school, now fallen on hard times, whose once grand manner, with its formal modes of address in Italian, bespoke not only his proud ancestry as a member of the lordly Venetian Mocenigo family but also his substantial mercantile contacts in Trieste. Prevelakis (1938:16–17) quotes a letter that Mocenigo wrote to his main Trieste colleague. The body of the text is all salutations and social news in the stilted neo-Classical Greek of the day. Only the postscript contains a few stylistically offhand but substantively precise instructions for purchase and sale. As we shall see, such affectations of unconcern for mere finance are a remembered mark of aristocratic mores that persist to this day.

If the most wealthy and established Rethemniots retain ideals of commercial modesty in their interactional styles, they also retain a respect for the long-lost Italianate culture of their predecessors. Further, they have assimilated that turn-of-the-century cultural idiom, and possibly the education which many of their children now seek in Italian universities, to a far more distant past. The enthusiasm that some Rethemniots profess for things Venetian entails an important dimension of historical forgetting: when the Turks invaded Crete in 1645, they were welcomed by the Orthodox population as liberators from harsh Venetian rule (Dimakopoulos 1971:325–326). In the early years of Turkish administration, at least, the comparative indifference of the Ottoman bureaucracy to the Greeks' internal affairs, and the removal of an interfering Catholic hierarchy, seemed to justify this initial popular optimism.

The modern Rethemniots' expressed preference for Venetian over

Turkish culture—"we have no war with the Italians"—demonstrates how well the nationalist ideology of the Greek state, embodied in a more or less continuous condition of hostility with Turkey and embedded in larger, neo-Classical claims to European status, has done its work. During the militantly nationalist regime of 1967–1974, one official had even wanted to demolish the proud minaret at the mosque of *gazi* Hüseyin Paşa, one of the highest in the Ottoman world, despite the fact that it had been designed by a Greek Christian architect. As long as it stood, he reasoned, the Turks could use this monument to make territorial claims on Crete. History has to be remodeled to make the present safe. Doubtless the Turks did prove cruel, capricious occupiers whose response to the slightest hint of rebellion was ferocious in the extreme; but they were scarcely worse than the Venetians, and the current rehabilitation of the latter indicates the force of a cultural economy that ranks the European stereotype over the Oriental. Speaking of the way in which residents use "Venetian" as a word of praise for architectural artifacts, in contrast to "Turkish," a senior member of the historic conservation office described this symbolic reworking of history—a reworking that ultimately deploys nationalist ideology against actual state policy:

> They believe that they got from the Venetians, the Venetians left them something. They never regarded them as conquerors. That is, the inhabitants of today don't regard them as conquerors, they've put them up on [a] high [pedestal], whereas they regard the Turks as tramplers (*katapatites*) who demolished the [local] manners and customs.

This, as a version of the official line, equips the residents with a symbolic weapon of some strength.

The rehabilitation of the Venetians thus fits the rhetoric of modern Greek nationalism. It also, not just coincidentally, fits the present political and economic absorption of Greece into the European Community. Monumentally, the state marks this stance by the holistic restoration of the Old Town as a Venetian monument. We must remember, however, that many of the buildings that "look" Venetian may in fact be later accretions built under Turkish rule—in part by Greek Christian masons—to patterns already well established under the Venetians and therefore often indistinguishable from their archetypes (e.g., Malagari and Stratigakis 1985–1986:58). That effort has received substantial monetary support from the peripheral development programs of the European Community—an eloquent comment on the political status of Greece in the context of the Community's growing homogenization. We must also remember that this formal objectification of a living community in monumental terms departs significantly from earlier patterns of use. In the seventeenth century, when the Venetians were still in control, earlier building zones were already being ransacked for masonry for newer habitations (Dimakopoulos 1971:339). This pattern, which almost certainly goes back much further, certainly continued into the Turkish period and until after World War II. Historic conservation turns the makeshift familiarity of domestic space into something permanent and inelastic.

The architecture, thus monumentalized, recalls a grander age. It was an age with its own ranks of nobility, major and minor, Venetian and Cretan. These titles went for naught once the Turks were in charge. Rethemnos has nevertheless boasted an "aristocracy" in more recent times, at least since the end of the nineteenth century, when Crete became nominally free of Turkish control (1898). Until early in the present century, certain expectations of demeanor and dress—"looking neither to the right nor the left" as they walked down the street, riding on horseback to business, conducting conversation in French—appear to have obtained. These "aristocrats" were merchants rather than hereditary landowners and had acquired a good deal of local power through their appointment as trade representatives—"consuls" (konsoles)—for various foreign countries. In those days, massive mercantile interests were concentrated in Rethemnos, which was not only a depot for the passage of goods from the great trading ports of the Levant, but also a major production center for tannin (made from local acorns) and above all for a kind of soap greatly prized throughout the Balkans. The soap industry, attested in Turkish records as early as 1673 (Stavrinidis 1986, II:156–157), and lively throughout Crete well into the nineteenth century (Kremmidas 1974; see Spratt 1865, II:112, on Rethemnos), was the last major commercial interest in Rethemnos to collapse before the rise of tourism. Its demise in the early 1960s gave the coup de grace to those few hardy families of the old upper class who had managed to cling to their interests in the town. At that point, many of the suddenly impoverished merchants left for Athens, where construction labor was in high demand, or for Germany and other countries where cheap labor fueled a spiraling economic boom. Some, having realized their hopes of better fortune though chastened awareness of new constraints, have returned to Rethemnos, where they have opened boutiques or tried to profit directly from the sudden access of tourism. Urban and European fashion has now become the prerogative of all; but as a merchant with powerful nostalgia for the past lamented, all these things are ready-made and nothing entails the cooperative mutuality that used to bind trader, craftsman, and customer.

At the turn of the century, however, such mass-produced urbanity was unknown. French affectations were the prerogative of the few. The disdainful konsoles constituted a highly endogamous caste, as property could more easily be conserved among a few families than through the acquisition of impecunious and poorly connected affines. After World

War I, however, a new class of merchants appeared and mocked the social pretensions of the old "consular families." Some of the latter nonetheless adapted successfully; but, after World War II, in the 1950s, virtually all the remaining old families started to move away for good. The new *aristokratia* adopted some of the pretensions of the old, notably the affectation of modesty in all matters relating to personal wealth. Its members also affected "European" styles of dress such as the monocles worn by the men. Even those of relatively modest cultural pretensions read or wrote poetry. The mark of this culture was, above all, a cosmopolitanism that the poor, insofar as they took any notice of it at all, resented and despised.

This cosmopolitanism partially consisted in a well-sustained disregard for what were perceived as the conventions of village tradition. This was especially true in the area of sexual morality, not so much in any greater degree of permissiveness as in a more aggressive and individualistic display of respectably bourgeois romanticism. Paradoxically, for example, only the wealthy could afford to ignore the stern requirements of the dowry: just as the old aristokratia could affect modesty in its public mien because its entitlements were known to all, so now the rich did not need to prove their ability to dower their daughters in the way that a poor father might be expected to by his neighbors. Love could thus be portrayed as the product of an understanding, or "feeling" (*esthima*) as it is still rather demurely labeled, even though the usual processes of brokerage were required before such sentiments could lead to the only acceptable form of romantic attachment, engagement to be married. The emblematic display of self-restraint, rather than of sexual prudery, was crucial. The same father who disdained the dowry for his twin daughters, and who was willing to let his twin daughters travel unattended by boat to visit their uncle in Athens at the age of thirteen, might also forbid them the public intimacy of walking hand-in-hand in the streets of the market area. Poorer girls, whose chastity was a necesssary component of their marriageable value (*timi*),[1] might hold hands without embarrassment. For them, the shield that such mutual chaperonage afforded against scandal was more important than making a display of self-discipline for its own sake.

Women of wealthier families might go—under chaperonage if they were still young enough to be liable to suspicion—to some of the coffeehouses. This was certainly a substantial departure from village and urban proletariat practice. Today, female students attending the University of Crete frequent the many pastry shops (*zakharoplastia*), and even local girls and young women gather there for sociable chats in the full glare of public inspection. For the pre–World War II women of rank, however, such actions proclaimed their independence, not from strict fathers and prying neighbors, but from the rural stamp of female submissiveness. They were almost certainly more a mark of class identity and of an emergent bourgeois style than the unfettered expression of personal choice (see Cowan's [1990:82, 87] nuanced account of such patterns in modern Macedonia).

The new style was self-consciously European. A woman recalls her father's own coffeehouse before World War II:

> The aristocracy of Rethimno went there. That is: the ladies with their official, their weekend dresses, now, went to the coffeehouse, they didn't have anywhere else to go.

One particularly eccentric lady "used to wear some wide, long dresses, and always a hat, and she always carried an umbrella." Such striking affectations were vouchsafed to only a prominent few. Style was more important than wealth; if one had style, one's *moral* right to wealth was not in question. The coffeehouse owner's wife would call their customers "the rich" (*i plousii*), even though she and her husband were quite well-to-do themselves; he was a skin-tanner and itinerant merchant as well as coffeehouse proprietor—not occupations for an educated man of the world, and thus not passports to the domain of "wealth" in this sense.

As several writers have recently shown (e.g., Douglas and Isherwood 1979; Appadurai 1986), both the circulation and the restriction of material goods encode ideas about leisure, the ultimate privilege of rank and wealth. In its extreme form, this becomes a revaluation of goods ("rubbish," "junk") that have fallen into disrepair or disuse, and whose reactivation can therefore *only* symbolize and reaffirm the economic and social independence of those who have the time for them (Thompson 1979). The truly wealthy have the power to parade either eccentricity or simplicity: they can afford not to care. The economy of manners in Rethemnos deserves further discussion here.

For the poor, the path to moral superiority consists in frugal self-management that still permits lavish, ostentatious hospitality to others. This is the way to the moral high ground. For the "aristocrats," by contrast, frugality is replaced by the obligation of charity *de haut en bas*, by ostentatious nonostentatiousness in the more obvious trappings of wealth, and by the adoption of style for its own sake over displays of material acquisition. Disdain for showing off may protect actors from the very question of whether they have as much to show off as their attitude suggests.

The hospitality of the poor and the charity of the rich thus both fit a pattern of social investment. The poor made much of giving up everything they owned because this was often their sole means of investing in social capital. The wealthy, conversely, were careful not to display their charity—a rhetoric of self-effacement that still allows a few to sneer at the flashiness of new wealth. One extremely wealthy man, an Asia Minor refugee, used to send parcels of food to all the indigent townspeople but instructed the boys who delivered them to say nothing about their source. His daughter recalls:

> I know that he used to help very many people. That is: I've been stopped in the street and told, "Did you know, your father helped me, my donkey had died on me and he bought me a donkey." But he never used to *talk* about this! Never! Never! Very few people knew about it.

Austerity and simplicity reigned at home, and these acts of generosity were subject to the same code of self-effacement. This man would tell his daughters that he had no money to give them for luxury purchases, but if a customer came and told him his wife was ill, he would immediately help with cash.

Simplicity is something that aristocrats and the poor share as an ideal, much as they share the affectation of indifference to money. Within this discourse, however, there is plenty of room for testing class attitudes. A young pharmacist of "aristocratic" status, whose wife was of village origin, could not—he claimed—bring himself to eat with his hands as she did; since they were both ardent communists, this comment was probably little more than self-ironic banter. But when he was eating fish with some villagers, they objected when he asked for cutlery, saying he just wanted to show that he was the scion of a good family. A former road sweeper recalled that a pretentious local woman visiting a restaurant had claimed not to know what *ameletita* (literally, "things one shouldn't study") were; the cook asked her whether she minded if he explained, as she might not like it; she told him to go ahead and yet was furious when he said, "*Arkhidhia* [balls]!" He retorted that it was her own fault: he had asked her first! Such tales seek out signs of insincerity behind the simplicity affected by the rich. For in that simplicity, which Bourdieu (1984:95) has called "the privilege of indifference to their own manner (so they never have to *put on* a manner)," may well lurk the affectation of not needing to be affected. In de Certeau's (1984:35–37) terms, the poor use the *tactics* of irony and trickery to flush out the deeply embedded rhetorical *strategies* that sustain the social position of the established and wealthy.

Affectations of simplicity may take the form of converting old or useless objects into repositories of value. This calls for plentiful funds, and sometimes, especially in the restoration of decrepit private houses, political connections as well. Only the well-to-do can afford this secular piety, in which a humble setting presents renovation as nostalgia.

With the general rise in standards of living, however, even the poor have begun to invest in bourgeois symbolism, if on a necessarily less lavish scale. The fireplace is one mark of this reconstituted rurality: a "European" and "traditional" item in modern materials that has largely replaced the functional stone fireplaces of the old buildings. Most surprisingly, perhaps, men—especially—have ostentatiously made pets of cats. A burly ex-policeman, originally from a rugged highland area where cats are considered useless at best and a menace to young lambs and babies at worst, coos and fusses over several furry felines in the street. Perhaps unable to afford the elaborate simplicity of a "simple" home, he has nonetheless found in his pets a way, one that undoubtedly would have earned him ridicule at home, of showing that he has risen above the unsentimental utilitarianism of village ways.

ETHNIC HOMOGENEITY AND THE *MIKRASIATES*

Long before the present embourgeoisement of Rethemnos, other cultural changes had already taken place. The withering of local ethnic diversity— notable at the time of Cretan independence in 1899—took place in a relatively short time span. In addition to the Turks, there were a few Jewish households, although the old Venetian ghetto (*Zudecca*) near the port had been demographically diluted and its boundaries enlarged (Ankori 1968:314–315). The Venetian-period synagogue, allowed to open for at least the second time in 1386, has vanished without trace (Moutsopoulos 1973, I:84); its successor near the Fortezza, wrecked by the Nazis, became a brothel before falling into total disrepair. The few Jewish merchants who remained in Rethemnos by this time all perished with their families when the old transport ship onto which they had been herded was deliberately sunk in Khania harbor by the Nazis.

Armenians, like Jews, were prominent in commerce. In 1740, an Armenian goldsmith appears to have been one of the more successful merchants in town (Malagari and Stratidakis 1985–1986:62). The majority of the Armenians left in 1948–1949, lured by the prospect of an Armenian homeland in the Soviet Union of Stalin, whence they wrote enthusiastic letters in which their erstwhile neighbors could decipher extremely indirect hints that things were not at all as wonderful as the letters overtly asserted. Almost all the Turks had left by 1924. Among the few who managed to remain were the bath attendant Fatme, who turned out to be a Frenchwoman from Provence and who became known as Madame Hortense (Prevelakis 1938:79–84; photograph in Louloudakis 1984:17), and an itinerant vendor known as Tourkoyoryis ("Turkish George") who preferred to change his faith rather than his home.[2] The few Catholics migrated to Athens. By 1960, Rethemnos was an almost solidly Greek Orthodox town.

The one major cultural change among the Greek population was the arrival of the Asia Minor refugees. The collapse of Greek irredentist dreams before the walls of Istanbul in 1922, the rout of the Greek armies, and the massacre and sack of Smyrna had huge numbers of refugees fleeing the carnage. A few more prescient families had arrived in the decade before the Asia Minor campaign. In Rethemnos, these early arrivals had to compete with the established Cretan population for the chance to buy up the properties of Muslims; since autonomy in 1899, the latter had been leaving in large numbers for Smyrna and the Dardanelles. These first refugees from Asia Minor remained at a great disadvantage: their early arrival did not entitle them to the compensation granted to the far larger numbers who left under the provisions of the Treaty of Lausanne (30 January 1923; see Pentzopoulos 1962:52). At that point, the government simply made over the Muslim-owned houses—some 3,352 on Crete alone—to the newest arrivals (Pentzopoulos 1962:103 n.34, citing League of Nations 1926:73–74, 82).

Some of the newcomers were settled in the countryside, while others made straight for the sequestered Turkish properties in town. On the whole, the refugees who had been assigned to rural properties fared better. By introducing new cash crops such as tobacco, they were able to improve the value of the lands they received. Jealous locals still remark that the refugees got all the best land on Crete, land that the Turks had sequestered for themselves and that was now redistributed to the newcomers. This resentment allows little sympathy for the rural refugees' complaint that they had been far wealthier in Asia Minor than they ever became on Crete. Such claims, never easy to evaluate, became effectively meaningless when the Ankara Convention of 1930 transferred ownership of all the sequestered property into the hands of the two national governments and thus bypassed the refugees' claims completely (Pentzopoulos 1962:117–119).

In town, however, opportunities were cramped at best. It was only in 1957 that the government finally set up an office and methodical procedures for selling the Muslim properties to their present inhabitants in order to raise more money for alleviating the plight of the shantytown dwellers (Pentzopoulos 1962:233). Until then, many urban refugees had lived in appalling conditions, their distress compounded by uncertainty about the future. The Muslim houses were often in bad repair. Most were small and had tiny windows that let in scant sunlight. They had been homes nonetheless. Muslims, who returned on sentimental pilgrimages three decades later and more, were overcome with emotion when they saw their old homes again. One former coffee shop owner went into his erstwhile establishment, still in use. Announcing, "I'm going to drink water"—an emotive marker of place for Greeks—he made for the cold water faucet, where he promptly burst into tears.

These *Tourki* had been neighbors and friends. On special feast days they had presented gifts (*peskesa*) to their Christian neighbors (see also Hirschon 1989:29). Kalomenopoulos (1964:130) records some remarkable friendships ("At the end of each song, Nafi [a Turk] would good-heartedly say, 'My little Greek brothers, let's drink a[nother] round!' ") and recalls with tears the Muslim greengrocer who allowed a deranged old Christian beggar woman to sleep every night in his shop, "until, one winter's night, her bad Fate arranged for her to die on the bench from the cold" (Kalomenopoulos 1964:170).

The Muslims' departure was accompanied by immediate hostility toward the refugees who had taken their place. For the refugees, though suddenly destitute, were more cosmopolitan than the indigenous Cretan population, especially the villagers recently arrived in town. Unlike the departed Turks, they were, simply, not Cretan. Intense mutual dislike resulted. The refugees lamented a fate that placed them among rude peasants, while the rural Cretans called the refugees "Turks"—a clear acknowledgment that in some ways the newcomers were more alien than the *Tourkokritiki* who had departed. Prevelakis (1938:20) noted that the Turkish flavor of the market street actually intensified when the refugees replaced the Muslims. The departing Muslims, too, were transported to a foreign country. The local Turks among whom they landed called them "chattels" (*yaouridhes*, a term usually reserved for the infidel Christians). Most of the Muslims had indeed been very reluctant to leave (see Elliadi 1933:38). All that their forced departure achieved was to ensure homes for the arriving Christians, who did not think much of these dwellings either then or later (see Pentzopoulos 1962:70).

The attachment to place is rooted in social experience. Muslims and Christians who have made the pilgrimage back to their former homes have invariably greeted their old neighbors with deep affection. Within a decade of the exchange, too, a party of Cretan Christians was warmly welcomed in Turkey by Muslims from Crete (Elliadi 1933:39). The rifts forced on memory by the arbitrariness of international politics hurt deeply and cry out for erasure. Forced to leave Crete, some Muslims suddenly began to tear the wooden window boxes (*kioskia*, plates 24, 25, 26) and other ornaments off their houses, not wishing to leave them behind or give them to strangers and enemies from Asia Minor (Prevelakis 1938:73). Gradually, however, nationalistic history recasts these events even in the popular memory. Today, some Rethemniots claim that it was the Christians who destroyed all the window boxes, so that all these—now—obviously "Turkish" traces would vanish. Here, once again, the official fear of Turkish claims echoes increasingly in the recast memories of everyday life.

The refugees, although divided among themselves by both class and place of origin, struck the local people as forming a closely knit and unified community of their own. The newcomers soon came to sense the local hostility to their presence, which they reciprocated with an attitude of cultural condescension (see also Cowan 1990:44; Hirschon 1989:30–33). They reacted by developing strongly commensal forms of solidarity:

At that time, all the Mikrasiates were very united (*dhemeni*) who had settled in Rethimno, and they held many shared parties (*ghlendia*). Very fine parties. It seems that at Apokries [pre-Lenten Carnival] they made merry each evening at one house, all of them together! Each one brought his meal, and they gathered in the particular house—each time at a different one—[and] each knew, most of them at least, how to play some [musical] instrument; my mother could play the mandolin when she was young; and they held parties from one night until the next, perhaps these parties might last for days.

Not all the refugees were so urbane or cosmopolitan. The daughter of a *Mikrasiatissa* explained:

I have the impression that the Mikrasiates are, like, of two kinds. The first, the one kind are subtle and urbane (*eksevyenismeni*), who know a lot about housekeeping (*pou kseroun poli apo nikokirio*), very fine housekeeping, and all that; and there are the others, who, you know, the women get all snarled up (*anaskoumbononde*) and swear at each other in the streets and speak nasty words.

This observation accords with other evidence for divisions of class and education among the refugee population (see Hirschon 1989). The refugees were largely hostile to the monarchy, which they blamed for the political adventurism that had cast them from their homes. This put most of them staunchly in the Liberal camp, at least in the early years after resettlement. Increasingly disgruntled with government inaction during the 1930s, their poorer urban component swung sharply toward the Communist Party and remained largely faithful to it during the long years of its proscription from the Civil War until 1975 (see Pentzopoulos 1962:190–195; Hirschon 1989:44, 47). Rethemnos offered the wealthier and more cosmopolitan immigrants few opportunities for self-advancement, and they soon left. Some of those who remained began to advance up the socioeconomic ladder, and in the process shifted politically away from the Left and Center both out of disillusion and because of their progressive attachment to large industrial and commercial interests (see also Hirschon 1989:44–45; but cf. Salamone 1987:155). Many refugees nonetheless continued to vote for candidates, whether communist or socialist, whom they saw as critical of the right-wing establishment.

These various kinds of difference—between indigenous Cretans and refugees, and between rich and poor—are upsetting to Rethemniots because they suggest cracks in Greek homogeneity, a tenet of both state and popular ideology. Against statements to the effect that there are no tensions between indigenous Cretans and Asia Minor refugees, we may recall that as recently as ten years ago a schoolgirl might be taunted as a "refugee" even though her mother was Cretan and her father was locally born.

NOSTALGIA

Both Cretans and refugees entertain images of a past in which people kept their word and could rely upon one another, hospitality was always offered and never abused, craftsmen and customers enfolded their dealings within the social ties of mutual dependence that had not yet been undercut by mass-produced and impersonal goods, uneducated older people showed respect to young students who reciprocated by adopting a measured and unextravagant demeanor instead of the guitars, earrings, and beards of today. The key to this kind of nostalgia is indeed *reciprocity*. It is the unquenchable, because pragmatically insatiable, longing for a condition of mutuality that overcomes class, educational, political, personal, and cultural differences—an idealized, improbable past in which, toward the "aristocracy" as bearers of Rethemniot culture and identity, all others were willing to erase their own demanding particularities in the name of a mutual but by no means socially egalitarian "respect" (*sevas*). In its extreme form, such respect was what the konsoles demanded in exchange for their haughty patronage: the poor "loved" the rich because they had need of them and could not afford to express a hatred fostered by their barefoot childhood.[3]

This kind of nostalgia is a key strategy in the claims people make to cultural legitimacy. Those who now bewail the loss of "aristocratic" values are rarely able to claim that status for themselves. Virtually all the major commercial families that governed Rethemnos's fortunes in the early years of the century have departed, and many of those who today constitute the commercial elite are of Asia Minor origin. The cosmetics retailer mentioned above acknowledged as much when, speaking of a prewar pastry shop (the pâtisserie-confiserie mentioned in the first chapter), he remarked that it was not for "the likes of me and you" but was frequented by "prosecutors" and other elevated members of the community "with their French [language]." The Mikrasiates found the indigenous Cretans lacking in any extensive knowledge of the cosmopolitan world of trade, and so they easily took on the mantle of the departed worthies whose houses they inhabited and whose place in the local commerce they very visibly filled. Much of their contempt today is directed against the newer arrivals from the villages. The social space over which they compete with them is that vacated by the departed "aristocracy" of fifty years ago. The recently urban, for their part, sometimes make great play with the "Venetian" or "Byzantine" origins of their surnames, and this is one arena in which the Mikrasiates cannot compete for nobility.

When the refugees first arrived in Rethemnos, the local dignitaries did not have much time for them. The old families were few and dispirited. A journalist declared in 1940 that at that time there were only eighty-six "old Rethemniots" left in the town; Prevelakis's account makes it clear that much the same perception had obtained in the preceding two decades as well. Even supposing one could calculate the emigration rate precisely, and even allowing for a greater rapidity of change in the post–World War II years than previously, it becomes clear that laments for the passing of an era of fine social distinctions are part of the strategy whereby, at any point in the process, people lay claim to cultural and social superiority over those they dismiss as parvenus.

This also appears in the idealization of poverty that one still hears from those who mourn the passing of the old order. For these essentially conservative and relatively well-to-do citizens, a Rethemniot of old was more dependable (besalis) and had a stronger sense of obligation. This was true of both the upper classes, consisting of the "merchants" (embori) and "professionals" (epistimones),[4] and the poor. Each side knew its debt of mutual respect toward the other, and sevas ("respect") is a characteristic feature of this nostalgic moral landscape—a respect, however, that unequal relations of patronage were to a great extent responsible for imposing. Those who were poor then express the same memories with vituperatively funny imitations of the aristocrats' precious, self-consciously European mannerisms.

The external mutuality of sevas thus actually defined a hierarchy of class. The rise of a newly wealthy bourgeoisie, however, has by now blurred the categorical distinctions between classes as well as the distinguishing marks of respectability. Scandalized by topless bathers, one elderly carpenter wondered how it was that foreigners were able "to live without a boundary to anything." Tourism has led local women to appear "trouserless" (ksevrakotes), a term that, when applied to local people, implies poverty and above all a lack of parental or other protection, hence a low position in the social order (see also Hirschon 1989:116). A man who might tolerate his own wife's bathing topless said that he nonetheless could not allow her to go topless in Rethemnos in case her father or some other close male relative saw her. The issue is less what she does then who sees her doing it and who will be held responsible for her good conduct: respect for "society" is at stake. Thus, too, the female practice of sitting on one's doorstep with one's back turned to possible passersby (see also Hirschon 1989: 189) is said not to be a matter of a personal sense of embarrassment (dropi), but of *ithos, public* morality, or "being re-strained" (*na ise sinestalmenos*; on *sistoli*, see Gallant 1990:509–510). In a social world that has lost its form, however, this sense of respect becomes increasingly hard to sustain. "Ugliness" (*ask[h]imia*, literally, "formlessness") abounds. To those who idealize the past as a time of structured, hierarchical reciprocities, the modern age is truly a time of moral pollution in Douglas's (1966) sense of "matter out of place."

But the ugliness of poverty was real enough to those who had to put up with it. Before and for some years after World War II, the children of the poor went barefoot, warming themselves in winter by burning a few scraps of secretively scrounged paper in a street corner and feeding on wild greens in the spring. The little money the poor possessed they stored in sacks, since chests of drawers were an inconceivable luxury and banks were deemed untrustworthy. As soon as they could, they turned that money into real estate, as a defense against the manic fluctuations of currency. The poor became ever more beholden to the merchants, who extended credit to them for sometimes minuscule sums of money. The poorer refugees, lacking even the security of social networks, often found it difficult to get credit, and lagged further and further behind.

OIL AND SOAP: SLIPPERY ECONOMICS

Most Rethemniots were nevertheless able to eke out some sort of living. In the hinterland villages, from which so many of the Cretan element hailed, olives were a major crop, and the oil they produced provided them with both domestic nutrition and, in a good year, a source of income. Above all, it provided the mainstay of the once-flourishing soap industry.

The collapse of the soap industry around 1960, however, suddenly left almost the entire town temporarily destitute. It is probably to this sudden economic collapse that we can attribute the preservation of so much of the Old Town. Residents were simply too poor to contemplate major rebuilding, so they did the best they could with the damp, drafty houses that have since become one of the town's major economic assets.

In the early 1950s, there were seventeen soap factories in Rethemnos. Each of the larger factories could produce 100–150 tons per month, and even smaller operations regularly made about 130 tons. They sold all over the Greek world, from Alexandropolis to the Peloponnese; the demand was highest in northern Greece, since Athens-Piraeus had cornered the rest of the mainland market. The olive crop of the Rethimni prefecture was high in acid content, and this made it exceptionally suitable for high-grade soap. The milling of the olives was then a much slower affair than it is with today's collectively organized and modern production methods, with the result that much of the crop rotted and the oil was consequently of poor quality. The only solution was to turn it into soap. Each factory had its representatives in the main towns—Larissa, Thessaloniki, Agrinio, and so on—just as the major food manufacturing companies have their trade agents in Rethemnos today. It was difficult to control the agents' rake-off—"things were crazy" (*yinotane tis mourlis*)—as, even when an agent got 20 drachmas a kilo but reported only 19, it was hardly worth the merchant's while to check on him at a time when travel around Greece was still far from easy. An agent's tactic was to present an impenetrably complex account. He would undertake distribution of, say, sixty 150-kilogram sacks of soap and report that he had sold five at 19.80 drachmas, four at 20 drachmas, the rest at 18 drachmas! Such complex knavery notwithstanding, the soap industry brought steady revenues to the town.

Within the period 1960–1965, almost the entire Cretan soap industry collapsed as a direct result of the competitive prices and qualities offered by industrial production. Thus began a process of radical change, for the genteel pretense of avoiding competition with one's fellow Rethemniots, socially mandatory up to this point, could not easily withstand the external pressure to develop an economic ideology that favored competition both within and beyond the local society. The mainland agents all demanded new shipments as a *condition* of paying for those already received. If the agent already had in hand as much as, for example, one hundred tons of soap, this demand was catastrophic for the producer; indeed, the larger the producer, the harder it was to meet such an ultimatum and thereby avoid the crushing blow of bankruptcy and perhaps even jail. This last was the fate of suppliers, who, lacking sufficient storage space, had *akopo ladhi* (literally, "uncut oil"):

> Akopo ladhi is the following. You are a producer, you have many olive trees, and you have no storage area in your house. That's *very* bad: if you make two tons of oil, you should have storage space for two tons' worth. So you, what do you do? You grind the olive oil at the mill, and after that you say, "Go and unload it at such-and-such a merchant's."

The merchant gives the producer a receipt, which can be converted at any time into cash ("cut," hence the term "uncut oil")[5] at the going rate:

> With this paper in hand, you, so to speak, can marry off your daughter, and say, "I'll let two or three years go by and keep my oil there, and maybe some lad, some boy, will turn up so I can marry off my daughter and then I'll take my paper and 'cut' it at the price current on the day that I cash it."

With that money, the young woman's father could buy a house for the dowry. In this way, he would also avoid having to put his trust in banks and paper money; inflation would increase the drachma value of his oil over the period in question. For the merchant, however, it was unprofitable to store the oil without putting it back on the market. Merchants—who were thus oil dealers (*ladhadhes*) as well as soap makers—thus speculated on the shifting value of oil, selling when it was high and buying new supplies as soon as it dropped significantly again. As operators who might be managing two million kilos of oil at any one time, they usually maintained a position of considerable ascendancy over the small-time producers (*sakouladhori*, literally, "bagmen"), whose profit margins were always small. Many sakouladhori were town dwellers from Rethemnos who could not support themselves adequately in town, and who worked in villages where they had ties at regular intervals throughout the olive-picking season (October through February). The owners of the larger olive groves were in a somewhat better condition, since their access to storage gave them more flexibility in playing the market. As far as possible, the larger merchants preferred to deal directly with village-dwelling producers, whom they could more easily bind to them by ties of spiritual kinship. Merchants who were wealthy enough to be able to exercise a degree of choice would prefer to baptize children from the larger *fares* (patrigroups),[6] as the resulting spiritual relationship would be spread over a larger number of people and thus secure them larger and therefore more risk-free supplies of olives.

When the crash came, these merchants were suddenly deprived of purchasers for their oil supplies, and it was this that drove them into debt. The disaster was general, but it affected the suppliers much more drastically than it did the wealthier merchants. The suppliers were suddenly left facing bankrupt debtors. Moreover, in addition to the regular sakouladhori and olive-picking young women (*sillektries*), there were others who had converted their entire meager incomes into oil in anticipation of selling it at a profit to the merchants. These unfortunate people—female servants, for example, who made a monthly wage of 300 drachmas—were suddenly destitute. As for the merchant-manufacturers, most had shown enough foresight to diversify their activities and were able to absorb the losses through other commercial activities. Of those who had not done so, and who as a result faced total ruin, most filed bankruptcy in order to avoid repaying their debts by selling off their stock and equipment. One man adopted a different strategy, one that allowed him to keep his best asset—his good standing as a merchant—"which I won't sell however much you pay me." He sold off what he could and destroyed the rest at his own expense. Instead of pursuing those who still owed him money, moreover, he wrote off their debts. Fortunately for him, he had enough real estate to protect him from complete financial eclipse. He sold most of this property at extremely low prices; one villa, for example, which he estimates has a present-day value of 5 million drachmas, he sold for

40,000 drachmas. He took off for Piraeus with his family and opened a small handicraft factory there:

> I lived in Piraeus, in a neighborhood [called] Kaminia (Smokestacks). There it so happened that I was neighbor to some Mykoniates, who were pure-minded (*aghni*) islanders, they too were consumed by poverty and misery in their barren islet, Mykonos, because if you take away from them Delos with its antiquities, the rest of it's two and a half, two and a half or three thousand inhabitants, there are no trees, there's no water, but they've managed if you go in July, August, to be two and half, three thousand inhabitants and eight thousand visitors (kseni). That's a lot of people even though the island's barren, but they have this great treasure—Delos—let's say. So, there I saw how their people came there and bought bags, and bought—"Hey, what are they doing?"—not to go on at length to you, I went there to Mykonos, let's say, once or twice, in this way, so I got into the system (*čikloma*) and I bought wool and I had some ten little women [working for me in Piraeus] and they made pullovers, such things, and I used to sell them, I took them to various tourist shops, I sold them on Mykonos.

He also sold some in Rhodes. He began to sell in Crete as well:

> And I saw gradually that this work could not be confined to Mykonos, to that island, since tourism was spreading. Crete wouldn't stay behind. And I experimentally made five or six rooms, that is, I didn't have money to create a whole unit even though all who were in debt made *monadhes*[7]—because for the last fifteen years anyone who is in debt came out well!

These others gambled on big bank loans for tourist development. (A few, building on their business experience from such trades as carpentry and metalworking, did very well and provided the basis of the town's modern tourist development.) After his bitter experiences with the soap factory, however, and ever mindful of the dangers of indebtedness, the former soap manufacturer preferred a smaller scale of operation and a greater degree of reliance on personal obligation. Because he had been so careful to pay off his debts from the collapse of his soap factory before leaving for Piraeus, his erstwhile creditors—who undoubtedly would hope to benefit commercially from their association with him if he succeeded—were now eager to lend him money. Today, it is his proud boast that when he enters a coffeehouse in any village, he will usually be treated by someone whose debt he wrote off at the time of the crash, and whose friendship is far more valuable—in both the commercial and the emotional senses—than a paltry five hundred drachmas would have been. But there is no doubt that, for small-scale operations, the recognition of obligations constitutes an investment of social capital that may easily be redeemed with monetary interest when material conditions permit.

This example sounds a central theme. Residents who moved to the New Town had many opportunities for commercial expansion. Some of those who remained within the confines of the Old Town have also expanded economically, although on a much smaller scale. Their social and symbolic capital does not convert into the financial credit of big banks and legal obligations, however, and yet the intrusion of the bureaucracy into their operations—in the form of the town-planning and historic conservation agencies, or as new tax levies and inheritance regulations—compels them to remain dependent on these newly wealthy former neighbors and kin. The former soap maker acidulously compared the profits that the new landowners were making on hotel construction in the New Town with the paltry dividends he and others like him had been able to get from their investments:

> It went well for all because the hotel which at that time was worth a hundred, a hundred million, is now worth a billion. . . . [W]hereas I'd given [i.e., invested] 20,000 drachmas—because that was the cost of a funeral twenty, fifteen years ago—to a funeral parlor to do my funeral, now the funeral parlor tells me that it's not enough: "We'll get you as far as the church; after that you'll have to pay the difference, d'you understand?" Whereas the 20,000 I had was enough for my funeral to take place, a *good* funeral, today it's not enough!

It is hardly surprising that to this day poorer Rethemniots take a very dim view of the stability of banks and currency. But today their alternative, real estate, has become as divided into two rapidly separating classes as they have themselves. A client who wishes to secure a bank loan must also take out insurance on his business. The superficial attraction of these policies is that, if no claims are made, the capital can be reclaimed—without interest—after twenty years. Anyone who bought a policy at 4,500 drachmas per annum around 1965 would have been able to buy a house in the Old Town at about the aggregate price (i.e., 45,000 drachmas) ten years later, whereas today the accrued value of the policy has dramatically failed to keep up with rising property costs even within the Old Town:

> What has he bought with these 100,000 drachmas [*sic*]? A door, a window. A door [is all] he's bought! Whereas the others [i.e., the owners of the insurance company] have "eaten" a house! This is how things are in Greece (*afta ine ta ellinika pramata*)!

And even that "door" is predicated on the client's not having had to use any of the insurance money—in case of sickness, for example—at an earlier date. On the other hand, by keeping the money and buying the house instead, the client would have been the owner of property worth around

1 million drachmas by the mid-1980s! A shop on the main market street (Arkadiou) that cost 200,000 drachmas in the mid-1960s would be worth between 15 and 20 million drachmas twenty years later. One of the soap manufacturers owned fifteen shops on Arkadiou Street, of which the largest was worth 160,000 drachmas in about 1965. Although this constituted wealth in local terms, the entrepreneur would have become rich even by international standards had he managed to hold on to his properties until tourism inflated their value. Gloomier voices predict that those who have succeeded in keeping their properties may suffer a similar fate when tourism, in its turn, breaks down under the pressure of competition from the cheaper resorts of Turkey and Morocco.[8]

The major economic change brought by tourism came in the form of a massive revaluation of land outside the Old Town after the military seized power in Athens in 1967. Large, agriculturally feeble seashore plots of sandy, windblown desert could, in the 1940s and 1950s, be bought with a single barrel of oil. These properties, formerly the best that hitherto despised poor refugees and backwoodsmen could hope for in the way of dowries, suddenly became immensely valuable and enabled their owners to develop into a class of nouveaux riches. A few enterprising leaders of the old merchant families played the most seminal role, however, and reaped the most significant first profits, because they were in the most advantageous financial position to take immediate advantage of the military junta's indiscriminate stimulation of tourist development. When I first visited Rethemnos in 1971, no Old Town hotel boasted private bathrooms. By 1973, the first major hotel was going up on the edge of the Old Town. Now, by the late 1980s, the entire coastline had become an endless tract of such installations.

Today, then, tourism has created a new situation for those who managed to survive the crash of the early 1960s or who have returned from economic exile in Athens to take advantage of the new conditions. The population is also swelled by a new influx of villagers eager to take advantage of this rich and seemingly unlimited source of enterprise. Typifying the new possibilities for adaptation is the member of an *arkhondoi-koyenia* (upper-class family) who married within his own class and set up in business as a producer of ironwork and timber fittings. In the early 1960s, at a time when many merchants faced bankruptcy, and when his own business crashed, he was still sufficiently solvent to open a hotel bearing his own name but basically financed and managed by his wife. She had worked in a bank before their marriage, and, in addition to accounting skills, she had a good understanding of French and English—a mark of high status in those Eurocentric days. These skills were a practical asset in the new conditions of life—one of the few features of the "aristocratic" culture of which that could truly be said.

Those who today regret the passing of this elevated minority contrast it with the rise of a new class of parvenus lacking education, finesse, and, above all, the kind of cultural initiative that formerly had the town's leaders reading and writing poetry, borrowing from the libraries, glorying in Rethemnos's proverbial reputation as the town of letters. They scoff at the numerous nouveaux riches who made their wealth from tourism. "Now the layabouts (*alites*) have become big merchants, the aristocrats!" grumbled an elderly cosmetics retailer, whose small but steady business was founded by his father, an Asia Minor refugee. They know that it was a few well-established merchants whose calculated risks opened up the new economy from which the inexperienced and uncouth are now so eager to snatch quick profits. Above all, these nostalgic grumblers feel that they have lost the moral advantage: once really *needed* by the poor, today they find themselves despised for their effeteness and snobbery, their cultural values an antiquarian relic. They associate this catastrophic change, not only with the rise of tourism and its exploitation by fortune hunters, but also with the sudden inflation that occurred at the same time. This inflation is not simply an economic problem. Rather, it is seen as a decline of stability and tradition, a consequence of cultural as well as managerial failure, a loss of that quality of life that they call "fine" (*oreo*): "Manners and customs have changed, social interactions, everything!" And "everything" includes whatever made social life possible: mutual trust and respect between classes, cultural standards, the possibility of extending and receiving credit, recognition of social boundaries that might not be transgressed.

Another resident, a critic of vested interests and thus occupying a very different place on the political spectrum, voiced a strikingly similar plaint—that the restaurateurs spawned by the modern restaurant trade are mostly cheats and opportunists who do not fit the style of "old Rethemnos":

Fish? At less than six hundred *franga*[9] I can't find any. And I buy frozen ones—red mullet, bass—which cost four or five hundred. But how nice they are! See how this unfortunate tavern keeper sets aside two kilos for you,[10] frozen, and tells you to give him seven thousand drachmas! Eh? It's, well . . . ! Why do they buy them? They buy them at six hundred franga a kilo so as to find two or three fresh ones to use them as camouflage so as to sell the frozen ones for fresh. They aren't. . . . You should know [this much]: of today's tavern keepers who exist in Rethimno, it's questionable whether there are ten left of the old ones. All the others . . . [who are] harbor workers . . . bearers . . . porters, suchlike—these are the prof[essionals] of today, whose sole interest is how they are going to take it [your money] off you! And many of them—bravo to them!—each year change [to] a [new] apartment [i.e., restaurant premises], frying potatoes, selling.

This ironic comment comes from a man who prides himself on both his sense of fair commercial practice and his insight into the iniquities of the bureaucratic establishment and of the wealthy, but who—as a good fellow in the social sense—cannot quite suppress a sneaking admiration for these tricks of the newly rich. But he also longs for the days when "here in Crete people had grown up with the triptych:[11] religion, fatherland, family"—this, moreover, from a self-declared supporter of Florakis, the Communist Party's general secretary:

> You used to be able to destroy yourself because your second cousin's, your *second cousin's* granddaughter was raped by someone. And you could destroy your house! By going to jail: that is, by killing him, you'd go to jail.

Today, parents complain, a daughter will not even tell her father where she has been.

These attitudes, which cross party-political allegiances and even the broader barriers of class, are an especially elaborate and articulate form of *structural nostalgia*. In each generation, people attribute the superior qualities of the past to its more perfect adherence to a set of structured rules and principles for the conduct of social life.[12] In the villages and town alike, sexual morality was once more nearly perfect than it is today, these people claim, as their predecessors had also claimed before them. In town, the high cultural standards of a haughty, self-regarding aristocracy allegedly once came closer to the European ideal. Above all, equals and neighbors were bound together by ties of mutual assistance and affection:

> People were more united (dhemeni) then, among themselves. That is: the neighborhood was a [true] neighborhood, where you went out, you saw your neighbor woman (*yitonissa*), the neighbor woman knocked on your door, where the children came out and played in the street, where the neighbor woman had the meaning that if something happened to you, she'd come and help you, come and ask you [if she could help], whereas now she's begun to see you from a distance.

Images generated by this kind of nostalgia put the poor firmly in their place and eradicate all memory of class differences.

CLASS AND CONFLICT: NOSTALGIA FOR DIFFERENCE?

While it is hard to estimate the respective size of social classes in interwar Rethemnos, one can gain some sense of it from the fact that the "aristocracy"—which included all such professionals as doctors and lawyers—

wholly supported the rightist Popular Party. The liberal Venizelists, whose eponymous leader was a popular Cretan politician before becoming an international figure, are generally thought to have had about 85 percent of the vote. After 1932, refugee disillusionment increased the communists' local influence, while the mantle of Venizelos had to be shared among an ever-widening spectrum of parties and leaders. The result was that it became increasingly difficult for any party to gain a clear majority. In the 1986 municipal elections, the right-wing candidate was denied victory over his socialist rival only when, at the last moment, the communists threw in their lot with the socialists (see below).

Embourgeoisement has not abolished the rhetoric of class in Rethemnos but has invested it with a new indirection. Class is something to be admitted to with embarrassment, if at all (see also Bennett 1987), but to be utilized as a weapon in the day-to-day negotiation of social resources. For the wealthy, money is the key determinant of class status; for those bearing local family names of many generations' standing, ancestry; for those excluded by virtue of their former or present poverty, political affiliations such as membership in the KKE (the [pro-Moscow] Communist Party of Greece)—the only political party whose members I heard talk of themselves as dhiki mas, "insiders," a term more commonly used of kinship or cultural identity. Class relations in Rethemnos still labor under the shadow of the Civil War (1944–1949) and its several aftershocks, but wealth and kinship distort the more predictable patterns.

Shifting alignments give the whole topic of class a curious evanescence in local conversation. In the management of Rethemnos history, the negotiation of class identities is both perceptual prism and processual motor. The politically conservative tend to reify the past, to structure their nostalgia and to view the present as a fractured version of past perfection. The political Left also sees the past in absolute terms, but then rather as an unmitigated misery from which their own efforts are slowly beginning to redeem them—a curiously theological metaphor, but a pervasive one, and one that has powerful echoes in modern Greek culture generally.[13] The crusty reminiscers of the Right tend to equate the people of Rethemnos with a generalized "aristocracy," a wealthy merchant class whose very pretensions to European culture entitled them, even in the most grudging memories, to a collective mantle that never had any formal status after the bedraggled departure of the Venetian forces in 1646. These nostalgic curmudgeons insist that the reciprocities of respect were more nearly perfect in those days. One former coffee shop proprietor claimed that the typical Rethemniot of old was more besalis (morally dependable). The "respect" that these people remember as the characteristic relationship between people of different class was thus presented as a mutuality but turns out to have been quite the reverse. It is exemplified by the strictly unilateral use of honorific titles (e.g., *kirie kathiyita*, cf. the French *M. le professeur*) to people of professional status. The nouveaux riches, by contrast, show little interest in either receiving or affecting such courtesies.

Throughout Greek society, the premise of moral equality interacts with strategies of advantage among widely separated class or professional interests. Campbell (1964) gives a finely nuanced account of *filotimo*, the proud dependability that assumes *both* a parity of *moral* respect *and* the possibility of a strong *social asymmetry*. Moral respect is both a mask and the enabling condition for the mutual dependence of shepherds, merchants, and politicians—or, in Rethemnos, workers, traders, community leaders, and bureaucrats. The inbuilt contradictions, however, can barely withstand the combined onslaught of sardonic contempt from the populist Left, the impatience of the newly wealthy with the prettified ways of the erstwhile "aristocracy," and the undisguised competitiveness of modern commercial life. It is no longer so easy for the wealthy to disguise inequalities by their performances of mutual *sevas* and by demonstrative affectations of "simplicity."

The carpers on the conservative Right emphasize the sense of crumbling social hierarchy. Today's wealthy, they grumble, are not *truly* wealthy: aside from some ten or twenty individuals, it is simply that many have managed to elevate themselves economically to the point where they live comfortably and think they have achieved something socially significant as a result. The old rich were *laofilis*: they performed acts of charity and sat at the coffeehouses frequented by the poor, with whom they would engage in discussion: "That's why the people loved them." Note again the affectation of simplicity and mutual affection—an idiom that resembles nothing so much as Victorian philanthropy. A former coffeehouse proprietor recalls that a wealthy wholesaler would shop for himself with a straw bag in hand, after which he would come to the speaker's uncle's coffeehouse (as it then was); the proprietor made much of the fact that this distinguished notable would use the first name without a prefixed *kirie* ("Mr."): "There was no *kiriliki* [gentlemanly status] then"—*except* when other customers were present. This account of past social relations, which seems oblivious to the irony that the powerful are those who can *choose* whether to use such formal titles, is impregnated with nostalgia: *real* friendship existed then, in contrast with the *false* friendship of today. Nostalgia literalizes the spurious equality that the formal etiquette implied. Each *kafetzis* (coffeehouse proprietor) would stand in his doorway, holding his tray discreetly behind his back so that his competitors would not see it, and would greet each passerby with an unctuous *kalimera kirie Yanni* ("Good day, Mr. John"). The kindness of the "equalizing" response did not leave much doubt about the economic or political realities of such a relationship. Those who were poor at that time are more inclined to recall—and to mimic with savage resentment—the stately courtesies that the well-to-do affected among themselves.

It is a relationship in which praise easily becomes a form of condescension:

> ELDERLY LADY, *pausing at door of a coffeehouse*: You've whitewashed?
> CO-OWNER (a woman): I have whitewashed.
> LADY: *I* [can] see you've made it like a little [white] dove. *Exit, grandly.*

The recipient of this kindly attention claimed to be most touched by it.

Condescending praise and affectations of simplicity go hand in hand. Demonstrative restraint expresses—and reproduces—an economy of power. Like members of powerful village factions whose quiet mien tests the limits of self-regard by showing they have no need to demonstrate it, those Rethemniots who were indeed to the money born use their restraint as a rhetorical claim to their freedom of choice. As with money, so also in speech, economy of style was a luxury of taste. The wealthy measured their words as they measured their money. In contrast with the vernacular habit of speaking *koutourou* ("every which way"), they only said *singekrimena pramata* ("specific things") and "everything they did was measured (*metrimena*)." Expressive modesty signals superior class identity: "whoever says less is better." Measured speech, like modest dress or architectural facades, follows a long-standing Eurocentric rhetoric of restraint. Loquacity, said one bitter observer of nouveau riche manners, is "parasangs"[14] from courtesy.

That did not mean that speech and dress are not carefully styled, but simply that stylishness could include deliberate understatement. Men might wear beards, for example, despite the fact that in the villages these were the prerogative of priests and mourners. In town, however, men favored the French-style goatee (*mousi*). Especially in Venizelos's time, and partially in imitation of him, the goatee was de rigueur for all "aristocratic" men. A local sports promoter still wears a goatee and the kind of lamb's wool hat that the great Cretan liberal favored—a nice conflation of the "European" and the "nativist" styles. *Mousi*, a singular noun, is contrasted with *yenia*, a *plural* noun used of the more uncontrolled and flamboyant beards worn by hippies and priests. As Stewart (1985:60) observes, plurality has negative symbolic implications in Greece, and the wildness of the yenia suggests the very antithesis of the bodily restraint espoused by the elite.

Personal dress links individuals to the social body, much as architecture clothes collective identities. Dress makes a social statement about the self: it disguises the intimacies of the body and presents the formalities of the social persona, thereby providing powerful metaphors for the expression of cultural tensions between intimacy and display. So strongly is this felt that townsfolk contrast the *eghoismos* of the Greek, who always wants to appear well dressed abroad because he sees his personal self-presentation as both a reflection and a representation of the national image, with the simplicity and underdressing of the tourists they see around them. The upper class, who view such displays with disdain, are the only ones who have the freedom to imitate the foreigners' "simplicity."

The state of one's clothing is therefore, at the very least, an index of self-respect. Dress has gender-coded moral implications: an ex-policeman wanted to set a man wearing earrings to cutting wood all day. The coding is explicit and should be kept that way. A housepainter, returning from work in soiled clothes, refused to sit down in the coffeehouse, because he was concerned that people might see him that way and wonder "what role he was playing." A baker keeps a standing order for trousers with a tailor who knows that he dislikes dark colors as these show up the flour; when he got married, his bride-to-be nearly had second thoughts because her family kept commenting on how "dirty" life would be amid a constant swirl of flour, and both of them—now happily married for a quarter of a century—express embarrassment whenever someone catches them still in their flour-smeared clothes. An elderly returned Athenian wears a high-crowned, formal hat and a necktie in the coffeehouse, "for official [wear]"; when he goes home, he switches the hat for a cloth cap, which is more comfortable but is considered working-class apparel. He will not appear with his head bare anywhere, however, as he professes to be embarrassed by his baldness and even wears the more snugly fitting cloth cap in public on windy days. Those who long for the good old days recall that the suits of the aristocracy were all "European." The best were English, and this was in part taken to symbolize the Cretans' pre-Cyprus Anglophilia. Working-class men may also wear Cretan dress, particularly in winter when the long boots and jodhpurs (*čilotes*) offer some protection against the damp and cold of Old Town housing; these items thus constitute something of an admission that one is not living in luxurious (or even moderately comfortable) conditions. Cretans also thereby make a statement about their local identity—an option open to them long before the cultivation of such exotic details by the tourist industry, if we may judge by a document of 1900 that mentions a Muslim "tailor of Cretan costumes." One Mikrasiatis (Asia Minor refugee), however, strenuously denied the connection between dress and identity. It may have implied excessive differentiation from his point of view. Some country-dwelling refugees adopted Cretan dress for a while, probably out of a desire to assimilate (see Eddy 1931:167–168).

From these examples, it is clear that even such apparently innocuous details as dress and hairstyle are components of the contest over the past as much as the obviously antique buildings and the bureaucratic agencies entrusted with their preservation. As vehicles of embodiment (see Cowan 1990), they are not so much the unconscious elements of a reified habitus (see de Certeau 1984:58 on Bourdieu 1977:78–79) as a resource for spirited resistance to the state's attempts to produce just such an environment through massive counterinculcation. What is more, the state tries to objectify certain elements, not necessarily those currently in vogue, and thereby to expropriate them to its own version of "tradition." At the same time, the citizens themselves—who are after all the object of this sustained proselytization—expropriate fragments of the official discourse in defense of their own renditions of Cretan and Rethemniot identity. The common language the state and its citizens share is that of tradition, history, identity. They differ, however, in precisely what they respectively ascribe to those resounding categories. A struggle like the current one over the regulation of the old buildings in which they live brings these contradictions to the surface. Then, suddenly, the swaggering male pride that delights in Cretan costume, Cretan dances, and Cretan drinking customs swerves sharply away from the cultivation of a glorious architectural heritage. For the state's interference in people's homes, however benignly intended, is, in the most visceral and at the same time literal sense, a breach of intimacy.

In the next two chapters, we shall look at the social basis of the Rethemniots' current sense of identity. We shall explore their work, their neighborhood practices, and their uses of kinship and other tried and trusted media of consociation. We shall find that an androcentric kinship ideology and a sense of local identity sometimes merge, and that in so doing they pose a discourse radically alienated from the unifying pabulum of the nation-state. It is, in fact, a warlike discourse, and on occasion it sets the local actors against the state to which, at other times, they profess deep loyalty and prove it unto death. Being Rethemniot is hardly a simple matter. When the state intercedes in the processes of self-definition, and when above all it intervenes in the material context that gives that social life its physical shape, the complexities sometimes spill over into open conflict. It is these vagaries that may lead us to a better understanding of the negotiation of power between citizen and bureaucracy, between two present-day perspectives informed by two divergent visions of the past. The challenge is thus both to relate the mundane details of everyday life to the grandiloquent locutions of officialdom and, at the same time, to differentiate between them.

Chapter Three

HOSTS, NEIGHBORS, AND RIVALS

Hospitality: Semantic Ambiguities and Moral Certainties

Hospitality is a hotly contested moral good in Rethemnos. It is a claim of some antiquity: "The inhabitants . . . are, as everywhere in Crete, lively, cheerful, busy, and caring to strangers in an extreme degree" (Khatzidakis 1881:67). Did the very next generation of a people thus described really force Lilika Nakou to live outside the walls? Nonsense, retorts one man who knew her; people just didn't have the ready space for renting then that they do today. But what if her morals were suspect—would that not explain her exclusion? No, came the response again; for to admit that would mean accepting the likelihood that the right-wing journalist and thug she portrays had really succeeded in broadcasting slanders on her chastity before she arrived—and that would constitute a slander against the entire town. For a visitor's criticism of Rethemniot hospitality violates the canon of reciprocal hospitality itself. Hospitality does not mark acceptance of the stranger so much as the moral superiority of the host. In such a moral hierarchy, Rethemniots rank themselves highest among all Greeks.

Rethemniot hospitality is certainly lavish and frequent. From the groaning formal tables that our hosts deprecatingly dismissed as "makeshift" to the sudden arrival of a bottle of wine when we dined out— "So-and-so's treating you," a restaurant owner would announce as he thumped it down on the table—our social life seemed at times to be one of unceasing ingestion. Village rules partially apply: one who enters the coffeehouse may not treat those already present, except under very exceptional circumstances (usually a major celebration). Personal experience can subject these practices to the invidious comparison of past and present that constitutes nostalgia. A visiting expatriate grumbled that whenever he walked into the coffeehouse, his friends failed to notice him, but they always greeted him when they found him already ensconced there: the corrupt world of the town has reduced the sociable spirit of kerasma to a cheap play for gain. But one should set against this view another Rethemniot's principled refusal to accept a kerasma on the grounds that he always arrived at the coffeehouse later than his would-be benefactor and so was never able to reciprocate.

While coffeehouse clients do not automatically treat strangers to drinks as they do in most villages, the most casual conversation brings payment for the newcomer's drink in its train. A new friend called me out of the coffeehouse next to his shop to go and "lift the fridge"—which turned out to mean drinking from a chilled bottle of retsina at his patrilateral cousin's coffeehouse round the corner and nibbling on some boiled sardines. When he asked his cousin how much he owed and the latter said, "A hundred [drachmas] or so (*kana katostariko*)," he put down 150 drachmas, thereby demonstrating generosity to both his cousin and this stranger and emphasizing the importance of studied imprecision in informal social relations. We shall return later to the theme of this reciprocal, intentional vagueness in economic interactions. Fussing over small change is an embarrassment because it forces the material basis of a kindly gesture into the foreground.

Small-scale treating of drinks and nuts is still common among neighbors in the tiny side streets of the Old Town, while it has virtually died amid the impersonal high-rises of the New Town. Men who have moved to the latter often spend the early evenings back in Old Town coffeehouses in pursuit of a familiar sociability. The principle of treating remains highly charged with affective and moral implications, but its forms may change under the pressure of urban life. The direct exchange of bottles of wine at the same sitting, for example, would violate village canons.[1] For modern Rethemniots, this is quite acceptable unless one is sitting at the next table in an open space, in which case both parties have to act out the model of village propriety. At a distance, or in the crush of an enclosed but busy restaurant, the elaborate pretenses of long-term exchange are abandoned. One can no longer count on daily encounters to maintain the rough balance of reciprocation. People are aware, however, that this is a departure from the ideal, and they become extremely sensitive to the suspicion of scrounging. When a man joined me at my table for some conversation and I paid for the coffee he had already drunk, he remarked that he had not come over so that I would treat him! The nuances of treating can still be deployed to a variety of strategic ends. A socialist and victim of the 1967–1974 military junta was furious when an ultrarightist sat at his table and clumsily ignored the clear signal of deep displeasure the socialist gave by, quite simply, not offering to treat him.

On one early occasion, I responded in mountain village style to being treated[2] by telling the kafetzis to treat the entire company. He seemed surprised, although he acted on my request with fair alacrity, and another townsman later commented that in this action I had been *oreos* ("fine, socially right")[3]—reaffirming, in this remark, the association Rethemniots make between rural values and an idealized version of their own past. Such minor gestures on my part certainly pale in comparison with the outpouring of warm words (and drink) that accompanied the meals lavished on us upon our every return from a significant absence. However slight the expense, the rhetoric of hospitality is always one of total commitment. "If it isn't cut it doesn't get eaten (*ama dhen kopi, dhen droete*)," remarked our kindly landlord when I demurred at his cutting into a fresh cabbage just to treat me. The pun on *dhen droete*, which means "is unbearable, antisocial" when used of a person, suggests the uselessness of mere things fetishized and divorced from the realities of everyday life.

How can one reconcile the occasional demonstrations of real unfriendliness to strangers, or a Rethemniot's criticism of a neighbor for not keeping a totally "open" house,[4] with the overwhelmingly warm, generous, and freely extended hospitality that we so often experienced? The contrast between these two images is not an irresolvable paradox, nor is it simply the result of different observers' perceptions. It lies, rather, in the shifting conditions under which people bring others into their homes, and in their changeable evaluations of strangers. People may offer great and disinterested kindness while deriving substantial benefit from their actions. Hospitality has a noblesse oblige dimension that makes it an ideal medium for renegotiating social inequalities (Herzfeld 1987b). Rethemniots are sensitive to the oppressive aspect of treating: "I don't have to ruin myself just because you want me to (*dhen ine na pa' na khalaso to eafto mou epidhi to thelis esi*)!" But lavish hospitality, whatever the obligations it imposes, may also express deep affection as well as warm curiosity. Conversely, the occasional closed door or insulting gesture reflects, as we shall see, the fear of outsiders' ability to undermine both the entire social order and the individual's domestic harmony. Such multiple ambiguities inform a housewife's hyperbolic observation—delicately ironic (cf. Chock 1987)? warmly affectionate?—that we were "our [i.e., their] people" (*dhiči mas anthropi*) and should not feel like "outsiders" (*kseni*). These terms, which divide kin from non-kin, also separate neighbors from strangers and Greeks from foreigners. Hospitality is a multilayered edifice of complex relationships.

Hospitality serves, too, as a means of expressing Cretan identity. A merchant informed me *prokatavolika* ("as prepayment") that the evening's entertainment was on him, as this kind of absolute hospitality was what Cretans did. My protests were to no avail whatsoever. As a challenge to his lien on local identity, they threatened the very rules of hospitality itself. On another occasion, three nonlocal laborers—members of a new immigration wave inspired by the New Town construction boom— walked into a tourist goods shop. The proprietor insisted on treating them from a bottle of grappa he kept mainly for tourists, and as he spoke to them he used an increasingly noticeable proportion of dialect forms—

a subtler but no less forceful idiom of cultural intimidation. These contests over identity can wax fierce, but they may respond to other pressures. One round of particularly proprietorial evocations of local *ethimo* ("custom") made me feel quite helpless, until the kafetzis intervened, having decided that it was more in his interest to let me treat others like any local. By controlling the right to treat, locals maintain moral advantage over strangers who may represent offices and countries of much greater political power.

The corollary is no less significant. Foreigners (a generic category) do *not* have these customs and are thus morally weaker: "they are used to [having each of them] paying for each service (*ine sinithismeni na plironi tin gathe eksipiretisi*)." Germans, the old foe, are thought especially incapable of understanding the value of treating. When a tailor mended a German's torn pair of trousers but refused to take any payment, the embarrassed customer bought him a bottle of retsina—apparently thinking, said the tailor, that "since he doesn't want money I'll get him a bottle of wine." The desire to pay money for such a trivial service underscores, to the Rethemniot, the fragility of the tourist's presence. The tourist will not have time to develop real social relationships. His almost bureaucratic reaction—immediate repayment, in whatever form—cuts him off from two of the main features of Rethemniot social engagement: the creative manipulation of time, and the cultivation of a devil-may-care rhetoric toward material wealth. His well-intentioned gesture made it seem as though he was *too* conscious of his own greater economic ease and at the same time short-circuited the temporal play that is locally the means of creating active friendship.

Tourists, as transients, are unlikely to become regular customers. There is thus little interest (in both senses) in cultivating affective relationships with them. In my favorite coffeehouse, I would find myself retreating to the stuffy, smoke-ridden interior along with the local men when the tourists began to flood the outside tables in summer. The visual effect of this cultural segregation was stark: in the shadowy interior, huddles of laborers and pensioners, all men, gazed out at a vista of male and female tourists' bright and often skimpy clothing, their faces turned beatifically to the burning sun. The locals derided the proprietor's obsessive greed for more and more money and criticized his habit of charging the foreigners much higher prices. Such a coffeehouse owner may even tell locals not to pay while foreigners are present to observe the discrepancy; the local ethos of credit virtually guarantees him eventual payment. Showing great enthusiasm to tourists who come back a second time, he sometimes nevertheless forgets what he charged them the day before. In commercial relations that lack any social basis, the pose of affect soon wears thin.

Locals find it hard to get any service while tourists are around. "*Eksoteriko perivallon* (foreign/outside environment)," punned an irritated regular. Recognizing the exploitation of outsiders as an owner's moral right, however, they rarely fail to abandon the pleasanter outside space to the tourists. Tourists, for their part, usually hesitate to enter the interior, perhaps because—a visiting expatriate suggested—they find the raucous backgammon players and gamblers intimidating. When a group of tourists who have braved the interior get up to leave, the gamblers at the next table may immediately spread out around their own table with every suggestion of sudden relaxation.

The regular customers at my usual coffeehouse claimed to detect only political or commercial motives behind the owner's many effusive claims of friendship for me: "for us Greeks he has no smile." (Of course I often became a pawn in these social tussles. One day, for example, a customer warned me that our genial host was calling me a spy; the very next day the kafetzis himself asserted that some [other] people had suspected me of being one!) The enlargement of the Rethemniots' daily cultural exposure has not led to greater intimacy either with the visitors or among the local population. Educated Rethemniots bewail the alienation that they attribute to the more formal, bureaucratic ways of doing business which modern circumstances dictate.

What were once gestures of friendship have become stylized as local commodities. One of our most hospitable friends in town once remarked that tourism had destroyed local patterns of interaction. Because it is an easy and fast source of money, he suggested, merchants do not spend time and money treating regular customers as they used to. The few tourist operators who treated customers to a drink, he went on, were thereby simply playing on the visitors' presumed filotimo (here, sense of obligation)—a sentiment that they would not now have to reciprocate![5] It is not clear that such actions represent a radical change; perhaps the observation is simply an instance of structural nostalgia. The use of kerasma as an idiom of ingratiation is certainly not new. It has apparently long been customary, for example, for a customer to treat a politician visiting the coffeehouse in the course of a campaign, both as a way of reminding the candidate of favors expected and, at the same time, of demonstrating his own important connections to the coffeehouse audience.

The generous rhetoric of hospitality and kerasma, then, may disguise ulterior motives. Anthropologists, however, have little to gain from speculating about these.[6] But they can perhaps more usefully tap the attributions and recriminations that local people bring to bear on each other's acts of incorporation and exclusion. Like the mutual recriminations of bureaucrats and citizens to which so much of this study is devoted, these attributions have material consequences. Fear is a commonly cited motive: fear of what others will say, fear of betrayal to hostile neighbors or to the authorities, fear of economic and social loss. Sometimes people are willing to take all these social risks. One couple who befriended two foreigners and often invited them to share meals found that their neighbors "made fun [of them] a lot (*koroidhevan poli*)." But then the foreigners reciprocated by treating them to a three-day Easter feast. It was this unexpected social vindication, rather than its material delights, that apparently made it all worthwhile.

Even as the forms and intensity of kerasma change, people still try through it to recast all their bureaucratic and commercial relationships in intimate, personal terms. But it is becoming increasingly difficult to maintain such social fictions. Tourists do not easily fit the role of guests because they rarely know how to manage the rhetorical forms of hospitality; their hosts, conversely, justify their more obviously exploitative use of such relationships by pointing to the visitors' boorishness. What begins as an amiable englobing of the tourist in local "custom"—such as the sharing of traditional Easter foods—rapidly proceeds to an *expectation* that the visitor will feel obliged to return. Sometimes this does indeed happen, and I was often shown photographs of Rethemniots affectionately embraced by their tourist friends and "regulars." Some go so far as to insist that a high proportion of the town's attraction lies in its hospitality, contributing to an increasing proportion of return visitors. Others, however, have reluctantly understood that most foreigners are not interested in creating serious social relationships. Indeed, these thoughtful local observers object to the commercialization of social relations—"tradition"—that has moved, in a short time, from hospitable spontaneity to "servility" (*dhouloprepia*). What is worse from their point of view, this servility is based on commercial calculation. Unlike the older men's coffeehouses, many of the new cafés do not serve Greek coffee because it is too complicated and time consuming.[7] The few establishments that try to cater to both kinds of custom are brusque indeed to any locals brave enough to request Greek coffee when there are Nescafé-drinking tourists to serve at the same time. Only when a local reporter investigated the problem did several proprietors declare their principled devotion to the national drink. As one of them told the reporter (Yiparaki 1987), "We are Greeks, and woe betide us if we did not serve Greek coffee!"[8] Yet refusals are in fact the norm during the tourist season, and the absence of any official complaint is not so much proof of their rarity as an indication of the Rethemniots' reluctance to invoke official sanctions of any sort. The lure of profit all too easily opens "traditional hospitality" to an alienating rationality.

THE NEIGHBORHOOD

The Old Town is divided into two major segments, each of which is symbolically represented by its own *Epitafios* (bier of Christ) in the great Good Friday procession to the Church of the Four Martyrs on the border between the old and new parts of town (plate 14). These segments cluster around two churches of the Mother of God, the Cathedral and the so-called Little Panaghia. These churches also provide the foci for the equally impressive religious processions on Easter Sunday (plate 15). Smaller subdivisions of the Old Town, while without any legal significance (see de Certeau 1984:106), organize the memories of an intimately shared past for the inhabitants.

If the coffeehouses provide a focus for male sociability much as they do in the villages, the narrow, shaded side streets of the Old Town provide an equally sociable setting for the women. Households typically consist of a married couple, their unmarried children, and occasionally an aged and widowed parent or other dependent kin. The houses are too small for larger concentrations of people.[9] Women exercise a good deal of financial control over day-to-day expenditure, although they will check with their husbands before purchasing expensive appliances. Their skill at fielding the importunities of itinerant vendors provides entertainment and material for mutual evaluation among the women of each small neighborhood. Although men spend a greater amount of time at home than is customary in the villages, house and neighborhood are clearly the primary areas of female authority.

Many men owe their houses to their wives' families, having received

14. On Good Friday, each quarter carries its own Epitafios—the bier of Christ—to the Church of the Four Martyrs. (1987)

15. An Easter Sunday procession moves along the street near the cathedral.
(1987)

them as part of their dowries. Expansion from this initial point of family
settlement is also often directed by concern for, and by, the female members of the family. House contracts often show house owners acquiring
properties in their own street of residence, and dowry houses are commonly additions, vertical or horizontal, to the parental home. The neighborhood defines a woman's social life; straying beyond it occasions suspicion. In Lilika Nakou's time, one young woman who simply went for a
walk out of sight of her street was sent away, never to return. The hostile
incomprehension that Nakou reports was probably the consequence of
her own tactlessness, presumably unintentional, in flaunting the freedom
that the local women did not possess, a freedom from both the constraints
and the companionship of this spatial solidarity.

The *vengera*—the evening gathering on the sidewalk or the yard outside a home—is largely, though not exclusively, female. In the summer
twilight, clusters of women sit talking earnestly, sometimes with two or
three men perched on the periphery while children race up and down with
excited screams and, from the boys, occasional bursts of anger that sound
like adult coffeehouse squabbles played at high speed and pitch. During
the daytime, women often sit with their backs to the open but narrow
streets, their feet resting on the lintel as they knit or crochet or peel vegetables. This stance also enables them to observe without being too closely

watched themselves. Everything counts as information: rich, meaty smells announce the quality of the other housewives' food; passersby, the arrival of visitors and the political alliances of the neighborhood. By the evening, the vengera gives form and currency to these observations.

The introversion of the neighborhood women's lives gives them a pre-occupation with sexual conduct that recent contact with foreign ways—many of them have taken cleaning jobs in the New Town hotels—has not entirely dispelled. Formerly, contact between the sexes was severely re-stricted, and marriages were arranged. This practice, known as *proksenio* (literally, "[acting] for an outsider"), brought young couples from differ-ent villages into town and their first homes. Townspeople are thought to be good matchmakers because of their access to resources; one man, who was entertaining two families from different villages at his home for this very purpose, insisted that wealth was not an issue. Rather, the bride's family sought assurances that the groom had good and regular work, and that he was not a drunkard or habitual gambler; the concern, as we shall see in chapter 5, arises from a wife's relative helplessness when her hus-band wastes the entire family's resources. Marriage brokers try to work within social and professional classes. One elderly man told me, in all seriousness, that he had encountered an Athenian woman schoolteacher and suggested to her that he should fix her up with a local doctor. She protested that she did not want to get married but agreed "because of your good words" to discuss it with him again. Clearly, she did not resent his suggestion, although she may have been amused by it; he felt he was doing God's work, as a woman "is the weak partner" and "should not remain [unmarried] (*na min 'pomini*)." Besides, a doctor, he said firmly, "is superior, he is, to the teacher." But he has many more candidates if this one should fail to please. Now an old man, he had met his own wife through proksenio. A neighbor woman went to his future mother-in-law and said, "I have taken a liking to your daughter and want to make a niece of her. I have a nephew, and I want to put him in order and make a human being of him." The girl's mother said that she would discuss it with her husband and their kin, which they did; and soon the engagement was announced.

Matchmaking gives strategically skilled actors creative opportunities. Of two brothers, the younger had a lasting health problem that required constant injections. When the older brother fell sick briefly, and was treated at home by a hospital nurse, he proposed to her that she marry the younger man, whom she had already treated. In this way, the younger brother would secure, free of charge, the relatively small amount of con-tinuing medical care he needed, while the nurse's salary from the hospital would also provide financial support. It would also free the older brother to continue his search for a groom for their sister, who should have been married first (according to the generally accepted norm) and who would soon be beyond marriageable age. The nurse, also not in the first flush of youth, lacked a property settlement of her own. Since the groom had built himself a house, however, doubtless as security against a future in which his illness might prove an insurmountable barrier to marriage with its usual expectations of uxorilocal residence, the proposal held out attractions to both sides. Negotiations were swift and decisive. In the groom's words, "In three days I was engaged, and in three [more] days I got married!"

Clearly, the arranged marriage had, and to some extent still has, a place in Rethemniot life. An old man who needs to "pass his time" may not be particularly effective at matchmaking, but neighborhood women engage in it continually. Today, at least, young people do not enter the relationship without any knowledge of each other, although such interest as they may express openly is often impersonal and economic. Increased emigration to Athens and elsewhere since the early 1960s, moreover, has created a new demand for marriage brokers. A lawyer of Rethemniot origin came back to the Old Town and was visiting his sister when a neighbor woman dropped by. When he happened to mention that he would like to marry off his son, a bank clerk, the neighbor immediately came up with a young woman on the outskirts of town who, she thought, would be just right, particularly as she owned a plot of land. They went over together to visit, and in short order—not without the question, "What do you have to give her?"—the deal was done. The groom owned a plot of land in Athens, and this enabled the bride, in her turn, to achieve the desired goal of big city life with some assurance of security. Although in urban Greece it is now usual for the bride to provide the house, such exceptions are not uncommon. In Rethemnos, some couples of village origin achieve an independent home through the provision by *both* families of funds for the purchase of a house, which saves them from the draining expense of rental payments and thus offers an attractive prospect of early financial independence. The form of such arrangements depends, again, as much on the negotiating skills of the marriage brokers as on the economic circumstances of the two families.

Marriage brokerage, then, is a highly deliberate form of negotiation. This may appear to belie the claim, often heard, that marriage is a matter of luck. But the process of brokerage is itself described as a "question of luck" (*zitima tišis*). In practice, this means that the bride and groom have very little to do with the initial selection of partners. They may have no previous knowledge of each other at all. Gossip, especially if the young people are from a small village, may make it quite unpleasant to marry within the home community, and outside brokerage increases the element of "luck." Describing the brokerage process in terms of luck and personal circumstances is a precaution that reduces the accountability of all concerned. If an offer is refused, the prospective groom may claim afterward that he had not seriously entertained plans to marry, an excuse that also absolves the brokers of blame for the breakdown. The brokers, for their part, can always justify their failure by claiming that they were misinformed about the character of the candidates. Rethemniots often anticipate the possibility of failure in this way (see also Hirschon 1989:111). They present their own contributions in the best possible light, while seeking the cause of breakdown either in a malign destiny or in the equally deficient personalities of other actors.

The actual outcome is today quite unpredictable. In earlier times, the poor had fewer choices, and their marriage options seem to have been more severely constrained. Emigration to the United States, for example, created a new marriage market. Octogenarian widowers, having achieved a comfortable standard of living in the States, could expect upon their return to Crete to find and marry young women sixty years their junior. The hapless brides' destitute fathers—especially if they had several more daughters—might actually be pleased to get them respectably married off so easily. A young woman's father would, in local parlance, accept such a deal "in order to save [sic] her." In times of great poverty, choices were few, and the solutions desperate. Today, however, the arrangement of marriages gives much greater rein to the wishes of the young people themselves, leaving the would-be marriage brokers searching ever harder for plausible explanations of failed negotiations and appearances of meddling. Fate, it seems, has turned its harsh attentions from the brides to the brokers.

BETRAYAL AND SUSPICION

This play of personality and fate has a truly practical significance. It is especially useful in dealing with the bureaucracy, where highly visible failure carries the further risk of embarrassment before one's ever-prying neighbors. Where the arbitrariness of luck or the bureaucracy does not suffice as an explanation for failure, the neighborhood itself provides a conventional object of blame. Behind the cheeriest neighborly greeting may lurk a vile betrayal to the authorities. How else is a household head to explain why his worldly competence did not suffice to get him a much-needed permit or to save him from the litigious wrath of the historic conservation office? He cannot admit to having bungled his business or to having been let down by his own kin, since these explanations would expose him to the ridicule he is at such pains to evade. The neighborhood, an unpredictable amalgam of the familiar and the unknown, ranks high in the etiology of disaster.

Rethemniots also find here a ready explanation for the apparent paradox that, while they accuse the authorities of indifference and inaction, they themselves seem to get into trouble with some frequency. Every interference by police or bureaucracy is laid at the door of *roufiania*—literally "pimping," and a contemptuous metaphor for the tale-telling that some Rethemniots insist is one of their least endearing features. (Others, under other circumstances, deny that it is at all characteristic.) People, maintain the carpers, dislike seeing a neighbor make good. We should not read such claims as clear evidence for some active principle of limited good whereby people consider the available resources to be finite and unexpandable.[10] It is entirely possible that the actual incidence of betrayal to the authorities is much lower than the frequency of such accusations might imply—but the impression of frequency is an important factor in maintaining their force, as, perhaps, is past experience (especially the persecution of the political Left that followed the Civil War) of police attempts to recruit informers.

These accusations are important, then, not because they are necessarily true, but because, by invoking conventional wisdom, they lubricate otherwise difficult social situations. Commonly encountered in the poetics of Rethemniot social interaction, they are subject to some degree of variation. Their success, however, lies in conjuring up a highly formulaic type of grievance that others, who may need similar devices soon thereafter, are reluctant to undermine.[11] Like the attribution of police inaction to vested political interests, they are ploys to justify failure by means of a conventional formula. Limited good is a reality for Rethemniots, not because people necessarily believe in it or act as though they did, but because repeated usage has stylized it as a form of common sense. Most defenses of personal and family integrity follow just this tactic of explaining one's own setbacks by means of a generic negative truth about society at large.

A dreadfully damp, leaking, collapsing house whose owner would like to demolish and replace it lies within full view of the historic conservation office. On either side stand the properties of close kin. Every time the owner tries to effect some (illegal) repairs, someone from the conservation office shows up. Despite the obvious explanation—they could hardly have failed to see him at work—he still prefers to attribute this frequent persecution by the authorities to the roufiania of neighbors, their identity unspecified but their collective character jealous by definition. The explanation gains strength from his equally strong conviction that no bureaucratic agency will show initiative in pursuing violators except when a sneaking neighbor forces its hand.

Another man moved from his home village to Rethemnos, where he acquired a house in the Old Town. He began making a series of alterations to the fabric of the building, as a result of which he wound up in court six times. He was sure that his neighbors resented him as a new-comer, and he insisted that it was a "put-up (*karfoti*, literally, 'nailed')" job.

Like witchcraft or evil eye accusations, such charges enable people to define the range of their enemies without specifying them by name and therefore without serious risk of a destructive direct confrontation. This is important in the social circle of Rethemnos, where, moreover, law en-forcement officers—many of whom have concluded long careers with the purchase of homes in the town—have a deep and complex personal in-vestment in the community. On the one hand, this makes them reluctant to act; but, when they need sources of information, they have no trouble finding them. "Each [of us] is jealous of the next [person]," say some Rethemniots, and no further explanation is necessary. "Pimping" can be attributed to a generic meanness (*kačia*) on the assumption that others cannot bear to witness one's own success. In other words, the image of limited good is not the principle by which Rethemniots actually operate; it is, rather, the form taken by the vicious stupidity they attribute to each other.

Trust is certainly fragile. While, for example, everyone recognizes the ubiquity of tax evasion, getting expert advice on how to do it entails the risk of treachery from one's mentors. Similarly, roufiania is the only rea-son people are prepared to contemplate for the arrest of gamblers. With-out the roufiani, so the argument runs, the state authorities—widely as-sumed to be venal—would do nothing: "If the other guy doesn't give them the means, they don't budge!" This conventional view furnishes a double explanation of communal problems: people can cast the blame for noise pollution, for example, on police unwillingness to prosecute with-out being prompted,[12] while excusing their own reluctance to report of-fenders on the grounds that they disapprove of roufiania and fear its con-sequences. Charges of roufiania can rarely be substantiated even when they are directed at specific individuals, but they do mark lines of more or less covert hostility. A coffeehouse proprietor who regularly skimmed profits from the gambling in his establishment was immune to police ha-rassment because he reported other offenses to the authorities—so claimed a disaffected customer whom the proprietor, in turn, similarly accused of being a police informer. If this description seems bewildering at times, it does in that respect accurately convey something of what it is like to participate in everyday conversation.

No one ever admits to being an informer. If everyone were truly reluc-tant to "pimp," however, it would be hard to blame one's clashes with the law on the virtual certainty that everyone *else* was doing so. Making excuses is more a matter of convention than of factual evidence (Austin

1971). Like blaming fate or the equally intransigent bureaucracy (see Herzfeld 1982a), attributions of roufiania operate by hindsight. They are excuses for failures already experienced. Far from expressing resignation to the whims of fate, they are determined strategies to buy time and social acceptance while one sets about repairing the damage as determinedly as possible.

The key to the roufiania metaphor is the selling of one's own flesh and blood to outsiders. As in the other echoes of the theme of prostitution that we have already heard, it expresses a concern with maintaining boundaries. The sale of sexuality breaches fundamental ideas about the integrity of the home and its female embodiments. It suggests that neighbors who fail to live up to their moral obligations are outsiders within. At its broadest, roufiania means collaboration with enemy invaders such as the Nazis, or with the post–Civil War state authorities. A moderate socialist refugee from Asia Minor, musing on the adulation that King Constantine I of Greece had enjoyed before his irredentism and pro-German sympathies led him into conflict with the liberal leader Venizelos (a Cretan) and ultimately into the Asia Minor disaster of 1922, suddenly burst out, "You pimp, shit upon your bones!" The Germanophile king, himself of German ancestry, had betrayed the Greeks' hopes and ambitions by urging them into a war they could not expect to win—a historic prototype for the rightist adventurism that, at the local level, encouraged informers and collaborators at every turn.

As rhetoric, the strategic effectiveness of the "pimping" charge is thus historically grounded. It lies in bitter personal as well as national experience of betrayal, and of the fragility of trust in the face of political force. During the last years of Turkish rule on Crete, Christians from the notoriously ferocious highland village of Asighonia (on which, see Machin 1983) wanted a co-villager who lived in town to direct them to the Turkish houses. He refused, knowing that he would automatically have been blamed for the massacre that must surely have ensued (see Nenedakis 1979:[xi]). Since he told them that if they wanted to kill Turkish women and children, they should "go to Smyrna" (that is, join the war in Asia Minor), it seems that he was less against the massacre as such than against collaborating with collective power—even that of his own side—against old neighbors. It is worth noting that this story shows pride in the *avoidance* of the very type of antisocial action which more negative voices claim as typical of the town.

Memories of roufiania have certainly scarred the lives of present-day inhabitants. Leftists, in particular, maintain that they must now ruefully share the social spaces of coffee shop and marketplace with those whose "pimping" had led to their arrest and torture in crueler times. Even though the searing horrors of the Civil War have receded, the pettier irritations of local bureaucracy still keep the fear of roufiania in running order.

The charge of betrayal, then, is ubiquitous. The physical environment provides a poignant metaphor, for, I was told, the very walls are full of humidity, a *roufiana* ("madam") who hands one over to the tender mercies of arthritis and so colludes with nature as well as with the authorities to make life a physical torment the whole year round. Rethemnos, its more embittered citizens accuse each other, is the "mother of roufiania,"[13] and all of Crete is riddled with it. If roufiania allows people to explain away their personal mishaps, however, structural nostalgia comes to the rescue of the Cretans' collective identity. The Cretans *no longer* maintain their customary sense of honor, complained an elderly refugee and ardent communist; now they have all become roufiani. And he handed me a copy of *Rizospastis* (Radical), the official newspaper of the Communist Party of Greece (KKE), telling me—as a test, perhaps, of my reactions[14]—not to tell any policemen that he had given it to me.

The authorities are not immune to similar fears of their own. Police inaction may result from a concern that they may be accused of mishandling suspects, a charge against which they have less protection in today's democratic polity than under military regimes of the past. They must also be responsive to shifts in the political messages emanating from Athens. Sometimes, when tourists make trouble, the police are afraid to initiate actions that could involve their superiors in some international incident and result in their own sudden, punitive transfer. Police officers do not serve in their home prefectures, but they may stay in one place long enough to establish families or for their spouses to have found good employment. An ex-policeman explained, "It's a very big matter . . . to tell an employee today, or a policeman, or let's say anyone else, you know, 'Pick up your things and go to Thrace, for example, or go to the Dodecanese!' " However unrealistic such fears may perhaps now be, the fact that long-serving officials can entertain them can do little to inspire civilian confidence.

Whether the authorities are capricious in practice is perhaps less clear, and less significant, than that people expect them to be so. Local bureaucrats and law officers, no less than their clients, take measures to shift responsibility for their social failures onto other shoulders. Just after the 1989 parliamentary elections had toppled the PASOK government in Athens, rumors began to circulate that the new, more predictably pro-Western authorities had specifically urged the police to be tolerant of minor offenses (such as excessive noise) by tourist shop owners. Whatever the truth behind such allegations, their force lies in the way they fit the canonical idiom of self-justification by appealing to the plausible bogey of fickle superiors. Ostracism or exile? This may be the nastiest dilemma a policeman faces.

From the citizens' perspective, any dealings with the forces of law and order constitute roufiania. The habit of identifying the authorities with a repressive right-wing tyranny dies hard. The bitter memories of roufiania and torture leave little room for sympathy with hard-pressed officials trying to do their duty. Of late, however, even this pattern has begun to fade. One speaker even justified roufiania, not when it was done for party-political reasons, but in order to catch a criminal. Even this individual, however, prefers to use mediation to deal with local thieves, and his continuing use of the uncomplimentary metaphor of "pimping" suggests that reporting to the police is still an act of last resort. The fear of state tyranny has not evaporated altogether, and it continues to sustain an ideal of communal solidarity before the intrusive mechanisms of the state.

The Other Side of the Coin: Solidarity before the Law

Others' roufiania works as an excuse for one's own trouble with the authorities because it fits a popular etiology of power. Aside from the fact that they generally follow rather than precede embarrassments with the law and ruptures between former friends, there is another reason why allegations of roufiania are unlikely always to be true. This is the frequency of reports in which the victims of theft, assault, or fraud protect the perpetrators from the authorities. Solidarity before the state remains a strong moral imperative.

A coffeehouse proprietor whose regular customers included a number of retired policemen and others of allegedly less than democratic principles was himself widely thought to be a police informer. Yet this same man, when a neighbor went berserk one day and smashed up the contents of the coffeehouse, later untruthfully told the police that the offender had already compensated him for the damage and should therefore not be prosecuted. While this story would not necessarily absolve the coffeeshop proprietor from the suspicion of having collaborated with the authorities in other matters, it does illustrate the horror with which charges of roufiania are viewed even as they are bandied about. This, too, is why a man who had lost a valuable gold cross refused to report its loss to the police *in case* someone had stolen it. No piece of gold is worth the loss of so much social capital—and there would be no guarantee of recovering the lost object either.

In another incident, three witnesses saw a woman shoplift three gold chains. They informed the jeweler, who, instead of reporting the theft to the authorities, asked a cousin of the miscreant to mediate. She denied everything and sent her husband to shout at the jeweler that the latter was "exposing" his wife (that is, to disgrace). The jeweler decided not to press charges. Although he had witnesses, he reasoned that the social pressure to back down would be enormous and might threaten his business. Above all, others would keep on trying to mediate right through to the bitter end, arguing (the jeweler suspected) that the shoplifter had been forced to commit the theft against her will, presumably by her husband, and producing various other mitigating scenarios as well.

Another example shows that the authorities may be complicit in favoring mediation over the law. A thief brought a watch back to the shop from which he had stolen it, hoping to get it repaired. The watchmakers, two brothers, recognized it as one of their own. They had reported the theft to the police—appropriately enough at that point, as there had been no *specific person* to accuse of the crime.[15] The thief refused to confess. Losing patience at last, the brothers went ahead and reported him to the police. Under questioning, and faced with the incontrovertible evidence of the match between the watchmakers' records and the police report on the theft, he finally owned up. The police made the thief return the watch but advised the watchmakers not to take the case to court. They argued that the evidence was so clear that it would be preferable to avoid the agony of a court case. Their apparently paradoxical argument makes better sense when we note that the lower courts' interest is less in the punishment of crime than in ending potentially disruptive disputes—a key feature in the regulation of the historic conservation regime, as we shall see.

The watchmakers were actually rather relieved at being presented with such a socially reasonable argument. One of the brothers had been best man at the thief's sister's wedding. Why would he steal from someone so closely connected to himself? To Rethemniots, this is not strange at all. Local rhetoric, deprecating the idea of involving the police, has it that "if he does such a thing, he would seem to be someone from my circle." As an insider, the thief was morally entitled to help himself; only an intimate would take my goods without asking me (or paying), and the only question that remains is why he did so in such a secretive way. This socially convenient syllogism, a deliberate fiction in which the victim plays hurt only at the thief's apparent assumption that he might not have voluntarily given the stolen object to so close a person, serves the principals' wish to restore harmony. It also dovetails happily with the authorities' preference for staying out of such minor disputes. It is less likely to have "consequences" (*proektasis*), as an ex-policeman explained, than would legal proceedings. There is communal pressure on the offender to desist from criminal activity, and on the victim to refrain from further action. A victim who insists on going to the authorities not only risks charges of roufianiá but may face violent revenge at the offender's hands as well. In local terms, betrayal to the authorities justifies vengeance; mere petty theft does not.

Thus, the local preference for mediation meshes neatly with official practicality. The police would rather avoid the risk of a contagious feud. They are also bureaucrats and, as such, try to keep their involvement minimal. As we shall see when we come to examine the role of courts in enforcing the historic conservation laws, judges are anxious to put as much distance as possible between volatile townspeople and themselves. On Crete, where men may take it upon themselves to threaten prosecutors and judges with physical violence, there is an added incentive to push all official responsibility as far away as possible.

Mediation and the hatred of roufiania are both expressions of communal solidarity in relation to the state. Bureaucrats and police officers accept them as means of reducing the practical difficulties of law enforcement. Yet the frequency of mediation does not mean that roufiania is necessarily unconvincing as an explanation of events. A self-styled victim may affirm that he knows who is guilty of betrayal—this, customarily, with an angry little nod of certainty, chin jutting forward, lips pursed. That performance alone so fully conforms to a social norm that no further discussion is either necessary or desirable. For one does not name names. To accuse a particular neighbor suggests that one is oneself capable of roufiania. When a Rethemniot does make a public display of helping the authorities, it must always appear to be for the common good against an anonymous opponent, as when people join in the hue and cry for an as yet unidentified fugitive thief.

Even giving someone else's game away to a fellow citizen calls for circumspection. An elderly refugee reacted with deep outrage when one after another of his coffeehouse companions solemnly informed him that they had converted to the religion of the *Iekhovadhes* (Jehovah's Witnesses). His gullibility fanned their ingenuity, and soon he was receiving telephone calls in the coffeehouse from "the bishop" thanking him for his steadfast refusal to join the general apostasy. The pious old man was beside himself with grief and anger as his companions furnished more and more "evidence" of their perfidy. His neighbors soon heard about his torment. What, they wondered, had this simple old man done to deserve such treatment? Eventually, one of the more compassionate neighborhood women dropped an anonymous note through his door, telling him that the "apostasy" was all a hoax. The anonymity of the note suggests that, even in this relatively trivial context, the fear of roufiania accusations is not to be taken lightly.

COMPETITION

The jealousy that leads a neighbor to report one to the authorities for building a drainage cistern too close to his house and to add some libelous remarks about the product one is making on the premises smacks of a strong sense of competition. A brief examination of commercial relations, however, will show that there have been changes in the *expression* of competitive relations, and that these are a fair index of major changes in the relationships themselves. In particular, they point up some of the social consequences of the shift from an agro-town and guild economy to one penetrated by mass production and the tourist trade. These include the gradual breakdown of effective resistance to bureaucratic control, as more and more external interests breach the solidary walls of Rethemniot localism.

Commercial attitudes have changed enormously within living memory. Above all, competition has become much more open and aggressive. Many businesses—shoemakers (plate 16), butchers, oil merchants, tailors—were once clustered in tight enclaves. The butchers huddled around

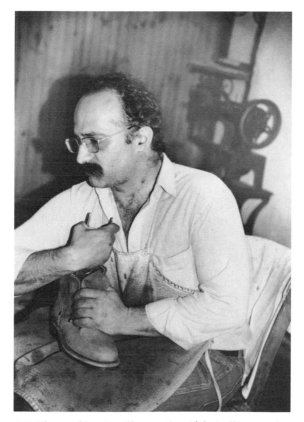

16. Shoemaking is still an active, if dwindling, craft. (1987)

the slaughterhouses on the edge of the Old Town where formerly shepherds would appear from the villages with single animals draped over their shoulders, looking for a quick sale. Where nearly forty tailors clustered together in a row, the present Arabatzoglou Street now sports a mixture of tourist shops, carpenters' workshops, restaurant-coffeehouses, and rooms for rent.[16]

Within the enclaves devoted to particular businesses and crafts, people avoided overt competition as socially disruptive. The craftsmen mostly knew each other well; many, indeed, were the former apprentices of their senior neighbors, who had often begun their own professional lives through exactly the same process of entrepreneurial fission. Because competition for custom was potentially intense, tradesmen sought diffuse ways of pursuing their advantages. There were some areas of moral solidarity into which competition might not enter at all. Even today, for example, a customer may openly prefer to buy his cigarettes from a more distant kiosk because he knows that the owner is poorer than the kiosk operator next to the coffeehouse he frequents.

The intrusion of a larger, bureaucratically regulated economy is responsible for most of the changes in the style of competition. Instead of disguising limited competition with the rhetoric of guild solidarity, tradespeople now watch the actions of bureaucrats with deep suspicion and are quick to complain that the latter are favoring their rivals. The management of economic relations has come under more public scrutiny, while the actions of tradespeople are no longer constrained by the intense neighborliness of the old professional districts. The butchers, for example, have become scrupulous about hygiene. This is less a consequence of greater medical awareness than it is of the bureaucratization of professional practices. All butchers must submit to veterinary inspection. Were the official veterinarians to prosecute one errant butcher more zealously than another, there would be a great outcry. In earlier times, customers came to butchers with whom they had personal ties, and few knew or cared enough to insist on clean butchering practices. Nowadays, open competition exacts strict hygiene from all, and butchers could not afford to tolerate favoritism on the veterinarians' part. As a result, they too have become "doctors." The abstract and at least implicitly measurable criterion of quality has replaced social ties as the primary determinant of customer loyalty. The state itself must now adopt the disinterested stance that formerly characterized the interactions of business rivals. This is the price of its penetration of the local economy, and it is the state's minor functionaries—usually locals themselves—who pay that price when merchants complain of unequal treatment.

The attitude of a tourist shop operator who has decided to sell off his stock is indicative of the contrast between the older, indirect mode of competition and the new brashness. He could easily follow the new fashion, familiar from the supermarkets that have sprung up in the past few years, putting up large signs with the old prices slashed through and with the new prices juxtaposed for contrast. He, however, prefers to put small new price tags on instead, thereby reducing the sense of direct competition with other shops that are still in business for the long term. He wants to be able to greet each colleague affably: "Why should he look at me with a jaundiced eye (*kako mati*, literally 'bad eye'), why should he see me as an enemy?" Since the "bad eye" symbolizes envy, this man—unlike some of his rivals and neighbors—still places high value on the maintenance of cordial relations with the latter.

The muting of competition also affected the evaluation of the quality of goods. As recently as the 1960s, dissatisfied customers did not complain. They either accepted the poor work or transferred their custom elsewhere. Craftsmen, faced with such defections, were expected not to inquire directly into the reasons. Such questions would have been an overt expression of competitiveness, while customers were similarly "embarrassed" to voice dissatisfaction lest in so doing they might threaten the decorum of public interaction. While some craftsmen were thought to be more skilled than others, they manifested their superiority in the range of products they made and sold rather than in the claims to the variety or quality of a specific item that modern advertising advances.

The shoemakers, who thirty years ago occupied perhaps half the shops in Souliou Street, had a particularly close guild organization, and decorum among potential competitors was strictly observed. Competition in the modern sense, with open vying for the attention of passersby, has become the bane of the tourists who walk along the same street today. Only two full-time shoemakers ply their craft there still; the remainder of the street has filled with tourist shops, and the contest can become fierce. Before 1970, by contrast, the competition was all carried out behind the scenes, in attempts to secure patronage through kinship ties and through the establishment of spiritual kinship with out-of-town customers, especially shepherds needing a regular supply of boots. Some merchants still try to forge bonds of mutual obligation: a butcher, for example, made a point of buying from the same shoemaker, in order to make sure of the latter's custom in turn. Watchmakers continue to ply their financially rather unrewarding skill in the hope of persuading their customers to buy gold jewelery from them as well (plate 17), just as in earlier years the jewelery business served as a front for illegal usury. Many grocers cling to customers' loyalty by extending credit—a high-risk investment, since there is no law that lets them prosecute defaulters, except those who fail to pay for alcohol. Some grocers do a small but useful line in portable gas-bottles, gambling on occasional scarcity; they can use their control of

17. A jeweler—surrounded by clocks, his wrist
resting on a newspaper—uses his weighing
equipment.

this occasionally quite scarce and essential commodity to remind customers that they would be ill-advised to stray. I tried to get a gas-bottle from
one of these grocers and was told, quite abruptly, that he was out of
stock. A friend who knew that this was untrue offered to help. He came
from a village near the home community of a second supplier, which
made them *kondokhoriani* (literally, "close-villagers"), and the supplier's
sister had also married into my friend's village. Claiming the bottle as his
own, my friend was easily able to persuade the second supplier to fill it.

Competition can thus be vindictive and monopolistic. Wealthier artisans, for example, would rent all the good workplaces in order to seal
them off from potential rivals, while one kafetzis—to his customers'
slightly scandalized amusement—bought up all the chairs and tables of
the neighboring establishment for the same reason. Nowadays, wealthy

newcomers offer the owners of desirable commercial properties huge financial inducements—four million drachmas in one instance—to sell out. Merchants wrap goods carefully so that rivals will not be tempted to challenge their customers to change allegiance. Even among close kin, competition today may be merciless. A merchant who co-owned a shop with his female first cousin (FBD) spread rumors about her persistent ill health in order to scare off the already reluctant and very wealthy family of her prospective husband, whose likely dominance over the continuing partnership he feared. When this devious ruse failed, he waited a few years and then opened an independent store of his own.

Overt, quarrelsome competition for custom is clearly the result of the recent penetration of local markets by much larger-scale forms of capitalism, with their relentless spiral of demands for more and more different kinds of mass-produced goods. Another important change has been the proliferation of shops serving the tourist industry. This, too, has greatly intensified the open bitterness of competition. A local shop owner told his teenage assistants to pretend to be orphans in order to gain customers' sympathy and, eventually, tips. This went on until a boy who had lived overseas and knew several languages the proprietor did not speak started telling the customers that the proprietor's mind had been turned by too much sex with his beautiful young wife! Most locals seem to have sympathized with the lad, and to have been properly scandalized by his employer's debasement of commercial mores.

Tourism has transformed the practices and organization of other kinds of business as well. Pastry shops and other suppliers of tourist establishments have multiplied, and the competition between them has put skilled workers, once grateful to find work at all, in a seller's market. This in turn fuels the bitterness of competition among entrepreneurs, since state price controls and the constant threat of competition from low supermarket prices restricts their ability to offer higher wages. The old trades, like those of tailor and barber, that catered to a local clientele, are now greatly depleted. A few new service trades have emerged, notably a laundromat that opened in June 1986; this last enterprise, useful to foreign visitors, depends on small hotels for regular business as it seems to attract only a very small amount of household custom.

Viewed against the decline in established local trades, the tourist economy is almost irresistibly seductive. One tailor has managed to survive by identifying a few regular customers among the foreign tourists, since his prices compete well with those of countries to the north. Shoemakers, on the other hand, are increasingly tempted to abandon their craft in favor of large-scale handbag production for the tourists. Souvlaki vendors, the first of whom introduced this trade to Rethemnos in 1964 (and who was locally thought quite eccentric at the time), milk the flow of tourists along

the main commercial thoroughfare. But it is the *fastfoodadhika* and souvenir shops that have proliferated more than any other. After peaking in
1981, many of the pioneers in this area are retiring from the fray to attend
to their rapidly appreciating New Town properties. Those who remain
committed to tourist enterprises must face an increasing level of competition and a growing number of non-Rethemniot competitors. The pie has
not grown appreciably bigger, but the number of slices has multiplied.

The practice of employing touts to pull in passing custom represents
another way in which the new economy has led to more direct competition. There is now a long gap between the time when one of the founders
of the first major hotel came in person to the bus stop to catch such custom as ours (1973), and the present difficulty that non–package tour visitors encounter in finding a hotel room at all. Where coffeehouse proprietors, half a century ago, lined up ingratiatingly with their trays, in the
silent hope of attracting custom, touts now prey on the avowed principle
that "the Scandinavians *want* you to ask them in." A coffeehouse proprietor bustles up to some bemused tourist couples with stentorian shouts of
"Siddown! Siddown!" and embarrasses them into sitting in his forecourt,
while his local customers quietly retreat to the overheated interior of the
establishment—in part to allow him to garner more custom at the specially inflated prices he charges tourists, in part to protect their privacy
and their illegal card games from amused but uncomprehending foreign
eyes.

On the edge of the very street where shoemakers once plied their trade,
raucous price wars—replete with screaming matches and threats of violence and litigation—have erupted between the owners of competing
tourist shops. Meanwhile, on the next corner, two restaurateurs accuse
each other of touting to steal customers already making their way to one
or the other restaurant. One of them called this *kamaki*, a term literally
meaning "fishhook" and more usually associated with sexual "fishing"
for foreign women (see Zinovieff 1991). Nothing more fully underscores
the depersonalizing of commercial relations than the rise of these preda-
tory patterns, especially in contrast with the *telalidhes*—criers who (at a
pre–World War II wage of fifteen to twenty drachmas per day) would go
about advertising the current stock of meat and other perishables that
their merchant employers wished to dispose of. The profession of telalis,
remembered today as a distinctive local tradition, became defunct in the
early 1970s—significantly, just when the tourist boom was about to begin
in earnest.

Old Town shopkeepers now see a noticeable rise in the proportion of
customers whom they do not know personally. Once-dependable reciprocities are steadily disintegrating under the combined pressures of the
larger market, an increasing residential drift to the New Town, and rap-

idly growing consumer awareness of the finer distinctions among pur-
chasable goods. Quality itself has become objectified: even older objects,
now collected and sold by Gypsies to antique shops in the towns, become
subject to qualititative judgments (and corresponding price assessments)
that had no meaning at the time the objects were originally made. Such
commoditization is a far cry from the usurer-jewelers who used to buy up
hoards of old coins from the Fortezza simply for the value of their gold
or silver content.

Another, complementary interpretation of the shift in the idiom and
level of competition illustrates what happens when people come to feel
less constrained by the pressure of social disapproval. Older merchants
were supposedly too proud to beg for custom, just as local politicians—
who cannot so easily throw off the bonds of kinship and neighborly obligation—similarly claim that they do not "beg" (parakalao)[17] for votes
because the embarrassment this might cause would make social interaction difficult as soon as elections were over. In the same way, residents
refuse to "beg" bureaucrats for favors, especially once it has become clear
that the bureaucrats have no intention of yielding; and merchants and
artisans do not "beg" dissatisfied customers to give them a second chance.
To do so merely invites rebuff and consequent social rupture. Such self-
abasement only enters the community with the weakening of face-to-face
relationships, when the fear of breaking off social links may lie concealed
behind a pose of dignified reserve. If the new merchants can afford to tout
their wares, this is largely because their social investments in the community are correspondingly weak, and because their interactions with
strangers pose no lasting threat to their self-esteem.

For all these changes, Old Rethemnos is still largely a town of small
shopkeepers. Some have purely service trades, notably the coffee shop
and restaurant proprietors. Many are heirs to a long local tradition: bakers, barbers, butchers, fishmongers, grocers, jeweler-watchmakers, pastry
cooks, tailors, shoemakers, even one man who makes donkey saddles for
villagers (plate 18). Metalworkers and soap cutters have been displaced
by mass production, and mattress making is a dying art. Occasional artisans, notably an onyx worker, have discovered that they can earn small
amounts with their handcrafted souvenir items (plate 19). A few vendors
ply their trade, some of them laborers making a little extra on special
occasions (plate 20). The visible signs of changing times are the numerous
fast-food bars, hotels, tourist restaurants, nightclubs, and souvenir shops.
The old-style groceries, with sacks of dried pulses flopping in dark doorways and crates of vegetables spilling onto the sidewalk, are yielding with
ill grace to small but comprehensive supermarkets. A lone couple makes
filo and kataifi pastry (plates 21, 22), and they have discovered that the
owners of supermarkets—which sell the more friable and less tasty com-

18. A saddle maker plies his craft, with a fairly complete saddle in the foreground, right. (1987)

19. Using simple machinery, an onyx worker prepares items for the tourist trade. (1987)

18

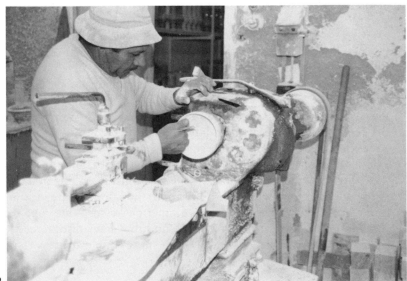

19

20. Selling Easter candles. (1987)

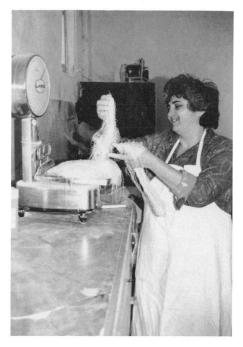

22. Weighing kataifi pastry for sale. (1987)

21. The preparation of filo pastry entails stretching a lump of dough over a large table before trimming it and drying it under sacking. It can then be folded and cut for sale. (1987)

mercial brands—buy the handmade product for their own domestic use. Of such differentiations of access to both the creation and the consumption of rarity are visible new class distinctions made (Thompson 1979; Bourdieu 1984).

APPRENTICES AND ASSISTANTS: THE END OF LABOR SCARCITY

Today's entrepreneurs must also compete for hired help; skilled workers, trained in state-run technical schools, sell their services to the most generous bidder. This was not always so. Until quite recently, apprentices clamored to be taken on at minimal wages, and they acquired their skills at work. There, they began to prepare for their own eventual professional independence. Their employers treated them roughly, but the long hours carried their own reward of practical experience. Their paltry wages were barely enough to secure them food (if they were not fed on the premises) and a bed.

Half a century ago, an advanced apprentice carpenter might earn a daily wage of 12 drachmas. Village lads just starting out would be glad to get the experience for as little as half that tiny wage per *week*. The competition for apprenticeships was fierce, and boys from more distant villages or from refugee families often lacked the personal connections to obtain comfortable positions for themselves. Only after military service might a senior apprentice graduate to 15 drachmas a day; a better sense of the scale of these wages is conveyed by the fact that a master craftsman could expect 130 drachmas per day in 1936.

Senior apprentices in skilled crafts such as carpentry or shoemaking were called *kalfadhes* or *kalfes*.[18] *Parayi* were apprentices of lesser age, rank, and experience, and the term, which means "foster-sons," implies a highly paternalistic relationship between employer and apprentice. All apprentices had a difficult life. The craftsmen for whom they worked, autocrats in manner as well as substance, could pick and choose: the town was full of young boys looking for work, many of them from families too poor to buy the books needed for the high-school entrance that their schoolwork had already earned them. The pay was so bad that apprentices often had to resort to subterfuge in order to find places to live: when one of them ran out of rent money, his mates would come during the night and help him decamp to new quarters. Nighttime illegalities, which today include the clandestine destruction of houses marked for historic preservation, are nothing new in Rethemnos.

The apprentices' hours were grueling, especially until the Metaxas dictatorship introduced a ten-hour working day. Before that, apprentices were expected to work for as much as twelve or thirteen hours in the summer, although a daily total of nine or ten was more usual in the winter months. Conditions were rough and the pay was minimal.[19] Once the apprentice had learned his trade, however, his increased income gave him more freedom of action. Prices were both low and stable, so that he could now survive by working only two days a week. His employer, however, would insist on a good return on the daily wage.[20] Even today, such part-time labor is far from uncommon. Occasional skilled jobbers from the villages augment the official work force, while some retired carpenters find work in the same way; one of these, for example, has an agreement whereby for 30 percent of his working hours he is employed at regular wages, while he pays the workshop owner for the hire of equipment to do his own piecework in the remaining time.

Apprenticeship was a way into town for the sons of ambitious village parents, and a way young men could learn a trade with which they would eventually become independent. Understandably, this aspect caused a good deal of friction between apprentices and masters. Two apprentice carpenters, after achieving their independence and working for seven years, bought a property for 150,000 drachmas, which now, twenty-two years later, is worth about 10 million drachmas and serves as their professional headquarters; while they meanwhile became wealthy enough to reside in the New Town, the Old Town provides them with a better work environment—for example, they can work in the open (plate 23)—and they like the low rents for storage in houses that are, in the general view, fit for little else.

The place of carpenters in Rethemniot society provides useful insight into the town's economic history. In the very early years of the Turkish occupation, they were so badly needed for the constant repairs required in the newly occupied Fortezza that, in 1659, nine Christian carpenters and one recent convert to Islam felt safe in petitioning for special treatment (Stavrinidis 1986, I:122):

> Your Excellency, Governor of Rethimni Ibrahim Pasha, and [you,] Most Wise in Learning, Holy Judge of Rethimni—may your wisdom be [ever] increased:

> It is brought to your attention that, since it is never easy to find carpenters for the repeated repairs to the fortress of Rethimno, and given that we always have need of carpenters, for this reason the above . . . were appointed permanent carpenters of the Fortress, on condition of their exemption from the capitation tax, and being exempted from the arbitrary forced labor that goes with it.

The carpenters never lacked for work. Turkish architectural styles added wooden window boxes (kioskia, plates 24, 25, 26), some with lattice-

23. Carpenters put the finishing touches to modern
furniture within the arches of a Venetian building.
(1987)

work shutters (*kafasia*) that functioned exactly as did the veils (*fere-
dzedhes*) that Muslim women wore: to permit observation from behind
them while defending against intrusive male stares. These were the marks
of the Turkish presence whose destruction occasioned such conflicting
memories. Turkish buildings also grafted winding internal staircases onto
the Venetian structures and inserted extra internal storeys for wood-
floored reception rooms (*ondadhes*). Where the Venetians had stripped
away the island's trees to make ships, the Turks turned a significant part
of what was left into the domestic architecture that has become, for locals
and tourists alike, the most visible reminder of their passing.

To this day, carpenters remain something of an elite among the traders
and craftspeople. They have become doubly successful since the mid-

25. The same house (cf. plate 24) after restoration and conversion of the downstairs area to use as a restaurant. (1989)

24. A Venetian house before restoration, with one complete and one partially damaged archway and a Turkish window box. Over the damaged arched doorway, a sign indicates that this is a wine store. (1970)

26. A characteristic conjuncture: electric light pole,
Venetian masonry, shattered Turkish window box.
(1986)

1970s: their services are much in demand in the new construction work
in the New Town (although, for reasons already discussed as well as because of the cheaper rent, they prefer to do as much work as possible in
the Old Town), and some of them get commissions for doors and windows from the historic conservation office. Today, they make Venetian-
style doors (plate 7) *and* "Turkish" window boxes (plate 27). The financial rewards for such work are relatively small in relation to the massive
construction efforts going forward in the New Town, however, and a carpenter sneered at the historic conservation office as the "bottom rung [of
the ladder]." This is one area in which specialized craftsmen are still in
great demand, although even they must compete for the services of young
assistants.

In the large establishments of old, each carpenter was given a specific

27. A modern replica of a Turkish window box
nears completion. (1989)

job. There is very little work available for these specialists today, and
those who are sage have diversified their interests. One such carpenter,
whose long sojourn in Europe as a migrant worker has equipped him with
practical fluency in several languages, opened a souvenir shop virtually as
soon as tourism began to develop in Rethemnos (1972), working on new
products during the winter months and selling them in the tourist season;
during the latter period, too, he also worked as a waiter in one of the big
hotels. The commonest pattern of seasonal labor combines winter farming with summer tourism. This man, however, uses his more specialized
skills as a precautionary strategy, recognizing that by diversifying he may
be able to escape the worst effects of overheating in the tourist economy.
He also varies his stock with items from the villages, from Athens, and
from abroad.

Another successful adaptation, although on a smaller scale economically, is that of the bakers (plates 21, 22, 28–31). Their presence, too, can be seen, heard, and smelled on many a street. The yeasty aroma of warm dough mingles with the more astringent vapor of sawdust-laden varnish to create an enduring sense-memory, especially in the quiet morning hours before the shadows retreat and motorcycle fumes and suntan oils overpower the smell of the past.

Bakeries maintain their hardworking, small-scale mode in the face of mass-produced goods because they supply distinctive local tastes in bread and *paksimadhia*, the hard rusks that Cretans like to dunk in tea or chamomile. Specialist bakeries continue to supply the enormous tourist hotels because their products are fresher and more manageable, if not necessarily cheaper. All Old Town bakeries (about thirteen in number) are family businesses. Rarely employing additional staff, they can lighten the summertime burden by "exchanging" work. Their products are few and vary only slightly. Innovation only comes about through occasional attempts to imitate Athens. One baker learned how to make *pita* dough (plate 29), for example, while doing his military service there. The summertime interchangeability of these shops, which in a more competitive and less per-

28. A pastry baker cuts his product. (1987)

29. Making pita bread. (1987)

30. A baker's oven, built into the old masonry. (1987)

31. A customer in village garb buys from a neighborhood baker. Over the window hang bags of tiny rusks (*paksimadhakia*). Note the curvature of the old masonry doorway into which the glass and wood front has been set, and the incised pattern on the plasterwork. (1987)

sonally based economy would be disastrous, is especially desirable for Rethemniot bakers who move their actual domiciles out of the Old Town.

This willingness to take turns in the summer is fortunate for another reason. Bakers, too, find it difficult to get assistants to work for them. Their hours are tough: bread must be started at 5:00 A.M. Specialty doughs impose additional burdens: the only two bakeries that produce pita for the souvlaki shops must then, once the ordinary bread is on sale, start the pita at 10:00 A.M. in order to be ready for the souvlaki sellers' early evening trade. Other special products absorb long days of back-breaking labor: the production of filo pastry sheets and the wirelike dessert pastry called kataifi can take a married couple, working together most of the time, from 7:00 A.M. until after midnight, with only the briefest lunchtime nap to lighten the day. The wages that a semiskilled worker can now command (about 2,500 drachmas a day for a baker's assistant in 1987, for example, as against the 6,000 drachmas that a husband-and-wife business may expect to make) are beyond the means of most Old Town small entrepreneurs. The survival of such ventures is moot at best. Without a regular supply of cheap labor, older entrepreneurs are thrown back on their own hard work. The very motive that so commonly drives them, their desire to educate their children for a better life, deprives them of a predictable succession. Their own children will not replace the supply of cheap apprentice labor on which their predecessors of only three decades ago had still been able to rely.

STUDENTS AND TOURISTS: THE THICKER END OF THE WEDGE?

Today, a largely new economic resource has become apparent: houses. Rethemniots have long rented rooms to apprentices and schoolchildren, an activity that carried high risks (apprentices were liable to disappear overnight when they could not pay) and low profits. With the advent of tourism and then also of the University of Crete, however, room renting has become decidedly more profitable.

It also brings increased social strain. Accepting tenants (*nikaridhes*) turns hospitality into a business. In the old days, most of the tenants were village boys, whose actions were at least fairly predictable and whose families understood the rules of reciprocity. Today, few tenants offer any such reassurance. Rental arrangements let intruders into the neighborhood without any guarantee of moral conformity or social reciprocity. People speculate and complain by turns about the outsiders.

Students and tourists pose almost as many economic risks as benefits. To a poor lodging house owner, the petty theft of sheets and blankets is a serious loss—as well as an abuse, given the still prevalent rhetoric of "hospitality." More seriously, local women resent the power of young female tourists, students, and professionals to disrupt their households. Dramatic acts of rejection—men's shoes left pointing toward a young woman's room, garbage thrown in from the street, a pair of women's knickers left hanging on the doorknob—are less the expression of moral repugnance than of the local women's fear of sirens who will lure their husbands away from earning the family bread (Herzfeld 1991); it is significant that they are apparently never directed at short-term tourists.

In house sale contracts, female buyers and sellers are predominantly listed as "housewives."[21] Lacking economic independence, these women have a good deal to fear. The androcentric public morality provides them with virtually the only acceptable means of expressing their alarm. Their apparent hostility to the strangers is very much of a piece with their attitude toward divorced women, whom they sometimes call "widows" (*khires*, apparently from the commoner *zondokhires*, "widows of the living"). The latter term has no male counterpart, as Cowan (1990:50) justly observes, and both forms evoke images of a sexual appetite once aroused and now frustrated (on this, see du Boulay 1974:123). Women do not necessarily thereby endorse the men's moral condemnation of open female sexuality. They know that the men will take advantage of it whenever it is offered. Concomitantly, however, they resent the degree to which their own limited options are bound up with their economic dependence. Nor are their husbands unambiguously benevolent toward educated women. Men, too, can call on the prevailing gender ideology to justify their baffled fury against the "girls" (see Cowan 1990:50 and n.3) who have been placed in charge of government offices—a source of frequent friction with the historic conservation office in particular; and here, at least, they can make common cause with their wives, using a shared moral rhetoric to express their displeasure. Professional women, many of them born elsewhere and often foreign-trained, can easily seem to rub salt into the existing wounds of class and gender relations.

Outsiders have also brought certain tangible benefits to the residents, and attitudes are not always condemnatory. Long before the arrival of the university, couples would take in more advanced high school students, not only as a source of income, but also a model for their own children. Nor are attitudes toward morality uniform. One elderly (male) supporter of tourism claimed that sexual freedom actually represented a moral improvement. Recalling that his own first girlfriend (*gommena*)[22] had been his first cousin, he suggested—with every indication of seriousness—that the strict moral surveillance of his youth had been the cause of the supposedly high rate of incest on Crete![23]

As the expression of a united front to the outside world, however, morality remains a focal convention. Drug addiction, sexual freedom, and above all the fear of AIDS have become major sources of anxiety for mothers with children of student age. And students, who are often rather vaguely dubbed "anarchists" by their detractors, do not necessarily enjoy living in the morally stifling confines of a "traditional neighborhood." One even admitted to his landlord that some of his friends were deliberately damaging the houses so that people would get upset, refuse to take students, and so goad the latter into demonstrating in the street. In this way, he reasoned, the state would be compelled to provide free dormitories.

This is a contest over resources, not only because they are limited, but because *both* sides have prospects of expanding them. Despite government subsidies,[24] some landlords, thinking that the tourists represent a better investment, abruptly evict student lodgers as soon as the tourist season starts. This evaluation, however, rests on the assumption that a lodging house can be treated like an olive grove—that it requires only intermittent attention. The men, moreover, happily leave the details to their wives. A young French couple rented a room for the night and then discovered, as so many do, that it was too hot and windowless. Their landlady, having first taken their passports for registration purposes and locked them away, meanwhile disappeared to her home village. The visitors were furious. Attempts to telephone the errant landlady at her village failed, and eventually a message—apparently effective—was left threatening that the tourist police would break in if she did not show up. She simply did not think of herself as living solely in Rethemnos; she had bought the house more than twenty years earlier as an investment for her children's future and treated her new role as that of caretaker rather than hotelier.

Tourism is thus a mixed blessing, and even its most direct beneficiaries harbor their own special resentments. A motorcycle rental agent sourly remarked that, while the tourists come to enjoy the sea and sand, "we are slaves on Saturdays [and] Sundays." Those with boardinghouses often empty even the smallest room of all personal possessions so that they can rent it, spending the summer months in warm but uncomfortable surroundings on the roof. And although such thrifty behavior may eventually earn one a modern apartment in the New Town, those who have moved there complain that they are isolated and depressed in their new surroundings.

The entrepreneurs, moreover, are divided among themselves. Most noticeable is the serious rivalry between the large hotels (mostly situated in the New Town) and the small, usually family-run boardinghouses. The latter accuse the hoteliers of trying to exclude them from competition until they need an "overflow" mechanism. But the boardinghouse owners are further divided, between those who remained loyal to an early attempt to create a professional association with its own centralized office and those who splintered off to form a separate group. A similar split developed between the original Tourist Shopkeepers' Union and a rebel group of localists. The Union's leadership largely consisted of non-Rethemniot entrepreneurs (*ksenoba[n]des*, "people from other parts"), who had bought up the expensive shorefront shop properties and who only operated in the tourist season, returning to their hometowns in winter; they tried to have legislation enacted to curtail the winter hours of the local shopkeepers, who promptly seceded. These various levels of dispute, which also had class and party political dimensions, follow a pattern of segmentary fission around degrees of outsiderhood ranging from tourists to New Town and out-of-town competitors.

THE POLITICAL ARENA: MUNICIPAL ELECTIONS

As one might expect, these tensions take their most overtly political form during elections. The municipal elections of 1986 played extensively on problems of identity. They concerned all Rethemniots, not just the residents of the Old Town, and the shift of economic power to the New Town is clearly reflected in the fact that the politicians' suggestions for addressing Old Town problems—notably the historic conservation issue—were long on sentiment but noticeably short on practical ideas.

In these elections, contested by mayoral candidates with slates of candidates for all the seats on the town council,[25] the two major parties—the socialists (PASOK) and the conservatives (New Democracy)—fielded full slates. A third slate, led by an independent, was supported by a coalition of the Left, including the two major communist parties. Officially, these slates did not represent the national parties of whose loyal supporters they were composed. One member of the rightist team was particularly firm on this point, arguing that even the rightists' candidate for mayor was standing on the strength of his personal abilities rather than of his party affiliations. Since the rightist leader had been appointed mayor by the military dictatorship, an ineradicable part of his past of which the other mayoral candidates made as much use as they could, the rightist slate as a whole had a clear interest in emphasizing its purely local concerns. Nonetheless, the slogans and vociferous electioneering style of all candidates except the third-party leader left identification unambiguous.

The third-party candidate, Babis Pramateftakis (see plate 9), was actually hurt quite badly by his strong association with representatives of the communist parties. Some Rethemniots who admired him personally, and who might have voted for him had he stood as a socialist, adamantly would not vote for his slate. Despite the legalization of the communist parties in 1974, the Left remained a bogey for those who still nurtured bad Civil War memories; moreover, few believed that a successful third-party candidate, if elected, would manage to remain independent of the strongly centralized communist party organizations. Voters even refused to support those of their own kin who stood in the communist-supported slate.[26] Against this, and perhaps as a sign of the way in which social ties undercut party politics, one ultrarightist activist decided to vote for Pramateftakis because the leftist leader was the voter's uncle by marriage (WFB)—a more telling link than the common village origin he shared with the incumbent mayor, the socialist Khristos Skouloudis, and suggesting that affinal connections play a much greater role in town than they do in the villages.

Much of the preelection rhetoric focused on the mayoral candidates' respective claims to community membership. The *others* were always the outsiders. Thus, Pramateftakis was, for his supporters, *yennima ke threma* ("born and bred") in the Old Town and a man of letters as well—a potent combination:

> As a shoeless kid he went around these little alleys and played like all the small children we were in that era. So: he has the education, he has the ability, and above all he has the humanity (*anthropia*).

His detractors turned this on its head: in their view, he had spent too long in foreign places acquiring his erudition both as a musical composer and as an engineer.

Dimitris Arkhondakis, chosen by the rightists to lead their slate, was a local man, a high school teacher and philologist much admired for his learning in the "town of letters." Moreover, even his political enemies conceded his willingness to work well with those who differed with him in political matters—a real asset in his attempt to background his political affiliations. His main problem lay in his earlier mayoralty under the junta. Khristos Skouloudis, the socialist incumbent, had equipped Rethemnos with many fine new public works. He, however, came from a village to grow up in the New Town, so that he had never experienced the rigors of local life in the raw:

> Skouloudis . . . hasn't slept a single night in the Old Town to see what "Old Town" means, to see in the morning when he gets up how the sheet is raw (*nopo*) from damp.

Skouloudis, a professional chemist whose brothers were major building contractors, was suspected of favoring the engineering companies (including his family's enterprise) that operated in the New Town, thereby attracting tourism away from the Old Town and doing it considerable damage in the process. In an interview,[27] he insisted that this was mere mudslinging on Arkhondakis's part. The accusation of favoritism toward kin and professional colleagues is so stereotypical, however, that no amount of denial, however fervent and however well documented, could ever deflect it. Rethemniots assume that *all* politicians and civil servants "steal." Many of the Old Town voters are already New Town residents, and this, pertinently, is a development that Skouloudis professed to deplore since the transformation of the Old Town into a huge tourist dormitory could only lead to a loss of local "color" and further deterioration in the architectural fabric. Whether active commercial interest in the New Town means indifference to the fate of the Old depends on the voter's current circumstances.

The question of loyalty to place, so insistent a campaign theme, revolves around employment. Thus, it informs much of the concern over the siting and eventual size of the University of Crete, the fate of the much-mismanaged harbor, and, most recently, the demand for a Rethemnos airport. The provision of a new cemetery was also a matter of concern. The water supply remained problematical—an issue since at least the Venetian period, when successive sieges made sources beyond the walls a dangerous risk (Dimakopoulos 1977:12–13). Today, the strain on the water supply comes more from the exigencies of the tourist industry. The brown liquid that dribbles out of the faucets on bad days is a constant irritant. Water also presented another kind of problem, the humidity that plagued the Old Town, but here none of the politicians really had a satisfactory answer, and the historic conservation office furnished all the politicians with a convincing scapegoat. European Community funding for projects in the Old Town was also a bone of contention. Playing on the always emotive theme of competition with the other towns of Crete, which had gained in asperity since Khania and Iraklio had succeeded in getting important segments of the University of Crete relocated to their own environs and away from Rethemnos, Arkhondakis demanded to know why Khania had received extensive funding for its Venetian quarter and Rethemnos nothing (*Rethemniotika Nea*, 28 September 1986, p. 3). Skouloudis, in the interview quoted above as well as in his public appearances, retorted that Arkhondakis must have known perfectly well that the charge was not even true.

Despite the utility to all parties of this theme of external funding, which gave some substance to the entailment of "Europe" in the reconstruction of historic Rethemnos, the "Old Town problem" was probably the issue on which the contenders most assiduously avoided taking specific positions. Whatever stance one took was a political mine field. All agreed that something must be done. Pramateftakis and Arkhondakis, in particular, called for a more liberal conservation law that would allow a third storey to be added to some buildings. It was Arkhondakis, however, who, in 1968, had (in his own words)[28] "provoked" the declaration of the Old

Town as a scheduled monument and so arrested the rush to complete redevelopment. There was thus some irony in the fact that it was now Skouloudis, as a representative of the governing party, who seemed less interested in changing the situation. Old Town residents complained that Skouloudis was simply not concerned with their district, since virtually any restriction on new construction made the Old Town irrelevant to his family's commercial interests, and especially to those of his brothers' building company. Skouloudis hotly denied these charges. It was, in fact, the local building firms who had first sought to turn public opinion—originally proconservation—against Arkhondakis's intervention in 1968. Arkhondakis, however, had meanwhile developed a plan that would permit interior alterations except in the case of houses with special architectural features, and it was this plan that he had almost brought to completion when he finished his second, and elected, term of office as mayor in 1982. With some further modifications, the plan was put into effect under the socialist government that had meanwhile (1981) come to power. Thus, in effect, the two leading contenders were perceived, rightly or wrongly, as having switched sides on the issue of the Old Town. Residents who accepted such charges of inconsistency and special interest did not hope for much from either candidate.

Behind the rhetoric about issues and capabilities, however, social relationships continued to play a decisive role. Blunter residents even admitted that issues were effectively irrelevant. This too, of course, is a rhetorical stance. People's choices actually depended on where they saw their interests best served. Some preferred to concentrate on larger questions such as the availability of work, while others looked to the more immediate problems of placing their children in good jobs, binding more customers to their businesses, and investing in social credit for the unpredictable future. Their cheerful cynicism was predicated on a probably fair assessment of what they could expect from the politicians, who were assumed to be concerned only with self-interest and *mandza* (literally, "eating," i.e., profit). Voters' self-interest, in turn, could be rendered morally valid through the rhetoric of "being embarrassed" (*drepome*)—that is, at even hesitating to support those closest to themselves. Although this ostensibly affective concern with closeness is expressed in terms of a fixed, morally secure hierarchy of value, in practice it is a matter for opportunistic calculation—as some acknowledge in moments of candor.

Personality also played a part. People complained about Skouloudis's blunt, authoritarian manner, sometimes attributing to it the partial desertion to the Pramateftakis camp of his slate of four years earlier. More significant, but also interpreted in a contingent and opportunistic fashion, were ties of kinship and residence. While such ties could not determine voting patterns in the almost regimented way that we frequently meet in village elections (see Herzfeld 1985:99–111), they often served to justify the choices that individual voters made. A few men, and fewer women, insisted that they voted without regard to personal ties or party affiliations. These claims, again, were often tactical ways of dealing with outsiders such as myself. Among intimates, however, social strategies worked in the opposite direction. People defended their choices in terms of social relationships. In this way, they at once justified self-interest in moral terms and rationalized the morality of mutual obligation in terms of practical interest.

A taciturn few refused to declare political allegiances at all, hoping thereby to extract favors from both the major parties. This raises the stakes, because success can give one a great deal of social standing but failure easily arises from suspicions that one is being grossly opportunistic. Those who adopt this strategy must be very aggressive in defending their right *not* to be aggressive on behalf of any political party or slate. One canny voter, within a few years, placed his son in a New Democracy candidate's firm and forced concessions out of the PASOK government–controlled historic conservation office. This is a rare talent among people who can more easily reap instant glory, and practical advantage, by bragging about their political connections. The more passionately a voter declares allegiance to a leader or party, the harder it is to switch without embarrassment, but commitment of this sort may be a small price to pay for a measure of dependable patronage.

A sharp difference did appear in the ways in which women and men spoke of such matters. Because women supposedly do not handle their households' external relations, they tended to express their voting preferences in terms either of loyalty to their husbands' choices or, more commonly, in terms of solidarity with women and their needs—terms that did not match their husbands' views at all.

In particular, women showed considerable contempt for the questions of political ideology that so preoccupied the men's public posturing. One woman went so far as to tell me that she, unlike her husband (a fervent *pasoktzis*), would vote "for the person, not the party." By this she meant that she would vote for Arkhondakis, who, in addition to being her grandson's (SS) godfather, exuded a genteel charm that supposedly held special appeal for women. Men and women alike acknowledged this quality. It allowed men to sneer at their wives for being politically irresponsible—a compensation, perhaps, for the loss of control that men usually exercise over their wives' voting in the rural communities from which most of them hailed. Arkhondakis was the "scholar" who treated the poor and uneducated as his equals, Skouloudis the villager who made good and now had no time for anyone. In practical terms, too, Arkhondakis's promise to reduce the cost of water had great appeal for the generally poorer Old Town housewives.

For the women of the Old Town, Arkhondakis's suave urbanity contrasted tellingly, not only with Skouloudis's rather abrupt style, but also with their husbands' domestic roughness and party fanaticism. Two contrasted political styles thus evinced two distinctively gendered and class-based Rethemniot identities: the raw and the cultivated. It also allowed them to poke fun at the snobbery of the nouveau riche New Towners: *they* are engineers (i.e., educated people, usually men), said one housewife, but we are just "little women" (*yinekoules*) in the Old Town. It does not appear that these attitudes directly affected the way in which votes were cast. Indirectly, however, it served to legitimate decisions to cast one's vote either way. Gender was important in these elections, not because it materially affected voters' decisions in the Old Town, but because it provided an acceptable (if scarcely impermeable) camouflage for individual motives and allegiances.

Conversely, the Skouloudis (socialist) slate operated most successfully on the rhetoric of male values. It also traded on the male Cretan posture of resistance to right-wing power. Even among the men, however, the mayor's reputation for brusque behavior nearly proved fatal to his hopes. He had succeeded in alienating his original colleagues from the previous election and had infuriated whole groups of civil servants whose traditional privileges he supposedly ignored.

In the event, however, it appears that gendered preferences were much more a matter of rhetoric and perception than of actual voting preferences. The differences between men's and women's votes cast for each candidate in the Old Town during the first round of voting were very small, as the accompanying table reveals.

First Round: Municipal elections, 19 October 1986: Old Town

	Skouloudis	Arkhondakis	Pramateftakis
Total votes	1153	1375	442
Men/women	555/598	674/701	226/216
Men/women	48.1%/51.9%	51.1%/48.9%	49.0%/51.0%

Source: *Rethemniotika Nea*, 21 October 1986, p. 1.

Nonetheless, Skouloudis's forthright stance could convey a message of rough, manly sincerity. On the eve of the election, at a huge rally before the town hall, he demanded to know why the authorities had still failed to identify the perpetrators of the car-bomb assassination attempt against him some two years earlier (on 24 October 1985). There are many in Rethemnos who still automatically identify the police with the repressive political Right. When I interviewed Skouloudis, he refused to be more specific, but evoked a popular (and populist) rhetoric by insisting that the attempt against him sprang from (commercial and political) "interests" that had been hurt by his efforts as mayor to further "the general good." Although he also adamantly denied that it had been a traditional family feud, his stance appealed to the image of Cretan manhood because it showed that he was unafraid of unseen but powerful forces.

His accusations challenged the authorities. They were also, in the context, somewhat paradoxical. The "state" that he criticized in these remarks, as also in his interview with me, was at that time still under his own party's control.[29] Moreover, as he spoke, and later when he came down to receive the adulation of the crowd, he was everywhere under the protective gaze of a very senior policeman.

Paradox and ambiguity make for good political negotiation. His stand attacked the vague bogey of government yet supported the ruling party, still more popular in Crete than in any other region. His election workers, meanwhile, put their efforts into activating kinship and other local-level ties. Despite the party's stand against patronage and manipulation, these tactics were necessary to the slate's eventual success. A specific illustration will show how they worked—when they worked.

A former communist, who took advantage of the rhetoric of local interests above party politics to assert that he "had never been" a New Democracy supporter, stood on the slate of the conservative Arkhondakis. A PASOK supporter decided to damage this man's chances as best he could. The fact that the candidate was a deserter from the communist camp constituted a first strike against him. Even the right-wing voters would see this candidate as an *anemazoksaris*—a Johnny-come-lately.[30] Worse was to come. This man "has no patriline (*soi*),[31]" complained his detractor; he would not get any votes from his own kin. Thus, he would be compelled to do the worst thing that a true man could: he would have to plead for votes. "He's sitting in beggary now (*sti zitiania kathete tora*)," sneered his foe. Those who longed for the return of the military dictators would support their own representative, an ex-policeman, in preference to this unfortunate. The candidate's own nephew, although also a right-winger, would vote for another candidate because his son worked for the latter—a bond that might, if only for reasons of obvious practical self-interest, be set against other such moral obligations as neighborly relations.

There was a good deal of wishful thinking, and some hope of making it stick, in these charges. This is also the logic of all the predictions, ranging from the cautious to the absurd, that supporters put forward on their chosen candidates' behalf up to the very last moment. One tries to persuade others that one's own slate will win; for who wants to be associated with a loser—except perhaps to render a close kinsperson's defeat less humiliating? The huge wagers that supporters risk on their favored candidates—two million drachmas against a new car in one case—are another part of this practical rhetoric, which also includes the practice of busing party supporters in from the nearby villages in order to swell the impression of electoral strength at the major campaign rallies.

In the event, the communist-turned-rightist garnered 139 votes, about 30 of which apparently came from people who usually, in national elections, could be counted on to vote socialist or communist. This was not, under the circumstances, a bad showing.[32] The candidate was himself no mean politician. He had a glib tongue, as even his bitterest enemies recognized, and could call on a wide range of customers (he owned a centrally located store) and ritual kin. Moreover, he could appeal to a residue of loyalty from fellow Mikrasiates, and, as a declared Venizelist, he did what all sensible Cretan politicians do: he claimed his own particular piece of the local heritage of liberalism, now diffused among the entire spectrum of political parties from extreme Left to extreme Right.[33]

Nevertheless, he could not count on all the votes on which he considered himself to have a moral lien. Most voters face difficult choices. Whereas, in village elections, segmentary agnatic loyalties may provide a relatively straightforward baseline of allegiance,[34] in the town they must compete with the claims of neighborhood, ritual kinship, commercial association, and uterine kinship and affinity, not to speak of political party membership. One of his close neighbors, deducing from past experience that the candidate would be upset if he did not vote for him but feeling a strong obligation to vote for his *koumbaros* (the brother of his daughter's deceased godfather, who also happened to be the PASOK slate's vicemayoral candidate), told him that he had to prefer the ties of ritual kinship. While everyone recognizes the electioneering nature of such excuses, it enabled the candidate and his wife to remain coldly friendly with their neighbor: they were understandably unhappy with the voter's decision, but, because the voter had thought to tell him in advance and to give him a socially acceptable excuse, the candidate's dignity had not been affronted to the point at which he and his wife would have felt socially *compelled* to break off relations. Since the voter had also told the head of the slate, who had courteously accepted this defection by the parents of a former pupil of his, a subordinate candidate really did not have much choice.

The communists, although relatively immune to appeals based on kinship and other purely social loyalties, also showed signs of more willingly heeding agnatic links. For example, one communist refused to vote for a PASOK candidate who was his son-in-law, whereas another voted for his nephew (FBS) even though the latter belonged to the ideologically far

more unattractive New Democracy party. An ex-communist who still favored the Pramateftakis coalition, and who expressed complete alienation from the Skouloudis camp despite a substantial favor that the
mayor had done him in the past, said that he would vote for an agnate
(FBS) of his, who was standing on the conservative platform, if this man
could get no other votes. A zero tally would have shamed the entire
patrigroup.

Agnatic loyalties die hard indeed. For the communists, however, "insiders" (dhiki mas) were fellow communists rather than kin or covillag-
ers. Although there were defectors, the communists' generally solid dis-
cipline made them a force to be reckoned with when, after the first round
of voting, Arkhondakis emerged slightly ahead but without a sufficient
margin to declare outright victory. The runoff election was held a week
later. This time, votes were cast only for the mayoral candidates. This
enabled voters to ignore all but direct personal connections with the mayoral candidates themselves, although the slate candidates continued to
whip up support for their respective leaders, perhaps in part because they
hoped to gain seats themselves in the process. The major parties brought
in substantial numbers of expatriate Rethemniots who had retained voting rights in the town,[35] and allegations of bribery were rife against both
large groups. Some thought that bribery was particularly used to get votes
for those candidates who did not have extensive kinship networks on
which they could rely, and it was generally believed that the heads of
larger families could expect larger bribes because they controlled more
votes. While I was never able to substantiate particular cases of bribery,
the rich circumstantial detail suggests that it may have occurred, at least
in the past. Once again, however, it is at least as likely that this charge
recurs with such frequency mainly because it provides a socially patterned—and, on occasion, preemptive—way of excusing the failures of
one's own side.[36]

Some erstwhile Arkhondakis supporters, especially Old Town women,
felt they had to support Skouloudis on the second round because it was
clear that, even if he did not win, he represented the government party
(and would be assured of a seat on the council at the very least). The
communists, after an ominous pause during which they individually speculated that they might have to cast blank ballots, received instructions
from party headquarters in Athens to support Skouloudis. The rough-
spoken but hardworking and well-organized incumbent survived—if narrowly—into a further term.

The foregoing does not pretend to be an exhaustive election analysis.
Much of the detail depends on hearsay, which is itself part of the rhetorical management of political relationships. These relationships in turn re-
volve around the risk-fraught but unavoidable necessity of weighing a

whole range of more or less exigent moral imperatives: kinship, spiritual kinship, neighborhood, professional association, and patronage—as well as ideological purity and party loyalty, these last two being by no means identical. The discussion is partial for other reasons also. Although the Old Town represents less than half of the Rethemniot electorate, I have avoided discussing aspects of the struggle that do not bear directly on its problems. Nonetheless, the personal machinations and alliances that I have described throw some light on the local aspect of Greek national politics, all too often absent from otherwise valuable historical analyses of electoral patterns (e.g., Legg 1969; Clogg 1987). These details suggest, for example, that generalizations about client-patron relationships, usually based on the elegantly described but historically specific and culturally idiosyncratic Sarakatsan case (Campbell 1964), miss the cut-and-thrust of daily political tactics. Such omissions circumscribe the explanatory value of general analyses. Only ethnographically does it become possible to suggest how national debates actually get converted into votes.

To understand how Skouloudis survived—when many socialist mayors, including those of Athens, Piraeus, and Thessaloniki, were defeated—means penetrating beyond the rhetoric of issues and worthy candidacies, and even beyond the hazy generalities of *simbathia* ("liking," a term that can be used to indicate warm approval ranging from appreciation of a candidate's qualities to a relationship based purely on spiritual kinship). Rethemnos is a town of merchants and craftsmen whose small profit margins are highly susceptible to political pressure. Sudden shifts in electoral allegiance attract notice, despite the secrecy of the ballot. Thus, for example, a slate candidate who serves simply to reinforce the total number of votes and who only gets two votes in a given district will know, since he knows whose votes these are, that they cannot have come from the neighbor who now pretends to have voted for him as well. Moreover, what look like practical measures for protecting the urban environment may be bad for business, and innovative policies may frighten voters. From the beginning, Pramateftakis waxed eloquent on the subject of "noise pollution" (e.g., *Rethemniotika Nea*, 13 August 1986, p. 1), but this was a weak theme at best in a town where people are less concerned with peace and quiet than with safeguarding their business and ensuring easy transportation of goods in and out of the protected zone of the Old Town.

These calculations are all part of the movement of social capital that is fundamental to the relationship between citizenry and bureaucracy. In the following chapters, we shall focus increasingly on the ways in which local and national concerns mesh with—or grate against—each other. This introduction to the mutual entangling of what, formally, are permanent social loyalties and official electoral possibilities should serve to prepare the way for an examination of the fluid but intense relations between citizen and bureaucrat. Having seen the negotiation of the political present, we are now in a better position to appreciate the negotiation of the cultural past.

Chapter Four

HOME SPACES

HOUSE AND NAME

Housing is both the core of Rethemnos's physical existence and the material and symbolic link between the generations of its inhabitants. Its symbolic and practical consequences are two facets of a single coin. Parents have strong obligations to house their children at marriage, through various combinations of dowry, inheritance, and gifts *intra vivos*, and these are described as expressions of affect as well as of a moral imperative.[1]

Behind the apparently haphazard distribution of property, or perhaps more accurately in front of it, lies an insistent rhetoric of impartiality. In practice, the division of property is rarely straightforward. Parents wryly observe that all their labor is directed toward setting their children up for life. The parental obligations are reciprocated in the form of moral expectations, although some aging parents invest considerable effort in avoiding dependency by renting a small place to live on their own. A good part of the children's social capital consists of a reputation for filial care. The common outcome of this pressure, insistence that surviving parents come and live with the children, can generate as much annoyance as would neglect. At the very least, there is tension about social expectations. An old man, living alone, explained, "It's not that my children don't want me, but I want to be on my own because I suffer from anxiety." The cause of this anxiety is his children's refusal to countenance his selling goods from a barrow. As they are fairly wealthy now, and socially mobile, "they would say that I am insulting them" by engaging in such a menial occupation in public.[2] He also refuses to frequent his son-in-law's coffeehouse, because he knows that the younger man will refuse to take his money. Many elderly people in Rethemnos value their independence.

Children are nevertheless expected to take their responsibilities to aged parents seriously. A retired carpenter likes to come to his familiar coffeehouse, near the place where he still occasionally does piecework, even though he lives in the New Town. His children regularly come by with the car to pick him up. Widowed parents, especially, expect to live in the home of a married child, and children are very reluctant to let them live alone—again, for fear of social comment. An inveterate gossip, one of our neighbors complained that she did not know the local news as well as formerly because she now had to tend to her elderly and sick mother, who had come from their village to live with her. Another neighbor, whose mother-in-law shouted incessantly in the street that she was possessed by demons, made a brave display of her sufferings—which were indeed considerable, if only because the tormented old lady rarely ceased her hoarse objurgations from dawn until dusk.

The moral obligations that bind children to their parents belong to a wider nexus that involves other kin as well as baptismal sponsors. Many such obligations are incurred through the establishment of residence in Rethemnos, both at the time of the initial search for work in the town and then later with the acquisition of residential and commercial property. This property is the object of the residents' repeated confrontations with the bureaucracy. Its origins are often obliquely expressed through the baptismal names the present owners bear. In order to understand the depth of the residents' moral commitment to their autonomy as home owners, we must therefore first focus briefly on the symbolic practices of naming through which this commitment is customarily established and validated.

There are important links among naming, kinship, and patronage.[3] Village youths seeking town employment as apprentices often turn to their godparents. In the past, these were often itinerant merchants who had earlier secured custom from the parents of male children by requesting the right to serve as baptismal sponsors; now it was their turn to translate the spiritual bond into material benefit. The godparent nominally has the right to choose a child's name. Whether this actually happens depends on several circumstances: the place of the child in the order of birth, the recent death of close kin calling for immediate commemoration, the status of godparent and natural parent. Each of these factors needs a brief explanation, as do the naming rules that in theory govern the choice.

The child whose name a father almost always insists on choosing is the first male, who should bear his paternal grandfather's name. In "resurrecting" his grandfather, a boy claims a special place in the latter's affections. The claim is a double one: there was no mistaking the pride of one elderly man who pointed out that his agnatic grandson had his surname *as well*. Again, the first daughter is likely to be named for her father's mother. Naming is a serious matter; one grandmother was deeply offended when, although none of her grandchildren had been named after her, the grown-up child with whom she lived proceeded to give a pet duck a humorous version of her name!

The second child of each sex may take the appropriate maternal grandparent's name. This seems especially likely when the conjugal relationship is a warm one, or if the mother's family has some advantage over the father's (for example, being Cretan when the father's family is of refugee origin). After that, the godparent's right to choose the name is rarely contested, unless one of the parents has recently lost a sibling; the sponsor, too, may confer the name of a recently deceased kinsperson. When the sponsors are willing, these secondary offspring may also receive names from the father's soi (group of agnates) or the mother's natal family.

But all these possibilities, even the preference for naming the first son for his paternal grandfather, may go by the board when the sponsor is too powerful or too important to be gainsaid. Among the children of the poorer Asia Minor refugees, especially, it is common to find first sons whose names result entirely from their local sponsors' decisions. The parents' strategy was to capture the material interest of affluent local families in the hope of securing work and connections: "They used to look for someone through whom they'd get to be known in the locality." It was not always easy to achieve this. In one refugee family, the mother's brother and sister baptized the first son and first daughter, who were duly named for the mother's own parents. Since this kind of "internal" spiritual kinship duplicates existing family ties, it gives no practical advantage, but it was only after the family had been on Crete some years that local sponsors would agree to baptize subsequent children.

The invitation to baptize implies a nominal superiority on the part of the sponsor. Cretans who agreed to baptize the children of refugees considered that superiority to be confirmed in the right to choose the child's name.[4] Cretans, again, who emigrated to Athens adopted some of the same tactics. One such migrant invited an engineer to baptize his daughter. The engineer happened to be the brother of a prominent Cretan politician and sometime government minister. The father felt obliged to allow so well connected a sponsor to name the girl after his own mother. "These people were of a higher class than me," he explained, and added that "I wanted to make a spiritual kinsman (sindekno[s])[5] of higher class" because everyone should think of possible future need. But he then added proudly, "Praise God, it never happened that I needed to ask him for anything!" He had through time converted his social and political dependence into moral self-sufficiency, and this was cause for abiding satisfaction.

The names that appear on a family's genealogy thus represent a calculus of status and interest. When the baptismal sponsors are more powerful or wealthier than the parents, the names they confer are less likely to be those the parents would choose of their own accord. But when the parents are rich or, conversely, are unable or unwilling to seek a powerful patron as sponsor, they exercise considerably greater control over the outcome. There may be material advantages to them in this also. The son of one of the wealthiest Rethemniots married a much poorer woman, and for a long time relations between the two families were strained. When they eventually improved, the well-off grandfather transferred considerable amounts of property to the two children (a girl and a boy) of this union. The boy received an especially large endowment because he was the sole bearer of his grandfather's full name; among his first cousins, the only patrilateral one is a girl. Not only would the grandfather's memory thus be perpetuated in the best of his numerous large properties, but the surname would guarantee the agnatic memory also.

The actual disposition of names thus encapsulates personal histories and relationships. It reflects both the obligations that are expected to subsist among children, parents, and sponsors, and the particular variations that circumstances and idiosyncrasies have wrought on these normative patterns. The houses and shops of the Old Town are not merely properties that people rent or buy as places to live. They are also material expressions of family relationships, political connections, and social status. Because their distribution is sometimes so intimately linked to that of names, they easily serve as the vehicle of passionate self-identification. Even in cases lacking a specific relationship between property and names, the general principle often seems to be sufficient to justify that kind of affective stance—at least vis-à-vis the bureaucracy.

The actual experience of living in these houses seems to be the primary focus in the construction of this kind of sentiment. In a few instances, where the house is large and architecturally prominent, relatively prosperous owners have lavished great care on creating a consciously traditional interior that incoporates the old fabric (Plate 32). Most of the houses, however, are small, uncomfortable, unhealthy, cramped, and dilapidated; but they are also homes. In the next section, we shall look at the kinds of immediate connection that build on family history in order to contrast the links that connect houses to personal experience and family history with the grander historical vision of the state bureaucracy.

RESIDENCE: FATHERS, BRIDES, AND CIVIL SERVANTS

Most Old Town houses are too small to admit of more than a nuclear family residence pattern, except for the occasional addition of a widowed parent. Newly married children move into a new house, most commonly supplied by the bride's parents. If they are too poor to do this, they may rent a house and save hard-won earnings to set up their own quarters as quickly as possible. Sometimes, parents may wish to divide a house with one or more children by floors—one of the problems that causes such irritation with the historic conservators' limits on vertical expansion.

Families of eligible young women usually seek to lure grooms with the promise of a good urban home. For the groom's family this mutually con-

32. The formal reception room of one of the grand
Venetian houses in Rethemnos; note the framed embroidery and the molded ceiling. (1987)

venient arrangement furnishes a solid foothold in the town. In rare cases,
the bride's family may not be able to afford a house but may take the
groom in as a temporary *soghambros*, or in-marrying groom, the potential opprobrium of this label[6] being offset here by the explanation that
"he is studying"—that is, to work his way into a coveted civil service
position, such as a job in the public telephone company. A civil service
post provides one of the few means for an ambitious and able village boy
to rise above menial or artisan status, and makes him a more attractive
"catch" for a family already resident in the town.

   Many Cretan villagers who moved to Rethemnos in the years between
1935 and the late 1950s saw their newly acquired houses as a reliable if
meager investment. Few trusted their wealth to banks or paper money.
Gold sovereigns (*lires*) were acceptable, if unwieldy. Real estate—fields in

the countryside, houses in town—represented something more lasting. Apparently, the first generation of these migrants viewed their new town houses without sentiment, much as they treated their fields; they were a source of income, either as a place of work or, when work itself did not yield good income, as a source of money from rents and as an eventual dowry for daughters not yet grown to adulthood.

Sentiment accrued with time. Parents' affection for a house represented an appreciation of the labor they had put into it. Their children became sentimentally attached to what sons, in particular, regard to this day as their "paternal house." Until the first child's marriage forces the beginning of the decision-making process, parents carefully avoid assigning any part of their possessions to particular children. When that division is made, it technically follows the legal principle of equal partible inheritance. In the home village, especially, this may entail a drawing of lots in order to prevent internecine conflict. Affective bonds with the "parental property," however, are problematical from the start. When the parental home has been divided up into several parts, perhaps through more than one death, it quickly becomes simplest for all the siblings and cousins to take their shares in the cash made on the sale of the property. Some of the divisions of tiny properties among multiple sets of heirs yield very small amounts of money (see chapter 7, figs. 7.4 and 7.5). Such dispersion certainly has the effect of dissipating any affective lien on the ancestral home, and men's rhetoric on this score has more to do with ideals of masculine identity than with any desire to preserve the old structure at any price.

An example will illustrate the point. A housepainter, who has seen (and indeed made) many a building change its appearance, and who therefore knows a great deal about the transience of such commemorative possessions, reflected:

> From my father I didn't get anything except a house with two [sic] rooms [and one kitchen, mentioned later], which was Turkish, a genuinely Turkish house, built during the time of Turkish rule. We preserved it, we stripped it down, we plastered it, we made various improvements so it wouldn't collapse, and it became, anyway, a habitable house, and we stayed (katsame, literally, "sat") in it.

The father, a refugee of Cretan descent who had fled the Smyrna holocaust of 1922, had managed to locate his own father's Cretan village property and sold it in order to set up house in the town. His new abode was a mean, physically confining environment for a family with three boys and two girls, each of the two main rooms a mere fourteen square meters in extent. When the children grew up, they stood to inherit a miserable fifth part apiece.

At this point, however, other considerations prevailed. The division of such tiny dwellings into several equal parts makes no practical sense, and their financial value, as we have just noted, is usually trivial. The sons were also obliged to consider their reputation as providers and protectors of their sisters. They thus conceded the house to the sister who had married a poorer husband. The transfer of this house ostensibly took the form of a direct sale at the precise taxable value—an unusual situation among siblings, and one that, in conjunction with its *social* representation as a dowry (*pro[u]čio, prika*),[7] almost certainly means that the money was put up by one of the brothers in the first place. The building was so inadequate for modern expectations that the sister—who had three daughters, one of them divorced with a child of her own—until recently preferred to pay rent on a damp-ridden but more commodious house (at 13,000 drachmas per month) and rented the old house out to a childless couple (at 10,000 drachmas per month). Now, at last, she and her husband, both of them crippled with illness, have managed to scrape together enough money from the proceeds of their newsstand—also rented—to demolish the old house and build anew.

Meanwhile, her brothers needed to find places of their own. Eventually, discovering a town garden plot, with lemon and tangerine trees, one of them bought a segment and built himself a house there. By renting the spare rooms to tourists he amassed enough funds to begin a second house destined for the same purpose. For all his sentimental attachment to his father's old house, the realities of residence have moved far away from the patrifocal patterns of the more conservatively agnatic villages. Attachment to the "paternal house" can seem like the last despairing clutch of nostalgia upon an increasingly recalcitrant modernity. It survives the material disappearance of the old: "An entire past comes to dwell in a new house" (Bachelard 1964:5), and with it the icons and family photographs that provide a more portable link with the past.

Not all sentimental attachments to property are agnatic. A coffee grinder owed his profession to his commitment to continuing a maternal uncle's (MZH) business, at the urging of the latter's widow "that it should not be wiped out (*na mi zvisi*)." A refugee who had taken his immediate household to Piraeus and acquired property there disposed of the Rethemnos house he had received in the post–population exchange settlement scheme by giving it to his uterine niece (ZD) who happened to bear his mother's name. While he could have built an additional house on the adjoining land, he had not done so, and her sister received nothing. He admitted that this was unjust, and that he had "liked" (*simbathise*) the one niece more than her sister simply because the former bore his mother's name. In the absence of agnatic claims, other aspects of kin ideology tightly channel the permissible range of affect.

Most of the recent rural immigrants to Rethemnos hail from villages where it is customary for the bridegroom to provide the house. As has happened throughout Greece (and Cyprus: Loizos 1975), however, male emigration and massive migration to the towns have increased the competition among women for eligible husbands. One strategy, part of an extremely volatile calculus of symbolic as well as economic advantage (see Bourdieu 1972), has been to include the provision of a house in the dowry. Such practices, which have a long history in urban Greece (see now Sant Cassia, forthcoming), leave men scrambling for rhetorical means to reassert their moral authority in physical locations over which, technically at least, they exercise only a restricted degree of control: hence much of the talk about "paternal houses." Such reconstructions of family history mark attempts to make sense of a new moral and economic order in which aggressive masculinity does not have the moral force it possesses in village social life, and where it is beset by nuance and ambiguity.

Men and women alike attest to the sentiment that now binds them to their old houses. In the interwar years, many rural migrants preferred to think of their newly acquired town houses simply as an investment, much like the fields they had left behind. But within a single generation, the bond of memory became strong. The mean condition of the houses sometimes seems inversely proportionate to the affective value placed on them, as in the "blood" that ran in the incised plaster of the meanest. Even with today's prosperity, a ramshackle hovel commands this agony-laden affection. The housepainter again: "the father feels pain for it (*ti bonai*), and, and each wall (*douvari*) has many memories each person could tell." So he went twice a day "to see my father's house, the door, I go for a ride with my car, like that, *tsak!*"—and the brief visit, endlessly repeated until the house was finally demolished, satisfied his need. New construction on the old site helped ease nostalgia into a less intense emotion. This affective attachment to the physical fabric of a past home, although less traumatically disrupted, is of the same order as the Cretan Muslims' sentimental pilgrimages to their former homeland.

In chapter 6, we shall meet a woman who fought against the damp that riddled her house until the dilatoriness of competing bureaucracies eventually forced her to move elsewhere. "Feeling pain" (*ponao*), like the pain (*ponos*) of bereavement (see Caraveli 1986), suggests eviction from familiar contexts, the death of something valued. People "feel pain for" their houses, and for the town itself, as increasing commercialization opens it to ridicule and criticism from foreign visitors. Often, there is little to be done about the disappearance of the past. The housepainter's sister eventually demolished their father's house, as we have seen, along with her brother's dream of reconstituting it as a place to which he could retreat for a quiet coffee alone with his memories. Sentiment carries all the pain of knowing that even the most robust dwelling can rot away or fall victim to the needs of modern living.

DOWRIES

While West Cretan village parents usually provide their sons with a house at marriage, the pattern has been largely reversed in the towns. Strategy and affect coincide: the much more diffuse social ties of the urban setting throw a greater burden of mutual reliance on the immediate family and undercut the larger agnatic solidarity. Parents who provide property for their sons effectively free the latter from any kind of dependence on their affines; but those who *fail* to provide housing for their daughters attract only contempt—except when daughters find husbands whose educational sophistication or cosmopolitanism leads them to disdain such "backward" practices in favor of the approved Western ideal of disinterested romantic love. These are calculations of cultural as well as economic value.

Parents usually provide housing for their children out of their existing properties and, if space is scarce, rent properties for their own old age. Every effort is made to keep as many daughters as possible close to the parental home. A common tactic is to build a *plaka* (concrete roof) over the existing *ondas* (wood-floored room), thereby creating two dwellings in place of one. For this reason, the conservation order restricting additional storeys in Old Town houses formerly occasioned much anger. This has in part dissipated in the last few years, however, both because the restrictions themselves have been partially eased, and because the exodus to the New Town that resulted from their initial imposition led to a massive building boom—partly still fueled by the need for dowry apartments—in the New Town. There, properties have become an extremely profitable investment.

The male refugees, no less than the village Cretans around them, described house ownership in agnatic terms. Having been granted their houses as "exchange" (*andallaksima*) property, they were required to pay the state whatever a locally constituted committee assessed as the difference between their Asia Minor estates and their new homes, if the latter were rated at a higher price; those who could not afford to pay the whole amount were assessed for a rental charge instead. Unlike the refugees who had settled in the more expensive cities such as Piraeus and Athens, and long before the 1988 act of parliament that completed the process there, all those who lived in Rethemnos had managed to buy up the freehold from the state. Many did so soon after arrival. In 1942, exploiting one of the few advantages of the catastrophic wartime inflation, the remainder were suddenly able to pay off the outstanding amount at the 1924 drachma assessment. A house valued at 150,000 drachmas could suddenly be bought for two eggs or a basket of peaches; one man, who had paid half the value of his house to the state and was paying rent on the other half, now acquired the latter with the wages he earned in kind on a single day's labor.[8] In this way, refugee house owners became as independent as their Cretan neighbors, and the men could in consequence talk more convincingly in terms of the ideology of male possession.

Women of both groups, however, saw these houses more as a dowry that would ensure them social advancement or at least solvency. Only the wealthy few who married outside Crete generally escaped this constraint—for example, the lawyer whose wife, a Thessaloniki woman, received her judge father's retirement pay (*ef'apaks*) as dowry and used it to buy a magnificent old house on the main commercial thoroughfare: "I wasn't even present at the contract[-signing], my husband it was and the refugee [who had previously received the house as andallaksimo who] signed." Her own daughter is in Athens, so "the air from here on up is our own"—a slightly ironical use of the legal usufruct term, given that for the foreseeable future further upward construction remains prohibited. Nonetheless: "Once they were saying that they would 'give' the 'air,' [so] they said; but even if they were to give it, I'm telling you once again, I shan't 'bother' [i.e., build on, damage] it!"

If the only economically feasible means for parents to dower a daughter is to build an extra storey, what are they now to do? There are alternative forms of endowment to housing. A working mother spoke of her children:

> They're doing fine at their school. If they want to study, I'll help them. I'll help them of course, but I will *not* start buying up property in order to create a dowry (prika), either for my son [*sic*] or for my daughter.

She added, however, that many residents still ask of a new bride, "What prika did she get?" It hardly matters that a recently enacted family law abolished the legal category of prika, "since people's mentality doesn't change!" And the same mother mimicked the condescension of neighbor women:

> "But she's good, of course. She's a good girl, those things. But not to have a house? She should have a house! She should have a house!"

But she justifies the practice of providing poor young couples with a house because the local rents are high—twenty-five to thirty thousand drachmas for a two-room apartment—and a working husband can barely afford the rent charges. House ownership protects the poor from the constant and inflationary drain on their weak resources.

Nonetheless, the institution of dowry seems always to have been

viewed in Rethemnos, as elsewhere (see Herzfeld 1980), with some ambivalence. It became a shibboleth for various kinds of social discrimination, particularly between rich and poor. Some refugees, too, complained
that the Cretans were "dowry hunters," but this was probably more an
expression of frustration at the refugees' economic disadvantages in a society they despised than an assessment of actual differences. Both refugees
and indigenous Cretans claimed that good looks and a reputation for
chastity could obviate a dowry. A male refugee, on the other hand, could
strike an effective pose when asked about his "demands": "I don't want
anything. Whatever belongs to the girl . . . I'm not a dowry hunter," said
a young man of refugee parentage who was seeking a local village woman's hand in 1960. He actually turned down the parents' offer of 100,000
drachmas and told them instead to use the money to buy a house for the
young woman. Here, in fact, he was being quite canny. He was a Rethemnos merchant, and merchants always face a certain level of economic risk.
By making sure that the house would be in his wife's name alone rather
than as a dowry in which he had a legal interest, he was protecting their
future home from the consequences of his own debts. At the same time,
he paid the parents the ultimate compliment of asking for their daughter
for her own virtues alone. In general, attempts to invoke the romantic
ideal play a big part in the strategic calculations that lead to marriage,
especially when the partners are economically unequal.

The wealthy, too, had their reasons for questioning the institution of
dowry. Indeed, for them, the conspicuous rejection of prika could be as
viable a strategy for social advancement as its retention had been for earlier, poorer generations of the same family. This has to do with the fact
that wealth does not automatically buy admission to the highest ranks of
the establishment. Once an entrepreneur has reached a certain affluence,
the one thing that remains potentially out of his children's reach is the
social acceptance that goes with good education. In the years following
World War II, for example, a soap manufacturer and sheepskin mer-
chant-tanner—who had risen from humble village origins and marriage
to a Mikrasiatissa to become one of the richest men in the town, with
huge landholdings outside the town proper—made no attempt to acquire
real estate for his four daughters. It was a deliberate stance:

> I remember that he didn't give my mother money to buy cloth, linen, which
> makes sheets, so she could make a prika for us. Never did he give her any.
> "When they grow up, they'll work, they'll make their prika on their own!"

Note that the trousseau items are also included in the notion of dowry.
Dowry contracts from the turn of the century list every single item of
embroidery, bedding, and silverware, and every household utensil and
ornament, as well as the house itself. They also mention icons and specify

the name of the saint depicted in each; these were items of great symbolic import and closely associated with the identity of the family the bride was leaving behind (see Plate 33; cf. Kenna 1985). In one such contract, dated 1899, a goldsmith and his wife, betrothing their daughter to a Piraeus merchant, detailed an elaborate inventory of jewelry as well as the very clothes that the bride would wear. These included "a dozen pair of women's trousers [*sic*], various; six (6) nightdresses and six (6) frocks, of which one [is] of silk; two women's overcoats; three women's woollen shawls; three hats; two umbrellas"—and so the list, which also includes some items of dress for the groom, goes on. Such detail contrasts strongly with the terse documents that confer only real estate in more recent years. In those early days, however, when a house could be bought for the price of two oxen, the precise detailing of smaller items did not seem at all incongruous.

Trousseau items continued to be important long after they faded from the legal documentation. They served as a mark of the bride's dependency on her husband, and of her relegation to the domestic sphere. A father who wanted something better for his daughters could play on the symbolism of dowry to put such ambitions into effect. This, not stinginess, is apparently what motivated the soap manufacturer. His often repeated injunction to his daughters to "make a prika on their own" was pedagogical. He wanted the young women to become fully independent of their

33. Personal icons, household items, a doll. (1987)

husbands in financial matters, although his own first married quarters had come to him from his father-in-law, and he did give his four daughters houses some years *after* their marriages. From the perspective of social mobility, subsequent events justified his delaying tactics. Two of the four became teachers. The two younger women live and work in Athens, their inheritance a ruin that some architects—former neighbors in the same street—only recently bought and have tried to restore.

Professionals like these, however, are now virtually the only people who can afford to achieve what formerly every father attempted, the gathering of the offspring and their children in a single close neighborhood. A member of just such a family, too, became an official of the historic conservation office, and has consequently found herself obliged to prohibit others from their own, architecturally indefensible, strategies for achieving the same kind of clustering—that is, by building modern accretions atop their antique houses. Resentment feeds easily on acts like this, which seem to claim special privilege for the bureaucrats.

Strict regulation, however, has also partially changed the social pressures. Given the severity with which it is now enforced, Old Town properties have little value for those who are not interested in tourism and only want to start a family. Many consequently prefer to acquire their first homes elsewhere. While New Town properties may also be given as dowry, the ever-present unease about dowry as a social institution may combine with an increasing willingness to educate daughters as well as sons and thus to erode the institution itself.

Moreover, even though dowry is often presented as a "traditional" obligation, its absence a basis for criticism of the parents, providing a house was often more than some earlier residents could afford. They would rent a small home—perhaps just a room or two—until some improvement in their financial condition permitted them to acquire a house of their own. This often meant a period of absence in Athens or abroad, where work was more plentiful and wages better. Income from rents, supplemented by the produce of their village lands, meanwhile enabled those who had already acquired houses to eke out a living, though usually without a surplus that would permit investment against the uncertain future. In this way, generation after generation of newlywed couples, often the discomfited beneficiaries of matchmaking between their respective villages, moved into a Rethemnos of cramped expectations and intense social proximity. Unable to build outward, reluctant to relocate to what were then cheap lands outside the Old Town walls, they could only refurbish their interiors and build vertically. For them, the sale-contract stipulation of ownership regarding the "air column"—the space immediately above the existing built area—was the only escape from the narrowness of their existence, and one that they voluntarily closed off with a new layer of in-marrying sons-in-law.

Houses acquired before the early beginnings of the historic conservation program in 1968 were often radically altered outside and in. Additional storeys met both dowry requirements and the hope of commercial development through the addition of more rentable space (afterward to be converted into still further dowry accommodation) or shop areas. Internally, the first elements to disappear were usually the *ghournes* (stone tubs) and *tzakia* (fireplaces; plate 34); while these were dysfunctional in modern terms, taking up a large proportion of the often-limited kitchen space, a further consideration lay in the intimations of primitive, "un-European" living that they conveyed. Larger changes usually entailed reinforcing rather than drastically reforming existing structures. For example, in one house given to a woman from Smyrna in the refugee settlement scheme, her son and daughter-in-law replaced the partitions of wood and plaster (*sandouma*) with walls of a more permanent material, but without reorganizing the space as such except to move the lavatory away from its "Turkish" position close to the entrance.

CONTESTED OWNERSHIP: GENDER AND THE HOUSE

The possession of houses is full of ambiguities. From a strictly legal perspective, the dowry house belonged to the bride on whose behalf the groom (*prikoliptis*, literally, "dowry taker") exercised managerial con-

34. Icons flank the old stone fireplace, into which the elderly woman living here has set her gas stove. (1987)

trol. When a young couple from a village arrived in the town already married and purchased a new home for themselves, they would often appear on the contract as equal co-owners. Women view these houses as the locus of their moral authority as well as the entitlement of their neighborly social interaction. Men, even when they live in houses acquired by their wives or mothers as dowry, tend to think of the physical building as *patroghoniko* (literally, "patro-parental"). In short, talk about houses usually entails a more or less explicit symbolic struggle between two idioms of social identification: the agnatic group on the one hand, and the residential cluster—which may actually be quite dispersed—created by a group of sisters' houses on the other.

These are not mutually exclusive identities. First of all, they are not of the same kind. Although both are based on kinship, the agnatic allegiance remains conceptual, while the ideal of clustering the daughters around the parents translates kinship into the physical fact of residence. Moreover, her father's social standing requires a bride to be adequately housed: the two ideologies converge on this point. What is "his" in his dealings with other men becomes "hers" in her relationship with the neighborhood (*yitonia*), both kinds of possession being essential to the parents' pride. In a society where men from virilocal villages are lured into marriage by the promise of an uxorilocal arrangement, the effective loss of the man's status as an independent actor supported financially and politically by his agnates is compensated by a rhetoric of ancestral possession and by the pride that he takes, in turn, in providing for his own daughters.

It is this male self-assertion that the state crosses whenever it imposes conservation and safety regulations on new construction and renovation. The effects of this interference fall at least as heavily on the women, whose lives are spent in and around their homes. But the men's pride fuels resistance no less forcefully than the women's unhappiness. When a retired policeman lost a prospective son-in-law because litigation begun by the conservation office held up the construction of the dowry house, his anger was violent. Another man whose application, approved in Athens five years earlier, was still stuck in the local bureaucracy, demanded rhetorically whether he should go to "beg" (parakalao), his humiliation further compounded by his apparent conviction that he was suffering discrimination from the socialist government because he was an ultra-rightist.

Men contrast their male pride with their wives' timidity in the face of state power. After paying a huge fine (at least 270,000 drachmas) in 1973 for making unauthorized alterations to the house that his wife had bought with her own money (as a "dowry" [proučio] some fifteen years earlier), a man stormed:

Say I, "The house I want to make, I'm going to fix it up just as I want. It had no balcony, it had no windows. I'll tear the whole thing down! I'll pull it down, mate. How else are we going to cope? Am I to live in the house like a rat?"

Says my wife to me, "No! They'll lock you up!"

"Let them lock me up a thousand times! *Let* them lock me up! What does it matter to me if they lock me up?"

I tell the workman, "Get going!"

Says he, "No," he says, "I'm afraid to."

"I," say I, "will. . . . Give me the wrecking ball." And I take the wrecking ball, and knock everything down. There's the cops again! There's the "Archaeology" again! Again, [I'm] put inside! Again to court! Again, more money! And [on again] from the beginning!

The fact that men are usually the ones who deal directly with officialdom does not, however, exclude women from the fight. On the contrary, women may turn the idiom of male contest against both the functionaries of state and the pretensions of all men in general. Once, when several of the historic conservation office's notoriously easygoing workers were making a particularly slow business of rebuilding a wall, a woman from the adjoining house came out and upbraided them, asserting that they were "not men" to take so long and do so little!

This woman and her husband were meanwhile awaiting a decision from the conservators about their own house. The historic conservation office wanted simply to replace the battered, blue-painted, carved wooden doors with a pair of the smoothly varnished ones that are rapidly becoming its trademark throughout the Old Town. The house owners, however, insisted that the conservators could only effect this change if they also agreed to refurbish the window frames and repaint the entire facade. The conservators were initially adamant that they could not do this: they did not dispose of sufficient funds but thought that perhaps the owners could afford to take care of the additional items at their own expense. Neither side was particularly concerned about structural changes; the argument concerned only the house's appearance from the street. For months the impasse continued. Both house owners remained firmly entrenched in their respective logics of possession, neither of which paid much regard to the fact that they had bought the house together some twenty years earlier. The wife announced, "It's my house, I do what I want!" Her husband, describing the door as "my grandfather's," would not let the conservators take the door's measurements unless they agreed to do the same for the windows.

Two days after the 1989 national parliamentary elections, however, a former staff member of the office (a PASOK appointee) and one of the local parliamentary deputies (a PASOK member who was fighting for his seat in a recount that eventually went against him) showed up in a state of some urgency. The husband, in order to embarrass the conservator, asked the politician why the conservation office had expected him to find his own funds for the obviously necessary restoration work. The visitors said very little but went away in apparent annoyance. Soon thereafter, conservation workers arrived, announcing that they were about to begin work on the door—only. The wife told them they could do the entire facade or nothing; they responded by saying that there were plenty of other doors they could do if she didn't want to be cooperative; and she retorted that no one had asked them to do hers anyway! The conservators went away. This edifying scene was soon repeated, again with no obvious result; but some days later, the conservation team appeared and began work on the whole facade. The house owners had won their battle. (The turn-of-the-century wooden staircase, however, continued to rot inside; the conservators' major concern remained with external appearances, and the more than thirty thousand drachmas needed for staircase restoration was simply too much.) Magnanimous in victory, the owners treated the workers with great generosity, putting them under a strong moral obligation (filotimo) to do a decent job—but simultaneously tempting them into new proofs of their indolence!

This episode illustrates a number of important dimensions of house ownership. Most prominent is the staunch defense of personal possession. This incident, in which householders who lacked political clout nonetheless won the day, shows all the more clearly that many of the common complaints to the effect that only those with *meso* ("means," i.e., influence, graft) can get their houses restored by the conservation office are retrospective conventions for explaining failure. Once again, the rhetoric of self-exoneration aims to belittle others' achievements or to minimize one's own weakness. Note, too, that the wife and husband used significantly different ways of expressing their sense of home ownership; yet their tactics converged, and to good effect. The wife's stance was particularly efficacious, as her husband proudly acknowledged: parodying the self-regard both of the men in the conservation crew and of the official functionaries, she made a hostage of what truly was a remarkable architectural feature, the inscribed and elaborately decorated baroque door frame. Lacking both financial and political resources, she nonetheless showed that a woman who could play male games in the equally male-centered worlds of community and state might be essential to the achievement of male ends—to the redrawing of history that made the wooden door her husband's "grandfather's" and that makes so many other recently acquired houses the "patro-parental" topoi of other family fictions.

Personal, family, and larger histories especially converge in the case of the leftist Civil War veteran, mentioned in chapter 1, who wanted to restore his house to the appearance it had displayed at the time his father was killed there. The house belonged to the present owner's grandmother (FM). But he wants it "to be heard" that it is his father's house: this is the single fact that now has commemorative significance for him, and that motivates his surreptitious restoration. As a mutual friend put it, the house has "history" (*istoria*) and needs "restoration" (anapaleosi, literally, "reantiquating")—the latter a term borrowed from the official discourse of historic conservation—"because it's his father's house (*to patriko spiti*) and he doesn't want it to fall into ruin, [he wants] his children, his grandchildren to see it."

Like the housepainter mentioned earlier, this man set great store by the idea that the house had belonged to his father. It was there that his father died at the hands of the right-wing nationalists. Whether a house originates as a mother's dowry is essentially irrelevant to the sentiment of patrifilial piety. This agnatic rereading of real estate history strengthens the slight evidence of sale contracts for an especially high valuation of agnatic relations in property transmission. Further evidence for it lies in the occasional practice of buying out sisters' shares in a property so that the paternal home may be maintained in its integral form. The channeling of affect among agnates is expressed, in part, through the transmission of property and the "pain" that this property evokes as the repository of a *temps perdu*.

KINSHIP AND THE TAX SYSTEM

The emphasis on agnatic transmission may become a serious inconvenience. One tolerably well established young man, for example, received a tiny and practically useless house as a bequest from an agnatic cousin in the ascending generation. For him, this was simply a taxable nuisance. Until the end of 1988, however, prevailing taxation practices did invest kinship loyalties with great advantages for many house owners and buyers.[9] The seemingly rigid rules of a bureaucratic system may actually lend themselves to an extraordinarily flexible mode of negotiation and bargaining. Tax evasion is a key locus for the struggle between the citizen and the state over the control, definition, and rights of the self.

National legal systems subordinate all other relationships to that between the contracting parties and the state. On Crete, as elsewhere in Greece, social morality and practical advantage conspire in the short term to give various kin-group interests a higher priority. Ultimately, however, the state has the long-term advantage. An example that illustrates these relative strengths sets the scene, not only for the discussion in this chapter of the negotiation of ownership and taxation, but also for the more dramatic themes of bureaucratic confrontation in the remaining chapters. We shall see here that short-term strategies based on kin relations eventually fall afoul of the state's greater power and of its regulation of the economy. Among kin, sales of real estate may never be put into contractual form as long as the original parties remain in close and amicable contact. While they thus evade the tax inspectorate for a while, since property taxes are only levied at the time of transfer, their tactic can backfire with the passage of time.

This, briefly, is what happened in the following case. A man bought a shop from six sisters, his FFBDs, for 370,000 drachmas. It may well have been convenient for them to sell their minute one-sixth shares to a kinsman even at a relatively low price, especially as they had all moved away from Crete. He failed to register the transfer at the time, however, and, two years later, the value of the property had risen so much that the authorities set the *tax* at 200,000 drachmas. The unfortunate purchaser now had good cause to regret his earlier procrastination!

One cannot calculate these value shifts from the contracts themselves. Too much of the relevant information is indirectly encoded. From 1974 until 1988, Rethemniot (and all Greek) house sale contracts usually bore two prices. One was the ostensible price—"the reasonable and agreed valuation," as the sale documents' legalistic jargon puts it—paid by the buyers. The other, usually considerably in excess of the first price, is the "provisional estimate by Mr. Economic Ephor [i.e., Tax Inspector] of Rethimni"—an identity both dignified ("Mr.") and yet utterly impersonal (the absence of his actual name). In addition, however, there are two further, shadowy prices that, while they do not (for good reason) appear in the actual document, strongly influence the two figures that do appear. One is what the buyer actually paid, a sum somewhere between the first two mentioned here. A large proportion of this real money changes hands without the notary's official knowledge (although the named sum is recorded as having been paid in his presence). The point of not listing this entire amount is that the lower sum enables the buyer to plead with the tax assessor not to set the value as high as he really thought appropriate— the other shadow value—so that the listed estimate is actually the end product of a negotiation. The assessors are mostly local and are thus most commonly connected with the contracting parties by ties of kinship, spiritual kinship, or neighborhood. Behind the sere legalisms of the contract, then, lies the social reality of a bargain struck.

It is difficult to get more than generic accounts of these negotiations. From the little I did manage to glean, it became apparent that the tax authorities find themselves compelled to resort to subterfuges and stratagems to match the inhabitants' own. We should not forget that they are themselves citizens, and often local people at that, caught between the demands of their official roles and their social obligations. A man had bought a house that had been sold to pay off its previous owner's debts. He declared its value at 100,000 drachmas. The Tax Office employee with whom he dealt, however, was familiar with the bankruptcy case that had brought the house onto the market and set the assessment at 135,000 drachmas. When the owner protested, he "rechecked" and brought the assessment down to 125,000 drachmas. The owner continued his complaints. Then the ephor (chief inspector) happened to hear the conversation and told him that he should count himself lucky that he would no longer have to pay rent; he should leave quickly before the ephor personally reset the value at 135,000 drachmas, which, insisted the ephor, was what it really was worth.

The generic accounts of these bargaining sessions confirm the sense of a hotly contested process. The tax people professed to long for the introduction of the "objective valuation" law, which finally supervened. Even this, however, is not proof against local pressures. Even within the very small blocks of land, there is a good deal of variation in the age and condition of properties. Townspeople resort to damaging comparisons that recall the disparaging real estate descriptions of the older contracts ("a house, very aged, and entirely ruined," etc.) and exert the rhetoric of personal obligation to which every locally born employee is prone. The high proportion of Rethemniots in local public service is a problem in all bureaucratic dealings—not least, as we shall see, in the historic conservation office. Nor is property the only area in which tax assessment has been a matter of negotiation.

Technically, the tax collector must have receipts as proof of evasion; this is why the market police often do sudden spot checks on customers, including unsuspecting tourists, in the hope of proving that the goods they are carrying away from a shop were sold without proper receipting. In much the same way, the historic conservation authorities constantly check on any loose bag of cement they find standing outside an old house in case secret renovations should be going on inside. This unpredictable but persistent surveillance breeds fear, for discovery can have expensive consequences.

Often, however, the tax officers do not bother to ascertain the details on site. They assume that citizens cheat as a matter of course, having (it is reciprocally assumed) done exactly the same thing as taxpayers themselves. One merchant reminded me of an apposite proverb: "Whoever has been an abbot has also been a simple monk (*kellaris*, literally, 'one who lives in a simple cell [*kelli*]'); and [so] the abbot [always] knew what the monk was up to!" People thus generally fail to declare about half the year's income; they *know* that the Tax Office will automatically compen-

sate for that presumed level of evasion. The alternative, if one declares
the full value, is to contest the virtually automatic overassessment in
court. This is too much of a hassle; "and so I give in to the Tax Office
employees' blackmail." Tax evasion of this kind was a classic chicken-
and-egg dilemma; both sides were engaged in a never-ending negotiation
in which placing the ultimate blame at the other side's door was part of
the shared rhetorical weaponry.

The tax officers' assumptions, it should be said, were based on historical experience and did not concern only the poorest people in town.
Around 1950, for example, a notary public rented a shop out to a former
itinerant merchant at thirty okadhes of oil per month. At that time, one
oka was worth thirty drachmas, and prices were sufficiently stable to allow them to agree upon this rent over a seven-year period. The shopkeeper would take his rent payment, first in oil and later on in cash, to
the notary's father, for whom it was virtual pocket money, and the notary
would then drop by the shop to sign the monthly receipt for half the rent
or less. In this way, the shopkeeper was co-opted into a cozy familial
arrangement, while the notary paid less than half the taxes the state was
entitled to receive from him.

Successful tax evasion entails strategic incompleteness in one's financial
records. At the most basic level, people are more than reluctant to give
away any information on their profits: "These things cannot be written
down or spoken about (*afta dhe leghonde ke dhen ghrafonde*)." "Writing
down" is the most characteristic symbolic and practical expression of the
bureaucracy's power to regulate. Writing is the instrument of official, punitive memory. But speech, too, is dangerous: it is the social means of
betrayal, and one cannot trust others in a world of potentially limited
opportunities and jealous neighbors. By refusing to commit the details of
their transactions to either medium, merchants engage with the state in a
game of information management. There are risks: for example, if one
does not provide receipts for all goods sold, one depends on the certain
knowledge that one's own suppliers—like *their* suppliers in turn—have
not recorded the passage of the undeclared goods. This is easiest in small
businesses, those with an annual profit of six million drachmas or less. A
butcher, to take a hypothetical example that I was offered, may want to
declare half his sales. It is as much to his supplier's profit as to his own
for the supplier to make a second run for the same set of receipts (*timo-
loyia*). Many small-scale products can also be brought in by taxi or private car, conveyances that disguise the commercial character of the transfer; only what has to be supplied from the mainland or in bulk need be
brought by truck.

Because so much taxation is done through a system of informal assessment, merchants try to make their declarations plausible, but this tactic

may cover a multitude of sins. To take a single example: a man who owned two apartments and a shop declared the full rent income on the shop because his tenant had to indicate his full expenditure; on one apartment, he declared half the rental income, while on the other, leased to three students of whom only one required a receipt, he logically enough only declared one-third. It would be virtually impossible to trace such infractions except with the help of local talebearers, and the authorities used to rely quite heavily on the latter as well as on their own sudden spot checks. Snooping was then the only effective solution. Now, however, the tax officers do not carry out on-site inspections but instead require a "sincerity declaration" that carries heavy sanctions against perjury. One small shopkeeper complained that this measure will be the ruin of his profession, so vital was tax evasion to economic survival.

The negotiated character of almost all tax decisions was, until 1988, particularly clear in regard to the sale of real estate. Here, the assumption that everyone evades tax as much as possible is so deeply rooted that the rare exact declaration can cause great trouble. A Greek-American bought some property in the Rethimni hinterland. The Old Town lawyer whom he asked to draw up the contract asked him what sum he wished to record as the cost. Astonished, the client responded, "My dear fellow, we'll put down the amount for which I bought it!" The lawyer remonstrated, warning that the tax office would automatically double the amount. The client refused to cheat: "That's the way we do things in America (*sto Amerika*)!"[10] When the tax inspector did exactly as the lawyer had predicted, the client insisted that the lawyer accompany him to the inspector's office. The client thumped his fist on the inspector's table and called him a cheat and a man of bad faith, but the tax inspector disdainfully told the lawyer, "Take him away and go outside." The tax inspector nevertheless realized that the client was in fact in the right, and so, when the case ended up in court, he agreed with the lawyer's recommendation. The judge was astounded: this was the first time that the tax inspectorate had ever accepted a taxpayer's appeal unchallenged.

On the whole, the closer the relationship between buyer and seller, the larger the gap between the declared price and the real one. It is nevertheless difficult to make generalizations about this. Not surprisingly, different degrees and kinds of relationship entail different degrees of trust and shared interest. These are not fixed formulae that people follow unreservedly. On the contrary, they are brittle and unstable. In practice, people do hale their kin before the law. One common source of contention is inheritance. It is better, of course, to anticipate that shamefully public but sometimes inevitable development. A young man visited a dying kinswoman (FFBD) outside Crete to remind her that, if she were to give him her apartment, "the [family] name would remain." He thus strategically displaced the connection between baptismal names and property to pride in a common surname, an appeal to agnatic loyalties that succeeded despite the fact that the donor was a woman and an Asia Minor refugee rather than a Cretan. Having appealed to a particular valuation of kinship, however, he had to guard against competing interpretations. In particular, because he was not her son, there was a serious risk that other and perhaps technically closer kin would contest the property transfer if he received it as a gift or as a posthumous bequest; the law does not recognize any precedence of agnatic over uterine kinship. For this reason, he persuaded her to transfer it to him by means of a sale contract, thereby removing it from the domain of inheritance altogether.[11]

The obligations of kinship are morally weighty, but such incidents as this clearly indicate that their realization depends upon the successful management of affective relations. Some Rethemniots angrily insist that a good neighbor is worth far more than any kinsperson. This is because kinship creates a level of expectation that personal feelings cannot always match. One's neighbor may help one at a time of sickness or sorrow without necessarily provoking dark thoughts about possible motives. Kin, on the other hand, act as though their interests in one's estate were both reasonable and legally enforceable; but, since they know that in practice they can take nothing for granted, their kindliest gestures of familial concern are suspect. They are probably less likely than others to report one to the tax officers; roufiania within the kin group exposes the entire group to derision and condemnation. By the same token, however, they also might not rally around in time of need unless they thought that their interests were threatened by other kin with potentially stronger claims. The play of interest and affect is both subtle and mercurial, entailing endless guessing games and attempts at anticipating others' moves (see Gambetta 1988). While genuine affection may often motivate acts of generosity, moreover, the pervasive rhetoric of distrust has a material effect on the way people interpret and react to them.

The idea of a rigidly prescriptive set of rights and obligations will not adequately explain the uses of kinship here (see especially Karp 1978). It does provide an ideological yardstick by which individuals gauge—and above all represent—each other's actions. The selective loyalty of agnates flickers fitfully, glowing into flame only when other ingredients feed it. What we can say with much greater confidence is that, in general, property sale contracts between kin show much larger discrepancies between the declared and assessed values.[12] This is a fair indication of the continuing importance of kinship in establishing the trust necessary to achieve a solidary advantage against the state.

Rethemnos houses exist apparently suspended in varying degrees of what is actually slow, creeping decline. Some are renovated, others demolished, yet others drastically altered; most, however—caught between the ponderous bureaucracies of historic conservation and environmental control on the one hand and the self-perpetuating poverty of their owners on the other—slowly crumble away. The occasional surreptitious patching of walls and plaster and the makeshift arrangements of corrugated iron and awnings—the latter placed to keep the sun off flat concrete roofs that would otherwise transmit the oppressive summer heat into already stuffy interiors—do little to disguise the effects of humidity and neglect. While one repercussion of the historic conservation effort has been the increased value of properties now made suitable for tourist occupancy, the selective and partial nature of this benefit heightens the despair and anger of the less fortunate.

Humidity is perhaps the houses' greatest enemy, not only because of the direct damage it does, but because its effects on the inhabitants' health engender an intense dislike of the houses themselves. Colds, influenza, and arthritis abound. The encroaching sea is ever close to the surface; live eels were found under the foundations of one house, while the salt of the winter spume is carried by violent winds into the heart of the Old Town, discoloring the whitewash and creating a preference for plain plaster or tile surfaces.[13] Even in the summer heat, the smell of mold is rarely absent; in winter, water often glistens on the blotched paintwork and stains the remaining wooden floors. Even the few new buildings are not immune; the old ones almost all leak badly. When the first refugees from Asia Minor arrived, the Turks whose houses they were taking over told them always to wear woolen underwear as the only real protection against the damp; and a few men still wear the heavy woolen jodhpurs (čilotes) and high village boots in winter, less for traditionalist reasons than because this clothing provides real insulation. For the old, especially, the Old Town is cruelly unhealthy, and many are too poor to move out and too proud to allow even their own children to help.

HOUSES AND RENTS

Some people never manage to become house owners in the Old Town. One man told me that he had lived there for thirty-three years, first in his father's (rented) house and then, for ten years until 1982, in his own. Finally, the damp and his own financial solvency served as the stick and carrot of his departure; he bought a five-room apartment on high ground in the New Town for some 3.15 million drachmas, a value that increased to 10.5 million drachmas in a mere five years. Once one can afford to move, the investment is excellent. Another man who bought a *garsoniera* in a seaside apartment block for 545,000 drachmas in 1984 calculated that in three years its value rose to 3 million drachmas. Had he invested the money in the bank at the highest annual compound interest rate of 21 percent instead, he would have ended up with a mere 420,501 drachmas in accrued interest; the standard rate (19 percent) would have given him only 373,412 drachmas. According to the figure one regards as significant, then, in three short years he had increased the value of his investment by seven or eight times the amount he would have earned in interest from the bank. He was one of the luckier citizens.

The most fortunate of all are those who bought such seaside properties before World War II, at a value of one barrel of oil per kilometer strip. These "bad grooms" (*kači ghambri*)—that is, men who were not thought to be a good catch—were said to be "building a house on the sand!" This remark expressed their poverty as much as the apparent unreality of their ambitions. They planted short-term domestic crops—onions, cabbages, tomatoes—and lived, rather desperately, for the moment. But with the advent of tourism, these scraggly beachside properties suddenly acquired enormous value. Property prices shot upward, owners exchanged their land for plush modern apartments through *andiparokhi* (a device that also allowed the descendants of the original purchasers not to give up "ancestral" property), and agriculture all but disappeared from the coastal strip adjoining the Old Town. For those who did not profit from this sudden boom, however, New Town property values are a moving (and accelerating) train; and increasingly the old and destitute are being left ever further behind in the Old Town.

Even in the Old Town, rents have risen sharply (see Appendix). Until the economic boom of the late 1970s, renters included poorer young village couples seeking a foothold in the town and lonely old people unable or reluctant to impose upon close family for lodging. With the advent of tourism, however, rent levels began to jump in huge increments, leaving behind only the dampest and most dilapidated properties. The gap between rich and poor suddenly widened; the wealthier Old Town merchants became absentee landlords of rental properties, working nearby in the daytime but returning to the comparative luxury of their new apartments every evening. The rent on a seafront restaurant went from 48,000 drachmas to 200,000 drachmas in one year (1986–1987).

A baker's family had lived for years in the Old Town in a house much afflicted with damp but boasting one of the prized courtyards that are so cool and tree-shaded in summer. They paid 10,000 drachmas a month for seven rooms—a remarkably cheap arrangement that allowed them to live almost next door to their bakery. Suddenly, the fairly wealthy owner decided upon renovation; rather than wait for the historic conservation office to help, he obtained permission and shouldered all the expenses himself. The building has now become a very smart set of "studio apartments" for tourists, leased through a travel agency and therefore costing the owner minimal effort. The baker might have been able to seek protection in the courts but preferred to avoid a major quarrel.

Making a virtue of (social) necessity, then, he decided that this was a good time to move his home to the New Town. He could now at least set against the expense both a more secure investment and freedom from the noisome humidity. His attempt, however, almost ended in disaster. Having contracted to pay 4.5 million drachmas for the new apartment, he learned that his application for a loan had been rejected. He only escaped bankruptcy when his retired sister and his wife's childless brother—both relatively flexible financially because of their particular situations—advanced him a total of 2.5 million drachmas. Moving into the modern world of the New Town fortunately does not mean leaving behind the nexus of kinship obligations and support of an older life-style; often, as in this case, it would be impossible without that network.

But it was also his continuing sense of neighborliness that prevented him from suing for rights of occupancy. As a relatively poor artisan-merchant, he could not wholly escape the social order of the old district—an order that no longer interested his absentee landlord—even as he moved to the new. The same held true for an extremely wealthy landowner who wanted to maintain a small shop in the core of the Old Town. Although he found the *fivefold* rent increase ludicrous, he remarked, "I, too, do not want to quarrel, and [so] I shall leave." He would not have made himself very popular locally by protesting too much. Local ethics frown on any interference in the profiteering of fellow citizens, especially by someone who is on the verge of inheriting properties from which he may benefit just as much.

Renting out houses in the Old Town has been a major source of income throughout most of this century and well into the 1970s. Only the advent of mass tourism transformed its character. The possibility of renting was the key to the logic whereby Rethemniots saw investment in houses as a safeguard against the radical corrosion of currency inflation. Every Rethemniot household head, moreover, desired above all else to become residentially independent. In that enviable state, he could then cultivate his house "like a field"—that is, as a source of further earnings through rental fees. There were always young apprentices from the villages who could be crammed into these tiny houses, several to a room, their cooking done on a *parasčios* (a metal frame set over a communal fire in the old stone hearth. The various branches of the bureaucracy, the schools, and the police all provided grander custom. Rethemniots who had no room to spare still owned solid pieces of property that, if they did not accrue much value until the 1970s, at least did not depreciate either.

Indeed, until the advent of tourism, Rethemnos was not a lively real estate market. Those who wanted to make a fast profit went elsewhere, notably to Athens. An example will show how such opportunities arose. During the difficult days of World War II, a young man went from village to village as an itinerant merchant (*yirologhos*), his donkey laden with bales of cloth. Upon the cessation of hostilities, he decided to settle in town. He paid rent on a coffee shop (at 300 drachmas a month then) on one of the two main commercial thoroughfares. Gradually he was able to accumulate a considerable sum in savings; by his own estimate, he purchased about twenty gold sovereigns at the post–World War II price of 175 drachmas apiece. The 1956 monetary reform of Papagos and Markezinis raised the value of the gold sovereign to 316 drachmas—and the young man shot off to Athens, over his wife's protests, "so the plots of land wouldn't have time to get expensive." And there he has remained ever since, returning each year only to spend the hot summers months in a rented room in his old Rethemnos haunts, away from the noise and pollution of the capital. His children take their summer vacations abroad and insistently invite him to accompany them; but he, unlike them, still enjoys the bonds of memory with the place from which his financial acumen severed their most immediate links.

The wealthiest families have all moved out of the Old Town. Rich and poor alike, the emigrants either—like the enterprising young merchant—sought their fortunes in Athens or, from about 1970 on, took advantage of the sudden development of the New Town. In these more recent stages, renting out properties has become both commoner and more profitable. But this threatens the autonomy of the poor with no properties of their own. Elderly people who have so far preferred to remain independent of their children may be forced to accept their hospitality.[14] Merchants like the baker just discussed, who keep their overhead expenses low in part by paying low rent on their homes, eventually aim to move to the New Town; but they would prefer to do so in a condition of solvency.

Laws protect squatters' rights. Although there has been an extraordinary escalation of rent prices in the past decade, those who have rented properties over long periods of time find themselves at a great advantage. This is especially true of the commercial areas, where shop rents have increased much faster than house prices. A merchant may be forced to retire in order to qualify for his pension; in such a case, the rental agreement may be transferred to his wife's name, and this is the owner's one opportunity to push the price up significantly—provided, of course, that the landlord's avarice does not cause the rent to outweigh the merchant's pension.

Poorer Rethemniots who have managed to jump aboard the tourist bandwagon are especially dependent on good rental arrangements for their premises. An artisan who in 1987 made at most 55,000 drachmas a month paid a comparatively cheap monthly rent of 7,000 drachmas.

Since he could sell his simple artifacts to tourists only during the season from May through September, however, his total annual rent exceeded 30 percent of his overall untaxed profit. Moreover, he is scared of expanding his business; as he pointed out, if he were to purchase new equipment, it would almost certainly attract the unwelcome attention of the tax authorities, who base their estimates of income as much on outward appearances as on declared earnings. Under these distinctly confining circumstances, any significant increase in his rent will be disastrous, even allowing for whatever he can earn as a winter laborer or through the sale of marginal agricultural produce. Many merchants preferred to buy small shops in good locations rather than face the dramatic rise in rents. One butcher, for example, paid 130,000 drachmas for a tiny house, which he then plastered and decorated himself. It is on the edge of what is now one of the tourist centers of the Old Town and represents a solid investment for the future, while he has built himself a new house outside the town as well and moved his family from the cramped upper floor of the old house into their new home. Those who were too late to make such moves, like those who failed to relocate to the New Town when affordable apartments were still to be found there (and they are often the same people), have now similarly been left hopelessly and irretrievably behind.

With these encroachments of the larger economic system on the local preserve, purely financial and bureaucratic reasoning tends to replace more immediately social considerations. Some businesses—coffeehouses are a good example—once served a social as much as a commercial function for their owners. Today, such concerns are ever harder to sustain; the social capital they once conferred is no longer so readily convertible into economic or political advantage. A childless and otherwise unemployed souvlaki shop manager and his wife, for example, maintained their little establishment, a pleasant and unredecorated old house with a well-preserved arch window as frontage, as a way for the wife—who did not have the option of whiling away the hours in the male domain of the coffee shop—to entertain herself better than she could within the confines of their New Town apartment. In 1987, they were barely breaking even. When I offered to write them out an English-language sign to attract tourists, the wife's enthusiasm was immediately tempered by the fear that this hint of bigger takings to come might induce the landlord to increase the rent still further. She suggested waiting a few days, as they had an appeal pending before a rent tribunal.

In response to the owner's increasingly exigent demands, they had offered to pay a 50 percent increase in the rent (to 18,000 drachmas a month), thinking that for him this might be an attractive alternative to spending legal fees on trying to secure an even higher amount or forcing them out of the building. The owner, however, pointed out that some properties in the same street were fetching as much as 100,000 drachmas. Apparently the case was not resolved to the souvlaki seller's satisfaction, and within two years he had moved out to make way for yet another clothing boutique. His tactic had been no more successful than that of the coffee shop proprietor who sought to keep his taxes low by removing the eye-catching drinks display he had hitherto used to impress his customers. Comparisons are always dangerous. Those who use them to argue for lower taxes, for example, may do themselves no good and may actually be hurting their neighbors in the longer term. This is because the tax authorities simply raise the valuation of *both* properties on the next round.

Forcing rents up faster and faster are increasing numbers of non-Rethemniots. Three Athenian partners rented a building on the seaside esplanade and turned the front section into a fashionable cafeteria, while the back part, which faced the main market street, became an expensive jewelry shop. No Rethemniot merchant was willing to pay the rent, rumored (in 1987) to be an astronomical 160,000 drachmas (slightly over $1,000) per month. The intrusion of nonlocal merchants, beginning in the earliest stages of the tourist development, provides nostalgic traditionalists with a face-saving explanation for the social anomie they perceive around them. These people, they claim, do not respect the old values. It is they who are to blame for the breakdown of the old reciprocities, the unconditionally offered hospitality that marks the image of an idealized Cretan past.

Whatever the truth of such charges, the fact is that rents are climbing very rapidly. For those who find their own houses uninhabitable but cannot obtain permission quickly enough to rebuild or renovate them, and especially for those who are too poor to buy quarters of their own, dogged refusal to move from rented quarters is the only alternative to the final erosion of their miserable savings. But this angers the rentiers, who not only constitute a growing proportion of the population but whose expectations of rapid wealth have fed on the tourist boom. While current laws do protect tenants' rights, the fear of eviction is never wholly allayed, and the tourists, who are the partial cause of this pressure, have become increasingly associated with the disenfranchisement of the very traditionality that they have come to seek (cf. Greger 1988:115). The goose that laid the golden egg is under the knife.

This discussion of the housing situation in the Old Town has linked my central theme with some of the larger economic patterns that have affected the Rethemniots' lives. It is now time to turn to their own ways of constructing economic reality, and to relate these to their attitudes toward the state bureaucracy. In this chapter, we have already seen that the houses are a locus of struggle between men and women for symbolic domination. They are also the focal point for a similar struggle between citizens and state. The economic appreciation of these houses has vastly exacerbated such tensions. Capital does not immediately permeate people's consciousness so that they adopt a common bureaucratic rationalism. On the contrary, their own alternative rationality recasts the relationship between themselves and the state in ways that are quite alien to official thinking. These perspectives channel and direct the reading, and rebuilding, of local history.

Chapter Five

GAMBLERS AND USURERS

Englobing Precision: An Archaeology of Social Knowledge

Bureaucracy is often in conflict with social values in Rethemniot life. While different segments of the national bureaucracy have different histories, and while all bureaucrats are drawn from the wider society, the very idea of bureaucracy engenders expectations that materially affect individual actions and decisions. Bureaucracy presents a highly inflexible face to its clients, yet its practices encompass extensive variation and reinterpretation. Its clients, conversely, deploy the legalistic trappings of bureaucracy in pursuit of their personal ends.[1]

This ambiguous tension appears in the Rethemniots' contrasted cultural models of economic interaction, as also in arguments about the conservation of the Old Town. The contest over whether the houses are "Turkish" (*tourkospita*) or Venetian[2] parallels the contrast of bazaar and regulated market. In both domains, idealizations of the familiar and "Oriental" vie with the formal and "Western." Here, however, the archaeology is conceptual rather than architectural, the counter-archaeology of social knowledge that I suggested in chapter 1.

Conceptual excavation reveals the close relationship between the politics of everyday life and the larger national and regional battles over cultural and economic resources. It shows how stereotypical cultural images rationalize relations of power from the most localized to the near-global, and how they adapt to meet changes in these relations. Above all, it illustrates the penetration of daily experience by hegemonic systems of cultural classification.[3]

The premise of economic (or indeed any other kind of numerical) precision suggests the formal—and, to most Greeks, stereotypically "cold"—character of "European" culture. Real social life, by contrast, appears much more "Oriental." It is characterized by economic practices for which the ordinary terms are all recognized as Turkish-derived: *pazari* ("bargaining," literally, "bazaar"—note the similar implications of the English-language etymological cognate—or "market"), *vereses* ("credit," for which the neo-Classical Greek term *pistosi[s]* is only used in connection with formal bank transactions), and *koumari* ("gambling"; the official equivalents are cumbersomely formal). The practices so labeled all conflict with official norms and with the calibration of Greek culture to the classicizing cultural canons of Western Europe. They are, however, the most familiar and even the most morally acceptable in daily life. Even bureaucrats—who are human too—recognize that engaging with perceived social realities is as crucial as getting their paperwork exactly right. Orient and Occident, practice and theory: the very polarity of these terms attests both to the power of Eurocentric cultural models and to the resistance that they encounter in Rethemniot social life.

Rethemniots adopt a pose of studied indifference to the demands of numerical precision or bureaucratic exactitude. This has important consequences for economic relations. It runs directly counter to the bureaucratic insistence on financial and legal exactitude. Wholly irrelevant to this official economism (cf. Bourdieu 1977:172) is the economy of manners—the canon of simplicity among the rich, the emphasis on social rather than financial capital among the poor—to which local people accord such importance.

Precision furnishes a rhetoric of power. Bureaucrats can wield statistics because their professional status leads to this expectation. Citizens are often actively averse to arithmetical scrutiny. Exactitude, traditionally a lure for the evil eye of jealousy, also attracts the more calculating attentions of the tax or conservation official. The very act of enumeration can be a solecism among ordinary folks, rich and (especially) poor.

The poor "englobe" (Ardener 1975:25) the social values of the wealthy. Significant economic wealth, although sometimes itself a means to social ends, imposes greater obligations. A comparatively wealthy male should treat his friends more generously in the coffeehouse and elsewhere, be good for more loans, ignore minor debts, and rise above petty attention to the details of short change or insufficient weight in the shops he frequents. In fact, wealthier people are noticeably less insouciant in these matters than poorer citizens, a fact that places their affectations of "simplicity" in question. The poor must compensate for their lack of material wealth by gaining social credit in the community. As a result, the wealthy often end up seeming a good deal less attentive to social morality than do the poor, and their economic advantages—which make them a more visible target for criticism—only serve to highlight their social failures. Poor people see themselves as the repository of those social values of reciprocity, mutual respect, and high-minded disdain for mere money that they believe the wealthy to have abandoned. How else, indeed, did the latter *become* wealthy? This is a logical question in a community where no one concedes the inherent superiority of any other person, and it suggests a defensive aspect to the pose of simplicity among the wealthy that the latter do not easily concede.

In all daily economic relations, and more particularly in those illegal domains where the state's authority is challenged and ridiculed, the acquisition of social capital is a more potent determinant of daily actions than direct economic calculation. It is true that social capital may be invested in the pursuit of purely material ends (though the reverse can apply no less frequently), and that the capitalist, bureaucratic state makes economic morality the touchstone of social value. For residents, however, the more operative concern is with a morality that encapsulates, but is not driven by, the economic—a morality in which the very logic of quantification is opportunistically denied even though its dictates are pragmatically pursued. Rethemniots are far from indifferent to economic advantage—their erstwhile poverty and the desire never to return to it are constant themes in conversation—but they know that its pursuit makes bad social rhetoric and undercuts itself. The social calculus requires that actors carefully perform noncalculation.

Any account of economic relations must therefore recognize the practical effects of the social rhetoric. It would be wholly artificial to separate the economic from other dimensions of the clash between the bureaucracy and social life. Moreover, it makes little sense to ask whether, for example, gambling should be seen as primarily an economic, a symbolic, or a gender-related activity; or whether the extension of credit and concepts of neighborliness can realistically be treated as discrete. What we see in all these and many other domains is the reluctance of local actors to accept the regulation of social relations by the bureaucracy. At one level, this is simply a recognition that modern commercial behavior is "spiritually alienating," as a retired bookseller expressed it. At another level, however, this high valuation of amiable roguery and haggling incorporates a sense of the practical advantages to be lost when control passes to the agencies of state. The reaction to governmental regulation of the historic urban environment will make better sense if we first examine some of the economic areas in which bureaucratic ideals of precision clash with the locals' studied inattention to exactness of any sort.

Imprecision is clearly understood to be a calculating strategy in its own right, and the possibilities for bluff and counterbluff are legion. The assumption, too, of a studied indifference to financial gain may mask an intent understanding of the best strategies for achieving *social* gain. Beginning with an ethnographic account of bargaining practices, we shall examine the rhetorical premise of imprecision in other economic modes as well: begging, gambling, cheating, and tax evasion. While they vary in several respects, they share the main characteristic of conflicting with the official social ethos and economic ideology. They are thus markers for a non-Classical ("Romeic") social order and serve to mark the intimate sociability of (especially) men in a sinful world.[4] When discovered in representatives of the cultural canon—in bureaucrats and politicians (who should know better because they are the bearers of the official ideology), or in West Europeans (who should know better because they claim to have inherited the mantle of Hellenic civilization)—all such domestically endearing traits become the object of public scorn and contempt.

Bargaining: Pazari as Ideology and Style ~~Chiseling~~

Bargaining is an ideal example with which to initiate this discussion. While the term *pazari* is an "Oriental" one, the usual double meaning of bargaining in several Middle Eastern cultures—both as locus of social relations and as economic practice (e.g., Geertz 1979; Rosen 1984)—is replaced here by a double *terminology*.[5] The obviously "Greek" (i.e., Classical) word *aghora* means physical marketplace as well as the imagined spaces of grand commerce. *Pazari*, by contrast, ever furtive and nomadic, has no place on the official map; but it is omnipresent in social life.

In some contexts, bargaining is not only acceptable but even, on occasion, socially mandatory. Technically, it always conflicts with the police regulation of prices. Although people associate it with a time of great poverty, there is a certain nostalgia for the days before the market police regulated all transactions. On the other hand, merchants recall much less fondly the kinds of pressure that social intimates could exert. One merchant actually claimed that kinship was a less precious bond than friendship because kin are especially likely to take advantage of the relationship.

It is in certain restricted and seemingly traditional areas of sale, or where the illegality of the transaction itself precludes legal inspection, that we find bargaining as a general practice. Here, however, it is often the expected mode. When borrowing money from a usurer, for example, one should expect to bargain over the interest rates. Any failure to pay up immediately will put the usurer in a stronger position, and the rate will go up accordingly. The profession of usurer is nowadays illegal and must be "fronted" by a more respectable identity (of its two practitioners, one is a goldsmith, the other a wholesale grocer). While this circumscribes the usurer's own ability to haggle, it also, paradoxically, means that usurer and customer can exercise some degree of control over each other. In a social milieu to which the law is intrusive, defaulting on such illegal contractual relations can do more lasting harm to a reputation than can any infraction of state law.

All mass-produced goods are subject to tight price controls. The market police are vigilant. Their agents keep surreptitious watch from half-hidden doorways in the hope of catching merchants at the moment of overcharging, just as tax inspectors may waylay unsuspecting out-of-town visitors in the hope of finding some irregularity in the receipts they have been given by local merchants. While illegal credit may be given to facilitate purchase, illegally low prices are easier to detect, and the alleged strictness of the regulations and their enforcement provides the merchant with a ready-made excuse to charge the correct, higher prices. This works against bargaining as much as it does against cheating. One area in which bargaining may occur is in the purchase of relatively small quantities of village produce (which is also a potential domain for cheating on tax declarations), and this notably affects the very commonplace sale of grappa to coffeehouses and to shops that need to have a little ready hospitality to hand. A tourist goods merchant who particularly resents the importunate haggling of foreigners saw nothing incongruous in fighting down the price of twenty-six kilos of grappa from 200 drachmas per kilo to 165 by offering 145. His grappa is not for sale. It is, on the contrary, kept for the purpose of demonstrating stereotypical "Cretan hospitality" to his customers. As such, it serves as both an act of kindness and a lure. It makes any attempt to bargain with this man seem as small-minded as failure to buy his goods.

Bargaining carries intimations of reciprocity, price regulation only the impersonal ethos of the supermarket. The tourist goods merchant just mentioned particularly approved of the Finns, who alone of all foreigners never tried to bargain his prices down. In local deals, by contrast, acts of hospitality are not perceived as a one-way street: they are part of the bargaining itself, and it is appropriate that a round of grappa—a local drink, often illegally produced and rarely available commercially—should itself mark the conclusion of a bargain. Unlike the local customer whose economic exchanges with the merchant are part of a larger social pattern, the foreigner can only reciprocate hospitality by accepting the merchant's prices. Locally, friends haggle; foreigners who haggle are not friends.

Once, a German woman wanted to buy a string of worry beads (*komboloi*) from the same merchant. She asked the price and was told it was 220 drachmas. "One hundred sixty!" she responded. The merchant, refusing, began to gather up the bunch of komboloya and put it back, but then, as though hesitating, offered her a price of 200 drachmas. She countered with 190 drachmas. The merchant at first refused; then, as she moved away, he shrugged his shoulders, ignored my rather feeble offer to mediate, and handed it to her. He afterward contemptuously remarked, "*Deutsch!*" Here was an ironic reversal of stereotypes: the Cretan merchant, perhaps still mindful of the rapacious German wartime occupation of Crete, rejecting a West European tourist's "Oriental" behavior.

Bargaining style involves a wide range of poses—above all, that of indifference to mere gain. In this, it illustrates a general principle of informal economic relations in Rethemnos. If one has something to sell, one may affect great indifference to the very possibility of selling it. One young man, for example, espied a potential renter of a suburban property he owned. He immediately ducked out of sight because, as he explained, he did not want to seem too eager. It was this tactic that the tourist goods merchant used with his German customer as the pretext for his contemptuous "capitulation."

Ordinary friendship provides a framework for interpreting outsiders' attitudes. In one tourist shop, a conscript serving locally came to buy souvenirs; then he returned a second time, apparently having liked the shopkeeper. The latter was so pleased with the conscript's straightforward purchase and avoidance of bargaining—though, as he pointed out, a conscript has no money and would have been within his moral rights had he tried to get a better price for himself—that he charged him 1,700 instead of 1,730 drachmas. This was a small but symbolically important difference. The shopkeeper observed that the conscript had not bargained because now they were "friends." "That's how friends are created," he noted, conflating cause and effect. Bargaining is incompatible with friendship in those transitory visitors, especially foreign tourists, who do not belong to the local market structures. Among insiders, by contrast, it is virtually commensurate with both the creation and the content of social relations among non-kin and rests on a degree of mutual respect and trust (cf. also Rosen 1984:136).

Rethemniots treat bargaining as characteristic of older times, when local culture had not become so "European" and state-dominated. Bargaining is a positive virtue when it entails resistance to the state—for example, as a means of reducing the taxable amount—but becomes evil in a foreigner who uses it to treat the locals as unequal partners and who is insensitive to the past hardships of which it reminds them. Indeed, the moral ambivalence of bargaining has historical as well as contemporary dimensions. Speaking of the years before World War II, Rethemniots mention bargaining as one of the discomforts of those tough times.

Thus, for example, they like to tell of houses roofed over with *lepidha*, a locally produced gravel that had to be replaced on a yearly basis. Inconvenience, the "primitive" past, and the taint of oriental business practices come together in this image of what Rethemniots no longer want to be. The lepidha was brought from the nearby villages of Prine and Aryiroupoli by those villagers fortunate enough to have *lepidholakki* (lepidha pits) on their properties and was sold in the Four Martyrs' Square out in the open. Villagers and townspeople, while sharing a fairly precise notion of what the price should be, nonetheless went through the motions of bargaining each and every time. This bargaining was unrelated to considerations of quality and had to do instead with the size of the sacks, for which there were two basic prices (20 drachmas and 25 drachmas; or, at an earlier time, 25 drachmas a pair). Although these prices were relatively stable, and despite the absence of real qualitative differences, pazari was considered essential to the transaction. Negotiability in all things social, including money, was a means of expressing and creating intimate relationships.

In bargaining, Greeks relegate themselves to a denigrated, orientalized past.[6] It is categorically not something that "Europeans" do. That Greeks do it nonetheless is a categorical flaw from the official perspective, a mark of retarded cultural development. For actors, by contrast, most bargaining—like informal credit and other appurtenances of the informal economy—is familiar and acceptable. It stands in contrast to the "alienation" that the formality of modern economic relations entails. A pharmacist with big plans for local development warned that people who started to rely on banks and similar institutions would find themselves entrapped by unfamiliar laws and practices.

So bargaining, viewed from the inside, marks the genuinely social person. It also provides a means of displaying a degree of cunning and skill, and life's losers get little sympathy. A man who had taken advantage of a bankrupt embezzler's plight to get his house at a low price announced with pride, "We bargained it down (to *pazarepsame*)!" Bargaining nevertheless evokes a sense of moral ambivalence, as when a merchant of tourist goods ruefully observed that bargaining was a key feature of the "Greek *mentalité*." (His use of a French term announces a "European" sophistication that places him in a judgmental position.) In his view, a Greek customer is not satisfied unless he can force the merchant to lower the price by means of pazari. "People don't have the so-called consumer mentality," he observed, adding that poverty—another negative image from the despised past—also encouraged haggling; but he also noted that changes in the local economy, primarily through the advent of "Saint Tourism," are inducing a more bureaucratic attitude toward monetary matters.

The association of bargaining with cultural inferiority is most clearly seen in the relations between townspeople and itinerant Gypsies, who frequently comb the narrow streets hawking their wares in strident calls rich with the accents of the rural Greek mainland. Throughout Greece, Gypsies are often treated as racially and culturally inferior beings. Because the Gypsy vendors' sole economic advantage is their willingness to offer prices uninflated by storekeepers' rents and overheads, townspeople associate them with bargaining as a matter of course. The townspeople also regard the Gyspies as thieves who will take every opportunity to cheat and deceive. They easily find moral solace in their fears for forcing the itinerants' prices down. They also often torment the vendors with illusory hopes of big sales by pretending to engage in haggling with them.

Thus, for example, a housewife had encountered some Gypsy women selling rugs and carpets, one of the commonest items of the itinerant trade. She did also buy a basin and small pail of plastic, but the main social interest of the encounter for the local housewife lay in the eagerness of one of the vendors to sell her a relatively expensive carpet. The Gypsy woman had wanted 5,000 drachmas for a rug that the housewife thought might do for everyday use; she first offered her 3,000 drachmas for it, which was indignantly declined. She and her husband then scared the Gypsy woman away by saying that a man who happened to pass by at that moment was from the Tax Office (which he was not) but then sent a little girl after her to offer her 3,200. Refusing this final offer, the Gypsy left for good. The housewife's final judgment: the rug might have been a reasonable buy at 2,000 drachmas. In other words, she did not have the slightest intention of buying the rug at all and simply engaged in the bargaining encounter to amuse herself at the vendor's expense; the latter clearly perceived that she was being teased, especially when the local woman returned to the attack after first scaring her away.

Ragging Gypsy vendors is a popular activity among Rethemniot women. Often, the locals offer outrageously low prices just for fun, though there seems to be a perception that in former times the Gypsy vendors were more gullible or at least had to make do with poorer customers. The local woman remarked that when a vendor had tried to sell her a towel set for 1,400 drachmas and she had offered 500 drachmas, the Gypsy had turned her down flat, and another of the neighborhood women remarked, "They've 'woken up,' eh?"—a term (*ksipnao*) associated with "intelligence" (*eksipnadha*), and specifically with self-liberation. The use of the term here seems to imply some recognition of the Gypsies' disadvantaged condition, and of the Greeks' exploitative treatment of them to date.

Perhaps the toughest negotiating of all takes place among local women who know each other. This is a dangerous game, because there is always the risk of giving irrevocable offense to neighbors or kin, and these women are adept at the diplomatic fencing that such fears engender. A young divorcée made a small additional income by selling silk embroideries from Macedonia. She approached a neighbor woman: "My little Mrs. Yannoula [Little Yanna], what'll you 'write down' [i.e., order] from me? A little *seme* [a kind of decorative runner]?" The wheedling use of diminutives, especially in conjunction with the honorific "Mrs." (*kiria*), did not move the prospective customer, who remarked to me that her daughter—whose trousseau would be the only likely destination for such items—did not even like them. The agent tried again, now emphasizing female solidarity at the level of domestic economics—"you who hold the all-good-accounting-book!" And she added, in a tone of exasperated entreaty, the familiar, Turkish-derived exhortation, "*Ade* (come *on*)!" To this transparent appeal, the prospect replied by switching to a formal code (polite plural) and peremptory tone toward her neighbor and friend: "Nothing doing! I've told you [that]!" Her usage, with its subtle threat of social rupture, placed the responsibility squarely on the other woman's shoulders and so brought the uncomfortable discussion to an end.

Among neighbor women, who usually control their daily household budgets, this kind of economic behavior is not necessarily disapproved. It is, however, only appropriate to situations of relative intimacy. Women usually play only a minimal role in public business.[7] Foreigners who attempt to bargain with shop staff, who are often women, are thus violating their status as outsiders and claiming a gender-marked intimacy to which they are not entitled. Since most come from European countries, their adoption of an orientalizing stance is also condescending. Viewed in these terms, their attitude is not an attractive one.

Pervasive Values: Precision against Social Life

Excessive precision is also opposed to practical learning. It is not part of the immediate social environment but belongs instead to the encompassing formalism of the state. At least one merchant (a seller of shoes and other leather goods) complains that the obsession with precise accounting is also increased by the current condition of the national economy: inflation reduces people's willingness to take risks—that is, to barter social capital for material. While this might seem paradoxical in a society where formerly people preferred to invest in real estate rather than place their money in the care of banks, it suggests that the penetration of social mores by the industrial economy has left those lacking real estate property, but possessing newly acquired monetary wealth, desperate for every drachma's worth of faint security.

The "humbler" and more "un-European" the context, the more probably will the actors evoke an attitude of economic carelessness that actually increases the likelihood of acquiring the paltry but much-needed profits anticipated from the situation. A fairly extreme example will illustrate the point. A former municipal road sweeper, a man of low social status whose misfortunes have been exacerbated since retirement by increasing lameness, collects empty plastic detergent bottles from local housewives all over the Old Town and sells them to paint stores and other retailers of liquid goods. He stores them in what was once the house of his destitute mother, where she had lived "in anxiety . . . a stinking place." He pays nothing for the containers, reciprocating charity with a humiliating courtesy that requires him to say, "I don't mind if I do" (*dhe me niazi na paro*), and he is always extremely careful not to let others who see him at this degrading task rile him too much. He may even lie to the uninitiated and say that he has filled them with lamp oil (*petreleo*) for his own use: "I don't want to give anyone grounds [i.e., to deride me]." When he gets to his customers, he either sells them the bottles at 2 drachmas each or sells a large collection of them for as much as 160 drachmas. In the latter case he sells them koutourou—that is, without counting them exactly. (This informal term is conceptually opposed to "specific things" [singe-krimena pramata], as in the conveying of information through measured and precise speech.)

It would not do for such a man to appear too calculating, since his ability to maintain his tenuous source of earnings depends on a fine balance on the very edge of social acceptability. In his dealings with suppliers and customers alike, he must perpetually maintain a respectful mien. Any attempt on his part to demand precise payment would provoke derision and, probably, the end of the whole enterprise. His precarious economic survival depends on equally precarious social skills. At best, he can express his anger only indirectly, through light sarcasm that again mocks his humble origins; when people tease him for this activity, he replies that he does it "for his [lame] leg" or "to recall his profession [of road sweeper]." In cringing beggary on the outer edges of a cruel modern economy, he must totter dangerously between a social pose of indifference to gain and the practical necessity of bowing and scraping for it.

The converse of this is that a man who can afford to disdain precision when it comes to claiming the small change due to him is his own boss (*afendiko*). He is thus much freer than those unfortunate supermarket drudges who, significantly like bureaucrats in this regard, must account for every drachma to their employers. Being poor but independent legally allows him even now to do a far less painstaking tax accounting than would be necessary if his gross income (*tziros*) were over 6 million drachmas annually. It also gives him social status in the Old Town that only material wealth of a very substantial kind could effectively replace. Equally free is the man who can make grand gestures with small sums. One bar owner took 250 drachmas instead of the 300 drachmas he was entitled to for our six glasses of grappa, on the grounds that we were now "daily [regulars]." Another took my 500-drachma note saying it covered my kerasma, although technically I owed 540 drachmas; he had also treated a round himself, even though in other matters he was a man of notorious stinginess and avarice who charged unsuspecting tourists much higher prices than he dared ask of locals.

Nonchalant imprecision is the very stuff of which good social relations are made. It also, not so incidentally, can make for material advantages. One specialty baker, for example, makes a point of adding scraps of pas-

try to whatever his less fussy—and, of course, regular—customers purchase. Those who complain and force him to cut off pieces of pastry because the weight has gone slightly over what they requested, by contrast,
enjoy no such favors. By accepting their pedantic parsimony to the letter,
he deprives them of small but, over a long period of commercial transaction, far from insignificant gains. If one buys his pastry for a hotel restaurant, for example, the profit of those useful scraps can be considerable.
When a customer forces him to cut off any surplus, it becomes scrap material that is in fact only suitable for such gifts, so the pedantic customers
end up paying for those whose attitudes are more social.

One woman habitually asks for "50 drachmas' worth," which, given
that 200 grams comes to 52 drachmas, makes exact calibration difficult.
When the baker's wife gives her 200 grams, she replies, with a whining,
rising intonation that the baker's wife scornfully mimicked for me, "*But*
it's too much! *But* I don't want it!" The baker's wife calls this woman
parakseni—"strange," but in the sense that she is so far beyond the pale
that she behaves worse than an outsider (kseni) would. Since, however,
she is a regular, some finesse is needed in resisting her more importunate
demands. On one occasion, she showed up after church and demanded
400 grams on credit, having not brought her money with her. The baker
was able to refuse on the grounds that he had not yet made any money
(*šeftes*) that day—the implication being that, according to custom, it
would be unlucky for him to give credit on the day's first purchase.

Such an awkward customer may be rare, but the reactions to her behavior are interesting for that very reason. They show how strongly the
attention to precise reckoning repels more "social" Rethemniots. (The
baker is particularly well known locally for his honesty and sociability,
and takes pride in the fact that, although poor, he is in debt to no one:
"In the marketplace I am not embarrassed.") What especially irritates the
baker and his wife is that the woman invariably makes a fuss about the
exact weight. Once, when she complained that the baker had given her
less than she had asked for, he derisively replied, "You'll have some left
over (*tha perissepsi*)!" And he grumbled that she always, impossibly,
wanted the quantities to come out just right.

The fussy customer represents what the poorer people of the Old Town
regard as typical behavior for the wealthy. This is the sort of thing that
makes nonsense of those grand pretensions of simplicity. Curiously, but
quite logically, it is in fact the poor who can least afford to fuss about
exact weights and prices, because they are more dependent than the
wealthy on being able to accumulate the relatively intangible benefits of
social capital. The former road sweeper represents an extreme, since he
has little or no material wealth with which to fill out the social capital
and must therefore depend on the latter all the more abjectly. But even in

more comfortable surroundings, the premise of poverty always seems to go hand in hand with that of inattention to precise calculation. Those who are wealthy, it seems, can afford to rise above this social convention. Local merchants complain that it is often the comparatively rich who watch their purchases being weighed with hawk eyed attention. In commercial relations among the poor, insouciance about money counts for a great deal. Even a relatively wealthy coffeehouse proprietor thought he might join a general strike because otherwise people would say he cared about money. Indeed he does, and that is just the point: he cannot afford to have this said about him if money is what he intends to go on making.

If the daily rhetoric of imprecision thus masks a certain degree of precise calculation, the converse is true of the more traditional forms of state control, especially in taxation practices. Here, the seemingly precise exercise of law is extraordinarily capricious. Until quite recently, the Tax Office more or less automatically assumed that taxable assets were always underdeclared by about half their total value and accordingly, as we saw in the last chapter, doubled the tax.

Tax assessors simply assumed that citizens would cheat on principle. Their results were as accurate as their methods were arbitrary. A baker told me, for example, that the tax people sometimes deduced that he had underdeclared his takings on the basis of their inspection of the ratio between his flour purchases and his declared sales. As citizens themselves, tax inspectors know how much they have cheated on their own taxes and project this onto others. In one building sale contract in which he was personally involved, a tax official declared the value at half of the assessment that his own office set!

Because they are social familiars, moreover, tax officials are expected to help their friends, and here again a determined imprecision conceals some precise calculation. A young couple bought a house and declared its value as 750,000 drachmas, exactly half of what they knew it to be. The tax clerk told the husband that this was an impossibly low value for a house in that area, so the house owner replied that he had bought the house at the unusually good price of 900,000 drachmas—he had taken advantage of the previous owner's bankruptcy and attendant legal difficulties—but knew that the Tax Office would assume that he had paid more and so declared a lower value. He hoped at this point that "honesty" would pay—that is, to disarm the clerk by admitting, not so much to having cheated, as to having shown a good understanding of the strategic games played by both sides. He also hoped to gain some advantage through the fact that the clerk was a local man and a personal acquaintance. The clerk, although unconvinced, offered on this basis to reduce the taxable value from thirty drachmas to twenty-eight drachmas per square meter (at 103 square meters), but the house owner did not think this was good enough and asked to see the ephor. The clerk took him in to see this mighty official, who reduced the rate a little more; the house owner believes that the ephor did so because he had come in, not protesting in anger at the outrageous rate the clerk had proposed to apply (which was in fact the legal rate), but with humble mien and pleading his poverty. The clerk knew that the owner's demand to speak to the ephor was also a way of absolving him, the clerk, of any personal responsibility and so was reciprocally willing to play the game in the hope of helping his friend.

While a very recent reform of the tax laws has introduced much more rigid criteria for the valuation of real estate—much to the annoyance of most inhabitants—the system just described was in general use until 1988. At that point, the introduction of Value Added Tax (V.A.T.) and the abolition of the old assessment system caused some radical changes in the overall conduct of taxpayers. A coffeehouse proprietor grumbled bitterly that he would now have to provide a "piece of paper" for every trivial cup of coffee he sold, and felt embarrassed at the idea. He acknowledged that economically the new system would work to his advantage, since he would be less at the mercy of assessors' caprice, but at least in the old system he knew how to play the game. Despite their constant complaints about the assessors' inconsistency, rapacity, and general inhumanity, all the locals knew how to play this game, and so—as necessarily skilled social actors—did the tax assessors. The new system has bureaucratized a local social relationship and recast it as a purely mechanical, national one.

The rhetoric of economic imprecision is a mark of the older and economically poorer way of doing things. Those who prefer more modern drinking establishments, by contrast, seem instead to appreciate knowing what they can expect to get. The owners of such establishments rarely treat their customers; the rhetoric of hospitality is inappropriate to the setting. As townspeople become wealthier or more staid, they gravitate to these places, which fulfill their expectations of "aristocratic" standards. An old-fashioned and politically conservative merchant despised the practice of pouring out drinks in a rough-and-ready fashion, as is done at the simpler coffeehouses, and expressed a strong preference for the exact measures provided by spigoted bottles in one of the newer and more expensive places. But, once again, wealth imposes its own obligations. A pharmacist, scion of a wealthy family, finds it convenient from time to time to exchange two 5,000-drachma notes for a bag of 50-drachma coins he gets from an elderly kiosk manager (*peripteras*) whom he addresses with familiar respect as "Uncle (*Barba*)[8] George," but he does not check how exact the exchange is: "If he's going to cheat you, so be it (*khalali tou*)." (This willingness to turn a blind eye to the possibility of a poor man's profiteering contrasts instructively with the anger provoked by an extremely wealthy merchant who "loads" his prices but gets away with it because his store is so conveniently located that customers are reluctant to give him up.) The richer patrons of *both* kinds of establishment must always tip generously; a relatively well-to-do Athenian resident, originally from a village near Rethemnos, pays 50 drachmas for a cup of coffee in both his old friend's coffee shop in the Old Town (where the official price is 40 drachmas) and in a pair of grander establishments on the main boulevard, at the edge of the New Town and on the waterfront (where it is 44 drachmas). This man is quite aware of how tipping functions socially: at the latter café, he recounted, he gave the waiter a 100-drachma banknote, and the latter gave him a 50-drachma note in change, pausing briefly—as the customer recalled—to give the customer a moment to tell him to keep the rest of the change: "This is a habit of mine (*to 'kho sinithio afto*)." Tipping is so conspicuously absent from the poorer places that even proprietors with a reputation for grasping avarice invariably make a big display of returning exact change. This is admittedly not always convincing; when I told a friend that one of the coffeehouse owners had started to search rather laboriously in his pocket for some loose change, the reaction was that he had probably tried to make it *seem* as though he was trying to find the money! The effort, in any case, must be made.

The same applies in other small establishments. A baker who sold me a 155-drachma bag of tiny rusks (paksimadhakia) protested when I gave her two 100-drachma notes and a 5-drachma coin, urging me to keep the latter, but soon picked up the coin and gave me the 50-drachma note she still owed me as change. Even with larger amounts, small businesses seem to depend on the goodwill that is created in this way. When a retailer bought 1,400 drachmas' worth of specially prepared pastry, he gave the baker 1,500 drachmas and announced, "Take a thousand and a half, only your effort can never be paid for [i.e., no money can really repay the laborious hand production of filo]!" But this was from a relatively wealthy customer. Poor individuals are even more careful to exhibit disdain for mere cash: relative poverty has its rhetorical obligations, if one is going to make social capital out of claiming that one is in fact poor.

Excessive attention to the weighing of goods, for example, may provoke anger. The merchant may rhetorically ask himself, "Doesn't he trust me?" The fact is that no customer ever does, completely. "Good faith" (*embistosini*) is less a matter of belief in the merchant's innate goodness— few are so ingenuous—than of a public attitude of trust. A wholesale merchant may check the scales or an invoice with great care, but this is far less offensive than the same action by a customer. Merchants expect to cheat each other, sometimes by such simple devices as writing out the bill extremely rapidly and then announcing the total with a flourish that removes the calculation from under the victim's very nose, or by throwing rotten produce in with the good. But this is a reciprocal distrust among professionals, and the game is very different from that in which the local customer appears to suspect his neighborhood grocer or baker of defrauding him of petty sums. Also, if the challenge comes from someone who represents the profession as a whole—for example, the guild president—it can be expressed quite acerbically: "Haven't you closed down your shop yet [i.e., because your frauds have driven away all the custom]?"

Precision in economic relationships with friends, kin, and neighbors challenges ideological assumptions about equality and reciprocity, and violates the boundaries of good taste. The closer the relationship, the less easy it is to resist appeals for economic support that will not be repaid. Excessive attention to pecuniary detail also invites equally annoying attention from the authorities. In particular, reticence about exact economic gains and losses stems from a pervasive fear that such information will reach the Tax Office. Speaking of this fear of bureaucratic spying, one merchant observed, "These things are not spoken about and are not written down"—gossip and roufiania being the media of betrayal, and writing the idiom of bureaucratic condemnation. Ironically, it is the Tax Office's very devotion to precise accounting that sets it up for one kind of tax evasion. A wily, elderly merchant, a former president of the local shopkeepers' guild, told a coffeehouse proprietor who had become terrified of the new tax laws that he should not declare his total purchase of supplies at a value of 550,000 drachmas because that figure is too round (artio, "whole") and recommended 506,000 or 520,000 instead.

The policing of prices is highly arbitrary in practice, though less so today than in the days of the military junta (1967–1974). A pastry maker sold 8.30 drachmas' worth of specialty dough to a girl for 8.00 drachmas. When she left the shop, the girl was stopped by a market police official, who inspected the package and then insisted that she allow him to weigh her package in one of the shops on the main market street—the aghora, that physical location whose openly displayed prices mark it out in practical as well as ideological and terminological opposition to the furtively "Oriental" pazari, the market of the moonlighter's discourse. The law does not tolerate ignorance, and the pastry maker—a man who had hitherto maintained an existence almost impossibly balanced between social skill and legal blamelessness—could not escape its inflexible dragnet. Unbeknownst to pastry maker and customer alike, there had been a drop in the officially regulated price to 7.60 drachmas. The receipt was made out and signed in the name of the pastry maker's partner—apparently as a means of evading all responsibility—so the partner was formally charged. He protested vigorously, and the policemen began to wonder whether

they had perhaps been a little too hasty; but, in accordance with the irreversible character of Greek bureaucratic decision making, they could
not now rescind the charge order and suggested that the unfortunate partner should come back on Monday—it now being the weekend—to talk
to the officer in charge. The latter peremptorily dismissed the partner as
"the one who's been overcharging" and told him that the police had done
well to take him in. So the case went to trial.

Despite the rhetoric of impartial and predictable justice, Greek lower
courts are often capricious. As du Boulay (1974:179) has pointed out,
their overt function seems to be less the discovery of the actual sequence
of events than the settling of disputes. Theirs is a social rather than a legal
task. As such, it gives unusual force to Austin's (1975[1962]:141) analysis of judicial pronouncements ("verdictives"), for it is truly the judges
who verbally constitute the legal status of the defendant, rather than the
circumstances of the case itself. We shall see in another law case about
illegal construction in the Old Town that the judges, when faced with a
decision the difficulty of which springs mainly from their own desire to
avoid ultimate responsibility, may condemn a defendant in the secure
knowledge that the final decision will be made in appellate court. In the
present instance, however, the problem arose from a conflict between
moral and technical considerations. The conduct of the three trial judges
who sat on the case was indicative of these. Although the prosecutor decided to recommend acquittal, the presiding judge called a recess. This
lasted for an hour and a half, after which the prosecutor demonstrated a
very different tone. He asked the defendant to produce his lawyer, and
the defendant replied that he did not have one. The prosecutor, interpreting this to mean that he could not afford one, nastily demanded, "Aha,
dough and cash, eh?"—meaning that the defendant made a lot of money
out of selling his pastry and was miserly about spending it when he
needed to. The prosecutor then went on to demand a forty-day sentence.
The presiding judge pronounced a sentence of thirty days, which one of
the associate judges said should be suspended because of the defendant's
hitherto blameless record. This led the presiding judge to call a second
recess that went on for several hours. When the court reconvened, the
defendant was given a three-year conditional suspension of his sentence.

The arbitrariness of these proceedings owes a great deal to the judges'
own precarious position. There is a perception on the part of local lawyers that judges are in general recruited from among the less talented and
knowledgeable members of the profession, since their wages as civil servants are considerably lower than what a skilled courtroom lawyer could
earn from satisfied clients. Whether or not this is so, the entire episode
illustrates the entanglement of bureaucrats—here, members of the judiciary—in the webs of social obligation that more obviously characterize

nonbureaucratic interactions. For the relationships seemingly begun at the trial had actually been initiated earlier and continued afterward. The lenient third judge was an occasional customer of the defendant's, although the defendant had simply failed to recognize him. Some considerable time after the trial, this judge came by the defendant's shop and told him that he could appeal to the Tax Office to have his prices returned to the level at which he had been caught setting them, on the grounds that his waxed wrapping paper was an additional expense. Why did the judge bother to offer this advice, which did in the event turn out to be sound? On the other hand, if he knew that the underlying argument was valid, why did he not suggest it as a mitigating factor at the trial? It was much more to his advantage to act as he did, because he could thus appear as a beneficent savior rather than as a technocrat, and so garner a measure of social capital. By unexpectedly stepping out from behind his official role, he made a fine display of his humanity.

GAMBLING: THE POLITICS OF INTIMATE RISK

Gambling (koumari) is perhaps the most obvious example of the highly specific practical ends served by the rhetoric of imprecision. Serious and regular gamblers prefer complicated card games to dice, which they regard as fit only for "Karagiozidhes"—mere shadow puppets, whose follies in the famous marionette theaters provoke predictable derision. The metaphor is even more apt than at first appears. For Karagiozis is also the quintessentially insubordinate Greek, and his antics permit the underdog in every Greek to laugh also at the oppressive bureaucrat and tyrant (Danforth 1976). Those who rule the gambling tables may not take the dice players seriously, but the very unpredictability of dice invests its devotees with a wild appeal that the more cautious cardplayers can never earn. Gambling with dice evidently appeared in Crete under Venetian rule and by the fourteenth century had become, along with prostitution, a matter for concern to the authorities because of its appeal to the dissolute young (Xanthoudidis 1980:408–410). Although the detailed rules of the game changed in Turkish times (Xanthoudidis 1980:414), the gambling addiction has lost none of its destructive power.

Dice are a matter of pure chance: two aces, twos, or fours lose; two threes, fives, and sixes win; while one plus two loses and five plus six wins—an equal play of possibilities, in which the likelihood of major gains over a long period of play is small but in which a single evening's gambling can put an entire personal fortune at risk. In their negative view of dice, the serious gamblers ironically concur in the view of those more religious or conservative members of the community who see dice both as very ancient (thereby affirming the essential continuity of Greek culture!)

and as diabolically inspired. They view gambling in general as a replacement for honest work and the good leisure of a game of backgammon—a game that is now comparatively rare in the town, as are the "village" card games. But dice, precisely because they provide virtually no play for skill and place the players entirely at the mercy of a mocking chance, allow men who are competent at quite a different kind of game—the contest over degrees of nonchalance—to demonstrate skills of a specifically social kind, and to show off their iron nerves and their disdain for mere money as opposed to the esteem of their peers. The paradox of prestige is that one's contempt for others must always be tempered by the realization that it is others who judge one. The villagers who swoop into town after an especially successful sheep-rustling raid have nothing to lose except their cash; and, if they do that, they have huge losses to boast about when they return to their home communities. They may be Karagiozidhes; but this makes them—from an insider's point of view—braver, tougher, more manly Greeks, the kind of Cretan montagnards of whom myths are told.

Today, Rethemniot gamblers usually operate in the all-male preserves provided by the coffeehouses. Unlike the dice-playing groups, which often come together on a strictly ad hoc basis, the cardplaying cliques in the coffeehouses are usually of long and stable duration. People who have migrated to the modern suburbs of Rethemnos tend to come back regularly in the evenings to their old haunts. The high-rise structures of the suburbs, especially their newest parts, are not conducive to the easy fellowship of the coffeehouse, and mutual trust is an important component of the cardplaying cliques.

In their confident occupancy of coffeehouse space, players demonstrate mastery over a setting that also incorporates the tourists. When tourists enter, players huddle closer together to make room for them, automatically spreading out again as soon as the visitors depart, all with the same practiced ease with which they void and refill the open area in front of the coffeehouse during the balmy months of the tourist season. The eagerness with which the right-wingers in one coffeehouse began to play led one communist observer to compare them, sarcastically, to devout churchgoers.

The political allegiance of this particular cardplaying group is mostly to the conservative New Democracy party. An impassioned socialist activist, although joining the odd game, more frequently sits nearby, watching, exchanging occasional pleasantries with the players. The coffeehouse allows him to rise above political differences, while maintaining a careful distance from those with whom he might, through an argument over the cards, become embroiled in political violence. One of the most faithful members of the cardplaying group, however, saw cardplaying as a means of *avoiding* entanglement in political discussion; but then, he belonged to

the majority! Those who belong to the same political party are less likely
to quarrel over cards, which can otherwise focalize political disputes in a
noisy and potentially violent fashion. At least one man avoids the coffeehouses altogether, as he feels that he would be forced to play cards and
that this would lead to fights.

Curiously, it was the puritanical military junta of 1967–1974 that
turned gambling into a more public activity. This came about because the
authorities of that time, believing that they would thereby undermine the
monetary dimension of gambling, permitted the playing of card games in
coffeehouses provided that no money was involved, and they closed
down the clubs that had permitted gambling to flourish in a good deal of
secrecy. One concession was preserved: it was permitted to play dice for
money on New Year's Eve. On this evening, although the excitement of
defying the law is absent, the huge sums that change hands provide a
different tension, and a real test of that studied indifference to mere
money. One active gambler, whose father's losses had already compelled
a move away from the town a generation before, remarked that he ought
to have been a millionaire by now but instead found himself still obliged
to work for his living—substituting, so to speak, the social capital that he
derives from his pose of manly indifference to money for the prestige of
actual wealth. Of course, there is an element of rationalization after the
fact in this stance—men do, after all, sometimes acquire impressive personal wealth—but working for a living is at least socially acceptable,
whereas preying on one's fellows is not.

No gambler can ever effectively predict the outcome of a game, and the
social pressure on male players to take huge risks is unrelenting. Any
demonstrated proclivity to predict the result of a game meets with derision. On the kibitzer's side, there is his own role in the contest over manhood, which consists largely in a constant play of dare and counterdare.
On the player's side, however, there may be an actual fear of hexing the
results. Ideas about the evil eye again provide a useful analogy: excessive
concentration on a specific, well-defined, material gain constitutes a social hubris that attacks the well-being of others. A young man from one
of the wealthier families told me that, while his kin were mostly big gamblers, he and his friends always agreed before any game that no one
would put down a stake larger than 1,000 drachmas. The winner would
then spend the money on treating all the others, rather than picking up
the cash, for it is always better to make a generous splash than to hoard
a miser's profit. Gamblers do cheat for the sake of gain, some extensively;
but to *admit* to an interest in specific monetary advantage is an unpar-
donable solecism. Serious gamblers, ever eager to boast of the size of their
losses, rarely speak of their gains and minimize them when forced to do
so.

A gloating winner violates two norms: he rejoices openly at another's expense, and he tempts fate, the evil eye, or sheer envy. One exception was that of the returned American, who told of winning $3,700 in Miami after a loss of $3,000; here, however, the point was rather to show that the profits are relatively trivial. Far more characteristic was the boast of a young man who had gone to Iraklio on the night of Christmas Day and had lost 200,000 drachmas in one session. To speak with extravagant disdain of one's losses is *khoui* (dramatic self-aggrandisement) in a way that boasting of one's gains cannot be, because it combines the intimation of access to huge resources with a fine insouciance. Remarked one habitual player, a man with serious personal problems, "You get over the financial problem. Human problems can't be gotten over." Amassing gains at the gambling tables is far less important than a reputation for social grace.

Reticence about gains and a willingness to boast of losses are the gambler's version of aristocratic "simplicity," a devil-may-care attitude toward money that also fits the image of aggressive masculinity. One man told me that he had lost 30 million drachmas in gambling during 1970–1986—"at real values," he amplified, not at the present low value of the drachma. This same individual recently lost 27,500 drachmas in a single evening of poker, a game of which he professed not even to be particularly fond: "I wasn't even moved [by it]!" Insouciance converts the loss into real social capital. Another man, now the owner of a profitable gambling coffeehouse, lost a five-room apartment in central Athens while gambling in Rethemnos in 1954; in the same period, he also gambled away a house then valued at 55,000 drachmas in Rethemnos in the course of three evenings' play. This man, who is now considered unusually rapacious as a businessman (he is said to have bought up the chairs from a neighboring coffeehouse rather than let it pass into new hands and start up again), has an additional reason to boast of his losses. As a gambler in his own right, he can present himself as "one of the boys," even though he is in fact better known for the percentage he takes from his customers than for his own bravura.

A gambler walks on a social knife-edge. On the one hand, by acknowledging his losses, he shows that he doesn't care and that he denies the permanence of his wealth, such as it is. On the other, serious loss suggests that he is ruining his family, which means that he may not be much of a man anyway. Losses should not, by bankrupting his family, show him to be his wife's moral inferior because she has no money to care for herself and the children of his house. Again, boasting of one's gains means that one is rejoicing in someone else's misfortune. While this may give satisfaction, it thereby provokes others' distaste, for it means that one has socially widowed and orphaned a family of fellow townsfolk. The balances are delicate and ephemeral, and the risks of slipping into addiction—an addiction far more widespread than the much more widely publicized use of drugs—lend excitement to the daily round. The effects of profligacy at the gambling tables can be catastrophic for later generations. A poor chestnut vendor, whose grandfather had emigrated to the United States, had entertained expectations of receiving a $1,500 legacy at the latter's death. Through the grandfather's gambling, however, he inherited instead a roughly equivalent amount in debts. "*Kali oreksi* (A good appetite [to you])!" he snarled, in an ironical comment on his "fortune."

What of the gamblers' wives? Men decry the compulsive gambler who reduces his family to penury. As many wives do not work—those who do so are usually involved in a family business such as a bakery and could therefore expect a limited amount of economic freedom—the compulsive gambler's wife is in a particularly difficult situation. Because she controls the daily budget of her home, her reputation as well as the brute facts of her survival depend entirely on her husband's continuing to fill the purse. More than one woman has summoned the police to arrest her husband where he was gambling; more probably apocryphal is the tale of the man who, having gambled away all his worldly goods, then put his own wife up—and lost her. A happily married local woman, when asked what she would do if her (extremely industrious and home-oriented) husband were to take up gambling, responded that she'd tell him, "[You go] to your mother's [house], and [I'll go] to my mother's!" The compulsive gambler illustrates the ambivalence of aggressive manhood: those who are too weak to resist its seductions forfeit their claims to embody it. A gambler must be able to balance on the edge of potential ruin without ever quite falling over. When such a man boasts of his losses, he draws attention to precisely this nerve-racking skill.

A particular incident illustrates the recognition by men that gamblers' wives must be enabled to hold the purse strings if they are to survive. The principal in this tale, who was also my informant, is a loudmouthed man who attacks those he dislikes as unmanly, but who also expresses deep respect for certain women of his own (communist) political persuasions. A friend, an inveterate gambler of New Democracy affiliation, ran into serious financial difficulties. After his father's death, which entailed a complex set of expenses, this man found himself owing 1.2 million drachmas on his house loan. When he expressed deep embarrassment at the prospect of having to approach his employer, who was also his political patron and the only individual of his acquaintance who was wealthy enough to extricate him from potential disaster, my informant insisted on accompanying him to see the patron, to whom he then described the gambler's plight. At first, the patron refused all involvement: " 'Eh,' he says to him, 'and what if you gamble it all away?' " So the mediator said that he would serve as guarantor, and that the money should be placed in care of the gambler's wife. This argument, significantly, persuaded the patron, who was probably reluctant in any case to refuse help to a loyal client and could hardly deny that this was an eminently reasonable solution. He agreed to the loan, stipulating only, as an additional condition, that he be allowed to retain half of the gambler's wage until such time as the debt was thereby repaid. Even with such a large sum of money, the wife could clearly be trusted to ensure that her husband would not be able to gamble any of it away; and the husband, of course, was hardly in a position to protest. Lack of the self-control that men idealize in themselves demands a surrender of power to the women of the house.

Gambling is one of the pivotal symbols of male identity in Rethemnos. Women have certainly also gambled for the past two or three decades. In the one licensed gambling club that formerly existed near the Venetian Harbor, gambling parties were often mixed. Women from poor families, however, do not gamble. To do so would threaten their reputation as housewives and erode their tenuous social capital—so much more vital to them than to the wealthy. The peculiar combination of secrecy and public bravado that marks coffeehouse gambling, however, seems to be exclusive to men.

There are several reasons for this. First of all, it is still unusual for women to frequent the coffeehouses. Then again, some of the biggest local gamblers are sheep thieves from the mountain villages of Upper Milopotamos, who descend to the town in order to gamble wildly on the proceeds of their raids. Then there is the social logic of success. The wealthier a man becomes, the more he feels he has to show how little he cares for his gains. He aspires to the camaraderie of men whose aggressive rhetorical devotion to poverty is matched only by their fierce desire for wealth. At the gambling tables, the excitement heightened by the risk of a police raid, these paradoxes attain dramatic force.

Gambling is an especially serious problem for those who are actually too poor to play large sums but can easily be tempted into risking what little they have. While explanations for this may include the obvious desire—rarely realized—to get rich quickly, and the sheer boredom of life in what was until recently an isolated and quiet provincial town, male values clearly play a major role. Not only may a habitual gambler cite his father's similar addiction as a legitimizing precedent in the agnatic idiom of the Cretan countryside, but taking chances puts the small-town gambler in a category together with the swashbuckling animal thieves of the mountain villages—from whom he may in fact be descended, and with whom he is liable to find himself engaged in games of chance, especially around Christmas and New Year.

A committed gambler spoke of his addiction in sexual terms. Since in former times the only way to have sexual relations with a woman was by agreeing to marry her (unless she happened to be a prostitute), he pointed out, gambling provided an outlet for frustrated youthful sexuality. But he then went on to say that if a gambler were to receive a message that a girlfriend (gommena) was waiting for him, "you can't get up" (dhe si-konese)—using an ambiguous verb that can mean both "get up from the gambling table" and "have an erection." Gambling, he said, provokes a strong emotion that "surpasses the erotic."

Certainly excitement runs high—especially on New Year's Eve, when men play dice for one thousand drachmas per single throw. Moreover, while one does not encounter much of the ribald sexual humor of village cardplayers among the town's coffeehouse customers, traces of it remain in the strong conviction that a woman's presence at a card game spells bad luck. A coffee shop proprietor took on one of his own customers and began losing, despite the presence of his wife (whom one of the bystanders, ironically aware that cardplaying in public was not normatively a woman's activity, described as a "ko-kan [card game] scientist"). Another observer told the proprietor, "Send her away, koumbare (ritual kinsman)—send her away, because you've gotten yourself 'burned'!" and then told the wife herself, "When you're near him, he loses." She, quite unabashed, insisted with a broad grin, "I'm his good luck (ghouri)." This joking exchange was quite comprehensible to customers, many of whom came from the mountain villages where the fear of female pollution at cards, and the metaphors of contest over feminized objects, are much more explicit. It is in this light, too, that we should interpret the jokes attributing winners' successes to their being Jehovah's Witnesses—that is, of a sect so stringently pure that its members are said to eschew even sex; the further context was that one slightly simple and deeply religious old man (mentioned above in chapter 3) had become very irate at being told—quite untruthfully—that his companions were all converting to the sect. The usual Rethemniot symbolic devices for shifting one's luck, however, seem more innocuous, not to say mechanistic—for example, moving one's chair from the position in which one has hit a bad losing streak, or refusing to play further after being asked for a loan of money (the logic being that money is now leaving the player). The key trope here is instrumental rather than sexual.

In most situations, the players have all known each other for a long time and form regular cliques. They start with stakes of 1,000 drachmas and keep on doubling: 2,000; 4,000; 8,000; 16,000; 32,000; and 64,000 drachmas. The actual money is concealed, because if the police were to arrive and find it in full evidence, they would—as someone remarked with slightly malicious whimsy (he was sure that this proprietor was in fact himself a police informer)—cart off the proprietor, the players, and even the chairs. The proprietor conventionally gets 10 percent of the money played: "He is the one who wins. The player is never a winner!"

Gambling provides a substantial part of the real—and, obviously, untaxed—profits of the coffeehouse. Any attempt to stop the practice systematically would spell economic disaster, although the almost legendary inactivity of the police probably owes less to economic concerns or to the officers' reputed venality than it does to the legal requirement that culprits be caught red-handed. Not all establishments are equally dependent on gambling. One proprietor, for example, decided that the gamblers' fierce concentration on their games gave him little profit and drove other customers away. Another owner's son liked to play a cassette recorder at such a volume that some of the fussier gamblers fled, at an estimated cost in lost custom of 1,500 drachmas or even 2,000 drachmas a night.

Nor do all customers approve of the rake-off. One critic sourly observed that the proprietors should really only take 3 percent at most (instead of 10 percent). He argued that these unofficial gambling profiteers had lower overheads than professional casino managers because they used the same pack of cards over and over. Estimates put the rake-off at as high as 500–1,000 drachmas per hour; the proprietor also gets an entry fee of 500 drachmas from each newcomer to arrive. A group of ten men may play away an entire evening. A conservative estimate suggests that one coffeehouse proprietor was making a total income of about 100,000 drachmas per month. Once I unwisely interrupted a gambler in midgame, which provoked a polite protest from one of the other players; afterward, the latter explained that 50,000 drachmas had been at stake. This gives a fair indication of what local workingmen, who may take an entire daily wage straight to the card table, regard as high stakes. The proprietor checks roughly at the end of each hour (about the length of a hand) and takes his cut at that point. A written tally has to be kept, although this also increases the element of risk from the authorities. The police, for their part, cannot do much about simpler games of chance in which a written tally is not needed unless they catch the players in the act of exchanging cash at the table.

The proprietor's profits are the subject of a good deal of mostly covert grumbling. On one rare occasion when this flared up into open anger, an émigré Rethemniot who liked to fling his money around in an expansive way objected to the high percentage, denied he was stingy, but said he wanted to "eat" his own money, not have it stolen by others. No-one openly took his side. However justifiable, complaints of this sort disrupt an activity that many customers still want to go on pursuing. Some coffeehouse proprietors may actually make the larger part of their profits in this way; the younger generation, however, is more interested in loud music and fast food—the kinds of profit that fit more easily, as it happens, with the current bureaucratic ethos.

There is a widespread perception that proprietors of gambling coffeehouses escape punishment by doing extensive favors for the authorities. This perception must be seen in the larger context of the general attitude toward the police as a parasitical body, inclined to take the easy route when the incentives are sufficiently generous and rarely sympathetic to the rights and needs of the citizens themselves. This is quite independent of the evaluation of particular police officers, some of whom are regarded with respect and even affection because they do not make a big issue of their power when arresting a suspect. I was told—with what accuracy, I was naturally unable to discover—that police sometimes gamble themselves, though never in uniform.

Residents claim that they can tell which coffeehouse owners work as police informers because those who do not are much more often raided for gambling and closed down for extended periods. An ex-policeman suggested, however, that one reason for the lack of police interference was that gamblers systematically change their haunts. He also complained that most citizens do *not* inform the police. This fear of getting involved, and of being known as an informer, gives the police a socially acceptable excuse for inaction. There is, of course, something of the self-fulfilling prophecy in both the police complaint about the lack of citizen support and the citizens' assumptions about informers.

Both views emphasize the authorities' dependence on social relations. "To do their work, the police must have friends." When the police are called in, they have no choice but to intervene, no matter how much collaboration they have previously received from the proprietor. In the past, when they carried out a raid, they made the gamblers carry the chairs and tables to the police station as a material admission that they had been caught red-handed—especially important because, presumably, no witnesses would come forward for the trial. Only in rare situations, such as that of the desperate wife,[9] will public opinion support appeals to the police.

A very few coffeehouse owners actively discourage gambling. One such proprietor has gathered around himself a regular group of those who despise koumari. The very mention of it elicits their pious disapproval and leads to a ritualistic chorus of condemnation. *Koumartzidhes* should be hanged, they declaim, koumari itself is the worst of all social problems, whole properties have been destroyed. Customers vie in telling cautionary tales about their own kinsmen who have succumbed to the lure of gambling in the big city, and who thus turned an ambitious start in life into a personal financial disaster. The tenor of these remarks does not differ factually from those of the habitual players, though the moral evaluation is exactly the opposite. But the existence of such a discourse shows that the moral status of gambling is at best highly ambiguous. This particular coffeehouse does not willingly countenance even innocent ("village") games that do not require monetary stakes but are simply played for a drink. Men who are intent on their cards do not drink and therefore do not bring the proprietor any profit. Gambling coffeehouse proprietors view their customers as a steady source of income, whereas the view of the antigambling people is that koumartzidhes actually *never* have any money and are thus bad for business. Note that *both* kinds of coffeehouse proprietor can come up with a rational-sounding economic explanation of their respective attitudes. The result in both cases is to squeeze out the simpler, "village" games like *koltsina* and *kseri*, and in fact I never encountered a single game of either throughout my fieldwork in Rethemnos.[10]

The poor are the big losers at the gambling tables. By far the most serious consequence of gambling is the risk of complete destitution. One man gambled away his shop and his taxi in an evening but had other properties to fall back on. Others were less fortunate, and a few gambled away their sole assets: the houses they lived in. Occasionally, luck takes an unexpected turn. A villager, pressed by his wife to move to town so that they could have direct access to good schools for the children, sold his rural properties and gambled away most of the money. With the little that was left, he bought a house in a poor section of the Old Town. Soon enough, "he fell into the mud again (*ksanalasposene*)." To avoid total ruin, he sold his house and, with a small part of the money from that sale, bought a property out on the coast. That property became relatively valuable with the appreciation of coastal land. His son, who recounted this tale, cheerfully admits to having inherited his father's love of cards, although he is a much more cautious gambler and takes pride in having set aside enough money to make sure of his children's future.

Properties that have been sequestrated by the courts as a result of gambling debts may become available to upwardly mobile, hitherto comparatively poor families. A customs officer embezzled public funds in order to supply his gambling habit. As a result of the trial that brought this sorry tale to light, the offender's home was put up for sale. An industrious entrepreneur bought it and turned it into a bakery, with domestic quarters upstairs. The court had set the value of the house at 100,000 drachmas; the convicted embezzler had remitted 25,000 drachmas to the court in partial repayment of his debts, while the new owner paid the balance of 75,000 drachmas plus back taxes; the assessor, who was a friend of the baker, ruled that the 6,000 drachmas of sales tax should be taken out of the 75,000 drachmas paid to the embezzler's wife (and hence, ultimately, out of the moneys being returned to the public weal), rather than out of his own meager financial resources; he also allowed the baker to pay gradually, in interest-free installments. Since the baker was able to develop a tidy trade, the reversal of fortune seems to have been complete.

Gambling to some extent follows the agricultural calendar. Most of it takes place between the end of August and mid-February, when there is relatively little agricultural labor to perform in the villages. The only time gamblers are demonstratively open about playing for money, however, is on New Year's Eve (*t'aï-Vasiliou*, literally, "St. Basil's [Day]"), an exception that the authorities continue to respect. On that day, the coffeehouse proprietors quite unsecretively get out special dice-pens, lined in green baize, and the customers sit around intently with cigarettes in one hand and rolls of 1,000-drachma notes in the other. At this point, they are also liable to be importuned. A beggar down on his luck, for example, will hope to find a happy (and generous) winner; boys singing the New Year *kalanda* (carols) may hope for better pickings if they can find someone who has just had a big win. One beggar actually asked which coffeehouses men were gambling in that night. He clearly expected and got amused tolerance from the customers, who ordinarily despised him precisely because of his habit of coming down every New Year's Eve from his proud Sfakian village to beg in the town.

That the profit motive certainly plays its part in gambling in Rethemnos is clear from the high incidence and variety of forms in which players systematically cheat. Dice fall into two categories: *timia* ("honest") and *kalpika* ("fake"), the latter usually being improvised through the addition of a little mercury to weight them toward a particular value. (Coffeehouse owners have introduced transparent dice as a precaution against this.) Crooked players do not consistently use the loaded dice but may slip them in after about five honest plays, having lulled their opponents into a false sense of security. When a Khaniot gambler arrived in Rethemnos and began taking large sums off the local players, one of the latter exclaimed, "The dice are fake ones!" They all rushed into the kitchen and cut the dice open. The dice were (as the local man knew) perfectly in order, but he took the opportunity of the general hubbub to slip fake dice onto the table, and the game then proceeded much more in accordance with his hopes.

Cheating, which can look like excessive devotion to financial gain, may nonetheless sometimes escape opprobrium through its sheer cleverness. The man who substituted the false dice for good ones boasted about his achievement. This indicates the level at which cheating is socially acceptable: "They're all friends, but they don't respect anyone!" On the other hand, professional, deliberate cardsharping and the systematic use of loaded dice invariably provoke outrage. They are simply ways of sacrificing good fellowship to monetary advantage. Moreover, they do not expose the player to the manly game of risk. On the contrary, he uses them to ensure a certainty incompatible with the necessary provisionality of true social life.

CREDIT AND CREDIBILITY

In gambling, the risk of crippling loss adds excitement. As the very antithesis of predictability, it is a socially positive vice as long as it does not condemn the gambler's family to destitution. In a sense, gambling is the ultimate replacement of dependable monetary resources with social capital: it suggests faith in one's opponent's honesty as a potentially massive debtor. But even the less dramatic economic risks of social existence entail comparable trust and promise comparable rewards. In extending credit, one gambles on another's honesty and punctuality; but then a series of well-conducted transactions may generate confidence in the long term. There is a direct link between the two practices, in that a person who may ordinarily be reluctant to lend money will happily do so when he is well ahead in a gambling session. Then, and only then, it is to his advantage to lend cash. In doing so, he avoids any temptation to squander it himself and he may well increase his own profit if he then wins from the creditor an amount based on the loan he has just given him. The only risk, not a small one, is that the creditor may by now be in such desperate straits that there is no chance of quick repayment. Here, however, social pressures may eventually secure it, since a committed gambler will always do his best to regain his right to play.

Before World War II, informal credit was the rule in most shops. Merchants would record all debts in a notebook (*tefteri*); coffeehouse proprietors would write the debts on a public blackboard, which shamed the recalcitrant into prompt repayment. Most workers received weekly wages (*savvadhiatika*, paid on Saturdays); on that day, they would pay the previous week's debts. Wages were so small that credit was normal for even so trivial an item as a cup of coffee. Once the Metaxas reforms and later union activities put wages on a monthly basis, and especially with recent prosperity that creates competition among employers for skilled workmen rather than the reverse, such practices have all but disappeared. A workman would today feel embarrassed to have the reputation of being a habitual debtor, especially for minor items. The absence of legal protection for informal credit arrangements has also made substantial inroads. In the process, however, it has also aided in the creation of a secretive sociality around the extension of credit among the poorest Rethemniots. These people's reliability as debtors remains their strongest claim to social respect—their only real capital.

The morality of credit persists still. A restaurateur's wife had borrowed a statuette on credit from a tourist goods merchant, in order to make a present to some regular customers, using the rhetoric of hospitality for commercial ends. After a week, and again after a second week, the merchant requested the money; finally, exasperated, he bought a roast chicken from the restaurant and paid only 400 drachmas out of the 700-drachma value of the chicken, explaining that the balance exactly covered the statuette. The restaurateur's wife snarled at him, and a major row flared; but the next day the restaurateur himself came in to put an end to the quarrel, and both men amicably agreed that the whole cause of the problem was the stupidity of women! (Note here again the use of *generic* wisdom to justify past actions. Had either man criticized the other's wife alone, the quarrel would probably have worsened [see also Herzfeld 1987a:176].) The platitudes of gender ideology came to the rescue in a situation that might otherwise have ended in litigation or violence.

This incident is also interesting because the merchant used a precise monetary calculation to bring his opponents' attention to their violation of social credit. His ploy worked partly because the stakes were, in monetary terms, quite trivial, so that his own use of precision could not be construed as other than ironic. Normally, the important parallel between gambling and the extension of credit lies in the element of risk that both entail; and the ability to take risks is what social esteem is all about. Creditors, like gamblers, deal in high stakes, though their risks may also be a sign of economic necessity. One pastry supplier, owed about 50,000 drachmas ($375) after some four months, shrugged his shoulders and said, "I just hope he keeps on buying [from us] (*makari na perni*)!" Sometimes social and commercial credit are mutually convertible to this degree. Credit is a necessary lure for business, and local merchants can couch their credit tactics in terms of a higher social morality.

The ethos of imprecision, however, primarily *opposes* the symbolic capital of good fellowship (and male self-confidence) to financial capital. It does this in two dimensions. First, in an obvious and almost Maussian idiom, it treats money as undermining the reciprocities of social life: those who count their cash in an overt and precise manner are antisocial. But second, those who are imprecise in paying their debts are equally antisocial. They force the myth of imprecision out into the open, so to speak, and so betray not only the creditor but the community as a whole. Conversely, punctilious repayment absolves the creditor of any need to seek it conspicuously and thus makes it possible for him to be "one of the boys"—not, in other words, just a heartily disliked usurer. A carpenter who had done 712,000 drachmas' worth of work gave his customer a 10 percent discount and agreed to give the customer a grace period to pay the final 110,000 drachmas. When the latter sent the final payment, it was 25,000 drachmas short. The carpenter was furious, less (ostensibly, at least) because he had been cheated than because he had shown his kindness to this man in sundry ways, from taking 10 percent off the original charge to allowing him to take a bath in his house, and resented the *akharistia* (ingratitude)—the very opposite of true social worth, or *filotimo*. The client was a mainland entrepreneur with only superficial social ties in Rethemnos; his action underscores the suspicion with which Rethemniots view the new breed of absentee entrepreneurs. The moral context allows most shopkeepers to feel socially safe in refusing credit to known, regular defaulters. Not only are such debtors socially inept, but creditors are as reluctant as any other Rethemniots to go to law and try to avoid reaching the point at which that is their only available recourse—to say nothing of the added financial cost. The carpenter, for example, preferred to reach an agreement by telephone whereby the debtor gained some extra time to redeem his credit.

One advantage for the merchant of an unequal credit relationship is that it secures regular amounts of small custom from poor townsfolk. The merchant must establish a reputation for fair dealing, even generosity; the rewards may be considerable. One pensioner, who must pay a 20,000-drachma monthly rent out of his pension of 38,400 drachmas, became very irritated with his son, who was dating a young woman but seemed indecisive about marrying her. Finally, he put his foot down and told the young man to get married.

The father then undertook to meet the necessary expenses. He went to a local clothier and asked for credit for the requisite wedding suit (at 22,500 drachmas) and borrowed 10,000 drachmas apiece from two other friends to cover the costs of the main gifts. The clothier was especially relaxed about the transaction: "Send me the boy, and let *me* do the worrying (*'ksia mou emena*)!" The father had already borrowed an additional 15,000 drachmas from another merchant; the latter, when offered his money back that same evening on the basis of the 40,000 drachmas contributed by the poor old man's son-in-law and sisters, told the father to hold off repayment for a couple of weeks so he would have ready money to cover all the expenses. The son himself had a mere 5,000 drachmas in hand and could not help. But these various contributions saved the day: the father began to scrape together some of his pension money and the meager proceeds of his vending cart (hastily brought out of retirement), and the son averted the growing embarrassment of his liaison by marrying the young woman with due dispatch.

This incident brings to the fore several of the themes that will be essential to an understanding of the Rethemniots' interactions with the historic conservation office. First, there is the preference for informal channels. In this case, the old father had no choice: no bank would extend him sufficient credit, but a happy combination of supportive kin and his own reputation as a good credit risk—in other words, solid social capital—served him well. Second, and behind this aspect, there lurk the pressing needs created by the exigencies of social process, and especially of marriage. Pressure to conform meant that he had to have recourse to credit, and his subsequent boasting about his success in this area suggests that he expected to capitalize on the added social standing that he could garner from this unofficial credit rating.

Pressure to conform is *always* an issue, of course, and we shall see in the last chapter that aesthetic as well as moral issues play a major part, as in the case of a man who destroyed a "rustic" (and perhaps Venetian) fireplace only to replace it later because by this time fireplaces were all the rage and somehow terribly "European." Commonly, too, the need to dower daughters with homes of their own will lead parents to defy the authorities: a fine is trivial in comparison with social ruin. The historic conservation office faces frequent difficulties because the law can make little or no provision for such immediate, social exigencies. Townspeople react strongly to the regulation of their social values by an intrusive state that does not understand—or cannot afford to recognize—their social world.

In both the local economy and in the development of the historic conservation effort, the persistence of informal modes has practical and material consequences for the continuing history of the politia whose tale these citizens inhabit and animate. In the conceptual archaeology of their social norms, practices, and tactics, we find a measure of explanation for the tensions they experience in their dealings with the state bureaucracy. Now we turn to the effects of these same modes on the progress of another "archaeology": the historic conservation effort. Tradition and modernity merge here; but which tradition, and whose modernity, are these?

Chapter Six

IMPATIENCE ON A MONUMENT

Bureaucracy and Dispute

We return now to the theme of time and the ways in which it is evaluated and negotiated. In the name "Old Town," Rethemnos recognizes a dual meaning. "Old" is not necessarily "good," and it may be synonymous with dank, unhealthy, tumbledown. The inhabitants complain that the Old Town no longer exists for them. It has been appropriated by forces they neither control nor particularly admire—government, foreign tourism, a few wealthy entrepreneurs from out of town.

The tourists, especially, are an ambivalent blessing. They bring money, though not as much as foreigners "ought." This makes them stingy and immoral in the eyes of Greeks who at once depend on them and resent that dependence. Who benefits from their presence? Once, perhaps, some of the shopkeepers did; but now so many would-be entrepreneurs have rushed in to take their shares of the bonanza that no one makes much money at all. "How does the wage earner benefit from tourism?" one resident demanded. Wage earners have to pay inflated rents, and the entire local economy depends on the very uncertain future of tourism. Or perhaps it is the government that benefits? Then let the government buy up the best-preserved houses and cordon off an area of the Old Town, renaming it "Good Town" (*Kali Poli*)—an aptly ironic euphemism, snarled with polite bitterness at the bureaucratic expropriation of taste and virtue. If citizens must be forced to live in a home that they feel they do not actually own, what is "good" about life in a badly drained monument?

Moreover, the Old Town is a constant reminder of inequality. It is not everybody who must live amid damp and drainage. Those who do are caught in a vicious economic spiral. The mere transportation of construction materials already costs them perhaps 50 percent more than in the New Town because the narrow streets impede ordinary trucking, and the additional requirements of historic conservation are often so cripplingly expensive that residents simply let their homes decay. Few, moreover, make their living from the construction industry or from the government agencies that regulate it here. Among the wealthier and more prominent residents of the New Town, by contrast, is a virtual subculture of civil engineers, most of whom are closely associated with the two government agencies with which this chapter is concerned: town planning and historic conservation.

In these circumstances, it is not surprising that Old Town residents' anger has a strongly ideological and class-oriented flavor. Among those defending private property rights and the citizen's right to compensation from the historic conservation office, we hear the improbable voice of a self-declared communist (but since the socialists came to power the communists have not been notably fussy about their choice of ideological slingshot):

> One thing is a fact: that, from the moment that a given [government] service intervenes in my own property, I think that's nonconstitutional.[1] That is to say: let these people sit down some time to examine certain things correctly, and make laws that are both correct for the citizen and correct for the state. Do you want this building? Pay me for it, get me out of it; you'll get me out, however, at the price one has to pay for an apartment of the kind the engineers sell on the seafront [at] 100,000 drachmas per square meter—that's how much you'll give me in order to get me out. Because, if we look at it another way, the old [building] is *more* expensive than the new [i.e., because of the costs of restoration]!

The anger is unmistakable. Residents resent their enforced role of picturesque peasants for the tourist trade while others glory in comfortable, modern homes in the New Town and reap the profits of renovated properties in the Old. Since it is received wisdom that any government, even a nominally socialist one, is always in alliance with the wealthy, the intervention of government services can only appear suspicious at best. From the New Town, the Old may look pleasantly picturesque. But residents who want to replace undistinguished remnants of old walls, in order to reproduce them faithfully as part of a modern building with proper watercourse insulation, must instead maintain the old structures, with all their uncontrollable damp and the health problems—mainly arthritis and respiratory diseases—that accompany it. It was largely to escape these chilly ills that so many of those who could afford to moved out of the Old Town. Growled one resident, "These gentlemen (*afti i čirii*) live . . . in the most luxurious villas and don't know where the [true] Rethemniot lives!"

While there has been some lessening of the bitterness in recent years, many there are for whom lost patience will never be regained. To many, indeed, the tourists are symptomatic of a humiliating dependency on the industrialized countries. The far from left-wing souvenir dealer who claimed that most tourists came, not for the Old Town, but either for Crete's natural beauties or for "hospitality" (*filoksenia*), was articulating this resentment with great clarity. For him, the government was simply acquiescing in the dominance of outsiders, to whom only *moral* superiority could be obtained by the hapless natives through the recasting of tourism as "hospitality."[2]

The Old Town is thus a multiple source of bitterness for its residents. As we explore the reasons, amid the storm of accusations and cries of bad faith, we shall not be able to determine who is "in the right." All the actors have moral commitments in the matter, or at least act as though they did. If, then, in what follows we seem to be focusing unduly on strategic manipulations, this is not to deny the existence of those moral commitments, but to understand the means used to achieve conflicting moral ends.

Bureaucrats and townspeople alike are theorizing agents (Giddens 1984:5–6) whose analytic sense of past and current events shapes their handling of future ones. Bureaucrats, lawyers, judges, engineers—these are people too. To deny their humanity is simply to take sides in the conflicts we are examining. When, on the other hand, we treat their actions as enmeshed in the same rhetorical nexus as those of the townspeople they are variously said to frustrate or serve, we see more clearly why and when citizens and bureaucrats alike invoke common models (see Appadurai 1981) of "how the system works." When, for example, they discuss the new "declarations of sincerity" that the tax laws require, they are not so ingenuous as to claim that this novel system can guarantee the taxpayers' honesty. Rather, in keeping with their habitual skepticism about mind reading in general, they recognize that this is the official strategy—using a moral framework—for justifying more severe sanctions against transgressors.

Rethemniots regard the civil service with deep ambivalence. Bureaucratic employment often seems to be little more than a sinecure in which lazy and overpaid petty tyrants invent ways of annoying the public in order to pass their time[3] and justify their fat pay. Bureaucrats are repeatedly charged with violating their own rules—which, of course, they frequently do. Bureaucratic practice "alienates you" (*s' apoksenoni*) because it combines antisocial rigidity with personal greed and indolence. Some of its supposedly worst features, however, derive less from clerical caprice than from the expectation—shared by client and bureaucrat—that personal accountability is dangerous and to be avoided at all costs. Thus, deferring to a superior's decision allows the employee (ipallilos) to evade personal responsibility before the impersonal machine of state. Written documents have so much evidential authority that everyone wants someone else to produce them and no one wants to sign them. The term *ipallilos*, which means "someone who works under someone else," conveys appropriately infinite vistas of receding responsibility.

The difference between bureaucrat and citizen (or between one bureaucrat and another) is thus one of position in relation to the apparatus of state. Within each category there are infinite further distinctions and shifts of situation. Every poor Rethemniot family tries to educate its children to the point where they can become ipallili. The very envy that civil servants attract is a sure sign of their collective prestige, a prestige that masks some very substantial differences in access to resources but that also springs from some common advantages. Civil service salaries, if never magnificent, are at least steady. For a minor bureaucrat, the brief late summer leave is an opportunity to attend to the olive and grape harvests in the home village.

Self-employed artisans and shopkeepers are disadvantaged by comparison, since they can ill afford even so brief an absence from work. They also have few means of acquiring the technical skills (such as accounting) needed in order to stand up to the bureaucracy in defense of their already-straitened finances. Strains between the groups came out into the open in early 1987, when small shopkeepers officially joined forces with civil servants in a strike for the first time. Individual shopkeepers, many of whom were puzzled at the call to cooperate with the despised ipallili, surreptitiously opened their doors in order not to lose commerce or offend old customers. Often, those who disobeyed the call to strike were supporters of the New Democracy party, which had supported—some thought even incited—the national call for the strike. Their unwillingness to join the strike thus expressed their resentment of civil servants, rather than of the political party that happened to be in power at the time. As one shopkeeper explained, most shop assistants could not hope for even half the wage of a civil servant.

Owners and employees of small businesses are fully aware of the advantages of finding their way—or, more accurately, their children's way—into the ranks of the civil service. Their awareness places a special burden of anxiety on those taking school and university entrance examinations, since a certain level of education is the key to government employment. Seeking civil service posts for one's children is a strategy for gaining advantage in a competitive and grudging material world. The alternative is the continued mystification of the cynically self-styled "illiterate" about the intricacies of filling out forms and the constant fear of the consequences of error. This way lies ever more importunate disenfranchisement. An onyx worker avoided buying new machinery for his workshop because of the bureaucratic complications this would entail: complex purchase arrangements, the difficulties of the new Value Added Tax, and above all the Tax Office's automatic and punitive assumption that his income must have risen significantly.

Recall, too, the small merchants' hostility to V.A.T. on the grounds, not of added expense, but of increased complexity and reduced social immediacy. Even a relatively wealthy young man complained that when

one wanted to plan business on a serious scale, one ran headlong into a
very different conception of how things should be done and had to adapt:
"They spoil your character. . . . [so that] you work with their laws and
not your own." The plurality of "laws" here is a segmentary "refraction"
through the divisions of self-interest that separate, not only citizens from
each other, but also all citizens from the state. Indeed, to think of "laws"
rather than of "the law" is already a departure from the repressively uni-
tary ideology of the state. As a PASOK enthusiast remarked on hearing
shots fired illegally by campaign supporters, Cretans pride themselves on
their freedom from "written laws" and have their own instead. They resist the symbolic and pragmatic power of the written word. In an ideal
world, their sword would prove mightier than the bureaucratic pen.

This is not to say that bureaucrats have greater freedom of decision.
On the contrary, they in turn are held rigidly accountable to the state.
Greeks routinely complain about the trammels of bureaucracy. Minor
officials are as thoroughly enmeshed in these as any client. A client's failure to pay a charge, moreover, can easily become the bureaucrat's out-of-
pocket responsibility.[4] What is more, the bureaucrat is also *socially* accountable. As the legalistic buck passes upward, it perpetually pushes
against the countervailing, everyday ethic of "obligation" (*ipokhreosi*)
among kin, friends, and neighbors. Such moral forces are all the stronger
in a culture in which the most ephemeral ties, even chance encounters,
can be deployed to create new social bonds—to define people as *dhiki
mas anthropi* ("our people") in relation to each other.

Historic conservation bureaucrats, then, are not simply automata serving a thoughtless machine. From local functionaries up to government
ministers in Athens, decision makers are all accountable to their superiors. While some may exercise power in a repressive and capricious manner, their more capricious or repressive actions usually reproduce similar
asymmetries in their own relationships with superiors, passing the load
of material disadvantage downward. When their actions provoke disre-
spect from below, they fall out of favor with those above. The rapid staff
turnover in these offices suggests that the tightrope they walk is extremely
slippery.

Townspeople take great delight in pointing out the failings of bureaucrats. When V.A.T. was introduced in accordance with European Community regulations, they discovered that tax officials seemed to have no
idea of the rules—a situation that was reproduced throughout the entire
country, as the media soon confirmed. In all agencies, including both the
Tax Office and the historic conservation service, a multiplicity of laws
defies the ability of most bureaucrats to discover a consistent and manageable scheme. The state's apparent inability to give the employees clear
guidelines left them with few forms of self-defense: abruptness, buck-

passing, stony silence. Bureaucratic efficiency is constantly circumscribed from above as well as from below.

Bureaucrats must also engage in ordinary social interaction, a circumstance that inevitably restricts their power over clients. A baker went to the bank to deal with a bill of exchange for his wife's sister's husband. The bank clerk, although not a government employee, wielded the same kind of conditional power, since access to funds is controlled in a similarly organized hierarchy and does ultimately depend upon official state sanctions. The baker asked the clerk whether he was in the right line. The clerk haughtily responded that he would be dealt with in due course, and that, if he was in a hurry, "there's the road!" The baker asked him whether he was married. "No," replied the puzzled clerk. So the baker explained that, when he did eventually marry, his wife would send him for pastry; he would then find out how he would be treated! "What's this pastry?" demanded the by now thoroughly mystified clerk. The baker told him he would find out in due course. And indeed, much later, the now-married clerk came to buy pastry at a time when there was a great shortage. The baker told him about the shortage and added that if his customer was in a hurry—"there's the road!" The customer had little choice but to show some humility; having transferred to himself the social pressure on his wife to produce the appropriate sweets made from the special pastry, he had no choice. Since that time, baker and clerk, having understood each other perfectly, have become firm friends.

The moral is clear. Bureaucrats exercise their evanescent power at a constant risk of social exclusion. Their willingness to meet clients halfway is less often a mark of venal favor peddling than it is the strategic compromise of social actors caught between what may not be entirely implacable forces. When a neighbor complained that the owner of a small home-based business had dug a sewage well too close to the neighbor's house, the sanitary inspector simply advised the businessman to dig a new one slightly closer to his own house. He hoped, presumably, that the compromise would keep both from complaining about what each would otherwise—in order to guard against their respective friends' jeering—have to represent as his favoritism to the other. The historic conservation and town-planning officials, too, faced with an explosive local situation as well as the guardianship of a somewhat unstably defined national heritage, frequently resort to compromise. They are effective negotiators of tensions, both among agencies and between government and citizenry. They make judicious choices, and these are inevitably and repeatedly called into question. That is not necessarily the result of poor judgment on their part. It arises because each decision itself becomes an element in the unceasing contest over power, identity, and the future evolution of local society.

Sources of Conflict: A Monumental Wound

These characteristics of bureaucratic interaction largely explain the peculiar dissonance between the good intentions that motivated the several historic conservation laws promulgated by the state and their actual implementation, as well as local reactions to them. The laws themselves have a complex history, and we should begin with a brief examination of its unstable and contradictory course.[5]

Within a year of the 1967 military coup, the then mayor, Dimitris Arkhondakis, persuaded the the Ministry of Culture to slap a severe historic conservation order on the Old Town of Rethemnos. In the period of military rule, two other events occurred, neither of them obviously consistent with the spirit of that order, but both consequential for its further development. First, a representative of the military government visited Rethemnos and suggested that the unusually tall minaret of the celebrated mosque of the gazi (warrior of the faith) Hüseyin Paşa should be torn down. It offered the Turks, he claimed, too great a temptation for their irredentist ambitions. Second, in a series of laws promulgated from 1970 on, the junta provided a variety of incentives for massive tourist development.

What binds all these events together is the premise of European identity that they variously serve. The preservation of antiquities, seen as a "European" practice in itself, would place the Venetian glories of Crete on a pedestal where all could see how Crete had been one of the centers of an indisputably European culture. The destruction of the minaret—built, be it noted, on the design of a Christian (Greek) architect—would have reinforced the selective bias toward European culture. The order was never carried out. The development of tourism brought rapidly increasing numbers of West Europeans to Crete, and with them a greater interest in conserving whatever was romantic and picturesque.

In 1973, a team of experts led by the architects N. Moutsopoulos and I. Zervas was approached by Arkhondakis, who persuaded them to conduct a careful survey of all the buildings (see Moutsopoulos 1973:ii). Moved at the time by Arkhondakis's pleading and enthusiasm—"He *begged* me to take it on!"—Moutsopoulos now argues that this work is the ethnological exploration of a people's soul, not a bureaucratic exercise. The greatest difficulty nonetheless remained, in his didactic view, that of teaching that same people the great significance of its buildings.[6]

The residents' own appraisal of the buildings' significance was much less complimentary and grew out of more immediate concerns. For some, the Moutsopoulos study was only the beginning of their problems. A resident recalls:

> Before the appearance of Mitsopoulos [*sic*], you could destroy and build and do whatever you wanted in the Old Town. If you wanted to make four- or even five-storey [buildings] you had no problem. Afterward, it was forbidden. One or two floors—ground and upper [floors].

It was not that most residents had the means to build anything so ambitious as skyscrapers. By the time significant numbers had achieved a measure of economic self-sufficiency, by the late 1970s, it was far too late even to try. Houses were being subdivided into ever smaller and more cramped units because they could not legally expand. Many of the residents simply left for the high-rises of the New Town, increasing the sentiment and substance of class differentiation by leaps and bounds. There is some irony in the fact that Moutsopoulos himself urged much greater sensitivity to the residents' social needs than the historic conservation staff ultimately proved able to provide.

For the failure to address these needs, the uncoordinated division of labor between the historic conservation and town-planning offices is widely blamed. While several local attempts have been made to call for a single local agency (*enieos foreas*) to deal with the problems as a whole, and while all the contenders in the 1986 election agreed on the necessity of achieving some degree of administrative unity, the national bureaucracy has proved structurally too inflexible to sustain such a solution. Everyone agrees on the basic principle. No agency, however, as Mayor Skouloudis pointed out, is willing to surrender any significant degree of bureaucratic jurisdiction:

> For example, the Archaeological Service should see the matter very clearly and understand that it will have to preserve whatever in the Old Town has archaeological or historical interest within its exclusive jurisdiction, and all the remaining part of the Old Town should be conserved by the Town-Planning Service, as is anyway provided for under the appropriate Presidential Decree.[7]

Disagreement, however, does not operate at this abstract level. Which parts go to which service? Skouloudis himself recognized that the tone of the disputes was highly personal—or, as he then moderated the charge, "[inter]professional." With all the scorn of a man whose family has long flourished in the building trade, he expressed serious misgivings as to whether a group of "archaeologists"—actually civil engineers and architects—could possibly have the requisite technical expertise to comment on structural problems. Everyone agrees, stereotypically, that it is impossible to agree. Within that common framework, the civil servants and politicians are free to situate the blame according to their differentiated interests—a relatively genteel version of the idiom of self-justification that we have already seen among the population at large. For it is not only in the bureaucracy that buck-passing is widespread. Indeed, it only works there because it closely follows the conventions of blame that we have already seen in the charges of roufiania, and that, in the final chapter and at the other extreme, we shall also find embedded in the normal practices of the legal profession.

To many, looking back, the entire progression of events now seems a cruel, generic conspiracy of the rich and powerful against the economic interests of the poor. That the majority of Old Town residents at this time were genuinely poor appears not to be in dispute. Dimitris Nianias, who as Minister of Culture made an on-site inspection in Rethemnos in 1978, forthrightly told me, "If the state wishes to create a traditional [i.e., historic conservation] policy, that is, so that the ten million Greeks [who make up the national population] can preserve the Rethemniots' houses, those ten million should pay the Rethemniots!"[8] Few indeed are the Rethemniots who would dispute such a sentiment, and indeed the idea that a few houses might be maintained by the state as a kind of open museum had considerable currency.[9]

In 1973, property values were still low and stagnant, and military law was still in force. Although tourism had begun, its future effects on the land market were not yet fully apparent. In comparative terms, Old Town houses were at least solid possessions, and a small house there might be worth as much as ten stremmata of coastal land. The architects did their work:

> So, they were writing away; we poor folks didn't know what these people were doing. And one fine morning, we wake up, and they tell us that "you can't put one stone on top of another!" Everyone blamed everyone else.

In reaction, a new society was formed. This was the Old Town House Owners' Association (hereafter abbreviated as OTHOA), which started out with a membership of around three hundred infuriated house owners.

That impressive number, however, soon dwindled to a mere handful. As soon as the wealthier members managed to take care of their immediate personal concerns, they drifted away. Soon the association was dead. If not a conspiracy of the rich, then certainly a coincidence of their interests had once again struck at the poorer residents. For it was particularly those with large properties (more than one thousand square meters) who saw in the sowing of general distrust in the conservation authorities an excellent chance to better their own situations. They pressured the authorities either to curb the restrictions on extensive rebuilding (which did not happen) or to buy off the association's leadership with prompt action on selected cases (which is allegedly what did take place).

While the wealthy leaders shared the general interest in adding extra floors, which for the poor was a relatively inexpensive way of dowering daughters or providing sons with a durable inheritance, they hoped to go beyond the "third floor" that the poor were demanding and create high-rise units within the Old Town. These wealthier property owners were also relatively well connected and could afford the legal advice and representation that advanced their particular causes. The less wealthy, who were almost always less well educated in the political machinery, hoped in vain that by imitating these leaders they would get their support. Each landowner, reaching the limits of what could be done, abandoned the collective effort in pursuit of more individual goals. It was several years before some of those whose properties were locked into the conservation regime began to appreciate the economic advantages of what was happening. By the late 1970s, some of them were reaping the benefits of the tourist trade, and the old landowners of the Old Town saw both the New Town upstarts and their own formerly destitute neighbors begin to catch up with or even surpass them in wealth.

The president of OTHOA stayed at the helm until the end and is very bitter about the collapse of his dreams. He attributes it above all to the "Green Guards"—a contemptuous description of PASOK enthusiasts based on the party's official color. These former allies in his struggle, he charges, wanted "to close our mouths" once they got into power. Indeed, when Minister of Culture Mercouri made an on-site inspection in 1982, the OTHOA president was chagrined to find local party workers redirecting her schedule to a pleasant interlude with lira playing in a picturesque bar and intensive sessions with the civil engineers who worked for the historic conservation office.[10] His actions when he encountered her again show that he was now anticipating likely failure. Mercouri had just noticed children playing in muddy, unpleasant conditions:

> So she says, "I couldn't have imagined that such things exist here in Re-thimno." At that very moment, they happened to tell her that there was an urgent telephone call from Athens and they should take her [to the telephone] because it was necessary.
>
> So she says to me, "We'll continue this in the afternoon."
>
> Say I, "Thank you," say I, "but it's over," I say, "this visit is. In the afternoon, you'll get up [from siesta] late, and in the evening we can't see either my house, so you could admire that great mansion, or any of the other things in the town."

But he did go to the general meeting that had been called, and there he argued again with the minister. He had established, at least to his own satisfaction, that she had been prevented from making a proper inspection; thus, he had already planted the seeds of his self-justification in the expectation that his campaign would fail. His tactics, in short, followed the pattern we have already noted for bureaucrat-client interactions in general. As such, they perhaps lacked the full conviction that just might have made a difference.

A further and more gradually apparent reason for the decline of OTHOA was the satisfaction of numerous residents with the advantages that historic conservation brought to their growing investments in the tourist industry. Now there is even talk of reviving OTHOA in a radically reversed form, under the leadership of a faction that repudiates the founders' virulent enmity toward the historic conservation office and includes in its ranks at least one major former critic of the original OTHOA. It remains to be seen whether this endeavor will take hold.

A certain sense of solidarity nevertheless still binds together those who have had difficulties with the historic conservation office. In the coffeehouses, the embittered growl on and on:

> I sit in the coffeehouse and say, "I've gotten into a mess with the 'Archaeology.' " (. . . .) Each one tells of his pain (*lei o kathenas to bono dou*).

Despite the bonds of shared adversity, however, there seems to be no practical way to join forces. Indeed, adversity may furnish a level of solidarity that some would prefer not to lose: better, perhaps, the companionship of disaffection than risking the stigma of individual failure.

Such, then, in outline, is the conflict that began in the late 1960s. It was a conflict that would, in time, engage the attentions of government ministers in Athens, local police and other officials, and, of course, the frustrated residents. For them, the historic conservation office is frequently a malign enemy, for whose creeping evil the metaphors of cancer and gangrene indicate the range of vituperation: "For us, it has burned our innards" (*mas ekapse ta sothika mas emas*). It is a "great wound" (*meghali pliyi*) because to open a little shop one needs to wait for months to get a permit even to do interior work, a financially crippling delay when budgetary margins are tiny. "The 'Archaeology' has destroyed people's houses," fulminated one expatriate Rethemniot: it does not allow people even to break up the offending kioskia, those window boxes that recall the days of Turkish oppression.

The rhetoric and practice of government puzzle the residents, who easily fall back on conventional cynicism about government in order to explain such incomprehensibly unpatriotic as well as arbitrary measures. Their own motives are not always much less opaque. To take a single illustration, they become very upset when they are told they may not build the shallow balconies that permit them to extend their domestic control of the street area. "The balcony (*balkonaki*, a diminutive form) is one of the elements that has destroyed what has remained in Rethimno," observed the architectural historian and conservator Ioanna Steriotou.[11]

"It's fifty centimeters [deep] and hasn't the space for a single chair!"
Nonetheless, it makes a claim both to social and to physical space, and it
exemplifies the sources of mutual incomprehension that continue to fuel
the dispute.

THE COSTS OF "TRADITION": FINANCES AND FAVORITISM

Most residents profess to believe either that, since the government consists of "thieves" (*kleftes*) at all levels, any form of resistance is justified;
or that the entire exercise is for the benefit of the foreign tourists—which
amounts to the same thing, inasmuch as the local officials stand to benefit
behind the scenes. On these terms, it is hardly surprising that the rationality of conservators usually looks instead like pure, malicious caprice.
Even those who live off the tourists and generally favor the idea of preserving old Rethemnos are puzzled by its logic. A man who, eight years
earlier, had built a new house on an open space in the Old Town, and
was expanding it as a rooming house for the summer tourist trade, asked
one of the conservation officials if he could get help from her office with
constructing a pair of kioskia to make it look like a "traditional house."
When she replied that they never provided funds for work on new buildings, he was deeply annoyed, pointing to the help they had recently given
with an admittedly much older house, which, however, he felt no tourist
could possibly distinguish as such—in part because, lacking help from the
conservators when they most needed it, the owners had already stripped
and plastered its walls instead of restoring the masonry surface. No ordinary citizen is prepared to accept the notion that the government agencies may have been short of money when *they* most needed it. If they
accept the idea of budgetary shortfalls at all, they attribute them to the
venality of civil servants.

The historic conservation office, however, faces an enormous obligation, if only because there are about two thousand houses for which a
plausible case for restoration could be made. To make matters worse,
earlier directors of the office may already have made commitments that
the current incumbent could not possibly meet. Residents were not only
promised financial support for authorized renovations but were encouraged to proceed with these before the money was actually paid. That they
often did so is a measure of their desperation. One woman, the interior
walls of whose house were literally dripping with mold and water, was
promised full recompense for redoing the wooden beams:

> Finally we fixed up the house. We were paid neither for the beams, nor any-
> thing! The only thing the "Archaeology" fixed was to varnish the beams for

us, and it fixed the sidewalk. That was all. And, all right, thus far well and good—if they'd allowed us to demolish the house and build it again in the same style. As it had been!

The solution, then, is ostensibly predicated on appearance. This would make perfectly good sense to the residents of the Old Town, who constantly worry about the opinions of others and claim to share official concern with the presentation of their town to visitors. Even here, however, the local residents find the bureaucrats' actions inconsistent. This same speaker's house shared a wall with the neighboring house. The historic conservation office scheduled the wall for conservation even though, once the other house was rebuilt (for which permission had been given), the wall itself would not show. In the end, permission to build over it was given, but the long process of getting to that stage had been pointlessly exasperating.

Expectations—or at least demands predicated on alleged commitments—have continued to rise among the inhabitants. Uncertainty does not necessarily dampen hopes, although it does increase tension. The Ministry of Culture has been unable, perhaps understandably, to make any long-term projections about how much money would be available for restoration work. In a situation in which local actors have an interest in heating up the rhetoric of obligation, it may be virtually impossible for any conservation regime to avoid the impression of reneging. From time to time, a resident will show up having conducted some piece of expensive restoration exactly in accordance with the regulations and will demand payment. An official of the historic conservation program called this "blackmail," although in the context of the social life of Rethemnos it might seem to be no more than a variation on some common strategic themes. Residents exert what pressure they can—on each other, if that looks like a promising tactic. The woman who paid for house beams only to find out that the conservation office would not recompense her then became especially irritated when her friends started to assume that, because she had taken possession of the beams, she had also received the money. In the end, she decided to move. She meanwhile took out a loan, which "I'll be paying back for twenty-five years, twenty-five years, without having a house!" On the very day she spoke to me about her plight, she was going to make arrangements to pay rent on a house in the New Town so that she would no longer have to put up with the damp: another reluctant refugee from the Old Town, still paying rent on her shop in the commercial district there but living in a drier, healthier place.

In the earliest phases, the conservation office had little money at its disposal. From 1981 on, after PASOK came to power, it had an operating budget that never fell below 5 million drachmas and by 1987 had reached

250 million drachmas (see the sign in plate 35). But concurrently political competition, inflation, and spiraling expectations, as well as a wider distribution of effort and money, have conspired against the achievement of consensual satisfaction. And the continuation of funding at present levels is by no means assured.

What is more, the money supply appears to be very erratic even for work that has been completed. This is a major reason why carpenters regard working for the historic conservation office as employment of the last resort—the "bottom rung of the ladder." Only with repeated visits could one carpenter eventually persuade some office employee to give him what was due, and the delays cost him expensive time lost from work. The arbitrariness of financing shows how the rhetoric of "limited good" originates, not in the local culture, but in the control exercised over it by the state bureaucracy.

35. Work in progress: advertising the latest funding that supports the restoration effort. (1986)

Other problems lie in the conflict of principle between the original designation of the Old Town as a "scheduled monument" (*dhiatiriteo mnimeo*, literally, "a monument to be preserved") and its later and more relaxed designation as a "traditional neighborhood" (*paradhosiaki sinikia*). Residents have much less difficulty with the "traditional" label than they do with the more ferociously official "monument." As with the absorption of the rooming house proprietor's trade into the stereotypical ideology of hospitality, the idea of a state-supported concept of tradition absorbs the more formal and less understandable notion of historic conservation. For tradition does not only come "from the top." It is not so much "invented" by a powerful elite (Hobsbawm and Ranger 1983) as *negotiated* and *contested* to meet the overlapping interests of elite and working class. Social actors adapt the sweeping generalizations of officialdom in order to promote some of their own ideas about what tradition might be. In this process, they gradually recast official concepts to meet personal experiences and aspirations.

In the same way, too, residents absorb the notion of *cultural heritage* into the much more immediate concern they have with *filial inheritance*. Not only do men resist interference with the "paternal house," as we have seen, but they recast the idea of a historic legacy as a form of intrafamilial endowment. In one sense, the whole Old Town became a vast agglomeration of potential dower properties, and when the historic conservation laws came into force they abruptly collided with the obligation of every father to dower his daughters even if this meant building extra, illegal storeys on their own houses. The residents recast the very idea of a national heritage as that of a dowry—a common trust whose beneficiaries should at least be able to make real use of it:

> This is the complaint of the Rethemniot: that his house essentially doesn't belong to him, and that the house he has belongs to the Archaeological Service. And, further to that, the entire secret [i.e., issue] is that the Old Town is a monument and you all live off it. All right. Nobody has any doubt about that. We said, we have it as a dowry (*pročio*); but we could exploit this dowry in a suitable way.

This speaker foresees the eventual collapse of the tourist industry, a far from improbable scenario (see *Rethemniotika Nea*, 7 June 1987, p. 1). Yet many Rethemniots treat tourism as the only possible raison d'être of conservation and argue that residents should be entitled to anticipate this development in order to avert a new economic disaster.

The historic conservation office operates on standard bureaucratic principles. It reports to the Thirteenth Inspectorate of Byzantine and Postbyzantine Antiquities, which is responsible for the whole of Crete, and is overseen from the Iraklio office. The local staff includes an architect, a civil engineer, and a draftswoman, two drivers, two guards (whose duties include reporting infractions), a secretary, three managers in charge of records and accounts, and some fifteen to twenty workmen. These last are on open-ended contract, and their number may fluctuate according to available funds and the work that is available. Mostly villagers from the Rethimni hinterland, they receive some training in restoration work.

These people live close to their work. One of the guards is himself an Old Town resident. One consequence of this is that the residents experience constant surveillance. Many residents, having received a permit, take it as carte blanche to make wholly different alterations from those indicated on the permit, and some get caught. Despite the conventional explanation of such social embarrassments as the consequence of roufiania, it is clear that many of these incidents arise from the frequency and intensity of day-to-day inspection by the authorities and from the residents' creative reinterpretations of the permits. Few infractions escape the net. In one gleefully recalled incident, a professional archaeologist was cited for making unauthorized alterations to his Venetian house. Since most residents do not see any great significance in the fact that the employees and directors of the conservation office are not, strictly speaking, archaeologists, such discomfitures of professional identity among the learned and rich are hugely entertaining to everyone else.

The conservation office insists on full documentation for absolutely every action taken. Sometimes, of course, this is a wise precaution. When a home owner decided to move the main doorway of his Venetian house round from its main-road location to one of the surrounding side streets and justified this highly convenient rearrangement on the grounds of "oral tradition," the historic conservation office was able to point to relatively recent architectural drawings that show the original formation. The need to justify every change with architectural drawings and photographs has created a veritable industry of civil engineers and architects, whom the residents collectively regard as overfed parasites living off the misfortunes of the poor and always hand in glove with one or the other of the rival government agencies.

"THIEVES" FALL OUT: BUREAUCRATIC INFIGHTING

The characterization of the bureaucrats as "thieves" reflects the conventional wisdom about government services in general. More critical observers admit that the "system" is more powerful than specific employees, and that the latter really only have the power to "give an opinion" without necessarily being able to translate it into bureaucratic action. Nonetheless, most residents represent their difficulties as embodied in the bureaucratic personalities of the officials involved. They level charges of indifference, favoritism, and pedantic adherence to the law against these officials, their expressed opinions often—but not always—following what they perceive as political party allegiances.

Central to the pervasive sense of indirection and missed opportunity are the effects of *internal* conflict. Sometimes, the only way to get satisfaction is to play one kind of bureaucratic foot-dragging against another. Thus, a resident who could not persuade the historic conservation office to let him replace his roof with a concrete slab was finally able to take action when—but only when—the old roof had become dangerous. Once he was able to persuade the town-planning office of this, the historic conservation officials had no choice but to issue him with the necessary permit. Such institutionalized procrastination strains the tolerance of residents and officials alike. Incidents in which one agency is able to force its way into the other's domain of jurisdiction also do little to calm the atmosphere of suspicion that colors interagency relations. In addition, there are often technical and personal disagreements within each agency, notably in the historic conservation office.

To make matters still worse, both agencies have had frequent clashes with the Municipality. The Municipality would like to develop tourist facilities and other moneymaking ventures—it sponsored a plan, ultimately rejected, to create a casino in the Fortezza—and spends a higher proportion of its funds on the New Town than the Old. The historic conservation office, in particular, objects to this set of priorities in strong and public terms. Sometimes the effects of these disagreements approach the ludicrous—as when the Municipality paved what used to be the shoe-makers' street with reproductions of the old "Maltese paving stones," only to have the historic conservation office, a few days later, order them removed again so that the archaeologists could first recover the original paving materials. Before this confrontation became known, a passing pharmacist teased one of the shoemakers: "You [people] must have big influence (meso)!" Little did he know what would happen next.

If the "Old Town problem" had only been a question of interagency strife, residents would probably become cynical enough. But it is more often the private citizen whose affairs get enmeshed in these administrative squabbles. The citizen gets a permit from one service, which offers every assurance that this is a comprehensive document; goes ahead with the construction or restoration in question; and is punished for failing to obtain permission from one of the other agencies as well. Usually, these disputes involve the historic conservation office and the town-planning office, rather than the municipal authorities. In such cases of contested jurisdiction, one senior local official of the Ministry of Justice, who was thoroughly fed up with having to disentangle them, told me, "the citizen is [morally] in the right" in becoming angry and rebellious. When the town-planning office opened a branch in the heart of the Old Town, its intention was to succeed in public relations exactly where the historic conservation office had most conspicuously failed: "so that people wouldn't be put to a lot of trouble," as one of its clients recalled, and especially so that permit applications could be processed rapidly. The idea was to grant conditional permits, which would require the correction of minor problems—a foreign-language sign,[12] an inappropriate use of cement—before they would formally take effect, but that could be issued within six to nine days from the time of the original application. The historic conservation office allegedly objected to this as trespassing on its own turf, and the branch town-planning office was soon shut down.

Yet only a few years earlier the historic conservation office had itself made a similar concession to local sentiment by opening a Rethemnos office, whereas previously the operation had been run from Iraklio. The town-planning office, which ordinarily restricts some of the wilder ambitions of would-be builders, looks generous and concerned about citizens' welfare by contrast. One town-planning official tried for a while to persuade the Rethemnos branch director to let the historic conservation office have a free rein, thinking that the social consequences of unthinkingly applied conservation rules would both emphasize the social ineptness of those rules and, by contrast, highlight the town planners' supposedly greater humanity.

But the faults certainly do not all lie on one side. In another incident, the historic conservation office had given permission for the addition of a third floor to a Venetian house, after the owner had gone to the trouble of checking with the authorities in Athens and had established that it was set back from the road by the legally acceptable distance of three meters. After a three-week delay, however, the town-planning office insisted that the distance should be four meters instead and that the permit should therefore not be granted. The house owner is convinced that this problem arose mainly because the architect who examined the site belonged to the immediate family of the managerial head of the historic conservation office—a classic illustration of the way in which the facts of local social ties influence, not so much the actual operation of the agencies, as people's perceptions of it. For whether the decision was actually influenced by the civil engineers' division into two mutually opposed cliques, each so firmly clustered around one of the two embattled agencies that a well-meant attempt to create a local architects' association foundered at birth, the client's perception of the matter certainly influenced *his* decision to go no further for the time being. His hope, in short, was that the historic conservation office would provide the necessary funding, and he was not prepared to alienate that office in exchange for a quicker approval from the town-planning authorities. Instead, he hoped that a gradualist approach would enable him to take advantage of his connections with the historic conservation team, while his own investigation of the legal situation convinced him that on strictly technical grounds he could eventually get around the town planners as well.

TRIED BUT NOT TRUSTED: CASES AT LAW

To understand how these charges and countercharges operate, we shall now examine three cases that ended—each more than once—in the courtroom. These cases allow us to perceive, not merely the formal role of bureaucracy and law, but their actual performance by agents who belong to the community whose members stand charged with breaking the law. What we shall see is that judges, lawyers, bureaucrats, and residents all share certain assumptions about the process, and that, despite their affectations of mutual hostility, they agree on the way in which their actions should be governed by those assumptions.

In the first case, a tourist guest-house proprietor wanted to alter the front wall of his building, which faces the "wild side" of the sea on the lower end of the Fortezza's sheer drop down to the water, but is set back on the inner side of the street and thus discreetly removed from the restaurants that have begun to fill up the seafront sidewalk. He had bought the house in 1946 as a "stone-built, earth-roofed, ruined house,"[13] had kept it (with a roofing of iron sheets) as a storage place for barrels and other odds and ends for his soap factory, and had recently transferred it to his son as a parental gift. He hired a civil engineer to prepare plans for rebuilding and duly filed for a permit:

> An inspection was done by the Old Town town-planning office, they came and saw that there was nothing [of antiquarian interest]. Just that there was about seventy motorbikes' worth[14] of rubble.

So he went ahead.

After he had virtually completed construction, a historic conservation official appeared at the site and demanded to see his papers. Sensing trouble, he soon thereafter took the entire file to the conservation office for confirmation. An official there told him, "The permit that you have I cannot keep. But I must keep some of the papers back in order to study them [further]." He told his engineer what had happened. The engineer was horrified: the innocent householder should never have gone there with the papers in the first place: "You have a permit, you're within the law, so as for *them*, let them talk!" he remonstrated.

Construction continued, and then, some three months after he had begun the rebuilding, the owner received notice from the historic conservation office to desist. This was soon followed by an official charge to the effect that he had covered up some old foundations, and he was summoned for trial. One harassment followed another, and, at the time of our discussion, he was facing a *third* court arbitration. The first time, the trial was postponed because the representative of the conservation office was "busy"; on the second try, it was postponed again. By this time, the owner had paid the engineer something in the region of 100,000 drachmas for the original inspection and drawing.[15] As he pointed out, he was caught between two quarreling government agencies. The town-planning office usually rules, not on questions of historic conservation, but simply on whether a plan conforms to safety and other planning requirements; but for this man, as for so many others, such fine distinctions of jurisdiction are academic: "But the substance [of the matter] was one: when we have a permit, do we have a permit or do we not have a permit?" Moreover, while he was in favor of preserving the Old Town, he resented what he saw as favoritism to the more powerful citizen who knows how to "maneuver" (*manouvrerni*) and can have his affairs settled in two or three years.

The data on the second case are much more detailed, in part at least because I was present at the trial and knew or came to know almost all the principals. A rooming house proprietor, Eftikhis Arvanitakis, had obtained town-planning permission to erect a new house on an open space in a side street in the Old Town. The town-planning office also assured him that their permit covered him against all eventualities, and that he did not need to check with the historic conservation office. The latter, however, served him with a notice to desist forthwith. When he refused, they took him to court.

The Public Prosecutor—who evinced considerable impatience with the legalistic maneuvering of the official bodies concerned—predicted that Eftikhis Arvanitakis would be acquitted if he was right in claiming that he had made sure of all the necessary paperwork by obtaining a permit from the town-planning office. The historic conservation office, however, cited him for failing to await their own issuance of a permit, required for any construction within the Old Town. After a lengthy discussion of the exact provisions of the law, he and his codefendants (his wife as co-owner, the two civil engineers who had drawn up his plans, and his contractor) were convicted and sentenced to two months in jail. The lawyer hired by one of the civil engineers requested an increase to three months for them all, as this, unlike the shorter sentence, was appealable.[16] The question that the local court as well as the Appeals Court in Khania had to decide was whether Eftikhis had actually broken the law; and whether, if he had, extenuating circumstances justified his acquittal. After two years of complex legal maneuvers and enormous expenditures of time and money, not to speak of peace of mind, he and his codefendants were finally acquitted. He and his building contractor lost earnings of two to three thousand drachmas each for every day spent in court. The latter may also have lost additional money through being unable to supervise his relatively inexperienced work crew. In general, their case situates the "Old Town problem" in relation to Greek legal culture. It particularly offers some valuable insights into the prevalent mood of irritation with the stance of the historic conservation office, as much on the part of prosecutors, judges, and lawyers as on that of the residents.

The first trial was postponed because the civil engineer who had designed the allegedly offending plans was ill. The next trial, which I attended, took place in the spring of 1987. In the early morning, before the trial, Eftikhis ran into the principal prosecution witness, the chief historic conservation officer. An acquaintance of long standing and herself born and bred in the Old Town, she assured him that she would find some way of presenting the evidence that would not harm his chances. This is especially interesting in the light of subsequent developments; for, in retrospect, it appears that she was thereby able to meet the social expectations of a friend and neighbor without implicating herself in collusion to deceive the prosecution, and her actions after the trial fit the same pattern. Every civil servant in this small town must negotiate a continual and difficult path between the competing traps of social confrontation and legal responsibility.

Three of the codefendants—the civil engineer arrived late from her home in the New Town—forgathered in the courthouse cafeteria to discuss their chances. At this point, the chief prosecution witness appeared again, and Eftikhis amiably introduced her to me. At my request for a meeting, she no less warmly invited me to visit her at her office later in the day. This curious—and, to those involved, apparently unsurprising—sociability between defendants and prosecution witness underscores the importance of maintaining affability in such a small community. The town-planning officer who had issued the original permit also wandered through and chatted with the defendants. The trial itself was scheduled as number sixty for the day. Even allowing for the summary style of these courts that such a high number suggests, it meant a fairly long wait. Defendants must also constantly check to see which trial is proceeding at any given moment. Their names are not called out outside the courtroom, and it would be quite easy to miss one's own trial, as the judge may decide to postpone any number of intermediate ones. If that happens, the defendant is in contempt of court and may be punished accordingly. It is not a system designed to console.

The codefendants maintained their innocence from the start. Eftikhis had gone to the town-planning office, and the official who had issued the permit was willing, even eager, to testify on his behalf. The contractor, too, was adamant that he would never have agreed to participate without first having satisfied himself that all legal requirements had been met: "I don't take on illegal jobs," he flatly declared, further insisting that the state-run electric company would not have cut off the local current in order to let construction proceed had they entertained the slightest suspicion that the project might be illegal. Eftikhis felt especially upset because the contested site is only about fifty meters' walk from the historic conservation office, and yet it took them about six weeks to lodge a complaint—after Eftikhis had laid down the concrete foundations and had begun bricklaying. At their first behest, he agreed to stop work—"I neither cursed them nor refused"—but after a further six months of delay he lost his patience and began again. "Couldn't they [have said], 'Stop, don't do it!' right from the start?" he demanded, aggrievedly.

Eventually, after watching several other matters being rapidly disposed of, Eftikhis and his codefendants were called to trial. The trial was relatively short, but at the end the judge decided to postpone his decision until he had tried another case. This new case, a complex inheritance dispute involving several key actors, lasted much longer than anyone had expected, and by the time the judge was ready to announce his decision, Eftikhis's nerves were clearly very frayed. Eftikhis tried to keep his spirits up by commenting on the judge's "politeness," but the civil engineer, perhaps made more perceptive by previous experience, thought the judge was twisting the knife quite deliberately by adding this new delay.

The conduct of the trial was, as the lawyer was later to observe, a blunt exercise of power. That final delay lent drama to the judge's negative ruling, when it finally came. His timing increased the force of his authority and deflected attention from the arbitrariness of his verdict. Eftikhis was particularly upset at the waste of time: "And [to think] that I have work [to do], and I'm drowning in it, do you see?" This reinforced the judge's display of power, which was also made explicit in his use of easy familiarity in a manner that hovered ambiguously between hectoring and bonhomie: double-edged irony safely beyond objection or challenge.[17] Defendants and prosecution witnesses alike never quite knew where his sympathies were leaning until he finally pronounced the verdict. That verdict was all the more unexpected in that most residents expect judges to be merciful in these cases because they have understood the absurdities of a situation in which the full majesty of the law is invoked over tiny properties of minimal historical or financial value. Certainly, the legal officials who spoke to me about the Old Town expressed impatience with the quarrels of the government agencies.

Much of the trial itself consisted of arguments about the precise interpretation of the law. The lawyer argued that the house in question was not a "monument" (*mnimio*) and could not, therefore, be subject to laws dealing with the treatment of monumental structures. He also suggested that once a permit of any sort had been issued, this should be the end of the matter. The prosecution witness, however, argued that the entire Old Town was subject to close regulation by the Archaeological Service. Legally, the ambiguity seems to have resided in another aspect of the problem. When Eftikhis applied for and was awarded his permit, the law permitted residents to obtain this document from the Old Town town-planning office; the permit was then approved by a council appointed by the Prefect. While he was building, however, a new Presidential Decree required the separate issuance of a historic conservation permit as well. He thus fell in the gap. Did this unfortunate timing make him legally culpable or not? Eftikhis felt that, as a layman, he could not be expected to know the details of current construction law. Indeed, the main prosecution witness afterward supported his claim that those who were really responsible in this regard were the civil engineers. She also castigated the town-planning office for the mischief they had done in giving Eftikhis bad advice.

Before the verdict was announced, this prosecution witness had to leave on other business, and, since I now had an appointment to see her later in the day, I found myself in the awkward position of being the one to tell her the outcome. She professed shocked surprise and immediately telephoned the owners to tell them that she was deeply embarrassed by what had happened. She assured them that they were not to blame, she had been certain that they would be acquitted, and they should get matters set to rights by suing the town-planning office or by exercising their right of appeal. For (we may presume) substantially different motives, she took a position that the civil engineers' lawyer was also willing to consider seriously: that the judge had been attempting to send a stern message to the town-planning office, against which another and more general suit was still pending, while still agreeing to a sentence that could be appealed; and that he had taken this action "so that the employees of the town-planning office might be terrorized a bit, and come to their senses a bit." She was especially incensed that town-planning officials would allegedly advise those to whom they gave permits that these covered the legal requirements of the historic conservation office as well.

The lawyer, however, also thought that the judge may have been attempting to relocate the responsibility for what would otherwise be a dangerous precedent, putting the historic conservation office on the defensive in the face of a likely flood of similar cases. Appeals, moreover, are heard by three judges, not one, and this diffuses the ethical responsibility still further. Interestingly, the historic conservation official tried to get the owners engaged in a common plaint about the machinations of Greek bureaucracy: "Greece, eh?" There is a strong tactical similarity here with Mayor Skouloudis's display of bitter disaffection (see note 7 above) from his own choice of activity. Having claimed that his worst error was to stand for election in the first place—this, after the *second* election of 1986!—he then announced: "Unfortunately, Greece is scourged by petty politics. This is the scourge. In every political situation. I am not a politician! I cannot and do not want to make petty politics; it's beyond my mentality and my tactics. I came here with a job to do." Every individual is innocent of the national character; tactics are above tactics.

These declarations show how deeply local officials are in fact enmeshed in social relations. While all officials are formally debarred from favor peddling, these relationships both enable them—and for practical reasons require them—to make common cause against the faceless apparatus of state. However conscientiously the historic conservation official intended to serve her agency, and there is no reason to suppose that she did not wish to do so, she still had to find a way of managing the social nexus of everyday interaction. The rhetoric of opposition to "the system" allowed her one strategy, although a continuing frostiness suggests that it did not entirely suffice on this occasion. Her protestations of "embarrassment" (using the verb *drepome*) clearly marked her perhaps unrealistic desire to separate her official persona from her social one. Other, obvious scapegoats were available. Either the judge had been trying to frighten the town-planning office, or the town-planning office itself was to blame, or the lawyer was too closely associated with the town-planning office, or the civil engineer—a member of the anti–historic conservation office faction—had been irresponsible. But the owners themselves, she insisted, were not morally to blame, and she would advise them on how to get their rights recognized.

Finally, on appeal, the defendants were indeed acquitted, ironically vindicating the predictions of town-planning officer, historic conservation official, lawyer, and even—if the others had read the situation correctly—the judge. Eftikhis had been determined to pursue his rights to the bitter end: "We shall struggle over it!" And he added that, while they might have been accidental "violators" (*paravates*) of the law, they were not "criminals" (*englimaties*). The judge's position was crucially different. As he subsequently explained, the defendants' tactic was to claim that the law did not obtain in their case. He, in contrast, "applied the law!" In this connection, it is only fair to record that a town-planning official not involved in the case admitted that the prosecution witness was herself trapped by the letter of the law.

The judge, in accordance with his prerogatives, declined to use the option of "mercy" (*epiikia*), a technical loophole that allows a judge to decide against punishment because a defendant is poor. Eftikhis, a generally successful small-time entrepreneur, felt that his financial position had been damaged beyond repair by expensive and time-consuming litigation. But again, the judge, like the prosecution witness, felt constrained to observe the *formal* requirements of the law. The *reasons* he did so were probably as much social and tactical as legal, and it is clear from the reactions of all concerned, himself included, that his verdict was in no sense the end of the affair. It did have the virtue of satisfying both the precepts of the legal code and the demands of a locally powerful official agency. Much more significant, however, is the way it defined the issue so that due process could now be safely removed from Rethemnos altogether, thereby averting a still nastier and more protracted fight.

Whatever the actual motives of the actors in the Arvanitakis case, it is clear that *attributions* of motive are an important tactical device. We cannot be sure how the kinship ties among officials and residents affect their actions, but we can see how *accusations* of interest may affect the outcome of those actions. In much the same way, we cannot be sure why judge, agency officers, and residents took the particular decisions they did, but we can discern the effects of some of the explanations offered by competing actors. Why did the historic conservation officer telephone the defendant and behave so apologetically? Why did the judge prevaricate to such a degree, and why did he reach a verdict so diametrically opposed to all predictions? Whatever the intrinsic interest of the answers to such questions, we can more easily see the actual *effects*, intended or otherwise, of the decisions made, and of the actors' own stated interpretations of what was happening.

One only has to consider that critics rarely mention the officials' dedication to the ideals of historic conservation, in order to see that the representation of motives is a poor source of insight into the motives themselves. Its value lies, rather, in what it tells us about the role of motive attribution in the political process. Accusations of favoritism are part of the conventional wisdom about patronage. Like self-justification (Herzfeld 1982a, following Austin 1971[1956–1957]), such accusations must be cast in a familiar rhetoric, rather than be literally convincing, in order to have any impact. One of the senior conservation officials, a member of a prominent local family, illustrates the other side of this rhetoric:

> When they want to get some matter passed on which the [Archaeological] Service may have an opposing view, they try by means of my people, my family, to persuade me that perhaps they're relatives of mine, perhaps they're friends of mine—because that's the only time they remember me—so that my family will bring me these [comments] and my family will tell me to give him [i.e., the client] special attention, and to serve him and to do what he asks for.

Close relatives are the worst of all. They ask the official to prepare their paperwork for them herself, presumably in the hope of so implicating her in the final decision that it would have to be in their favor. In this, their behavior recalls that of the kin whom the souvenir seller recalled with such distaste. The principle is the same: requests from close relatives are hard to resist. Appeals to even more distant ties of kinship and friendship always call for some degree of response in a small, close-knit community. This creates an almost impossible situation for any employee, let alone a relatively senior one who is visibly charged with decision-making powers (and may be thought to have more than is actually the case). The very people who object to an employee's alleged "amoral familism" equally protest that same employee's refusal to offer them favors.

A weakness not only of the "amoral familism" formulation but also of its critics' objections to it (Banfield 1958; cf. du Boulay and Williams 1987) is that both alike fail to recognize the role of the concept itself as a rhetorical weapon in strategic competition. Actors who want something champion the *morality* of familism, while those who fail to get what they want treat it as a travesty of the state's institutional morality. Officially, at least, the system is so constituted that the plans submitted by an official's close kin do not pass through that official's hands. Such rulings, however, have very little effect on the social pragmatics of reputation. The same principle is at work in allegations that the historic conservation office rejects as a matter of course all plans submitted by members of the "town-planning" clique of civil engineers (which now includes the previous historic conservation office director). The present director, well aware of these accusations, insisted that plans are only rejected for specific, technical reasons.

This discussion leads us to another case, in which one of the actors was a sibling of a historic conservation official and a civil engineer in her own right. Manolis Aridakis, an ex-policeman, became horribly enmeshed in both the social and the bureaucratic barbed wire that awaits the unwary Old Town resident. Another resident described him as "pitiable" (*aksiolipitos*).

In 1978, with a loan, Aridakis bought a house at 800,000 drachmas. He requested that the historic conservation office provide some financial help with the necessary refurbishing of the plaster, windows, and some other repair work. He paid the substantial sum (as it was then) of 15,000 drachmas for the engineer's plans. The entire cost was to be around 300,000 drachmas. A year or two after this application, the conservation office assigned him 40,000 drachmas, from which the engineer's fees had first to be deducted. He went to the conservation office: "With the money you've given me, so to speak, we shan't cover anything." The office director agreed to try again; note that the decision was not to be made by her but could always be attributed to a higher source. After further application, he received an additional 100,000 drachmas: "Of course, it was, so to speak, a sum that in any case did indeed cover part of my overall expense. In any case, I did get it, may those people be well!" In 1980–1981, he contemplated buying a neighboring building with a badly damaged roof and in danger of imminent, wholesale collapse. The town-planning office wanted this house demolished, as it was a public threat; the historic conservation office refused to contemplate its destruction and demanded that it be restored instead. The previous owner, absent in Athens, had suggested to Aridakis that he buy it. He demurred: not only had he no need of such an additional property, but he had no means of transporting the rubble that had accumulated, and the road was too narrow to get a truck through.

Eventually Grigoris Perakis, a civil engineer closely associated with the conservation office, bought the ruined house. "There and then began the waste of my time, my troubles, my worry, everything I suffered, from then on." Workmen came and demolished some of the old walls and the roof. A high wall with two small windows, however, remained in place. Aridakis, with a seasoned police officer's preference for avoiding unnecessary conflict, decided to extend a friendly gesture:

> And I say to him, "Excuse me very much. Are you," I ask him, "the buyer?"
>
> "Yes," he says, "we've bought it now, right here, we have."
>
> I say to him, "Look here. Health and joy to you, may it be blessed with good fortune. But I will ask you very kindly, since," I say, "I have children; I'm a neighbor here; we'll be neighbors, we should have good relations (*thel' 'a 'maste aghapimeni*); I like open discussions—to close up the windows here, now that you're fixing it [the house] up, the children, see, will want to build, and then we'll have complications (*bleksimata*), we'll have lawcourt [cases], we'll have quarreling (*istories*). Which we don't want to have. We'll be," I tell him, "friendly (*aghapimeni*) in this neighborhood," I tell him.[18]
>
> "You know," he tells me, "so as to close up the window," he tells me, "I'll get dark windows, so that nothing will show, so to speak, and they won't be openable."

But this was no solution. Aridakis pointed out that when, at some future point, he or his children decided to build, the newcomers would object, and that would lead to serious trouble. Perakis, however, refused to agree, arguing that the house needed light. When Perakis added not only windows but a balcony door as well, Aridakis went to the town-planning office to complain, and from there to the historic conservation office, where it was soon established that Perakis did not have a permit. As a result, work stopped for while, but soon resumed. Aridakis again called

in the authorities. There ensued a fiercely ironic confrontation between
the communist director of the conservation office and the socialist engineers, nicely swaddled in the ambiguities of the phrase *ti kanete* ("how
are you?" *or* "what are you up to?"). Cutting across party-political differences was the civility expected among professional colleagues, but
other ties only intensified the complexity: one member of the Perakis family worked in the conservation office, and another served on the prefectural council that vetted all the final decisions about building permits.
This was one event in a long series of such standoffs, culminating in the
director's abrupt dismissal and subsequent—and successful—court action in defense of her professional standing.

After another brief pause in operations, Perakis not only completed the
windows but began adding a whole new third-floor room. Finding photographic evidence in the historic conservation office that this extra room
had not existed in the old building, Aridakis confronted his neighbors
with the illegality of their new construction. Again work stopped but
shortly thereafter began anew. Aridakis phoned the historic conservation
office to get the director there at the exact moment that his neighbors
were laying the concrete upper floor section. She did not come. They completed the work, creating yet another window in the process. When the
case went to court, Aridakis was a witness for the prosecution. In the
corridor, one of the defendants accosted him and threatened him with
dire consequences. When he asked a passing employee whether he had
heard the threat, the latter—apparently just to evade possible consequences—denied that he had. When they got outside, the engineer accosted Aridakis again: " 'My village,' he tells me, 'is higher than your
village, we're tougher (*pio pallikaria*)!' " Aridakis responded with outraged dignity, saying he refused to engage in macho gestures (*pallikaries*)
and would prefer to resolve their differences in court. Since building still
continued, Aridakis now resorted to a formal complaint to the Public
Prosecutor, citing these threats as well. The case initially did not come to
court and was only brought when Aridakis reminded the authorities that
the charge included that of threatening behavior. This ruse to get the case
tried failed, as Aridakis could find no witness to the threats, and the entire
case was dismissed. Citizens occasionally threaten various senior officials—we have already noted some instances—and it is perhaps because
of this that the authorities are less interested than they might otherwise
be in pursuing allegations that highly placed persons have threatened ordinary townspeople.

Meanwhile, Aridakis thought he would add two rooms to his own
house as a dowry for his daughter, who was engaged. He got the necessary paperwork cleared through the town-planning office, whose special
Old Town branch was now operating—"so that," as he erroneously

thought, "the Archaeological Service had no business with the building permits of the Old Town." But the branch's days were already numbered. He fell into the same trap as had Eftikhis Arvanitakis. First, when he specifically asked, the town-planning authorities told him that, according to Law 7561/84, he was not required to check with the Archaeological Service, but that he should get the Prosecutor to set a compensation for Perakis's windows. The Prosecutor's response was to tell Aridakis to go ahead and build, and if Perakis wanted to bring the matter to court, it would be resolved there. The first sign of renewed trouble was the appearance of the police with a complaint from the neighbors, but this did not seem serious and they soon went away again. Next came an official from the town-planning service with a complaint that delayed matters further. Again, he was able to continue. Meanwhile, however, a Perakis connection had replaced the director of the town-planning office. She appeared on his doorstep one early afternoon: "Why are you working?" And she went on to threaten him as well as the town-planning officials with jail:

> "I'll put you all," she says, "in jail!"
>
> I say, "Listen here," I say, "I'm in this building. An unencumbered building. You see that very well. So, I have no complications. I'm asking you," say I, "to leave me in peace."
>
> "I'll send you to jail," she tells me, "you'd better know that!"
>
> "Do you know that I've got my daughter engaged to be married?"
>
> "What do I care," she says, "about your daughter?"
>
> So, in the end, I was forced to sue her.

He had explained about the dowry, but she showed no interest. So he went ahead and sued. This time he had a witness, as his wife had been present throughout the confrontation. The official was sentenced to forty-five days in jail.

The next day, however, the official counterattacked, by submitting a formal complaint about the building to the police and the prosecutor. Aridakis had only been served the order to desist *after* he had received the original permit from the town-planning service. The conservation order supervened, however, and the police once again forced him to stop despite all his protests. As a former policeman himself, moreover, he was caught in another social impasse: "Stop? Stop. I desist. What could I do?" So first he tried to get a written statement from the—rather reluctant—director of the town-planning office that indicated he could build. The police responded that the one document did not cancel out the other. Bureaucracy had struck again: "I was about to go crazy!"

He had some basis for concern. The young man who had become engaged to his daughter grew impatient with the slow progress of their future home (and investment) and broke off the engagement. The case dragged on for over a year. One day, by now utterly fed up, Aridakis began to build again. Again the police came; again, he agreed to desist; but this time, apparently irked by accusations that they had favored him as a former colleague, the police served a summons on him. Thus it was that he came to trial, this time as defendant.

The trial itself had elements of farce, notably when one of the witnesses for the historic conservation office accused the director of the town-planning office of being crazy (*paranoikos*) and of interpreting the law in accordance with his own wishes. The judge allegedly tried to help the witness avoid trouble by saying, "[He's] not crazy, the *matter* is crazy!" The conservation witness insisted that it was the town-planning director who was crazy. The town-planning director thereupon seized a copy of the civil code, checked the laws on libel, and demanded that the two conservation office witnesses be sued, calling on the accused—Aridakis—and a lawyer who happened to be present to serve as witnesses. The deeply embarrassed judge allegedly then told him that had she realized he was in the court while other witnesses were giving evidence (which he should not have been), they would not have spoken about him in this way! Aridakis's transformation from accused to prosecution witness cannot have been other than discomfiting to his opponents. Even better was yet to come. The court dismissed the case against him and ordered his neighbors to close up their windows and pay him costs as well. The neighbors appealed, so the case went to a five-member bench, which upheld the decision in Arikdakis's favor.

To cover himself, however, Aridakis asked the director of the town-planning office for documentary support. He took it to the police chief. He began demolishing the old toilet in order to make way for a modern one. Again he was stopped and again permitted to continue after due inspection. A series of legal maneuvers followed, enlivened by several attempts of the neighbors to goad Aridakis into violence with teasing, threats, and offensive names, while his wife tried to restrain him from committing mayhem. "The sky went below and the earth above, so distressed did I become." In his fury, he went again to the Public Prosecutor. The latter told him that, while the alleged infraction would come to court as a matter of course, he should not interrupt his work this time.

At first, the new trial was postponed. When it finally came about, however, the neighbors finally and definitively lost their case and were also ordered to close up their windows. An important factor was the lack of clear evidence that a window had previously existed in that position. A witness Aridakis encountered quite by chance about half an hour before the trial began recalled that in the old days there had been no window there. This witness was an old neighbor, and Aridakis, suspecting that he might be trying a little too eagerly to help, enjoined him not to commit perjury for his sake. Sentiments of neighborliness, which Aridakis had rightly suspected as the cause of this witness's initial eagerness, also made bad data for his case.

A very different argument appears to have clinched the decision in Aridakis's favor. The window, a mere three meters away from a window in Aridakis's own house, was the neighbors' bedroom window, "the window of the room where she [a Perakis family member] will be changing [her clothes], so I don't think that this thing is correct!" Note here the confluence of moral with architectonic concerns: covering is all, and the idea of avoiding future conflict between the children of the two parties coheres with that of their moral guardianship while they are still under their fathers' control.

Despite his victory in court, Aridakis felt himself very much a loser in practice. He had spent something on the order of one million drachmas on court costs, lawyers, special measurements and charts required in evidence, the 30 percent increase in the cost of materials over the year and a half of delay, and the 18 percent V.A.T. in the final stages, as well as additional, wasted wages for workmen. This is the financial loss of a man whose income derives mostly from his police pension and small agricultural holdings. The interminable bureaucratic convolutions strained his patience, especially when—he believes as a deliberate *koroidhia* (public humiliation)—he was promised advance warning of one hearing before the Prefectural Council, only to discover that it was taking place on the very day on which, exasperated at having heard nothing, he finally happened to inquire about it.

Above all, he was hurt in a moral and social sense: "If we speak about the moral damages, these can't be calculated. They're incalculable!" He lost a prospective son-in-law. This entailed a big risk to his daughter's future, whatever the benefits of getting rid of a dowry hunter. Spinsterhood is thought demeaning. In fact, his daughter did become engaged again, to a less impatient or greedy swain who was prepared not to insist on the house as a condition of marriage. The ramifications, however, did not end there. The money that Aridakis lost would have sufficed to buy an adequate house with which to endow his other daughter (they are twins). Now he thinks of splitting the present house in two and renting quarters elsewhere for himself and his wife.

AGENCIES IN CONFLICT: THE REFRACTION
OF NATIONAL DISPUTE

Residents complain bitterly about the inability of the two services, historic conservation and town planning, to unify their operations. To a significant degree, these internal conflicts reproduce intragovernmental tensions in Athens. During the period of my fieldwork, the Minister of Culture and the Minister of Environment, Planning, and Public Works, to whom the historic conservation office and town-planning office respectively reported, were engaged in highly public hostilities. While some local officials assured me that the squabbling in Athens had no effect on their actions, residents' accounts indicate that this denial may have been more of a feint to avoid discussing anything potentially so embarrassing.

There are some indications that the residents may be closer to the truth. When one infuriated entrepreneur, having begun to build a house with town-planning permission, was stopped by police order at the historic conservation office's behest, he went to the Prefect—the highest official in town. The Prefect showed some understanding of his frustration but initially could not help:

> And she tells me, "It's a little bit difficult, because, look here, we have a complication with the two ministries, the one ministry is this way, the other ministry is otherwise."
>
> And I, how am *I* to blame, then? Am I to become the billiard ball between the two ministries? I'm to become the billiard ball that the one ministry will kick from over here, and the other ministry will throw me from over there? It's impossible. I shall go to work. And whoever comes to stop me—I'll kill him!

The Prefect finally agreed to phone the historic conservation office and emphasize the point that where this man had built his house there had been no Venetian ruins of any kind at all. Her own reluctance to intervene may have been the sensible caution of an administrator who needs to know the facts, but it is surely indicative of the situation that this senior official could—with an immediately recognizable bureaucratic evasion of personal involvement—appeal to the most senior level of all.

The quarrelsome example so publicly set by the ministers and their staffs in the capital did at least mean that there was little to restrain local officials from similar conflicts at their own level. It was certainly not the sole cause of conflict. Officials at the Ministry of Culture in Athens assured me that Rethemnos was the only historic conservation project to be bedeviled by so many local public relations problems. While outbreaks of similar tension were reported from Rhodes, for example, the Rethemnos situation has been more consistently problematical. The local conservation office director also told me that she thought that no other town had been granted such a strong financial commitment for this kind of work. Perhaps, indeed, the puzzled irritation of ministry officials in Athens reflects concern over the fate of this massive investment.

At the same time, it is important to recognize that national disputes are refracted through the divisions of local conflict. Social ties of many kinds bind local officials to the citizens. These ties in turn may themselves be deployed as weapons and defenses. Local interpretation of the larger scene may also serve as an oddly selective filter of perceptions. A teacher—and thus an educated man—suggested quite seriously that the entire conflict was being stage-managed by the government, which, having run out of funds, now needed to find an alibi for reneging on its predecessors' commitments. Once again, the local actors' perceptions have a clear and material effect on the way in which events are played through. The theorizing actor may have only a stereotypical understanding of bureaucratic causality, but it is a model based on experience.

Beyond generalizations about the motives of bureaucrats, residents also express doubts about the historic conservation office's solvency at a more immediate level of concern. They worry especially about whether the money available to the office will dry up before their own houses have been restored. Delays are expensive. Repairs to a Turkish staircase that would have cost 25,000 drachmas in 1986 would cost 30,000 drachmas a year later; the owners, however, required by the historic conservation office to replace an entire set of broken tiles with comparable material at their own expense, could spare no further cash for restoring the staircase, which continues to crumble away. Next door, on the other hand, the tiling was replaced by the historic conservation office itself, after the office had interceded to prohibit its replacement by a concrete roof (plaka). In yet another case, a young woman wanted to place a plaka underneath the tiles, then reset them in place, so that leakage would be stopped without violence to the appearance of her house; here, the local explanation for the historic conservation office's refusal to countenance the plan rests on the idea of avoiding precedent—a concern also for courtroom judges. Whatever the reasons, and explanations both charitable and otherwise abound, the historic conservation office does not have infinite funds at its disposal, and its demands irritate impoverished residents when they are not financially supported.

A further problem lies in the lack of local autonomy. Most Rethemniots assume that the real decisions are taken in Iraklio or Athens. This, like the financial shortfalls reported in successive annual budgets, provides local officials with a much-needed alibi in their confrontations with residents. Since they are mostly local themselves, they need a basis on which to make common cause against "the system," as we have already seen in the aftermath of Eftikhis Arvanitakis's trial. Residents often complain that the historic conservation office is unrealistic in believing that it can restore the entire town rather than selected, important buildings. They also maintain that it initiates too many projects at once and then rarely finishes anything; certainly Rethemnos has the look of a place

where extensive restoration is always going on, although it is difficult to
see how the office could both focus on completing single projects *and*
reassure the impatient citizenry of its long-term desire to satisfy everyone.

In the battle over conservation, it is said that the poor—the *fouka-
radhes*—are the real sufferers. Since almost all Old Town householders so
identify themselves, this has the sense of a general complaint, an act of
identification with the oppressed in the best tradition of Cretan populist
rhetoric. The history of this sense of disenfranchisement long antedates
the introduction of historic conservation measures. In the mid-1930s,
when it seemed that the extension of one of the main commercial streets
would require demolition of the mansion of one of the leading local families (whose current head was governor of the Bank of Greece), the plan
was diverted to take in the house and shop of another citizen. The latter—
"the foukaras!"—climbed up on a tall column and threated to jump to
his death in front of the two thousand people who had gathered. It was
only when he was promised compensation that he agreed to come down
again.

Today, the situation is reversed in one important sense. Now it is the
poor who want to alter, demolish, and rebuild; and it is the educated rich
who can afford to take pride in the historic significance of their homes.
Poorer residents express particular resentment at the original leaders of
OTHOA who, they claim, managed to arrange for their own houses to
be restored without cost to themselves and then left their less well placed
supporters in the lurch. To reconstruct a Venetian house in accordance
with the requirements of both the historic conservation office and the
town-planning office can be quite expensive; a laundromat operator, for
example, received a loan of 6.7 million drachmas, which will have to be
repaid with 17 percent interest; it was based on an estimate calculated
before the historic conservation office withdrew 2 million drachmas from
the commitment it had made to his project. He feels utterly besieged, especially as, while carrying monthly utility bills totaling 57,000 drachmas
for the shop alone as well as heavy expenditures on equipment, he must
still persuade a suspicious local clientele that laundromats are a good
idea. For such a would-be entrepreneur, the requirements of the historic
conservation office are simply an added, and huge, burden imposed in an
already desperate situation.

This man at least began with some capital and credit. Those who are
poor to the point of destitution, and who had once entertained hopes of
being able to modify their homes in order to make more money from
them, now feel betrayed on all fronts: by the government, by the political
parties, even by OTHOA. They see fine houses that belong to wealthier,
absentee Rethemniots getting priority, and they wonder. For example, a
house allegedly slept in by Kornaros[19]—the present owner bought it for a

relatively small sum on the grounds that it could be turned into something useful, and he has been locally accused of playing on the previous owner's sentimentality—is now being extensively restored with a view to its eventual use as a folk art museum. One of the neighbors who has been trying to get authorization and funding for repairs to an equally impressive Venetian house commented, with savage irony, that the historic conservation office would do this for the present owner, because the owner is "poor" and "we have lots of money." They spent 11,000 drachmas on hiring a civil engineer to prepare their own restoration plans (fortunately he was a friend, as otherwise it would have cost them 15,000 drachmas), and the photographic work still has to be paid for separately. Since the historic conservation office rejected these plans, they were perhaps understandably bitter, even if the comparison with the wealthy neighbor was hardly fair either; they did eventually succeed in provoking some further action, but only on replacing the wooden doors framed by a monumental Venetian stone entrance.

These aspects of the conflict share one crucial feature. They all show that residents and bureaucrats communicate very erratically with each other at a variety of levels. This is in part the product of a long history of negative mutual expectations. The "non-European" self-image of the Greek, which represents civil servant and citizen as mutually antagonistic raiders, does not serve the development of a unified approach to the problem. Because, moreover, officialdom's very ideology prevents it from recognizing the existence of that alternative discourse in which its own functionaries are fully implicated, there are only the weakest of prospects for a concerted attempt to address the problems at the level where they hurt most: in the lives of those who, having no other homes, must chafe impotently at the constricting confines of a national monument.

HISTORIES IN THEIR PLACES

ANTIQUITY AS POLLUTION: CONTESTING THE VALUE OF THE PAST

This account of Rethemnos has been about conflicting visions of the past and their realization in the present. History is experienced both as an immanent property and as an external threat. The same question returns time and again: whose is the history, and whose the discourse about it? Who decides what constitutes the history of this place? What are the common places of its warring histories? The development of the Old Town gives shape, smell, and sound to a contested cultural topography.

The very name of antiquity provokes resentment. Some feel that it is arbitrarily applied, that it should be confined to monumental architecture. Certainly the perception that some of the antiquities are of "Turkish" date does not increase people's respect for them. Official historiography falls victim to decades of its own derision of anything Turkish and is hard put to defend its position, given the absence of a uniformly clear break in domestic architecture between the Venetian and Turkish periods. Conversely, an elderly refugee from Asia Minor described his house as *katharo*, "pure" or "clean," because it contained virtually nothing of antiquarian interest.[1]

In a town where house-proud women and fiercely independent men resent the intervention of bureaucratic archaeologists, this devaluation of antiquity symbolically reinforces the general distress that residents express at the physical dirt which crumbling, damp-ridden walls impose upon them. At the same time, most residents recognize that *some* buildings deserve to be preserved as monuments. These are not their houses but certain landmark constructions. Not all of them have survived into the present day, and poorer residents bitterly condemn the wealthy merchants who demolished them and thus deprived the town of major tourist attractions.

Thus, for example, it was a merchant who in 1945 demolished the Venetian sun-clock and tower, having first, in 1936–1938, removed a group of buildings serving as shops. The demolition was carried out secretly and in great haste in order to provide a better access route to the harbor storage area. In this way, the high and mighty struck at the collective interest of the town (see also Youmbakis 1970:29), depriving it of what might, in the long term, have drawn many visitors. The poor use this as an example of the selfishness of the rich. The old fabric of the town thus suffered on both sides of the main class division, for the poor, in turn, were not above reusing hewn Venetian masonry, as the Venetians themselves and then the Turks had done in earlier times.

By lending their rhetoric to the preservation of monumental architecture, the poor can thereby deploy the official ideology in support of their own goals. In so doing, they make a clear distinction between monumental and domestic architecture. Many also agree that the preservation of the monumental remains brings tourism and therefore also money. An elderly man mourned the old slaughterhouses, torn down in 1955. The state should not have done that even to beautify the area with a park, he complained, as these old slaughterhouses were *dhiatiritea* ("scheduled for conservation"). These, like the antics of the OTHOA leadership (if its critics are correct), are merely episodes in the shameful history of collusion between bureaucrats and wealthy citizens. Why should the state persecute the poor for doing with their own houses what the rich have already done, with impunity, with the entire monumental heritage of Rethemnos? Like the charge that the domestic architecture consists of tourkospita, these tactics turn official reasoning against itself. Once the rhetoric of national heritage has entered the protesters' vocabulary, it can be turned to their advantage. It may also reflect changes in attitude that themselves index changes in an individual's economic fortunes. Suddenly envisaging the benefits that might accrue to him from the tourist boom, for example, a suitably remorseful hotelier permits himself the cautious self-criticism that he has "perhaps committed a crime" against his own building by making illegal alterations to it. Now, instead, he takes care to conduct the remaining conversion work strictly within the rules, matching the antiquarian design of the house with a sanitized folk heritage of neatly organized wooden chairs and patterned hangings. While, to get his hotel started, he had first sought to demolish most of its distinguishing traces of antiquity, it now pays him to find new ways of endowing it with picturesque antiquity—a strategy into which bureaucrats and fellow entrepreneurs lost little time in initiating him.

Although increasing numbers of Rethemniots have similarly been drawn into the new economic nexus, resistance to the historic conservation office is certainly far from dead. The embittered logic of that resistance today may be summarized in a few sentences. The task of the office is to preserve the monuments of a glorious, European past. Instead of rescuing the last few true monuments from the rapacious rich, however, its detractors maintain that it foists "Turkish" misery upon a poor and victimized populace. To them, domestic quarters are not "archaeology," a term that most Greeks associate with such monuments as the Acropolis in Athens. Even some of those who are comparatively well-to-do and moderate in their opinions voice such objections. One lawyer, for example, echoed Nianias's position in arguing that, while the people of Rethemnos do not deny their history or their culture, the state should make sure that the burden of the expenses should not fall on private citizens. Others are less temperate. Money forces its will on the state, they say, and the state—which in turn is a "bandit" (*listriko*)[2] institution—forces the poor to become lawbreakers in a game whose rules are defined by the rich and bureaucratic: "The bonds that cannot be undone [i.e., regulations] are [simply] broken." In the multiply refracted contest over the meaning of the past and its relics, situated actors adopt attitudes that will serve their interests best. As they variously succeed or fail, their position in the nexus of power also shifts, and their engagement with the past alters with it. These changes are often reflected in tactical alterations of course, as we shall now see.

NEGOTIATING TACTICS AND CONTINGENT FACTS

In the previous chapter, we saw how conflicts among the various official agencies complicated the search for a solution. No less vexing are the power struggles of private interests. When some neighbors began agitating to have the space next to the Hüseyin Paşa mosque cleared of the rubble and weeds that presently litter it, the bank that owned the space refused to cooperate. The bank itself had wanted to build there, but the historic conservation office had succeeded in blocking its proposal. The only change on which neighbors, owners, and officialdom could agree was to close a short-lived "nightclub" that turned out to be a brothel and was promptly and decisively shut down. The Fortezza was the place for such establishments, not a neighborhood in the heart of town that had maintained its respectability since Turkish times. As a result, the open space has become a parking lot for the neighborhood, which suggests that in the end the residents were the sole beneficiaries of this impasse between the big power brokers.

This incident shows how each new disposition of space embodies the consequences of a particular negotiation of the relevant facts. As citizens and bureaucrats alike—and sometimes individuals trying to reconcile both these roles—pursue a variety of evanescent but intensely focused interests, they recast the history of the built environment, the classification of the buildings, and the relative pertinence of a set of often mutually incompatible regulations. Because these all appear to be matters of fact, they are paradoxically more liable to the grandstanding style of social debate that Rethemniots favor than are matters more openly labeled as opinions. To the extent that a building can be classified as Venetian or

Turkish, or that a law can be cited in defense of inaction rather than intervention, "self-evidence" (Douglas 1975) is not only a matter of cultural assumptions but an object of intense strategic manipulation. This is how bureaucracy actually works: official classification provides an uncompromisingly fixed point of reference around which swirl the eddies of intense, volatile negotiation over meaning and interpretation.

Residents can capitalize for short-term purposes on the state's sometimes crippling legalism. Cynics, proceeding from a personal rather than an institutional view of the state apparatus, even argue that the state cannot afford to suppress illegality. One went so far as to suggest that the state would never suppress drugs because then it would have no need of police or judiciary: "What is it [the state] going to do? Is it going to play church [a popular anticlerical metaphor for 'busy work']?" He went on: "The state saves (*ikonoma*), makes money, from illegality." The aggrieved citizen can thus claim to be the victim of state oppression and, as such, can justify the cunning and lawlessness to which the state leaves no alternative. This self-vindicating rhetoric deploys the morality of the state against itself and provides the framework for most of the tactics with which citizens pursue their interests against the law.

Citizens have a thoroughly practical view of the ways in which the state apparatus works. Thus, for example, they play adroitly on officials' fear of their superiors' possible wrath. A coffee shop in one of the best-preserved Venetian segments of the Old Town was connected with the opposite side of the street by a small buttress arch, which prevented the owner from putting up a modern glass frontage to make his establishment more attractive to potential customers. One rainy January night in 1974, he demolished the whole thing. Inside the building, he also constructed a lavatory and shower stall. He had proposed to perform this operation jointly with his neighbor, who backed off in fear at the very last moment. When the police eventually came to investigate at the request of the historic conservation office, he told them that the work had cost him 500,000 drachmas, and that if they wanted him to remove the glass frontage, they would have to finance the change. This aggressive stance protected him from further prosecution, since the authorities found themselves facing a fait accompli, which gave them a moral alibi for inaction.

Violence, too, may be effective against state functionaries, especially when conjoined with the rhetoric of citizens' rights. A knife-wielding butcher chased a historic conservation agent away from his brother-in-law's property and so gained the latter a short respite. Another resident, at a very early stage in the conservation effort (1972), having been thwarted for some twelve months in his desire to build a new house on an empty plot in the Old Town, went to Iraklio and burst in on the then ephor (superintendent), who at that stage still directed the entire Rethemnos operation from the larger city. When the Rethemniot refused to budge, and threatened to return and kill the ephor if he tried calling the police, the ephor checked his files and, as the client later claimed, discovering that the file had been sitting there all along, feigned anger at his subordinates' inefficiency. Sometimes one has to go higher still. One resident demanded an interview with the Prefect, then refused to leave until she agreed to telephone the historic conservation office and have matters sorted out to his satisfaction. In all such cases, violence served as an extreme means of making some change in the supposedly immutable dictates of existing paperwork; ultimately, the citizen must reckon with due process, but this does not preclude preemptive strikes. Violence and legal-mindedness actually do go hand-in-hand in Rethemnos. Like the urbanity and wildness that Prevelakis describes, they inform the practical dialectic of everyday life.

The state prosecutes offenders easily and wins many of its cases. Even this, however, does not necessarily represent a defeat for unruly citizens. Since the sanctions are weak—jail terms can be officially substituted by fines—many calculate that the fines cost less than waiting interminably for a permit that may never be granted and losing business because of the delay. This was the budgetary tactic of the man who altered his house six times and claims he was reported for this to the authorities by hostile neighbors (see chapter 3). Venetian houses had stone kitchen fireplaces, the form of which was stable well into Turkish times (see Dimakopoulos 1977:147). Local taste, uninterested in such historical niceties, held that fireplaces were too Turkish or too rustic. The householder feared that "[someone might] say, 'Are you in the village now, putting fireplaces in?' " He therefore destroyed the old fireplace, which he now admits was a fine feature of his house. Fashions change, and the meaning accorded to such features changes with them (see also Pavlides 1983). Accordingly, he later replaced the fireplace with a modern fireplace, at the substantial cost of 125,000 drachmas. This time, however, the fireplace went into the *saloni*, the public display area of the house, rather than into the intimacy of the kitchen. The social capital of modernity was worth more to him than avoiding a few cash fines.

This calls for some further comment about the significance of fireplaces in Rethemnos. For residents who move away to the New Town, keeping the old house as a place of work, the fireplace serves as an affective focus of memory. An elderly retiree, recently returned from Athens, whose well-preserved old house contains a fine stone tzaki, covered the whole fireplace with a tacked-up piece of oilcloth. He explained that the fireplace needed cleaning before it could be displayed, thereby showing that the functionally small value of these old tzakia has been displaced by their display value and by their objectification as the loci of nostalgia. Another resident, whose small house displayed all the signs of a carefully achieved respectability (matching upholstered furniture and a well-displayed multivolume encyclopedia), pointed with deep pride to the modern brick fireplace his brother had built for his living room (plate 36). On all sides, the status of the fireplace remains instructively ambiguous. Once the symbolic and practical center of domesticity, it has now become the carrier of conflicting ideologies. On the one hand, fireplaces are antiquities; on the other, the repositories of familiar but private memories. People do not adhere to the principles of conservation merely because the state tells them to. Rather, while increasingly using cultural criteria that the state

36. A modern fireplace blends Western and "oriental" artifacts into a statement about family and cultural tradition. Note the barometer and carefully arranged Cretan embroidery, as well as the *naryiles* (hubble-bubble pipe), candlestick, coffee grinder, and wedding photograph. (1986)

has taught them to represent the European essence of Greekness, they try to memorialize their own old life-style in terms that would give it value in a modern world hungry for nostalgia. Those who no longer own an old fireplace now turn instead to a more collective sense of "tradition," one that is more aggressively bourgeois and "European."

Different types of fireplace mark different accommodations to the objectification of tradition. The process whereby people negotiate these embodiments of nostalgia, however, are all effectively drawn from the practical calculus of the pazari rather than from the bureaucratic formalism of the official marketplace. Decisions that should ostensibly be proof against the subversion of precision and order are affected by a subtle drawing of the bureaucrats into the pazari idiom. As we have seen, the Tax Office provides another striking example of this process, with its former practice of basing assessments on the assumption that most citizens will automatically halve the value of any property being sold. Within the range of fiscal ambiguity thus established, a wide range of social negotiations balances personal relations against legal requirements.

In much the same way, historic conservation and town-planning officials alike must weigh social consequences against legal sanctions. The more they incline toward negotiation, the less convincing becomes their pose of disinterested public service—a pose that Greeks conventionally find hard to credit since they know that bureaucrats are always vulnerable to pressure from kin, neighbors, and business associates. By that same token, however, the more bureaucrats attempt to withdraw behind their official facade, with its ideological pretensions rooted in "European" ideals of civic probity, the more they become outsiders in a community where only insiders can function to full effect. Their skill as public officials may largely be measured in terms of how successfully they maintain this improbable balance.

It also turns on the ability to negotiate facts. Questions of precision and consistency, or whether a house is Venetian or Turkish, are surprisingly labile. While the historic conservation office strikes its more unwilling clients as merely capricious, it prides itself on the clarity of its guidelines and their application. Residents perceive its task as the preservation of "Venetian" monuments and object to its intervention on behalf of "Turkish" domestic quarters, as we have noted. They find it hard to understand why it forbids the destruction of definitively Turkish architectural elements such as the kioskia (wooden window extensions) that used to grace virtually all the old houses, for example (see plate 37), or why it allegedly opposes the construction of modern buildings opposite kioskia, even when open space is available, yet through its dilatory management encourages the destruction of many old stone structures. On the one hand, again, it turned down a request to place concrete underneath some so-

37. A Turkish window box and a Venetian corner ornament.

called "Byzantine" tiles; its rationale was that this might have entailed unnecessary structural strain. In a different project, on the other hand, the office director took great pride in a small guest house with an arched ground-floor room and heavy stone paving above, where precisely this technique held the older masonry in place—"because some weight was really needed to counteract the tendency to slip sideways"—and also put an end to water leakage. Such eminently practical decisions may, from an adversarial perspective, appear merely capricious.

Some residents ridicule what they see as the historic conservation office's dominant obsessions: arched doors and windows (plates 7, 9, 23–26, 31, 38, 39) (which "also"—though in very different style—exist in some modern buildings!), and walls of Sandorini earth. Of the latter, an irritated comment, that it doesn't "write" (*ghrafi*) what it is, expresses all the bafflement of citizens required to preserve apparently quite undistinguished and indistinguishable broken-down masonry. An inscription, by contrast, is something people can understand. Yet inscriptions are a form

38. Restoration leads toward the opening of a
new hotel. (1987)

of writing, and, as such, they are the visible reminder and the most potent
symbol of bureaucratic repression past and present. Those who are willing to concede that the control of interior construction has been lifted are
more willing to praise the conservation of buttresses and arched en-
trances, since these do not materially affect living conditions. (But we
should also remember that the term *kamara*, "arch," is a synonym for the
traditional "Turkish" house type that residents find so appallingly dark
and damp.) A nonlocal woman who wants to convert her proud mansion
on one of the main commercial streets into a hotel fumes that none of the
small houses currently receiving attention is "like mine." She would welcome the benison of antiquarian interest for sound commercial reasons
and so claims to envy the poorer residents the attention that the conservation office lavishes on their houses as much as they themselves resent
it. Here, as in virtually every encounter with the bureaucracy, the citizen

39. Work in progress: houses under restoration.
(1986)

seeks to effect advantageous change by playing with the rhetoric of an idealized impartiality with which none actually credit the bureaucracy in practice.

MANAGING TIME: BUREAUCRATIC TEMPO

One clear sign that bureaucrats are themselves engaged in negotiating rather than simply applying a set of semantically transparent laws is the extraordinary amount of procrastination and delay. It is not always clear how much this is the result of individual bureaucrats' caprice or cunning, and how much a consequence of the internal power structure of the bureaucracy.

Some residents apparently believe that the conservation office deliberately causes delay so that walls will molder and decay and thus be more

picturesque for the tourists—not a kindly assessment, but one that illustrates the ambivalence of attitudes toward the summer hordes. Yet delay
does not always serve the cause of tourism. It is said, for example, that
the slow pace of moving the archaeological museum from the tiny Loggia
to new quarters in the Fortezza arises from bureaucratic procrastination
at the highest level: "At one point he's away abroad, at another his wife
is giving birth, at the next he's giving birth himself, I don't know what
they're up to, the Museum doesn't get moved!"

Such delays also undercut the development of low-cost tourist lodging
in the town itself. One couple tried for two years to get a permit to have
their house restored. They had wanted to place larger windows in the
facade in order to let more light in (a common problem), as well as a
balcony overlooking the street, and these items were not approved. At the
end of the two years, the couple was thus left with a design that would
not be suitable for a private dwelling, although it would have served as a
tourist guest house or as a shop. Since the property was co-owned with a
neighbor, they agreed to convert the building into a small hotel. Suddenly,
the husband died, leaving a widow with two small children to bring up;
the co-owner, perhaps not coincidentally, decided that he wanted to turn
his share of the property into an independent unit. At this point, the
young widow gave up in despair and resolved to move as soon as possible
to her natal village. This tale exemplifies a general complaint about bureaucratic slowness: that property remains economically idle while the
procedures grind laboriously toward their uncertain and often capricious
conclusion.

Delay is an endemic problem. One day, I was talking with two brothers, both shoemakers, when one of them noticed that rainwater was leaking through the ceiling. The other brother would have to get up on the
roof to fix it, he observed ironically, because otherwise they would have
to go to the historic conservation office for a permit, and meanwhile the
entire building would collapse. Such bitter jests recall actual experience.
Stories abound of delays in issuing permits that lasted for as much as five
years.

Meanwhile, many find advantage in the strategic manipulation of the
inherent slowness of the bureaucracy itself. A tourist operator set up office in the Old Town and placed a neon sign at the entrance:

> And the devil so fixed it that at that very moment the "Archaeology"
> passes by.
> He asks me, "What are you doing here?"
> Eh! "Can't you see? Look! What are we doing? An office is being created,
> we're putting up signs."
> Says he, "Neon signs are prohibited in the Old Town."

Say I, "What should I, how could I know?"

Says he, "You should've asked us first."

"I don't [even] know that you *exist* in Rethimno, still less that I should *ask* you! You should," I tell him, "have announced it in the local press, that from such-and-such a date neon signs are prohibited. Because I can see that the entire street is full of neon signs. So how could I imagine that they're forbidden? If they didn't exist, then, yes: I'd have understood it."

He tells me, "No; we'll make you out a ticket."

A ticket was indeed sent to me a week later, telling me, "Within fifteen days, take them down!" I neither responded—I've got it here!—nor took them down.

[*At this point, I checked with him:* You took them down?]

No! [*I:* Ah!] Why should I take them down? Are you joking? I paid 200,000 [drachmas]! I should take them down?

[*I responded:* Yes, but now they'll serve you a summons. . . .]

If they do, while three years go by, until the case comes to trial, we have time. At least, let the office get advertised!

Evidently, then, its own sluggishness does not always work in the bureaucracy's favor. The operator admitted to me that he had indeed heard about the regulation about neon signs. As long as others still had them up, however, he was not prepared to sacrifice his own business—a fine illustration of both the competitiveness that legislation alone cannot fully undermine and the constant imputation of favoritism to government agencies. Delay is not, in fact, a prerogative of government agencies. Wherever the pen becomes the symbol of power, similar principles operate. Banks, for example, essential for much-needed loans to cover the costs of construction, can hold matters up over something as straightforward as a guarantor's signature.

Bureaucratic tardiness also contributes to what the townspeople see as the ultimate irony of historic conservation: that it actively participates in the destruction of the Old Town. One impatient house owner calculated that repeated fines for illegal demolition cost him at least 600,000 drachmas. It was, he insisted, well worth the expense to end up with "something fine" to live in. Such calculations are far from uncommon. They lend weight to the authorities' argument that the available sanctions are too light to be effective.

Bureaucratic delay is strongly reinforced by the residents' reluctance to plead their cases in court, and this takes some of the pressure off state functionaries. One angry young rightist, convinced that his troubles are all the result of a PASOK campaign of harassment, insists that he will not go to "beg." Another resident shrugs, "That's not going to profit us at all, to go and exchange 'words' (*loyia*, i.e., hostile words)—here it's deeds [we need]." The avoidance of conflict—"I may say some [bad] phrase (*kou-venda*) and regret it!"—is also a recognition that it is all too easy to end up humiliated. Far easier, then, to blame bureaucratic inactivity than to risk a confrontation that will lead nowhere. This is not resignation so much as a delicately tuned strategy, in which the actor tries to bring indirect social pressures to bear on officialdom while at the same time avoiding the risk of an embarrassingly public failure to achieve the desired result. It does, however, confirm the state in its overriding power. Ultimately the concessions that individuals can wrest from it in this way are usually quite paltry.

THE POWER OF THE STATE: RHETORIC CO-OPTED

At the beginning of the 1990s, it is clear that official policies have radically changed Rethemniot life. The economic benefits of tourism have undercut the stridency of opposition to the conservation program. While the transition to the new economy may be painful—some move their entire families onto the roof for the summer season, in order to exploit every square meter of rentable space within—the lure of a bourgeois, "European" life-style preys on the existing competitiveness and *eghoismos* of the householders. Despite all their complaints of bureaucratic indifference and insensitivity, some residents have clearly found the Archaeological Service to be a beneficent force in their lives. For example, a retired road sweeper found an arched structure in the front wall of his house and was told he must incorporate that wall in the front of his newly constructed abode, but he was allowed to choose whether the arch would adorn a window (his option) or the main entrance-door. A neighbor was similarly allowed to rebuild the ruinous inner structure, being required only to retain the front wall of the house. Having bought the house plot and attendant ruins for 310,000 drachmas (plus 40,000 drachmas in tax), this man is well satisfied with an initial investment that in some eight years has now risen to a value of between 6 and 7 million drachmas. Most, however, like Eftikhis Arvanitakis, complain that historic conservation employees spend inordinate amounts of time holding up work on houses that have no real archaeological value, or that are only three or four decades old, and that such delays are economically disastrous.

Even those who condemn the conservation office often feel constrained, at least in conversations with outsiders, to point out its advantages: some money has been made available for restoration, particularly of doorways; the tourists come because the ancient streets attract them (although many feel this to be a minor part of the tourist attractions that Rethemnos has to offer). The rhetoric clearly displays the effects of a slow but steady infiltration of official values, although individuals deploy these to unexpectedly diverse ends.

The rhetoric often also hints at the fear of official power to which some residents admit. This may also explain in part the qualifications with which many hedge their more bitter criticisms. The woman who had initially called the historic conservation office a "great wound" changed her story the very next day when my return made her realize that I was actively interested: the bureaucratic delay shrank from five months to three; the historic conservation office *might* cover some of the costs and would do all the planning; other people might have bigger problems, but "the 'archaeologist' got to know me afterwards"—that is, after her first encounter with the office—and he made sure that all was in order. Her revised account suggests, not only the fear that many associate with bureaucratic repression, but also the view that the only way to circumvent that repression is to acquire a personal contact—the official who "got to know me." If she believed me to be a government agent, she could at least now counter with one of her own. Official rhetoric to the contrary, influence (meso) has always been regarded as the most effective way to get things done and deflect petty harassment. A patron's rank in the wider hierarchy can be the most compelling of arguments. A struggling *pension* owner whose patron happened to be a government minister can terrorize a historic conservation official. As a beneficiary of just such protection was told by an intermediary: "One of his underlings told me, 'He couldn't *not* give it to you!' " From the perspective of most residents, then, state power is a far from abstract force in their lives. It is, on the contrary, an approachable human presence, the enabling condition of their attempts to negotiate each situation as it arises.

Even the wealthy and well regarded must operate in this way. The wife of one powerful local figure mused that she would have to ponder the question of whom she knew in the historic conservation office in order to have some aggravating delays taken care of: the bureaucrats were stalling on the grounds of lack of funds—"business as usual" (*ta sinithismena*). The wealthy and influential thus also have, or think they have, better access to the scanty funds that do exist, while those who are both poor and without influential friends are doubly disadvantaged. Limited in their tactical choices, the poor also cannot afford the kinds of alteration that the historic conservation office would allow them to make at their own expense. The poor thus treasure their contacts all the more lovingly. Fear of alienating such few sources of influence as they possess is the stick that goes with the carrot of genuinely effective patronage.

Fear is a real issue for the poor. However unjustified it may appear to be in a democratic state with guaranteed citizens' rights, it represents a tangible basis of state power and a realistic assessment of day-to-day experience. At the very least, residents suspect that bureaucratic interference or hostility could wreck their already pitiful finances through the vindictive creation of delay. The market police practice of carrying out spot checks recalls the more sinister forms of surveillance that were common in earlier, less democratic times. While most would agree that these days are irrevocably over, habits of discretion and creative misrepresentation die hard—as, perhaps, does the fear that actuated them. A local conspiracy theorist insists that NATO and the European Community, both very popular scapegoats for the country's international embarrassments, are also behind the historic conservation office's activities, and that the Municipality would not dare to oppose such powerful forces, which operate worldwide. While it is perhaps difficult to imagine what interest NATO might have in the preservation of the Old Town, it is true that the European Community has provided extensive funds for historic conservation, and the comment illustrates the kind of analogy that invests the conservation office with such terror for some.

Fear does not always take such extravagant forms. As an ethnographer asking questions, I was obviously suspect, at several levels: I might be a spy for the authorities, or I might represent one of these larger, more inchoate and sinister forces. The conspiracy theorist just mentioned—certainly not a man to mince his words—backed off from telling me about the bureaucratic adventures he had experienced in connection with his former home in the Old Town since, he said, he had given it to his daughter and "it's not mine" any more: while he might be willing to expose himself, he was not prepared to risk his family and was perhaps also relieved that in fact he really did not have to deal with the problematical house any longer. A neighbor with whom I had otherwise extremely cordial relations would not let me into his house to see the very alterations of which he had boasted to me in very precise terms, apparently for fear of becoming entangled with the authorities. "We should not speak!" said another—and disgruntled—citizen; he added, however, that he would make use of the town's rich crop of newspapers to describe his dispute with the archaeologists once it was settled, and he hinted darkly at iniquities which he constantly promised to specify but never did. Said another resident, explaining the general reluctance to discuss the difficulties citizens had experienced with the bureaucracy, "Not many people want to expose themselves." While eventually many did so, I found the confidence they thereby showed all the more impressive, as I now knew something about the deep unease that had previously inhibited them.

Such fears do have some basis in current experience. Skilled local actors play on residual fears, although the unscrupulous do sometimes meet their match. During the 1984 parliamentary elections, a local PASOK agent appeared at one house bearing posters and accompanied by two

young women employees of the historic conservation office. "You'd better put up a poster if you want your house done up," threatened the party
agent. The householder, who runs a small business on the ground floor,
agreed—on condition that he might put up a poster for the conservative
opposition as well. A less self-confident individual, or one for whom the
archaeologists' help was more crucial for business, might well have seen
in this encounter, not a heavy-handed jest, but a literal threat. Similarly,
a bitter critic of PASOK rule, son of a former policeman associated with
the extreme Right and himself a local representative of the ultraconser-
vative EPEN (National Political Union) movement, claimed to have received direct promises of funding and technical help from the Ministry of
Culture in 1982 and yet still, some four years later, to have seen no progress; and he interprets this as evidence of political discrimination, pointing out that his father's house is the only unrestored one in a long row of
buildings, the rest of which are inhabited by PASOK supporters. This
man is relatively well-to-do and refuses to go back to the ministry to
"beg." It seems that his complaint may be worth more, socially and politically, than eventual success with the ministry. A wealthy, conservative
housewife who had been unable to get action on her house averred, with
legalistic delicacy, that "if one isn't sure one cannot say" that political
favoritism has played a part; but then, with darkly cheerful humor, she
added, "I told you before that I had a [great] love—Karamanlis!"[3] Fueled
by impatience, suggestive hints break through a tired propriety, hints that
the fear of sanctions can no longer effectively suppress.

Historic conservation officials understandably deny all charges of political favoritism. The office director, for example, was at pains to point
out that her own house had been only half-completed while other projects
went forward, and that the office's workmen—despite the Rethemniots'
sneers—were "of all [political] stripes." Perhaps the Rethemniots' contempt for these men lies in part in the fact that the conservation office had
originally hired and trained men from the villages, and to such an extent
that the present management does not feel able to replace them with town
dwellers.[4]

Whatever one may think of the charges of political favoritism, many of
the truly poor genuinely do suffer from the conservation effort. There are
many reasons why the burden falls more heavily on them. Not only do
they lack the "friends" so necessary to having one's business taken care
of quickly (although supporters of the extreme Right now claim that the
socialists have turned the tables on them in this regard), but the consequences of a decision that in effect forces them to buy a new dowry apartment for a daughter, or to wait an extra few months for required alterations or bureaucratic delays, loom much larger in proportion to their
overall finances. Even a relatively well paid wage earner, a teacher, re-

counted a sad tale of losing a Post Office loan for reconstructing her
house because the paperwork took so long; after that, in order to get her
house properly finished, she had to take on extra work at school as well
as private employment at a tuition school (*frondistirio*).

For the truly poor and uneducated, the burden is enormous. At the very
first stage in the process, they can ill afford the expense of getting competent civil engineers to draw up their restoration plans for them (see the
fine examples in figs. 7.1, 7.2, 7.3) and so they more easily fall into the
hands of the unskilled or dishonest. One elderly man wanted to build a
small storeroom atop his two-storey house, which was not itself of any
great antiquity. He found a nearby civil engineer, who agreed to do the
plan for a relatively low fee of three thousand drachmas (still, however, a
substantial outlay for a man whose only income was his state pension).
The application was turned down because, responded the historic conservation office, the house itself overlooked the "Turkish School"—one of
the few monumental structures in the Old Town—so that any addition
would obstruct the view. As a result, the old man was out of pocket, disgruntled, and no better able to store his goods than before. A more
knowledgeable (or straightforward) civil engineer would have established
that the plan was not feasible at the outset, and would have told the client
so. It is obviously not always possible for the engineer to predict or control the outcome, popular cant to the contrary. At least, however, the
chances are demonstrably better for those who can protect themselves
with the services—official and unofficial—that money and influence can
buy.

LIMITATIONS AND POSSIBILITIES:
THE RANGE OF CHANGE

The belief that the historic conservation office controls the minutest detail
of each house interior dies hard. Thus, for example, a grocer, who serves
on the Old Town district council and should be well informed, gave as
his major complaint the "fact" that people could not do as they wished
with the *interiors* of their homes. In reality, the ability of the historic conservation office to interfere with what happens in the interiors has been
substantially restricted by the more recent legislation. Those who are
aware of this have come to believe that only "influence" will persuade the
office to authorize and undertake any interior work at all. Few, however,
admit to believing in the new dispensation, and it is not uncommon for
house owners to wait until nightfall before they get out their tools and
bags of cement and set to work. Indeed, whole houses have come down
in a single night, since the authorities can never reverse a fait accompli.

In part because of the health hazards of their ramshackle, humid

Figs. 7.1, 7.2, 7.3. Architectural Plans for Renovation (after K. Iliakis)
These plans show the incorporation of elements such as curved doorways, a
Turkish-style window box, and "Byzantine" tiling in accordance with the pre-
dominant idiom for the Old Town.

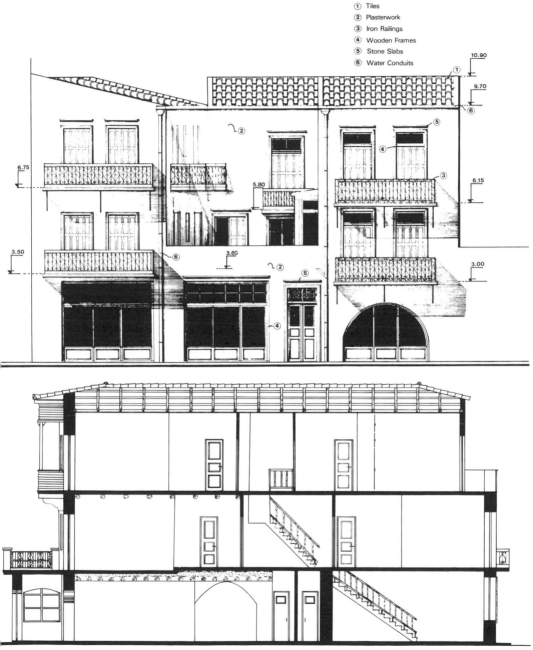

① Tiles
② Plasterwork
③ Iron Railings
④ Wooden Frames
⑤ Stone Slabs
⑥ Water Conduits

7.1

Fig. 7.2

homes, many owners are caught in a pitiless dilemma. Too poor to purchase alternative accommodation, they pay monthly rent for scarcely less
ruinous quarters, usually indeed in the vicinity of their own properties.
Meanwhile, the rising cost of living—fueled by the tourist boom that others have managed to exploit—perpetuates their homeless status. Those
who can afford to, simply leave, either for the New Town or for Iraklio
or Athens (although gambling, for example, may have been a more cogent
cause for emigration to Athens in search of work than the bitterest conflict with the archaeologists). The properties they leave behind are practically worthless, at least in terms of conversion to other kinds of property. The owner of a Venetian building with a floor plan of 299 square
meters, for example, plausibly argues that the 10 million-drachmas valuation which the historic conservation office placed on his property would
only buy him a "little box"—though actually somewhat more than the 5
square meters he claimed—in an apartment block in the New Town.
Meanwhile, who is going to find the 30 or 40 million drachmas needed
to carry out the full restoration the historic conservation office considers
his house to merit?

Nor is it necessarily an advantage to own a much smaller house, since
then it becomes virtually impossible to find people to rent the property.
Aside from souvlaki stands, with which the market is fairly saturated by

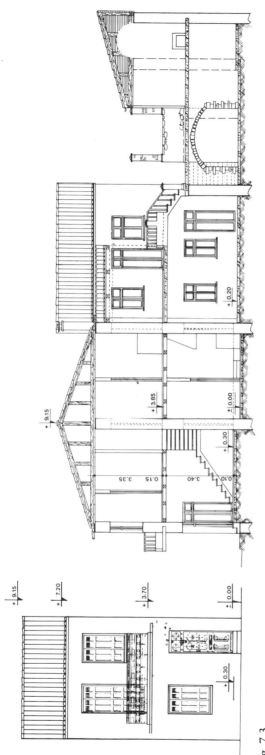

Fig. 7.3

now, the health inspectorate restricts the viability of such cramped quarters for would-be restaurateurs: "The law itself sabotages [us]," moaned one sad proprietor. "It doesn't support Rethemnos." In winter, this man served a restricted choice of food to local customers, including a company-loving amateur lira-player who would often provide lively accompaniment to an evening's exchange of ribald or philosophical verses, amid the surviving architectural fragments of the stable that originally occupied the ground floor—especially the *mantziadhoures*, or mangers (cf. Italian *mangiatori*). In summer, a few tourists would delight in the simplicity of cheap food at tables placed on the narrow corner sidewalks. The proprietor, however, would certainly have preferred something less picturesque and more profitable.

Others may prefer not to alter their properties, but this again stems from a pragmatic realization that any entanglement with the authorities is likely to bring trouble. A family that owned one of the fish restaurants in the Old Harbor was approached by the Tourist Police and advised to replace their old-fashioned frontage with glass display windows and other "modern" equipment. This would have earned them a higher official grade, permitting them to raise their prices. The owner's son, however, told the police that he intended to leave things as they were: "Consumption brings profit, and not profit consumption," as his grandfather had advised him.[5] He noted that the historic conservation office had money for such restorations, which have indeed become general all along the Old Harbor frontage, but his reluctance to take their advice clearly stemmed, at least in part, from the common perception that advice from any official quarter is always countermanded by someone else.

Few indeed are those who can afford the prohibitive cost of conforming to the requirements of the historic conservation office. Most who do so are entrepreneurs who, having made money in another business, can now afford to equip an entire house for tourist use and can meet other legal requirements as well. A butcher, who opened shop in the main market area, moved out of his Old Town house as soon as he was economically able to do so; then, after several years of renting it to a poor Old Town family, he evicted these tenants and converted the building into a superior rooming house ("studios"). He undertook all the expenses on his own account but consulted with the historic conservation office throughout the renovation process. Although many originally condemned the historic conservation office for not letting people "put their hands"[6] to their houses, this man, at least, now spoke warmly in favor of its actions. He even outdid it in one respect. While insisting that the office did not require complete uniformity in the windows of each house, he spent 700,000 drachmas on removing a balcony and an overhang and on making all the windows uniform. (Rumor set his expenses at 6 million drachmas!) But he had other ways of stating his individuality: the renovated building, clearly marked by an elaborate sign as a tourist establishment, was named for his daughter. Once everything was ready, he handed operation of the guest house to a tourist agency and thus has a moneymaking operation in which he presently needs to invest only a small amount of time and additional effort. In much the same way, a businessman who does not himself live in the Old Town was able to open a thriving rotisserie on one of the main streets. Although he stripped and painted the interior walls, he made no structural changes, and the historic conservation office has promised to restore the windows. He can afford to wait; his house is no longer used as a residence, and his business does not depend on architectural niceties.

The internal disposition of most of the older houses does not conform to the social and physical requirements of a modern family: plenty of light, individual bedrooms, adequate bathroom space. The walls are strong, but both the interiors and the decorative details of the facades need more thorough restoration. And it is here that the contest with the historic conservation office becomes especially pointed: the inhabitants argue that the office should not invest so much time on facades (or on the Turkish-style kioskia, for that matter—many Rethemniots recall the systematic destruction of scores of these reminders of the past at the behest of a mayor in the 1930s) but should help the inhabitants restore the house interiors in a way that would make them fit for modern living.

The situation is compounded by the curious circumstance that the historic conservation office is itself often cast as the agent of destruction. It is accused of having caused the town a "great injury," but this is ambiguous: does the charge evoke the misery of life in a neglected monument, or does it mean that the historic conservation office is actually to blame for the continuing destruction of the town's physical fabric? Which politia is suffering—the people, the physical town, or (in this case another possible meaning) the state itself? Whatever the answer, the collapse of the physical town serves as a bitter metonym for the condition of its inhabitants, and this curious irony deserves closer attention.

The reasons for which it can seem plausible to accuse the historic conservation office of direct responsibility may be summed up as follows: frustration, bureaucratic delay, and intransigence. There is also a widespread perception that once *afthereta* (unauthorized—literally, "arbitrary"—constructions) have been erected, no one will tear them down again. Generally speaking, this is true. No judge, for example, wishes to issue orders that will cause townspeople to remain homeless in any directly attributable sense, while the social disruption that would arise from the destruction of a dwelling unit built as a daughter's dowry cannot be contemplated (see also Hirschon 1989:118–128). There is thus a connection between the "fear of responsibility" (*efthinofovia*) evinced by judges and other locally accountable state officials (including the staff of the historic conservation office), and a high degree of institutional resignation to the apparently inevitable—an institutionalized form of "fatalism" that in this case represents a virtual triumph for the lawbreaker.

THE TEMPORALITY OF CONSTRUCTION AND THE CONSTRUCTION OF TIME

This resignation is a bureaucratic reincarnation of the traditional view of fate, that "what it writes it does not unwrite" (see Herzfeld 1982a:649–652). Irrevocable writ is the usual metaphor for the inevitability, retrospectively understood, of fate; and this image carries over, as we have seen, into the power of the bureaucratic pen. Conversely, a citizen's strategic manipulation of the bureaucracy largely consists in getting its functionaries to commit favorable decisions to writing before they can change their minds. Like bureaucratic classification, official time masks its own malleability. Ever eroding the inexorability of cultural history and political authority are the personal histories of social actors.

In the management of historic conservation, a common debate about time concerns the original form of buildings. Which evaluation holds usually depends on the discovery of written or pictorial evidence. A relatively recent cataloging of the buildings may displace oral tradition, because *written* evidence is more "real"—or at least more ineradicable—than oral. But official documents also displace personal mementos, even written or pictorial ones. When two sisters who shared a magnificent Venetian house discovered old photographs that showed a two-storey kioski on the facade, they wanted an appropriate reconstruction added to the house; their request was denied because an older photograph that showed the kioski had been temporarily misplaced. By the time it reappeared, the construction company that did the restoration work had instead built balcony supports which made a kioski unfeasible. As the sisters point out, matters were conducted on a very makeshift basis at that early stage in the historic conservation effort; nonetheless, the pattern is one that fits the more general pattern of bureaucratic concern with "covering" all likely sources of trouble by securing the fullest possible documentation before taking or permitting action.

It is not only the act of writing that creates irreversible conditions for the bureaucrat. So, too, does the physical construction of new buildings. To rephrase the proverb: what is built cannot be unbuilt. This applies to minor changes in interior structure and decoration as much as it does to wholly new, unauthorized buildings. Thus, to open a hotel, most local business people would *first* get the building restored or constructed and then, gradually, seek such permits as were still outstanding. Others, closer to the "system," may also test the ambiguous edges of the historic conservation laws. A well-connected civil engineer who wished to convert a Venetian house into a modern restaurant began the work, then applied to the historic conservation office for permission. The plans, although incomplete, were forwarded to a special meeting of the council that rules on all Old Town decisions of this kind; and no further objections were raised. Critics saw it as significant that the applicant was both a colleague of the civil engineers and architects who constituted a plurality on the council and closely related to a key functionary. Whatever the grounds for this highly circumstantial innuendo, the socially significant aspect is townspeople's automatic assumption that he would not have been fool enough to fail to exploit his advantages. A further irony of this incident is that the historic conservation office is said to have thereby lost the chance to record the original paving—the very element that they had forced the Municipality to let them preserve in the shoemakers' lane.

Not everyone even goes through the motions of obtaining a permit for privately undertaken restoration, which may follow the same logic, and the same assumptions of irreversibility, as modern afthereta. An elderly veteran of the leftist forces in the Civil War wanted to restore his house to its condition during his father's time. It was in this house that the royalists had killed his father. The son had been long absent from town, and now, in his old age, he sought to enshrine this personal history by removing the accretions of intermediate occupancy. He worked at night, behind a carefully closed door. He had to move some ten truckloads of rubble, left from the collapse of the roof and from additional detritus thrown into the house from next door. This was no "archaeological" conservation, nor, in fact, can it have been an exact reproduction of the house as it had been in his father's time, for he smashed a "traditional" washing trough (ghourna) and supported the front balcony with iron struts where none had previously existed.

He worked in extreme secrecy. Aside from the fear of roufiania, the old Resistance fighter, who customarily travels armed in case of sudden attack, was mindful of the many unsettled scores left by the Civil War. He did not care, however, what happened *after* the work was completed. The house had been deserted for thirty years while he had been away, first in various prison camps as a political detainee and then earning a living in Athens, and it would not be possible now to determine when the repairs had been effected. He could plausibly deny all knowledge of what had happened, and he was even willing to consider asking the historic conservation office for help with the restoration of the facade. This may explain why, passing his house, I discovered cement bags lying against the house front long after he had finished the interior remodeling; otherwise, such carelessness might have seemed to invite trouble. I have heard it said that whenever historic conservation officials see two bags of cement lying anywhere, "it [the "Archaeology"] has to go inside" to investigate. Conversely, sacks left lying outside are a sign of confidence that one is clear of all legal obstacles (plate 39).

The old veteran's goal was quite specific. He valued his own family's history far more than that purveyed by a state bureaucracy which he had long ago learned to detest, and he was not prepared to brook the delays and possible refusals to which officialdom would probably have subjected him had he gone through the required procedures. It was, of course, a particular version of that history: the house had earlier belonged to his grandmother (MM?) and thus probably came to his father as dowry property inherited from his grandmother by his mother, but it was the association with his father that moved him. Ironically, his effort was described to me as anapaleosi—one of the official terms for restoration. The question of *whose* history is to be celebrated in the physical facts of conservation determines what restorations or substitutions are actually made.

This means in effect that acts of demolition or restoration are preemptive. When the 1968 law was introduced, a former mayor urged all owners to modernize their houses before the law could take effect. Note that his call for action *anticipates* and thus *resists* legal closure. Whether as written edicts or as physical changes, barriers of this sort are only inevitable by hindsight. If what is written cannot be unwritten, it can at least be *re*written; and if what is built by a citizen cannot easily be unbuilt by the authorities, an old building can at least be induced to fall down. (In a democratic society, the state is arguably much more at the mercy of "fate" than are individuals: when I began fieldwork, not a single local construction declared afthereto had been pulled down by the government.) The severe literalism of official practice gives the tactically adroit citizen some real advantages. One Rethemniot remarked of the afthereta, with painful accuracy, "Here in Greece, nothing [is] more permanent than the temporary." He had specifically meant the phenomenon of afthereta functioning as restaurant-bars without either a building permit or a license, both of which require such lengthy procedures that anyone who failed to go ahead unofficially while awaiting the outcome of the official process would seem rather simpleminded. It is widely understood that the main priority in the construction of any afthereto is to get the roof on, as this makes a dwelling definitive (even if illegal) and thus more or less assures the building's continued existence. Today, some of the afthereta that were originally put up by Asia Minor refugees in the vicinity of the Fortezza are scheduled for demolition as part of the town-planning office's attempt to create a "Green Belt" around that majestic monument, and these will be the first afthereta to fall to the official wrecker's ball—doubtless hastened on their way by their unsavory reputation as bordellos.

The following incident demonstrates another way in which skilled tacticians can exploit the bureaucracy's legalistic paralysis. Approached by a customer for advice on getting a permit to pull a building down, a demolition expert told him simply to request a roof renewal permit instead. Although mystified, the customer did as he was told. When the permit arrived in due course, the demolition expert waited until an afternoon when the nearby Archaeological Museum was closed, then removed the old roof, taking care in the process to weaken one of the walls at the same time. As soon as the new roof was added, the wall collapsed and the building was rendered useless. As a result, the owner was able to replace the entire building after all, whereas an initial request for permission to do so would certainly have been denied. Another of the demolition expert's customers had a permit to make internal changes but wanted to replace his whole house. The demolisher had several workmen at the ready. When the inspector from the historic conservation office showed up, she fussed about the importance of protecting certain features, then started to leave. At that very moment, the workmen gave one of the walls a massive shove, and the whole building began to collapse. The demolisher called the official back to see for herself what had happened. Since she had not actually witnessed the sabotage, she could only certify that the building had indeed collapsed. Had she refused to do so, she would have found herself at the center of a storm that, without restoring the building, could have led her to court. The conspirators had managed to co-opt her, willy-nilly, into their scheme, showing thereby an understanding of bureaucratic process that contradicted the law's insistence on simple questions of right and wrong.

She had little choice. In the absence of proof, faced with an irreversible situation, she had just witnessed a demonstration of the way in which bureaucratic good intentions can become ensnared in their own logic of precise documentation. The wrecker timed his actions with strategic finesse, converting the exigencies of the moment into an act of permanent destruction. Nothing, it is true, is more permanent here than the temporary. Under the volatile conditions of historic conservation in Rethemnos, conversely, nothing is potentially more temporary than a building designated as a permanent monument to the past.

CONTRACTUAL CALCULATIONS

Citizens' tactics turn bureaucratic literalism against itself. At the same time, one must have explanations ready in case of failure, while those who do succeed are equally skilled at justifying what others are all too willing to represent as preferential treatment.

The contrast between the well connected and the effectively disenfranchised becomes clear from a comparison of cases. A construction laborer wanted to demolish his two-room house on one of the approach roads to the Fortezza because it had walls so thick that he could build a three-room modern house in its place. He denies that it is any older than he is, although the thickness of the walls makes that assertion improbable; more to the point, he maintains that the historic conservation office has been dragging its feet for ten years now, and he is particularly angry because a local entrepreneur has meanwhile succeeded in getting permission to construct an entirely new three-storey hotel only 200 meters below the Fortezza. Whatever the justice of his claims—some said that the hotel had been authorized by the European Community's local commission but *not* by the archaeologists!—the aggrieved workman's irritation at what he perceives to be his unequal treatment at the hands of the historic conservation office echoes a common complaint, one that fits the demonology of bureaucratic victimization and thus provides a socially acceptable excuse for his failure to have achieved any progress. This puts those with good connections on the defensive. A long-term resident with a history of government service and ties to the currently ruling party (in other words, a man who was used to being thought excessively well favored) responded to a jealous interlocutor by asking how *large* the latter's house was. "One hundred and twenty-five square meters," came the reply. "Mine's 360 square meters," retorted the other, thereby denying that he had received any benefits beyond his entitlement. His rival, also a government supporter, was unlikely to pursue the matter—although he did volunteer an exasperated, "I pay taxes!" It is easy to see why those lacking party connections or private wealth might find cause for complaint. Even the well-to-do and politically connected, however, report a wide range of frustrations.

The law itself makes for a high degree of negotiability in practice. Because the laws have been revised so frequently, documents relating to the transmission of property tend to be extremely complex. This is especially so when many heirs—in one case thirty-four, and not uncommonly more than ten—inherit a small, ramshackle, and unsalable urban property in equal shares; or, worse, when the living heirs have either already passed the first generation of the testator's children or claim widely varying degrees of consanguinity with the testator. The two examples given here (figs. 7.4, 7.5) will illustrate the effects of such fractionation. In the first example, the heirs, all children and grandchildren of the original testator but only some of them still resident in Rethemnos, divide a small property into equal shares. Thereafter, some intrafamilial sales will simplify the

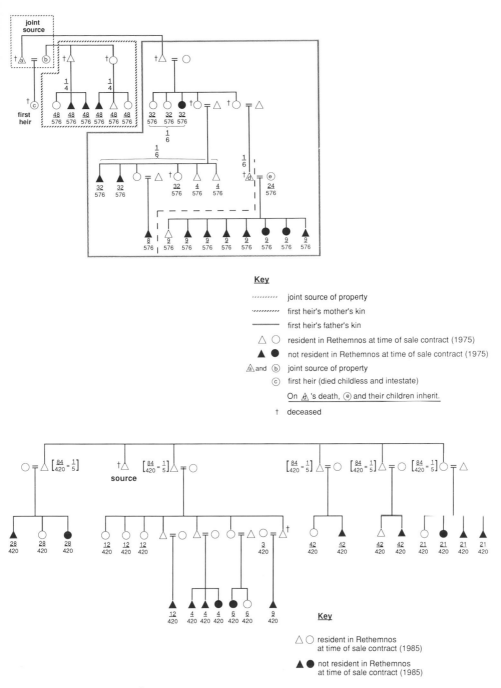

Figs. 7.4, 7.5. Division of Property: Two Cases

Fig. 7.4. (*Top*) This property was sold for 225,000 drachmas, so that one 576th part was worth slightly under 391 drachmas.

Fig. 7.5. (*Bottom*) The declared sale price of this property was 6.5 million drachmas, so that one 420th part was worth fractionally over 15,476 drachmas.

picture, but each such sale has to be separately negotiated and contracted and results in a further expenditure of tax payments. In the second case, the testator had no children of his own. The legatees inherit in proportion to their degree of kinship with the testator. In this instance, no subsequent sales are on record. It is not possible to discern from the records I have examined whether the greater geographical dispersion of the heirs and the more diffuse character of their common kinship contributed to the difficulty of resolution. Both of these eventualities, however, are clearly problems in the disposition of property transmitted in this laborious way.

Under this disposition, no heir inherits a particular piece of the property. Instead, all inherit shares in its value. In order to divide the property into separate freehold units, they must sign an additional contract. While this is often done as a means of separating floors, a device that especially serves the purpose of dowering daughters while continuing to keep these young women under a measure of parental observation, it is much less practicable when single floors or extremely small houses are under consideration. In such cases, the heirs may decide among themselves, and on an informal basis, how they want the space distributed. Since the stakes are likely to be small, and since in many such cases the initially cramped conditions of the house will have forced many of the children into early emigration, the likelihood of conflict is also comparatively small. In the absence of documentation, however, further litigation becomes impossible if the heirs should after all come to disagree, because their claims will be based on a legally indefensible—because unrecorded—agreement.

But should they remain in agreement, there are real advantages to avoiding a contractual division of the property, even when there are only two coheirs. Most obviously, they evade property taxes. The absence of legal documentation, moreover, makes it easy for one of them to erect an illegal building. This may even occur with the unwitting cooperation of the law, if the second heir already has a building of legal size and height on one segment of the property and can therefore plausibly seek permits from both the town-planning office and the historic conservation office to "add" on to the existing property.

In one such case, because the coheirs had not signed a contract dividing the original property, no official "caught" the fact that one two-storey building had now been separated from the courtyard that made it legal; while the second heir began to construct a second building in the courtyard—nominally as an extension of his own property, but in fact as an extension of the first coheir's original structure! Both were merchants, and some special deal appears to have compensated the second heir for his trouble. Neither unit of the property so divided now met planning standards for size. By the time the second coheir's building went up, masked from the town-planning office's vigilance by the fact that it had never been registered as a separate entity, the law—rather than the owner—was on the defensive. Nothing had been done without a permit, and no coheirs were clamoring for their portions. At the point when the second heir applied for a permit to build a third storey, however, an official of the town-planning office realized that something suspicious was going on: the proposed new building seemed to give no functional advantage to the second coheir. When challenged, however, the second coheir protested that the building was not his at all! At this point, the official could have haled both heirs into court, on several charges of illegal construction. He *threatened* the offending second heir with prosecution, whereupon the latter said, "I don't want a permit . . . you're right!" and begged him not to proceed. He agreed; for, as he argues, his effectiveness as a public servant depends on his ability to make compromises at appropriate moments. In the rhetoric that the heir and the official must share in order to "oil" their fraught relationship, the heir allegedly remarked, "He [the official] is a good lad. He didn't give me the permit. But he's right." This does not mean, of course, that the official does not expect the heir to make another attempt, and he concedes that he may even succeed on the second try. Bureaucratic regulation, whose self-legitimation rests on the premise of fixed laws and eternal truths, must always compromise; and this is why the face of Rethemnos keeps changing too.

A Facade: The Contestation of Surfaces

As we near the end of this account of historic conservation in Rethemnos, it will be useful to recall that the malleability of events described in this chapter does not only affect the fate of individual fortunes. It also affects the very appearance of the town. In the discussions that ensue, we encounter the same tactical adoption of official rhetoric against the prescriptions of official practice.

An Old Town hotelier had redecorated his neo-Classical building in blue, russet, ocher, and white. The conservation office demanded that he remove the blue and russet. His housepainter—who claimed that this was a symbolic concatenation of the national color (blue), the russet of Minoan columns, and the hue of the Greek soil (ocher)—was furious at this intervention. At the same time, as the housepainter wryly observed, the paint was subject to the wear and tear of the local weather, so that the conservators' anxiety to impose a permanent pattern—"The 'Archaeology' has big ambitions (*aksiosis*)," as he put it—began to seem rather silly.

> If I paint it yellow for you [now], I'll paint it white for you in September, that's not the end of the world . . . because in three months the [paint will]

have fallen off, do you see? It [will] have fallen off, I'll paint it for you as you wish.

On the seafront, the constant attrition of saline water on paint and white-wash was one factor that encouraged the use of the incised plaster designs. These, at least, did not wear away under the constant lashing of wind-driven spume.

The painting of the facade is an apt metaphor for the social process of compromising on the surface in order to cover up other problems. The painter pointed out to his angry employer that any confrontation with the historic conservation office would lead to the investigation of other illegalities of construction, and especially the building of a stairway that the office had expressly prohibited. Once again, compromise seems to operate on both sides, though neither owners nor bureaucrats will readily agree that this is what they are doing. Few actors openly admit the possibility of compromise, for that would be bad bargaining technique. Rather, they deploy political symbolism in support of arguments that ultimately concern their sense of ownership. The owner had not wanted to wait any longer for the historic conservation office's decision. Without any apparent sense of incongruity, the painter observed, "Inasmuch as we have, if you will, property rights which are, in any event, protected by the Constitution, you don't have the right to come, to come to me to tell me how to paint my house! I like to paint it red myself, because I'm a communist!" Everything, including ideology, is negotiable. The self-regard of (especially male) householders, expressed as a demonstrative individuation of house decor (Hirschon 1989:63; Hirschon and Gold 1982), draws authority from the intimation of larger and more encompassing political goals.

In the conversation that first made me aware of the "Old Town problem," my interlocutor on that occasion had grumbled about the government as "communists," presumably because the socialists were already in power then and seemed to him to be interfering with his private property rights. The failure of Pramateftakis's election campaign shows how damagingly the communist label can stick. Like the terms of official discourse absorbed by the language of local social relations, the rhetoric of political identity slithers easily between meanings. Its effectiveness must be judged, not on the literal grounds of veracity, but as one would judge the efficacy of any weapon designed to heighten an already polarized and well-defined local conflict in terms of larger but hazier issues.

The rhetoric of the confrontation also shows how aggrieved residents try to reappropriate the initiative from the state, mixing the ideological language of political formalism with the social jargon of obligation and respect: "In any case, it is a traditional house with many 'elements,'[7] which must be preserved." Bureaucratic rhetoric can be turned against itself. Thus, the housepainter justified his selection of russet as the "color of Crete" by saying, "This thing is a seal-stamp (*voula*)"[8]—the ultimate mark of official authority, and a metaphor for the approval that the owner had sought for the new color scheme. His indignation thus deployed the rhetoric of legality against the official agencies of the law.

ANCIENTS AS MODERNS: HISTORIES OF PAST AND PRESENT

The choice of pasts is negotiated in a shifting present. In this process, there are many components: the unceasing battle between the competing rhetorics of heritage and ownership; the humiliation of the citizen; the power struggles of owners and bureaucrats; and the gradual encroachment on the residents' attitudes of a carefully cultivated consciousness of historical heritage that often rebounds against the ideology that is its primary source of nourishment. As the housepainter who had to remove the two colors remarked, it was "our ancestors" (*i palii mas*) who decorated these houses "so that it would be something beautiful (*kati to omorfo*)." But he also insisted both that russet was a "Minoan" color and at the same time that older workers, including himself, could remember what the buildings used to look like before the conservators intervened—a convenient telescoping of the "traditional" with the "archaeological," and a characteristically idiosyncratic claim to the speaker's own piece of history.

The debate about the control of aesthetic standards is not only a debate about the state's political infiltration of everyday life. It is also the means whereby that infiltration is effected. Inasmuch as the state arrogates to itself the arbitration of taste, moreover, it devalues popular aesthetics—the disappearance of the plaster designs is a case in point—and simultaneously tries to define the "traditional." In the process, it introduces a new economic and political order, against which most resistance takes the form—not necessarily a politically effective one—of reinterpreting official ideology in familiar senses.

It is hard to doubt the pain, the bitterness, and the sheer frustration that residents of the Old Town have felt over the years. It would be equally wrongheaded to reject, in any categorical sense, the good intentions of many public servants whom the residents have portrayed only as venal, cunning, and unscrupulous. I have written at length about strategies and tactics, and these terms, like "manipulation," do evoke images of the cynical pursuit of self-interest. But self-interest and emotional commitment are not necessarily mutually exclusive, nor does a strategic rhetoric of affect necessarily cast doubt on the reality of the sentiments expressed.

The Old Town has seen its share of suffering—poverty, unhealthy and malodorous living conditions, thwarted social ambition and ruinously unrewarding hard work, a pervasive sense of official neglect that only recent reforms have begun to allay. In these materially shortchanged circumstances, people create opportunities for improving their lot or grasp them as they arise.

Officials also seek ways of improving the situation. One approach is bureaucratic consolidation through the proposed creation of a unified Old Town office. The responsibilities of such an office would combine those of the town-planning and historic conservation agencies, both of which would control its operation. Those who favor such a solution argue that it would eliminate the constant failures of communication between the two agencies, since the office would be run by civil engineers and conservators operating within a common framework, and above all in an organization designed to reduce bureaucratic delay and the contradictions that currently arise from separate supervision.

But a cynical response remains. First of all, would such a unified service be any more efficient? As it is, the inspectors of the historic conservation office are mostly local residents who pass the offending houses daily, it seems, for many weeks before they lodge an official complaint; under the new, unified administration, would this change? Then again, there is a widespread view according to which the multiplicity of services is seen as a device to perpetuate full employment among the ranks of government officials. Consolidation might entail a reduction in the number of office jobs available. Finally, while the Municipality does appear to favor such an office, especially as it might be able to control it and so realize some of its own plans, such as building a casino in the Fortezza, few expect the agencies in Athens to relinquish control to local government despite the heady rhetoric of "local self-government" (*topiki aftodhiikisi*) that came to the fore with the 1981 socialist election victory.

Rethemnos is a lived place, and its people must deal with the realities of social existence. It is also a real *topos*, both in literature and in architectural history. The cultural topology imposes strains on the experience of physical and social place that a less visible and ideologically less interesting cultural conjuncture might have escaped. The residents of this ancient town certainly exploit the benefits of tourism, boast of their heritage and their monuments, and pride themselves on the literary attention that today exposes them to some, at least, of the pressure they encounter. Conversely, however, they want to get on with the comforting ordinariness of their everyday lives.

It is this desire that makes them impatient on their monument. Their day-to-day concerns obliterate—physically and conceptually—the contested history of the official and touristic world, while their personal and familial histories have an immediacy that counts for a good deal more. As they engage with the rhetoric of official history, however, it co-opts them with thoughts of more immediate and tempting comforts. They begin to vie with each other in supporting historic conservation. The tourkospita disappear, not beneath a triumphantly returning Serene Republic, but a *Cretan* and *Greek* "traditional heritage" that encompasses and incorporates their parochial identities.

It is not merely that the material comforts of economic dependency have finally begun to overwhelm resistance, although that has undoubtedly been a large part of the process. It is, also and perhaps more significantly, that the sound and fury of cultural negotiation works in multiple directions. The official past may be in the process of gaining control of the living present; but the living population has domesticated substantial areas of the official—and once alien—historical past. These are "our" buildings now. This sometimes means that they are Greek, sometimes that they are Cretan; sometimes "paternal houses" and sometimes dowry houses; sometimes Venetian, sometimes reminders of the Turkish dominion. The tourists admire them and ignore them; the inhabitants praise them, or wish they could tear them down—and not infrequently do so. They embody different pasts for different actors. No attempt to monumentalize these histories in a single past can do justice to the complexities of its citizens' struggles for recognition. They are inscribed, not only on the walls that stand, but—like the symbolic blood in the incised plaster facings of the poorest houses—in the memories of walls that have crashed into rubble under the attacks of earthquakes,[9] wind and rain, cannon, bulldozers, and sheer commercial ambition. Monumental history has its place in Rethemnos, but Rethemnos has, and is, a place in many histories.

RENT CHARGES FOR
FIVE PRIVATE PROPERTIES
IN RETHEMNOS

	1.	2.[a]	3.	4.	5.
1963	500	200	242[b]	550	315
			U.S. $1.00 = 30.15 drx.		
1964	500 (0%)	200 (0%)	200 (−17.4%)	550 (0%)	315 (0%)
			U.S. $1.00 = 30.15 drx.		
1965	500 (0%)	200 (0%)	200 (0%)	550 (0%)	338 (8.9%)
			U.S. $1.00 = 30.12 drx.		
1966	500 (0%)	200 (0%)	200 (0%)	550 (0%)	350 (3.6%)
			U.S. $1.00 = 30.10 drx.		
1967	500 (0%)	200 (0%)	246 (23%)	550 (0%)	350 (0%)
			U.S. $1.00 = 30.10 drx.		
1968	525 (5%)	318 (59%)	308 (25.2%)	588 (6.9%)	392 (12%)[c]
			U.S. $1.00 = 30.10 drx.		
1969	650 (23.8%)	350 (10.1%)	350 (13.6%)	700 (19%)	400 (2%)
			U.S. $1.00 = 30.10 drx.		
1970	913 (40.5%)	350 (0%)	425 (21.4%)	767 (9.6%)	475 (18.8%)
			U.S. $1.00 − 30.10 drx.		
1971	1,000 (9.5%)	500 (42.9%)	500 (17.6%)	800 (4.3%)	500 (5.3%)
			U.S. $1.00 = 30.10 drx.		
1972	1,167 (16.7%)	583 (16.7%)	583 (16.7%)	800 (0%)	573 (14.6%)
			U.S. $1.00 = 30.10 drx.		
		Olive oil price increase from previous year: 0.8%			
1973	1,396 (19.6%)	698 (19.7%)	698 (19.7%)	917 (14.6%)	698 (21.8%)
			U.S. $1.00 = 29.72 drx.		
		Olive oil price increase from previous year: 23.5%.			
1974	1,958 (40.3%)	958 (37.2%)	979 (40.3%)	1,000 (9.1%)	823 (17.9%)
			U.S. $1.00 = 30.10 drx.		
		Olive oil price increase from previous year: 31.1%.			

	1.	2.[a]	3.	4.	5.
1975	2,083 (6.4%)	1,042 (6.4%)	1,042 (6.4%)	1,000 (0%)	958 (16.4%)

U.S. $1.00 = 32.279 drx.

Olive oil price increase from previous year: 22.2%.

	1.	2.[a]	3.	4.	5.
1976	2,625 (26%)	1,292 (24%)	1,313 (26%)	1,500 (50%)	1,021 (6.6%)

U.S. $1.00 = 36.889 drx.

Olive oil price increase from previous year: −0.2%.

	1.	2.[a]	3.	4.	5.
1977	3,000 (14.3%)	1,500 (16.1%)	1,500 (14.2%)	2,000 (33.3%)	1,250 (22.4%)

U.S. $1.00 = 37.209 drx.

Olive oil price increase from previous year: 12.7%.

	1.	2.[a]	3.	4.	5.
1978	4,000 (33.3%)	2,000 (33.3%)	2,000 (33.3%)	3,000 (50%)	1,500 (20%)

U.S. $1.00 = 37.107 drx.

Olive oil price increase from previous year: 17.4%.

	1.	2.[a]	3.	4.	5.
1979	4,000[d] (0%)	2,000[d] (0%)	2,000[e] (0%)	4,000 (33.3%)	2,000 (33.3%)

U.S. $1.00 = 37.416 drx.

Olive oil price increase from previous year: 13.1%.

	1.	2.[a]	3.	4.	5.
Feb. 1981			3,000 (50%)	5,000 (25%)	4,000 (100%)

U.S. $1.00 = ranged from 49.43 to 53.15 drx.[f]

Olive oil price increase from previous year: 26.7%.

	1.	2.[a]	3.	4.	5.
Jan. 1982[g]			3,000 (0%)	6,000 (20%)	4,000 (0%)
Mar. 1982[g]			4,000 (33.3%)	6,000 (0%)	

1972 and 1979 compared:[h]

	1.	2.[a]	3.	4.	5.
1972	1,167	583	583	800	573

Olive oil price increase, 1972–1979: 196%.

	1.	2.[a]	3.	4.	5.
1979	4,000 (242.8%)	2,000 (243.1%)	2,000 (243.1%)	4,000 (400%)	2,000 (249%)

Olive oil price increase, 1972–1988: 1,262%.

Note: Monthly rent charges received are given in drachmas, averaged for each year, to nearest drachma. Percentages indicate increase over previous figure for the same property, to nearest decimal point. Athens wholesale olive oil prices are given for comparative purposes (*source*: National Bank of Greece, *Monthly Statistical Bulletin*, August 1981 and February 1989).

[a] This property was leased to a public service company, the others all to private individuals.

[b] There appear to have been some extraordinary charges here, since the January and February rents were 550 and 350, respectively, dropping to a monthly rent of 200 for the remainder of the year.

[c] A new person pays rent on this property at this point, perhaps a wife replacing a retired or deceased husband.

ᵈ Figures are based on January–September only.

ᵉ Figures are based on January–November only.

ᶠ U.S. dollar equivalents for years not shown: 1957, 1958, 1959—30.10; 1960—30.13; 1961, 1962, 1963—30.15; 1965—30.12; 1983—98.76; 1984—128.48; 1985—147.76; 1986—138.76; 1987—125.93; 1988—148. *Source*: National Bank of Greece, *Monthly Statistical Bulletin*, August 1981, August 1987, and February 1989.)

ᵍ Missing data unavailable from source.

ʰ Percentage increases calculated over full period (1972–1979).

NOTES

Chapter One
The Town of the *Tale*

1. I have decided to use the form *Rethemnos*, as this neuter noun is the name by which the local people themselves have usually called their town, although I retain the form *Rethimno* in reported speech where such was the usage in Greek. The latter is the official form, otherwise spelled Rethymno(n); note also the ancient Rhithymna, and Rethimni (still the official name of the encompassing district (*eparkhia*) and prefecture (*nomos*). The Venetian name was Ret(t)imo, the Turkish Resime.

2. See especially the Greek title of Nikos Kazantzakis's *Zorba the Greek: Vios ke politia tou Aleksi Zorba* (1973) (The life and *politia* of Alexis Zorbas).

3. Rethemnos's fame derived especially from the presence there of such luminaries as the poet Khortatsis in Venetian times. A recent survey gave the illiteracy rate there as 27.2 percent, and a local newspaper commented that this "creates a contradiction with Rethemnos's tradition in Letters" (*Kritiki Epitheorisi*, 22 February 1987, p. 1).

4. Sieber (1823:48) gives a figure of about 4,000. Even allowing for the passage of time, Spratt's (1865, II:112) estimate of 10,000 seems far too high, unless he was counting troops barracked there.

5. I was fortunate in being enabled to inspect these and other documents relating to property transfer and housed in the Rethimni Records Office, by kind permission of the Ministry of Justice.

6. The powers in question were Russia, Great Britain, France, and Italy. Each had charge of one of the prefectures of Crete. After the island's incorporation in the Greek state, Skridloff Square was renamed for King George I and now commemorates the Heroes of the Polytechnic uprising that contributed to the colonels' fall in 1973–1974. It is popularly known by the name of the area surrounding it (Sokhora).

7. The review was originally published in the local newspaper that also provided the outlet for this collection of essays about books on Crete.

8. On the vraka, a ninety-year-old man recalled that when he emigrated from his village to Rethemnos in 1911, only three men wore European trousers. By the time he left for the Asia Minor campaign eleven years later, all the townsmen wore them.

9. The drug problem has become especially serious and seems to cut across common social divisions such as that between the local population and students attending the University of Crete; see, for example, the report on a police raid in the Old Town in *Rethemniotika Nea*, 27 May 1987 (p. 1), for one account of evidence for such symbiosis. Pharmacists on night duty, for which shops stay open on a roster basis, take particular care to prevent drug users from gaining access.

10. This is the term commonly translated in the literature as "shame." "Embarrassment" is a much clearer gloss here.

11. This is the infamous *kharatsi*. Sieber (1823:56–58) gives some evidence for the reverse process, the proselytization of Muslims to the Christian faith, in the early nineteenth century. Christians who were caught proselytizing Muslims faced punishment by death.

12. See Guy 1988 on the racist and nationalist implications of "white slavery" (prostitution) in Argentina. Mosse (1985) usefully discusses the relationship among sexuality, respectability, identity, and *embourgeoisement*.

13. Cf. Greger's (1988:138–139) view of village women in eastern Crete, where these fears appear to be much smaller.

14. From Turkish *sokak*, "street." The obviously Turkish origin of the term suggests a combination of intimacy and cultural inferiority to Greeks, as, perhaps, may the homonymy of the word ending with the standard diminutive marker -*akia* as well.

15. This is a segmentary term of social exclusion, contrasted with *dhiki (or dhiči) (mas)*. See Herzfeld 1987a:152–157.

16. Note the term, cognate with *ksenos* (n. 15), for "alienation." The rhetoric of incorporation is still strong here.

17. This is clearly the rhetoric of "blood," which brings discussions of ethnicity in anthropological terms into direct conflict with the symbolism of social relationships and made it a real challenge to try to explain my enduring discomfort with such characterizations. See Greenwood 1984:107–126.

18. This is a rhetorical device, like our "luckless" for "having bad luck," and it means that if there *is* democracy there, it is at best a bad one. Another such phrase, extremely common, has it that "we have no state (*kratos*)."

19. See above, n. 15. The palatalization of /k/ is a local form.

20. Kerasma takes highly agonistic forms in the highland villages. For a detailed account, see Herzfeld 1985:122–136, 149–162.

21. This word also means "meaning," and its use for an explicitly *silent* mode of communication indicates the value that the mountain villagers place on subtlety and cunning.

22. Literally, "gentleman, lord, Mr."

CHAPTER TWO
HISTORIES IN CONFLICT

1. There is an extensive literature on timi. Important ethnographic contributions are Campbell 1964 and du Boulay 1974. On the relationship of "honor and shame" to Mediterraneanism, see Davis 1977; Herzfeld 1987a, 1987b.

2. The name was evidently a scornful one, but this is not the same Tourkoyoryis who changed his religion in order to marry a Christian woman with whom he had fallen in love and with whom he was eventually forced to leave for Istanbul because he could not bear the derision his choice brought upon him (see *Kritiki Epitheorisi*, 26 November 1986, p. 2).

3. It is easy to fall into the logic of nostalgia oneself, especially when contemplating the effects of tourism; cf. Greger's (1988:115) allusion to "the 'real'

Crete," although her quotation marks and further comments do suggest that she is alert to the ironic predicament of such a perspective.

4. A term also meaning "scholar, scientist."

5. Another possible interpretation of the term is "without effort," from privative *a* + *kopos*, "effort."

6. I prefer this admitted neologism to the conventional "patrilineage," since it begs fewer questions about depth, etc.

7. A bureaucratic description: "units."

8. There is some justification for this gloom. In June 1987, tourist hotel room occupancy in the region was down by some 20–25 percent from the previous year (*Rethemniotika Nea*, 7 June 1987, p. 1).

9. Drachmas, literally, "francs."

10. The implication here is that "you" are receiving favored treatment, although frozen fish is usually regarded as inferior.

11. The allusion is to a kind of multiple icon, made in three parts.

12. For a more detailed treatment of structural nostalgia, see Herzfeld 1990.

13. I have suggested (Herzfeld 1987a:35) that the Fall of Constantinople in 1453 is the secular, cultural equivalent of the biblical Fall in Greek popular and official ideologies.

14. An ancient Persian measure of distance that he mentioned, using Classical syntax, in order to show his erudition.

CHAPTER THREE
HOSTS, NEIGHBORS, AND RIVALS

1. As Bourdieu (1977:6) has pointed out, such direct reciprocation suppresses the element of time. Mauss (1968[1923–1924]), too, recognized that it exposed the interest which lay behind reciprocity and would thus be unacceptable in many societies.

2. In Glendi, it is usual for a visitor from outside the village to do this in response to the initial treat, which of course comes from one or more of the locals.

3. Being oreos, for a Rethemniot male, is a social judgment and goal. For a woman to be orea is more a matter of physical beauty. Since physical beauty in a woman is often a reason for reducing or eliminating the requirement of a dowry, we can interpret the term as closely related in meaning to the notion of "social worth" (timi).

4. See Hirschon 1978, on the moral implications of "open" and "closed" states.

5. This is an excellent illustration of the dangers of translating *filotimo* as "honor." Not only would some circumlocution like "recognition of social obligation" serve immeasurably better here, but such usages as this imply that the *actual* content of that obligation is itself extremely labile and open to negotiation.

6. This is the old question of "psychological inner states." See Needham 1972 for the fullest account of the objections to attempting to describe these.

7. Because sugar is added *before* the coffee is heated, and also because the distinction between fully boiled and merely heated-up coffee is specified when one orders the local brew, each cup of coffee has to be made to order. Instant coffee

often comes in the form of an individual packet of coffee powder and a cup of (more or less) hot water.

8. There is a special irony here in that Greeks themselves more commonly called "Greek coffee" by the name *tourkikos kafes* ("Turkish coffee") until reaction to the Turkish invasion of Cyprus in 1974 led to the almost total disappearance of the Turkish name. One result of this was that the English-language column of the menu in a small café on the island of Nisiros offered, for a few drachmas, an item called, simply, "delight"—for which it retained the Turkish-derived name of *loukoumi* in Greek! Gastronomy brings a highly malleable symbolism to the service of national self-presentation.

9. In a survey conducted in February–March 1973, the population of the Old Town came to 5,133, or 34.29 percent (up from just under 100 percent in 1951) of the total urban population of Rethemnos. Of the persons surveyed, 423 lived alone. The remainder gave an average of 3.54 persons per family (household). These figures are approximate, as 40 dwellings were not investigated (Moutsopoulos 1973, I:117–118). Unfortunately, it is not possible to tell from these figures what proportion of those units listed as "families" consisted of married couples without children in residence.

It is at least clear that the pattern of residence has not changed greatly since that survey. Responses to a questionnaire I administered in 1987 to two classes of the "Turkish School," consisting of children born in 1975–1977 and currently living within the original Old Town, show family households with an average of 2.9 children (other than consanguineal kin or other visitors) ($n = 31$). In addition to the nuclear families, these households also included the following kin: 2 with MM, 1 with MB, 1 with FF, 1 with MF and MM, 1 with MBS, 1 with an unspecified male, and 1 with MB, MBW, MF, and MM (another sibling [not included in the above $n = 31$] omitted the MB and MBW). Children living in the New Town reported a very similar pattern, with the nuclear family living alone in the majority of cases.

10. Du Boulay and Williams (1987) rightly reject the model of limited good (see Foster 1965) in the Greek context. What their argument does not make clear, however, is that limited good *is* a *rhetorical* device in Greece and as such should not be dismissed from analysis altogether. See my related comments on "amoral familism" in chapter 6.

11. I use "poetics" here in the Jakobson-derived sense applied to social interaction that I developed in my earlier ethnographic study (Herzfeld 1985; see especially pp. 8–19). This approach calls for close attention to the balance between conventions and ways of deforming these in order to achieve social effects. Some readers may be inclined to view the present study as more "material" than its predecessor. A poetics of social life, however, treats the very distinction between the material and the symbolic as an analytical classification of *social use* rather than in the essentialist sense to which we are more accustomed. It can thus include rhetoric in the causal explanation of cultural and social change. I have also made use of Bourdieu's (1972, 1977) related recognition of the relationship between, and occasional mutual convertibility of, symbolic and economic capital, although

perhaps more heavily emphasizing the plasticity of cultural idiom (e.g., variations on the conventions of self-justification).

12. Local newspapers have not been slow to complain about "the tolerance of the appropriate authorities" toward illegal noise; see, e.g., *Rethimno*, 13 July 1987, p. 1.

13. In some Greek villages, the "mother of the water" is the metaphor for the main water source.

14. In Glendi, I was directly accused of being a spy for this purpose, and it may well be that similar—if slightly gentler—hints in Rethemnos were also tests of my reactions, which would then be interpreted as evidence of my "real" role.

15. Even in such a case, the fear of looking ridiculous for having been fooled may lead the victim of a theft to keep silent.

16. In 1948, Rethemnos had 12 butchers' shops with a total of 870 workers, 100 grocery stores with 130 workers, 17 bakeries employing 32 people, 40 tailors' establishments employing 150, and 80 barbers employing 106 people (Allbaugh 1953:309). Changes since that time reflect the decline in numbers of apprentices and the difficulty of running services of the last two kinds profitably.

17. The form *parakalo* is used to mean, simply, "please" (cf. Italian *prego*), but the slightly "folksier" sounding *parakalao* has just the right touch of class outrage.

18. *Kalfakia* is a diminutive form implying younger apprentices. For a detailed account of the categories and practices of apprenticeship, see Papayeoryiou 1986.

19. The poor children of the neighborhood would steal pieces of paper to make a fire merely to warm their hands. This must be seen in the context of other prices: a cup of coffee, which is today 50 drachmas, then cost 1.50 drachmas, while a *koulouri* (bagel-like bread) went for 0.50 drachmas; the regular wage for a skilled carpenter (50 drachmas a day) may similarly be compared with about 4,000 drachmas a day at the end of 1986. In 1930, just before the first labor laws, a senior apprentice made 20 drachmas for an 11-hour day. At that point, a meat meal in a local cookshop cost 6 drachmas, liver 5 drachmas, and spaghetti with meat sauce 3 drachmas.

20. A soap worker, for example, made two lires in 1946–1952 by working a three- or three-and-a-half-hour day, and that at a time when soap workers were paid by the cauldronful (*kazania*).

21. When they are listed as "farmers" or "landowners," this does not amount to much of a difference; it simply alludes to their village origin and the fact that, as daughters, they were given land as part of their dowries.

22. *Gommena*: a usually derogatory slang term.

23. Two further comments, made by other Rethemniots, were that monastic celibacy was responsible for incestuous relationships between prelates and their nieces; and that the old village custom of letting male first cousins serve as girls' chaperones had often led to incest.

24. Five thousand drachmas a month in 1985 for a corresponding payment by the student of 6,000–7,000 drachmas; in 1986, 6,000 drachmas against the student's 8,000–9,000 drachmas.

25. In the first round, there were three slates of 28 candidates each, plus a may-

oral candidate. If a slate had won an absolute majority of aggregated votes in the first round, its head would be mayor, with a town council consisting of the 12 slate members who received the largest numbers of votes. In the second round, fought between the two top mayoral candidates, a majority ensured the winner 7 council members, with 5 to go to the runner-up.

26. Such attitudes are very durable. As I have noted elsewhere, I was warned not to associate too freely with communists because this might create a bad impression.

27. Interview, 11 June 1987, Rethemnos Town Hall. The mayor's family took Arkhondakis's attacks seriously enough to initiate legal proceedings against him.

28. Interview in Rethemnos, 7 March 1987, in his private office.

29. The tension between his party allegiance and his tactics may nonetheless have proved unworkable. He has recently left PASOK and allied himself with a party further to the left. In the same interview, he noted the fear of political harassment that still worries voters and criticized PASOK for having thus far failed to "liberate the illiterate, simple, [indeed] the simplest person . . . of our place . . . [to understand] that 'you have rights.' " He was concerned that too many voters were still politically unformed and thus unable to resist the sloganeering of those he regarded as dishonest politicians.

30. The Cretan dialect term has the additional, and contemptuous, meaning of one who has married in from another village and agreed to live on his bride's property instead of his own.

31. "Having no *soi*": see n. 18, chapter 1, above. *Soi* is a term of variable meaning in Greece, but on Crete it appears to be invariably agnatic.

32. His 139 votes should be compared with the 436 won by the top candidate on the slate and the 29 garnered by the lowest. He was twelfth on the slate.

33. Eleftherios Venizelos, pre–World War II liberal politician and Prime Minister of Greece, was himself a Cretan. He is very much of an icon, even in the technical, semiotic sense of that term. One loyalist in Rethemnos continues to affect the lamb's wool hat, wire-rimmed glasses, and goatee that made Venizelos an easily recognized figure on the national and international stages.

34. In village elections. kinship plays a much more powerful role, although in recent years political party alliances have increasingly eclipsed this feature. In highland western and central Crete, agnatic solidarity, segmentarily organized, is still a potent force.

35. Two hundred kilometers is the minimum distance from one's registered voting place that permits one to abstain.

In the second round, each side charged the other with having spent a great deal of money on bringing in these optional voters in order to influence the outcome. Arkhondakis supporters were allegedly helped by private donors, notably one family offended by Skouloudis's failure to attend the unveiling of a bust of their politically most prominent, and recently deceased, member. Skouloudis may have benefited from an effective party organization. Certainly, the Skouloudis figure shows a much larger increase (414, = 35.9 percent), as against Arkhondakis's 145 (= 10.5 percent). Most of these votes, however, came from the supporters of Pramateftakis's slate (442, = 38.3 percent of Skouloudis's first-round performance). In Rethemnos as a whole, Skouloudis won by 166 votes, or 1.9 percent of all votes cast; in the Old Town, Skouloudis won by a mere 47 votes (1,567 to Arkhondakis's 1,520, or 1.6 percent of all votes cast)! The number of spoiled ballots was small throughout, and compulsory voting ensured a low abstention level. (Sources: *Rethemniotika Nea*, 21 October, 1986, p. 1; *Rethimno*, 21 October 1986, pp. 1, 3.) In the first round, the votes for all of Rethemnos had been: Arkhondakis, 3,866 (46.65 percent); Skouloudis 3,313 (39.98 percent); and Pramateftakis, 1,108 (13.37 percent). (Sources as above; *Rethimno*, 14 October 1986, p. 1; *Rethemniotika Nea*, 13 October 1986, p. 1.)

36. More probable are the charges of influence peddling for votes, a practice that seems to have been especially rife up to the 1967 military coup among members of both major political groupings (conservative and liberal). Both the desire to place children in civil service jobs and the frequent need to sidestep prosecution for various misdemeanors (including violations of the conservation and town-planning regulations) created fertile ground for such arrangements. Compare similar practices in rural communities (Campbell 1964; Herzfeld 1985).

CHAPTER FOUR
HOME SPACES

1. This last category is only advantageous up to a value of about 7 million drachmas, after which the tax level rises *above* that imposed on an ordinary sale. Basic property tax is 11 percent; *ghoniki parokhi* (parental transfer) is on a sliding scale of 6–27 percent, the highest level being applicable to properties worth 10 million drachmas and more. As a result, some parental gifts appear in contracts as "sales," even though in practice no money has really changed hands at all. Most recently, however, family legislation introduced by the PASOK government made ghoniki parokhi attractive by making a portion of the transfer tax-free.

2. On his monthly pensions of 11,000 drachmas, however, he cannot afford to move out of his miserable rented room in the Old Town.

3. Essentially these rest on the notion that the recognition incurred in naming reciprocates some material or spiritual benefit conferred in honor of the person commemorated in the name. As many Cretans wryly acknowledge, this lends itself to the symbolic cementing of patronage relations, and politicians are ever eager to seize on its advantages. See Herzfeld 1982b and 1985:234–238; Kenna 1976.

4. In some of the villages, especially more pastoral highland communities, the children of powerful shepherds often have many godfathers. Once there were forty godparents and they could not agree on the name, but, since they were all Cretans, one of them said, they should call the child Kriti, "so all of them should receive the favor."

5. Specifically, the reciprocal term between a child's parents and the baptismal sponsor. The equivalent reciprocal in marriage sponsorship is the more widespread *koumbaros*.

6. It carries particularly negative implications in virilocal communities because there the in-marrying groom's dependence on the bride's family attracts derision and undermines his manly reputation. In uxorilocal communities, the term means

very little, although in the endogamous and uxorilocal villages of western Rhodes the structural equivalent is the man who marries in from a different *village* (the *maepsari* or *maepsimi*; cf. Cretan *anemazoksaris*).

7. The terminology is very ambiguous. More detailed discussions of its semantic lability may be found in Herzfeld 1987a:144–149 and Skouteri-Didaskalou 1984:220–223.

8. For a general account of the monetary crisis and its variable effects, see especially Delivanis and Cleveland n.d.:78–82, 89.

9. At that time, a new system came into general use in Rethemnos, following its introduction in other parts of Greece. It is based on block valuations of sections of town and is less susceptible to special pleading.

10. The normal form of the phrase "in America" is *stin Ameriki*. By using the neuter article in conjunction with the English-language form of the country's name, the lawyer—who recounted these events to me—uses a common ironic form to suggest that the Greek-American was putting on airs, and that America is a very strange, very foreign sort of place where peculiar things such as honest tax declaration sometimes happen. If his client really did claim any such thing, of course, we may recognize it as the rhetorical use of a national stereotype reminiscent of similar plays on notions of Greekness.

11. It is possible for the seller or donor of any property to retain usufruct until death; I do not know whether this was done in the present case. Sales between close kin are often highly fictitious, in that money does not actually change hands even though the forms of a genuine sale are observed.

12. On a sample of property sale contracts drawn up in 1974–1976 ($n = 51$), 6 appeared to be between close kin. There was no way of establishing uterine links, so the following figures probably in fact *understate* the significance of kinship:

Declared Price as Percentage of Assessed Value

	a. All Contracts
$n = 51$	70.1 (max. 100, min. 19.3)
	b. Contracts between Close Kin
$n = 6$	51.3 (max. 100, min. 19.3)
	c. All "Others" ($= a - b$)
$n = 45$	73.5 (max. 100, min. 30.6)

Note that the difference between *b* and *c* is 22.2 percent. For this analysis, the mean for *c* is 74 percent. The mean for *b* is 46 percent.

Student's *t* is 2.59 with 49 d.f., significant at $p = 0.05$.

When the same calculation is performed on the absolute drachma figures rather than percentages, the mean for *c* is 84,800. For *b* the mean is 296,500. Student's *t* is 2.59 with 49 d.f., significant at $p = 0.0005$.

13. A practical advantage of the now scorned incised plaster surfaces is their resistance to severe discoloration or other damage.

14. Even those who own property may be forced through infirmity to move to their children's homes, and this may entail relocation far away, perhaps even out-

side Crete. Understandably, the elderly often express deep sadness at this uproot-
ing, however kindly it may have been intended.

CHAPTER FIVE
GAMBLERS AND USURERS

1. Compare Bourdieu's (1977:37) concept of "officializing strategies."

2. The form *tourkospita* is contemptuous; cf. *paliospita*, "rotten old houses,
brothels." The usage for the Venetian houses is always the more respectful *venet-
sianika spitia*.

3. See Gramsci 1971:349–350. State and elite penetration of the ideologies of
everyday life does, however, meet with resistance by appropriately situated actors,
and this leads to reformulation at all levels. As I have noted also in my discussion
of the "invention of tradition" model (see chapter 1), any attempt to see the
townspeople as incapable of recasting the terms of their domination to their own
at least passing advantage risks becoming complicit in the suppression of their
point of view. See also Cowan 1990:13; Scott 1985:317–318.

4. See Herzfeld 1987a:95–122, for a more extended discussion of the Hellenic-
Romeic dialectic in Greek cultural debate and its moral ramifications.

5. The official terms make some claim to the moral superiority of the practices
they denote, as the economy of linguistic exchange would lead one to expect (see
Bourdieu 1982:52). It is far less clear, however, that people internalize this claim
as unqualified respect for the official order on their own part.

6. See Fabian's (1983) discussion of the "denial of coevalness," where the
phrase is used to characterize anthropological discourse. The hegemony of "Western" discourse is nowhere more successful than in those places and cultural topoi,
such as Greece, in which its bearers persuade the local population to internalize it
to their own disadvantage.

7. Shop ownership may be transferred from an elderly man to his wife, but this
is usually only a cosmetic device designed to protect the man's pension after retirement.

8. More commonly used in address than the neo-Classical *thie*, *barba* is also a
much less stilted term, and it sets the context here for acts of collusion between
two men, one of whom is inferior to the other in age but superior to him in social
status—an ambiguity that is nicely conveyed by the coexistence in this term of
folk usage and kinship and generational asymmetry.

9. A male commentator may even indicate his disapproval to the point of gram-
matically feminizing her husband (i.e., as *mianou* for *enous*), a rather explicit way
of impugning his manhood; cf. Herzfeld 1985:216–217.

10. This contrasts markedly with my experience in "Glendi," where I played
both games often and with a wide range of male villagers.

CHAPTER SIX
IMPATIENCE ON A MONUMENT

1. The president of the Old Town House Owners' Association, G. Mousouros,
had also invoked the principle of constitutional property rights. In one of the most
acrimonious disputes to surround the question, the architect K. Iliakis (1981:4)—

an ardent PASOK supporter—responded, shortly before the elections that brought the socialists to power, that "the state, too, has a constitutional right, as does the social body as a whole, to preserve, make good use of, and develop in any way the Architectural heritage of the country." See below for other aspects of the dispute.

2. In evaluating his claim, however, we should bear in mind that the rooming house proprietors have repeatedly objected to the presence of "vagabond-tourists" (*alitotouristes*) on the beach in the hope of forcing them to rent rooms; and that, in turn, the hoteliers have tried to keep the rooming houses shut down for all but the two summer months—July and August—in which they overbook and need a safety valve to relieve the resulting pressure. On the other hand, an entrepreneur can still also claim paying guests as "our personal friends (*prosopiči mas fili*)." One couple "went as far as to send tickets for me to go with my wife to Germany and to France. Tickets, prepaid, return! That means in other words that these people left with the best impressions. (. . . .) No government ever helped us and gave us anything."

3. "Passing one's time" is a commonly offered reason for doing anything that is not, in an immediately obvious way, materially productive. The boredom of life requires it—but obviously some people are freer to do it than others, and do it on the taxpayers' money to boot.

4. For example, a clerk in any public telephone office will have to make restitution out of pocket if the client misdials (or gets a wrong number) and then refuses to pay for it.

5. The principal legal decrees of relevance here are:

   a. Ministerial Decision No. 24946 (26 August 1987) (*Government Gazette* [henceforward *GG*] 605[2], 3 October 1967, p. 4506) declaring the Old Town a "Historical Scheduled (*dhiatiriteo* i.e., for conservation) Monument";
   b. Presidential Decree, 1 December 1975 (*GG* 36[4], 31 January 1976, pp. 272–275), setting special terms and limits for building within the Rethemnos town division plan;
   c. Presidential Decree, 19 October 1978 (*GG* 594[4], 13 November 1978, pp. 6329–6336), declaring the Old Town a "traditional settlement";
   d. Presidential Decree, 10 November 1978 (*GG* 634[4], 1 December 1978, pp. 6770–6773), setting building proportions and limits within the Rethemnos town division plan;
   e. Presidential Decree No. 161, 30 April 1984 (*GG* 541[1], 30 April 1984, pp. 658–659), transferring jurisdiction over the supervision of historical sites from the Ministry of Culture to the Ministry of Environment, Planning, and Public Works;
   f. Presidential Decree, 25 October 1984 (*GG* 30[4], 14 February 1985, pp. 241–246), revision of the urban division plan and instructions for the design of restorations conducted under the instructions of the local committee on architectural inspection;
   g. Presidential Decree, 20 October 1987 (*GG* 30[4], 14 February 1985, pp. 241–258), revision of the urban division plan of Rethemnos, with particular reference to the disposition of currently unbuilt spaces.

Law c permitted the building of new structures on presently open spaces, while law d permitted additions such as balconies and water runnels, as long as they were "of traditional type," and also permitted television aerials "in places not visible from the street and until the establishment of a central mast for the entire city" (Article 2). Neon signs are prohibited, while the form and materials of doors and windows are narrowly specified (Articles 10–11). The new law permits the supervised demolition of old buildings and the removal of ornamental structures, subject to prior recording, inspection, and permission (Articles 18–19). In short, law d both permits architectural changes and demands complex bureaucratic procedures—from the definition of "traditional" to the criteria for permission to demolish or rebuild—that are clearly open to selective interpretation and operation.

6. Interview, 28 May 1987, Aristotle University of Thessaloniki.

7. Interview, 11 June 1987, Town Hall, Rethemnos. The relevant provision is Presidential Decree No. 161 (30 April 1984), Article 1(iii) (*GG* 541[1], p. 658). In fact, the several parties to the problem all agree in principle to the idea of the unified local service, which has been a legal option since 1964 (Law 1416/84), and the idea was strongly endorsed by a meeting of the Greek chapter of ICOMOS (the International Council on Monuments and Sites, a UNESCO agency) held in Rethemnos. (See *Rethimno*, 17 December 1985, pp. 1, 8; the *Rethemniotika Nea* for that time complained bitterly that the meeting was not attended by most of the senior officials whose involvement was essential to the successful merging of the various bureaucratic functions. See also the notice in *Enimerotiko Dheltio Tekhnikou Epimelitiriou Elladhas*, no. 1399, 27 January 1986, pp. 29–31.) Under the leadership of Vice-Mayor Stagakis, who had been directly involved in the discussions with ICOMOS, the Town Hall issued a draft document outlining the functions of the proposed new agency. The situation had become especially acute by this time because the Ministry of Culture, in a circular letter of 13 January 1986, had reclaimed some aspects of its former jurisdiction in the Old Town, thus effectively rescinding the 1984 legislation. Mayor Skouloudis sent a strongly worded letter to both ministries requesting that the decisions contained in the circular letter be annulled, as did the director of the local town-planning office and the general secretary of the West Cretan section of the Technical Inspectorate of Greece (T.E.E.) ("since it is not possible for a circular letter to rescind Laws and Presidential Decrees"). By the time of my 1989 visit, no further progress toward creating the new agency had eventuated.

8. Interview, 27 February 1989, DIANA (Democratic Renewal) party office, Parliament of the Hellenes, Athens.

9. During Nianias's incumbency, some funds were released for repairs and for small additions that would not damage the fabric. In the conservative government in which he served, however, he would probably have found it difficult to sustain such an argument for long.

To add to the complexity of the views expressed, the noted archaeologist Manolis Andronikos observed in a pro-PASOK newspaper and in a column cohosted by the same Italian-trained architect that the conditions under which Italian *palazzi* were maintained were very different from those obtaining in Rethemnos. Andronikos also expressed considerable impatience with what he saw as indiscriminate conservation promoted at the expense of the poor (*Allayi*, 10 June 1980, pp. 4, 8). He wondered how much of what was preserved genuinely constituted "the architectural expression of an age" and suggested that if some houses were to be preserved on this basis, then the authorities "should share the expenses of this salvage work among the social whole, and not dump it on the—as a rule— unfortunate, poor householder of this very old building."

10. His repeated outbursts got him into serious trouble. At one point, attacked in the local press by a civil engineer whose sister was a leading member of the historic conservation team, he sued his tormentor in court but lost the case.

11. Interview, 26 May 1987, Thessaloniki.

12. It is now illegal to hang shop signs on which the foreign-language lettering is as large as, or larger than, the Greek. The dramatically obvious failure of the authorities to enforce this law validates the insistent complaints about government inaction and indifference, especially in matters in which official intervention might disrupt the tourist operators' business.

13. This is a common formula in sale documents, and its frequency reflects the interest that all parties to such transactions have in emphasizing the dilapidated condition of the property.

14. The narrow streets do not easily permit access with larger modes of transportation. This phrase thus conveys a good sense of the frustration involved in working with Old Town buildings.

15. These expenses included the staff's social security (IKA) payments.

16. He was actually the lawyer of one of the other codefendants but seemed willing to represent all five at this point.

17. See Kendall's (1981) trenchant discussion of Brown and Gilman 1960.

18. There is a curious parallel here between local, civil etiology and ideas about original sin. *Aghapi* (universal love) is the prelapsarian condition, which disappeared with the advent of "history." Structural nostalgia always represents the old days as a time when people were more aghapimeni than now. Now, indeed, they have "histories"—fights, arguments, and legal tangles. Cosmology is indeed reproduced among the ordinary people (*kosmos*) (Herzfeld 1990).

19. Vitzentzos Kornaros, author of the *Erotokritos*, perhaps the best known literary work of the Veneto-Cretan Renaissance.

CHAPTER SEVEN
HISTORIES IN THEIR PLACES

1. This man once complained that a child's name, Nektarios, was not "Greek" (*elliniko*) *but* "ancient" (*arkheo*)—a reversal of the official equation of Greekness with Classical antiquity. To compound the irony still further, Nektarios was in fact a modern saint, canonized in 1961!

2. This is a nice example of the use of official rhetoric against the official state. The term *kleftes* ("thieves"), noted above, recalls the guerrillas who fought against Turkish domination before national independence. After independence, those who continued to fight against the state were branded "brigands" (*liste[s]*) and outlawed by the Greek authorities. Through a process of linguistic engineering, the distinction between listes and the erstwhile freedom fighters became increasingly unambiguous (see Herzfeld 1982c:60–69; Koliopoulos 1987). Today, describing the state as listriko is a strategic representation by citizens who recog-

nize that they can only achieve limited goals, and those only by working within the dominant discourse.

3. Constantine Karamanlis was the right-wing Prime Minister of Greece whose electoral defeat by George Papandreou in 1963 began a series of events leading to the military takeover of 1967. Recalled to lead the country back to democratic government after the colonels' fall in 1974, he remains a highly popular figure, especially among more conservative Greeks. The speaker did not of course literally mean that Karamanlis would personally help her. She is, rather, suggesting that her declared affection for him might militate against her effectiveness with the PASOK-controlled authorities. She may also be suggesting that, as a non-Rethemniot, she would have even greater difficulty than most; like Karamanlis, she originally came from Macedonia.

4. These workmen work on renewable contracts but are sufficiently steadily employed to get social security (IKA) benefits for their families, and this constitutes their major incentive to stay on.

5. This seems to be formulaically calqued on the well-known proverb, "The robe doesn't make the priest, but the priest [makes] the robe"—i.e., personality, not office, is what deserves credit. Another version of this, supposedly coined by the liberal politician Eleftherios Venizelos, has it that "the man makes the patrigroup and not the patrigroup the man" (see Herzfeld 1985:17).

6. This is the usual phrase for sexual contact.

7. *Stikhia*, a bureaucratic term for the recognizable features that the historic conservation office can list for its attention.

8. A Byzantine term, from Latin *bulla* (cf. "papal bull").

9. Although Rethemnos and Khania fared much better in this regard than Iraklio, earthquakes have wrought some damage (see, e.g., Spratt 1865, II:113).

REFERENCES

Aetoudakis, Dimitris. 1986. Ρεθεμνιώτικα—οδοιπορικό μέσα στο χρόνο (Of Rethemnos: Journey through time). Athens: n.p.

Allbaugh, Leland G. 1953. Crete: A Case Study of an Underdeveloped Area. Princeton: Princeton University Press.

Anderson, Benedict. 1983. Imagined Communities: Reflections on the Origin and Spread of Nationalism. London: Verso.

Ankori, Avi. 1968. Jews and the Jewish Community in the History of Medieval Crete. Πεπραγμένα του 2. Διεθνούς Κρητολογικού Συνεδρίου (Proceedings of the Second International Cretological Congress). (Athens: Khrisostomos Philological Society), 3:312–369.

Appadurai, Arjun, 1981. The Past as a Scarce Resource. Man (n.s.) 16:201–219.

———, ed. 1986. Introduction: Commodities and the Politics of Value. *In* The Social Life of Things, Appadurai, Arjun, ed., pp. 3–63. Cambridge: Cambridge University Press.

Ardener, Edwin. 1975. The "Problem" Revisited. *In* Perceiving Women, Shirley Ardener, ed., pp. 19–27. London: J. M. Dent.

Austin, J. L. 1971[1956–1957]. A Plea for Excuses. *In* Philosophy and Linguistics, Colin Lyas, ed., pp. 79–101. London: Macmillan.

———. 1975[1962]. How to Do Things With Words. 2d ed., ed. by J. O. Urmson and Marina Sbisà. Cambridge: Harvard University Press.

Bachelard, Gaston. 1964. The Poetics of Space. Trans. by Maria Jolas. New York: Orion.

Banfield, Edward C. 1958. The Moral Basis of a Backward Society. Glencoe: Free Press.

Bennett, Diane O. 1987. The Cultural Construction of Class: Resource Control, Social Relations, and Cultural Processes in a Community on the Pelion Peninsula of Greece. Ph.D. diss., Washington University, St. Louis.

Bourdieu, Pierre. 1972. Les stratégies matrimoniales dans le système de reproduction. Annales: Economies, Sociétés, Civilisations 27:1105–1125.

———. 1977. Outline of a Theory of Practice. Trans. by Richard Nice. Cambridge: Cambridge University Press.

———. 1982. Ce que parler veut dire: L'économie des échanges linguistiques. Paris: Fayard.

———. 1984. Distinction: A Social Critique of the Judgement of Taste. Trans. by Richard Nice. Cambridge: Harvard University Press.

Brown, Roger, and Albert Gilman. 1960. The Pronouns of Power and Solidarity. *In Style in Language*, Thomas A. Sebeok, ed., pp. 253–276. Cambridge: MIT Press.

Campbell, J. K. 1964. Honour, Family, and Patronage: A Study of Institutions and Moral Values in a Greek Mountain Community. Oxford: Clarendon Press.

Caraveli, Anna. 1986. The Bitter Wounding: The Lament as Social Protest in Rural Greece. *In* Gender and Power in Rural Greece, Jill Dubisch, ed., pp. 169–194. Princeton: Princeton University Press.

Chock, Phyllis P. 1987. The Irony of Stereotypes: Toward an Anthropology of Ethnicity. Cultural Anthropology 2:347–368.

Clogg, Richard. 1987. Parties and Elections in Greece: The Search for Legitimacy. London: C. Hurst.

Cowan, Jane K. 1988. Folk Truth: When the Scholar Comes to Carnival in a "Traditional" Community. Journal of Modern Greek Studies 6:245–260.

———. 1990. Dance and the Body Politic in Northern Greece. Princeton: Princeton University Press.

Danforth, Loring M. 1976. Humour and Status Reversal in Greek Shadow Theatre. Byzantine and Modern Greek Studies 5:141–163.

———. 1989. Firewalking and Religious Healing: The Anastenaria of Greece and the American Firewalking Movement. Princeton: Princeton University Press.

Davis, John. 1977. People of the Mediterranean: An Essay in Comparative Social Anthropology. London: Routledge & Kegan Paul.

de Certeau, Michel. 1984. The Practice of Everyday Life. Trans. by Steven Rendall. Berkeley: University of California Press.

Delivanis, Dimitrios, and William C. Cleveland. N.d. Greek Monetary Developments, 1939–1948. Social Science Series, 6. Bloomington: Indiana University.

Detorakis, Theokharous. 1986. Ιστορία της Κρήτης (History of Crete). Athens: n.p.

Dimakopoulos, Iordanis. 1971. Το Ρέθυμνο στο 1573—Μια σελίδα απο τις "Memorie" του Francesco da Molin (Rethimno in 1573—A page from Francesco da Molin's *Memorie*). Kritika Khronika 23:322–340.

———. 1977. Τα σπίτια του Ρεθέμνου: συμβολή στη μελέτη της αναγεννησιακής αρχιτεκτονικής της Κρήτης του 16ου και του 17ου αιώνα (The houses of Rethimno: Contribution to the study of the Renaissance architecture of Crete in the 16th and 17th centuries). Athens: Ministry of Culture and Sciences.

Dorst, John D. 1989. The Written Suburb: An American Site, an Ethnographic Dilemma. Philadelphia: University of Pennsylvania Press.

Douglas, Mary. 1966. Purity and Danger: An Analysis of Concepts of Pollution and Taboo. London: Routledge & Kegan Paul.

———. 1975. Implicit Meanings: Essays in Anthropology. London: Routledge & Kegan Paul.

Douglas, Mary, and Baron Isherwood. 1979. The World of Goods. New York: Basic Books.

du Boulay, Juliet. 1974. Portrait of a Greek Mountain Village. Oxford: Clarendon Press.

du Boulay, Juliet, and Rory Williams. 1987. Amoral Familism and the Image of Limited Good: A Critique from a European Perspective. Anthropological Quarterly 60:12–24.

Eddy, Charles B. 1931. Greece and the Greek Refugees. London: George Allen & Unwin.

Elliadi, M. N. 1933. Crete, Past and Present. London: Heath Cranton.

Evans-Pritchard, E. E. 1940. The Nuer: A Description of the Modes of Livelihood and Political Institutions of a Nilotic People. Oxford: Clarendon Press.

Fabian, Johannes. 1983. Time and the Other: How Anthropology Makes Its Object. New York: Columbia University Press.

Forbes, Hamish A. 1976. "We Have a Little of Everything": The Ecological Basis of Some Agricultural Practices in Methana, Trizinia. *In* Regional Variation in Modern Greece and Cyprus: Toward a Perspective on the Ethnography of Greece, Muriel Dimen and Ernestine Friedl, eds., pp. 236–250. Annals of the New York Academy of Sciences, 258:1–465. New York: New York Academy of Sciences.

Foster, George M. 1965. Peasant Society and the Image of Limited Good. American Anthropologist 67:293–315.

Gallant, Thomas. 1990. Peasant Ideology and Excommunication for Crime in a Colonial Context: The Ionian Islands (Greece), 1817–1864. Journal of Social History 23:485–512.

Gambetta, Diego, ed. 1988. Trust: Making and Breaking Cooperative Relations. Oxford: Basil Blackwell.

Geertz, Clifford. 1979. Suq: The Bazaar Economy in Sefrou. *In* Meaning and Order in Moroccan Society, by Clifford Geertz, Hildred Geertz, and Lawrence Rosen, pp. 123–313. Cambridge: Cambridge University Press.

Giddens, Anthony. 1984. The Constitution of Society: Introduction to the Theory of Structuration. Berkeley: University of California Press.

Gramsci, Antonio. 1971. Selections from the Prison Notebooks. Ed. by Quintin Hoare and Geoffrey Nowell Smith. New York: International Publishers.

Greenwood, Davydd J. 1984. The Taming of Evolution: The Persistence of Non-evolutionary Views in the Study of Humans. Ithaca: Cornell University Press.

Greger, Sonia. 1988. Village on the Plateau: Magoulas—A Mountain Village in Crete. Studley, Warwickshire: K.A.F. Brewin Books.

Guy, Donna J. 1988. White Slavery, Public Health, and the Socialist Position on Legalized Prostitution in Argentina, 1933–1936. Latin American Research Review 23:60–80.

Halbwachs, Maurice. 1980. The Collective Memory. Trans. by Francis J. Ditter, Jr., and Vida Yazdi Ditter. New York: Harper & Row.

Handler, Richard. 1988. Nationalism and the Politics of Culture in Quebec. Madison: University of Wisconsin Press.

Herzfeld, Michael. 1971. Cost and Culture: Observations on Incised Cement Designs in Crete. Kritika Khronika 23:189–198.

———. 1980. The Dowry in Greece: Terminological Usage and Historical Reconstruction. Ethnohistory 27:225–241.

———. 1982a. The Etymology of Excuses: Aspects of Rhetorical Performance in Greece. American Ethnologist 9:644–663.

———. 1982b. When Exceptions Define the Rules: Greek Baptismal Names and the Negotiation of Identity. Journal of Anthropological Research 38:288–302.

———. 1982c. Ours Once More: Folklore, Ideology, and the Making of Modern Greece. Austin: University of Texas Press.

Herzfeld, Michael. 1985. The Poetics of Manhood: Contest and Identity in a Cretan Mountain Village. Princeton: Princeton University Press.

———. 1987a. Anthropology through the Looking-Glass: Critical Ethnography in the Margins of Europe. Cambridge: Cambridge University Press.

———. 1987b. "As in Your Own House": Hospitality, Ethnography, and the Stereotype of Mediterranean Society. In Honor and Shame and the Unity of Mediterranean Society, David D. Gilmore, ed., pp. 75–89. Washington: American Anthropological Association (special publication no. 22).

———. 1990. Pride and Perjury: Time and the Oath in the Mountain Villages of Crete. Man (n.s.) 25:305–322.

———. 1991. Silence, Submission, and Subversion: Toward a Poetics of Womanhood. In Contested Identities: Gender and Kinship in Modern Greece, Peter Loizos and Evthymios Papataxiarchis, eds., pp. 79–97. Princeton: Princeton University Press.

Hirschon, Renée. 1978. Open Body/Closed Space: The Transformation of Female Sexuality. In Defining Females, Shirley Ardener, ed., pp. 66–88. London: Croom Helm.

———. 1981. Essential Objects and the Sacred: Interior and Exterior Space in an Urban Greek Locality. In Women and Space: Ground Rules and Social Maps, Shirley Ardener, ed., pp. 72–88. New York: St. Martin's Press.

———. 1989. Heirs of the Greek Catastrophe: The Social Life of Asia Minor Refugees in Piraeus. Oxford: Clarendon Press.

Hirschon, Renée, and John R. Gold. 1982. Territoriality and the Home Environment in a Greek Urban community. Anthropological Quarterly 55:63–73.

Hobsbawm, Eric, and Terence Ranger, eds. 1983. The Invention of Tradition. Cambridge: Cambridge University Press.

Hopkins, Adam. 1977. Crete: Its Past, Present and People. London: Faber and Faber.

Iliakis, Kostas. 1981. Ανοιχτή επιστολή: Αφήστε το μέλλος [sic] της Πολης στα χέρια της νέας γενιάς (Open letter: Leave the future of the town in the hands of the new generation). Allayi, 19 March, pp. 1, 4.

———. 1985. Παλιά Πόλη: Μέχρι πότε είναι το εξιλαστήριο θύμα του κρατικού παρεμβατισμού (Old Town: Until when is it to be the sacrificial victim of state interventionism?). Rethimno, 2 October, p. 3.

Kalomenopoulos, Yoryis. 1964. Ποιήματα (Poems). Athens: n.p.

Kaloyerakis, Yiannis. 1982. Ο Θεός σκοτώνει. Athens: Pasiphae. (English translation by Amy Mins: The Killing God [Rethymno: Pasiphae, 1988].)

Kapferer, Bruce. 1988. Legends of People, Myths of State: Violence, Intolerance, and Political Culture in Sri Lanka and Australia. Washington: Smithsonian Institution Press.

Karp, Ivan. 1978. New Guinea Models in the African Savannah. Africa 48:1–17.

Kazantzakis, Nikos. 1973. Βίος και πολιτεία του Αλέξη Ζορμπά (Usually translated as: Zorba the Greek). 7th ed. Athens: Eleni Kazantzaki Publications.

Kendall, Martha B. 1981. Toward a Semantic Approach to Terms of Address: A Critique of Deterministic Models in Sociolinguistics. Language and Communication 1:237–254.

Kenna, Margaret E. 1976. Houses, Fields, and Graves: Property and Ritual Obligation on a Greek Island. Ethnology 15:21–34.

———. 1985. Icons in Theory and Practice: An Orthodox Christian Example. History of Religions 24:345–368.

Khatzidakis, Iosif. 1881. Περιήγησις εις Κρήτην (Travels in Crete). Ermoupolis: Nikolaos Varvaresos.

Koliopoulos, John S. 1987. Brigands with a Cause: Brigandage and Irredentism in Modern Greece, 1821–1912. Oxford: Clarendon Press.

Kremmidas, V. 1974. Οι σαπουνοποιίες της Κρήτης στο 18o αιώνα (The soap factories of Crete in the eighteenth century). Athens.

League of Nations. 1926. Greek Refugee Settlement. Geneva: League of Nations (Economic and Financial 2:32).

Legg, Keith R. 1969. Politics in Modern Greece. Stanford: Stanford University Press.

Llewellyn Smith, Michael. 1973. Ionian Vision: Greece in Asia Minor, 1919–1922. London: Macmillan.

Löfgren, Orvar. 1989. The Nationalization of Culture. Ethnologia Europaea 19:5–24.

Loizos, Peter. 1975. Changes in Property Transfer among Greek Cypriot Villagers. Man (n.s.) 10:503–523.

Louloudakis, Th. 1984. Η κρητική φωτογραφία (Cretan photography). Athens: n.p.

Lowenthal, David. 1985. The Past Is a Foreign Country. Cambridge: Cambridge University Press.

———. 1986. Heritage—and Its Interpreters. Heritage Australia (Winter):42–45.

Machin, Barrie. 1983. Cultural Codes, Religion and Attitudes to the Body in a Cretan Mountain Village. Social Analysis 14:107–162.

Malagari, A., and H. Stratigakis. 1985–1986. Réthymno: A Guide to the Town and Its Surroundings. Athens: n.p.

Manousakas, M. I. 1949. Η παρά Trivan απογραφή της Κρήτης (1644) και ο δήθεν κατάλογος των Κρητικών Οίκων Κερκύρας (Trivan's census of Crete [1644] and the so-called list of Cretan houses of Corfu). Kritika Khronika 3:35–59.

Margaritis, Yorghos. 1986. Στης Κρήτης τ' όμορφο νησί (On the beautiful island of Crete). Dekapenthimeros Politis 57 (28 May):39.

Mauss, Marcel. 1968[1923–1924]. Essai sur le don. In Sociologie et anthropologie, pp. 143–279. Paris: Presses Universitaires de France.

Moatsos, Errikos. 1974. Η αρχοντικαί οικογένειαι του Ρεθύμνου επί Βενετοκρατίας (The noble families of Rethimno under Venetian rule). Πρακτικά του 3. κρητολογικού συνεδρίου (Proceedings of the Third Cretological Congress) (Athens), pp. 207–221.

Mosse, George L. 1985. Nationalism and Sexuality: Respectability and Abnormal Sexuality in Modern Europe. New York: Howard Fertig.

Moutsopoulos, N. K. 1973. Η Παλαιά Πόλις του Ρεθύμνου (The Old Town of Rethimno). Vol. 1. Thessaloniki: n.p.

Mouzelis, Nicos P. 1978. Modern Greece: Facets of Underdevelopment. London: Macmillan.

Nakou, Lilika. 1955. Η κυρία Ντορεμί (Madame Do-Re-Mi). Athens: Dhifros.

284 REFERENCES

National Bank of Greece. Various. Monthly Statistical Bulletin.

Needham, Rodney. 1972. Belief, Language, and Experience. Oxford: Basil Blackwell.

Nenedakis, A. N. 1979. [Preface] and Εισαγωγή (Introduction). In critical edition of Marinos Tzane Bounialis, Ο κρητικός πόλεμος (The Cretan War) 1645–1669), unpaginated and pp. 17–174. Athens: n.p.

————. 1983. Ρέθεμνος· Τριάντα αιώνες πολιτεία (Rethemnos: Thirty centuries of a town). Athens: published by the author.

Papataxiarchis, Evthymios. 1991. Friends of the Heart: Male Commensal Solidarity, Gender, and Kinship in Aegean Greece. In Contested Identities: Gender and Kinship in Modern Greece, Peter Loizos and Evthymios Papataxiarchis, eds., pp. 156–179. Princeton: Princeton University Press.

Papayeoryiou, Yorgos. 1986. Η μαθητεία στα επαγγέλματα (16ος—20ος αιώνας) (Apprenticeship in the professions [sixteenth–twentieth centuries]). Athens: Archive of Greek Youth.

Pashley, Robert. 1837. Travels in Crete. 2 vols. London: John Murray.

Pavlides, Eleftherios. 1983. Modernization and the Fireplace in Eressos, a Greek Rural Town. Oz 5:20–23.

Pavlides, Eleftherios, and Jana Hesser. 1986. Women's Roles and House Form and Decoration in Eressos, Greece. In Gender and Power in Rural Greece, Jill Dubisch, ed., pp. 68–96. Princeton: Princeton University Press.

Pentzopoulos, Dimitri. 1962. The Balkan Exchange of Minorities and Its Impact upon Greece. Paris, The Hague: Mouton.

Pitsidianaki, Stella. 1987. Έρευνα της κοινωνικής δομής στην Παλιά Πόλη του Ρεθύμνου (Research on social structure in the Old Town of Rethimno). Rethimno, no. 440, 12 February, pp. 3–4.

Politis, Nikolaos G. 1909. Η λαογραφία (Folklore). Laografia 1:3–18.

Prevelakis, Pandelis. 1938. Το χρονικό μιας πολιτείας (The tale of a town). Athens: n.p. [rpt. 1961, Galaxias].

Rabinow, Paul. 1989. French Modern: Norms and Forms of the Social Environment. Cambridge: MIT Press.

Rosen, Lawrence. 1984. Bargaining for Reality: The Construction of Social Relations in a Muslim Community. Chicago: University of Chicago Press.

Said, Edward. 1978. Orientalism. New York: Basic Books.

Salamone, Stephen D. 1987. In the Shadow of the Holy Mountain: The Genesis of a Rural Greek Community and Its Refugee Heritage. Boulder: East European Monographs.

Sant Cassia, Paul. Forthcoming. To the City: Kinship, Property and Family in 19th Century Athens. Cambridge: Cambridge University Press.

Scott, James C. 1985. Weapons of the Weak: Everyday Forms of Peasant Resistance. New Haven: Yale University Press.

Sieber, F. W. 1823. Travels in the Island of Crete in the Year 1817. London: Sir Richard Phillips.

Skouteri-Didaskalou, Nora. 1984. Ανθρωπολογικά για το γυναικείο ζήτημα (Anthropological writings on the women's question). Athens: O Politis.

Spooner, Brian. 1976. Concluding Essay 1: The Evil Eye in the Middle East. *In* The Evil Eye, Clarence Maloney, ed., pp. 76–84. New York: Columbia University Press.

Spratt, A. B. 1865. Travels and Researches in Crete. 2 vols. London: John Van Voorst.

Stavrakis, Nikolaos. 1890. Στατιστική του πληθυσμού της Κρήτης (Statistics of the population of Crete). 2 vols. Athens: Palingenesia.

Stavrinidis, Nikolaos S. 1986. Μεταφράσεις τουρκικών ιστορικών εγγράφων (Translations of Turkish historical documents). 2 vols. Iraklio: Municipality of Iraklio.

Stewart, Charles. 1985. *Exotika*: Greek Values and Their Supernatural Antitheses. Scandinavian Yearbook of Folklore 41:37–64.

Tannen, Deborah. 1983. Lilika Nakos. Boston: Twayne.

Thompson, Michael. 1979. Rubbish Theory: The Creation and Destruction of Value. Oxford: Oxford University Press.

Tsirimonaki, Maria. 1988. Απ' όσα πού 'παν τα βιβλία για την Κρήτη (From what books have told me about Crete). Rethemnos: Rethemniotika Nea. Review originally published in Rethemniotika Nea, no. 4307, 22 March 1987, p. 6.

Yiparaki, Yeoryia. 1987. Ντεμοντέ ο παραδοσιακός "γλυκύ βραστός" (The traditional "sweet [and] boiled [coffee]" is démodé). Rethemniotika Nea, no. 4405, 19 July, p. 3.

Youmbakis, Markos G. 1970. Fortezza: Η ιστορία του βενετσιάνικου φρουρίου του Ρεθύμνου (Fortezza: The history of the Venetian citadel of Rethimno). Rethemnos: n.p.

Xanthoudidis, Stefanos. 1980. Μελετήματα (Studies). Ed. by N. Panagiotakis and The Detorakis. Iraklio: Municipality of Iraklio.

Zinovieff, Sofka. 1991. Hunters and Hunted: *Kamaki* and the Ambiguities of Sexual Predation in a Greek Town. *In* Contested Identities: Gender and Kinship in Modern Greece, Peter Loizos and Evthymios Papataxiarchis, eds., pp. 203–220. Princeton: Princeton University Press.

PRINCETON MODERN GREEK STUDIES

This series is sponsored by the Princeton University Program
in Hellenic Studies under the auspices of the
Stanley J. Seeger Hellenic Fund

*Firewalking and Religious Healing: The Anastenaria of Greece
and the American Firewalking Movement* by Loring M. Danforth

Kazantzakis: Politics of the Spirit by Peter Bien

George Seferis: Complete Poems
translated by Edmund Keeley and Philip Sherrard

Dance and the Body Politic in Northern Greece
by Jane K. Cowan

Yannis Ritsos: Repetitions, Testimonies, Parentheses
translated by Edmund Keeley

Contested Identities: Gender and Kinship in Modern Greece
edited by Peter Loizos and Evthymios Papataxiarchis

*A Place in History: Social and Monumental Time
in a Cretan Town* by Michael Herzfeld

PRINCETON STUDIES IN CULTURE/POWER/HISTORY

*High Religion: A Cultural and Political History
of Sherpa Buddhism* by Sherry B. Ortner

*A Place in History: Social and Monumental Time
in a Cretan Town* by Michael Herzfeld